Labour, Work and Architecture

Dedicated to the memory of Hannah Arendt

Phaidon Press Limited
Regent's Wharf
All Saints Street
London N1 9PA

Phaidon Press Inc.
180 Varick Street
New York, NY 10014

www.phaidon.com

First published 2002

ISBN 0 7148 4080 7

A CIP catalogue record for this book
is available from the British Library.

Designed by Trickett & Webb Ltd
Printed in Hong Kong

Labour, Work and Architecture

Collected Essays on Architecture and Design

Kenneth Frampton

Contents

Preface

Those that can do, do and those that can't, teach, runs the old adage that discriminates in a prejudicial but cautionary manner between the rival provinces of theory and practice. I feel this to be of particular pertinence in my case for although I was initially trained as an architect in the AA School of Architecture in London, during the first half of the Fifties, I have, in fact, designed and realized relatively little. Instead, I have devoted most of my life to architectural education – despite the fact that it remains a moot point as to whether the prowess of an architect can really be acquired within the confines of the academy. At best, the academy is a prelude to mandatory apprenticeship; to that 'learning through doing' that is of paramount importance in the acquisition of a craft.

In addition to teaching, I am more strictly speaking a writer on architecture rather than an architect or even an architectural historian or, for that matter, a theorist or a critic, despite the fact that these essays, with the exception of the introduction, are arranged chronologically under the successive rubrics of *theory*, *history* and *criticism*. The only exception to this chronological sequence is the essay on the work of Hannah Arendt which has been brought forward for reasons that will be made clear in the introduction to the theory section.

The question may surely be raised as to whether any of these texts can be said to belong fully under any of these categories, quite apart from the fact that the boundaries separating such genres are not as determinable as we would like to imagine. Nevertheless, it may still be maintained that the first five pieces attempt to deal in a theoretical way with the socio-cultural context of architecture, with its ontological and productive limits, with the division of labour in industrial production and with the ideological debate over design education as these issues played themselves out in the second half of the twentieth century. This section concludes with two essays that attempt to establish the parameters for a critical, non-scenographic mode of practice within the constraints imposed by the overall context; that is, by topography, climate, and, where it still exists, some sense of regional identity.

As for the second set of essays, these may be seen as *historical* to the extent that they are attempts to address a series of episodes that either embodied the ethos of the avant-garde at the height of its commitment to the total transformation of society – most particularly under the then-promising aegis of the emergent Soviet state – or, alternatively, attempted to temper the fervour and conviction of the erstwhile avant-garde in various ways, without jeopardizing the potential of architectural culture to realize itself in relation to a progressive view of society. All of this was, in some sense, an attempt on my part to trace the *tradition of the new* as this seems to have evolved throughout the century, including even Adolf Loos's ironic dismissal of applied art as a contradiction in terms.

The nine essays gathered together under the rubric of *criticism* bring the material covered by this anthology closer to the present, covering as they do the 30-year span of my activity as an occasional reviewer of contemporary architectural developments. Much of this, I regret to say, comes under that which Manfredo Tafuri regarded as *operational criticism*, in as much as many of these pieces, despite certain reservations, largely supported the works and the architects under consideration; that is to say, they amount to an appraisal rather than a critique. There are three exceptions to this: the essays on the Ford Foundation and the German Ambassador's Residence in Washington, DC, and my overly moralistic not to say cursory treatment of Swiss German minimalism. Much is surely left out of this category, not only in terms of other architectural manifestations that I have written about over the years but also with regard to other equally pertinent achievements that so far I have never considered. Obviously the present anthology could have been very different: much could have been omitted, and an entirely different cluster of writings might have been included instead. This, then, is at best a sampler; a set of autodidactic reflections from the sidelines of history.

In one way or another, all my writing from the mid-Sixties onwards has been directly or indirectly influenced by the thought of Hannah Arendt, to whose memory this anthology is dedicated. This intellectual debt accounts for the title *Labour, Work and Architecture*, which is simultaneously a reference to Sigfried Gideon's *Space, Time and Architecture* of 1949 and to Arendt's canonical work *The Human Condition* of 1958. In this work she remarks on the socio-political and cultural connotations that may be ascribed to the terms *labour* and *work*, to the effect that 'Labor is the activity which corresponds to the biological process', with the human condition of labour being life itself, whereas, 'work is the activity which corresponds to the unnaturalness of human existence ... within its borders each individual life is housed, while this world itself is meant to outlast and transcend them all. The human condition of work is worldliness.'

On reading Arendt's book in 1965, I realized how these discriminations were able to illuminate the time-honoured but invariably confusing distinction between building (process) and architecture (stasis), with architecture having as its primary charge the creation of the public realm – within which her third term, namely *action*, plays itself out, testifying, as she puts it, to the fact that men, plural, inhabit the world. For Arendt this plurality was the precondition of all political life. It is this specifically politicized view of culture which launched my writing on its left-of-centre trajectory, which is paradoxical given the conservative dimensions of Arendt's thought – dimensions which are, in my view, redeemed by her insistence on the *polis* as the physical and institutional prerequisite for the continual enactment of democracy.

Introduction:
On the Predicament of Architecture at the Turn of the Century

> *... With the designation* experiment, *the avant-garde excuses its results, takes back, as it were, its 'actions', and unloads all responsibility on the receiver. Every boldness suits the avant-garde perfectly so long as it itself remains safe. The concept of the experiment is to insure it against the risk of all esthetic production. It serves both as trademark and as camouflage ... The historic avant-garde perished by its aporias. It was questionable, but it was not craven. Never did it try to play it safe with the excuse that what it was doing was nothing more than an 'experiment'; it never cloaked itself in science in order to be absolved of its results. That distinguishes it from the company of limited responsibility that is its successor; therein lies its greatness ... The path of the modern arts is not reversible. Let other harbor hopes for the end of modernity, for conversions and 're-integrations'. What is to be chalked up against today's avant-garde is not that it has gone too far but that it keeps the back doors open for itself, that it seeks support in doctrins and collectives, and that it does not become aware of its own aporias, long since disposed of by history. It deals in a future that does not belong to it. Its movement is regression. The avant-garde has become its opposite: anachronism. That inconspicuous, limitless risk, by which the artist's future lives – it cannot sustain it.*
>
> Hans Magnus Enzensberger, *The Consciousness Industry: On Literature, Politics and the Media*, 1974[1]

The Media and the Metier

It is necessary to recognize the limits of architecture as a *metier*; above all perhaps the fact that however much advanced techno-scientific methods may be employed in its realization, it is no more an applied science than it is a form of fine art. Despite the ubiquitous triumph of technological modernization, the practice of architecture is still to be more properly regarded as a craft, one which, at its full range, is dedicated to the significant formulation of the human environment. In this respect, it is always as much an ontological presence and an embodiment of societal value in spatial terms as it is an abstract or symbolic *representation*. Hence, it is doubtful whether it can ever be appropriately rendered as 'fine art writ large'. Unlike literature, music, painting and sculpture, or even theatre, photography and film, architecture cannot legitimately aspire to any kind of cultural automony since it is too intimately involved with the processes of everyday life and with that which Jürgen Habermas characterized as the unfinished modern project; in a word with that which Marshall Berman has since identified as the *pastoral* or caring mode as opposed to the *counter-pastoral* of the negative avant-garde.[2]

As Hal Foster has recently remarked, similar traits proliferate today in a great deal of architecture that presents itself as exuberantly plastic, wherein sculptural concatenations are proferred as the substance of an unprecedented 'value-free' expression. This kind of gratuitous plasticity is particularly evident in the work of the architect Frank Gehry, of which Foster has written:

With the putative passing of the industrial age, Modernist architecture was declared outmoded, and now the Pop aesthetic of Post-Modern architecture looks dated as well. The search for the architecture of the computer age is on; but, ironically, it has led Gehry and others to use academic sculpture as a model, at least to a degree . . . The disconnection between skin and structure represented by this academic model is at its most radical in Gehry's work in the Experimental Music Project (Seattle 1995–2000), commissioned by the Microsoft billionaire Paul Allen because of his love for Jimi Hendrix (a fellow Seattle-ite): its six exterior blobs clad in different colored metals have little apparent relationship to its many interior displays dedicated to pop music. Just as Gehry wanted to make Bilbao legible through an allusion to a splintered ship, here he makes an allusion to a smashed guitar (a broken 'fret' lies over two of the blobs). But neither image works, even as a Pop gesture, for you have to be well above the buildings to read them as images at all, or you have to see them in media reproduction – which is indeed a primary 'site' of this architecture.[3]

Many issues are enjoined in this perceptive passage, above all the recognition of the sculptural character of this genre and of the way in which this is closely connected to the spectacular, in as much as a great deal of its impact largely depends on its dissemination as an image through the media. Here, one can easily see how the cult of the free-standing aesthetic object is closely linked to the populist franchising of culture, to the so-called Bilbao effect, wherein spectacular imagery serves to stimulate global market forces, which play themselves out at many different levels, including the current competition between rival city-states as they struggle for their economic sovereignty in today's post-industrial, tourist-oriented, commodity culture.

Needless to say, one cannot exclude the sculptural from the full expressive range of architecture, as one may readily appreciate when one looks at the work of the Portuguese architect Alvaro Siza. In his work however, such plasticity is never divorced from the hierarchical articulation of the internal volume; that is to say, for Siza, the quasi-ergonomic inflection of the micro-space in a given architectonic sequence is just as important as the overall plastic arrangement of the space and form. That the sculptural need not be divorced from either the structural or the spatial is also surely borne out by the remarkably tectonic assemblies realized by the Catalan architect Enric Miralles.

As far as architecture is concerned, the limitations of the media-bound approach stem from the experiential 'distancing' effected by photography and film in the representation of architectural form – in that the camera unavoidably reduces architecture to the perspectival, that is, to an exclusively visual, reproducible image that, by definition, is removed from our everyday tactile and phenomenological experience of built form. However, we also need to acknowledge a dichotomous condition that now exists due to the universal proliferation of images: for while the mediatic facilitates fashion and stimulates desire it can also be beneficial in its capacity to disseminate information worldwide in such a way as to overcome the time-honoured schism between the centre and the periphery – between the dominance of the one and the subservience of the other. This is particularly evident in contemporary architecture, where some of the most sophisticated work realized today is being produced in countries that are variously distanced from the Eurocentric centres of influence – in countries such as Japan, Australia, India, Finland, Spain, Portugal, Norway, Ireland, Colombia and Mexico.

One can hardly assess the impact of the mediatic today without also addressing the uses and abuses of the computer in late modern society. In this regard it is clear that, as in every other field, architectural design cannot be pursued today in the developed and even in the undeveloped world without involving computer-aided design, although the way in which the digital should interface with other modes of representing architecture during the design process is by no means self-evident. It is clear that the use of the computer is not only indispensable for the preparation of working drawings and other documents but that it also has an important role to play in the calculation of structure, in the design and modelling of environmental services and in the design, realization and operation of servo-mechanisms of all kinds. However, its stochastic use for the generation of form as an end in itself is more questionable, since this can be just as gratuitously formalistic as any other heuristic device solely indulged in for the purposes of aesthetic display.

Gehry's penchant for exploiting the digital as a means to construct inconceivable and unresolvable formal conjunctions could hardly be further removed from the aspirations of the British engineer Peter Rice, who sought through cybernetic technique to restore to structural form its capacity to arouse the enthusiasm of the general public. Shortly before his death Rice wrote:

This is the positive role for the engineer's genius and skill: to use their understanding of materials and structure to make real the presence of the materials in use in the building, so that people warm to them, want to touch them, feel a sense of the material itself and of the people who made and designed it. To do this we have to avoid the worst excesses of the industrial hegemony. To maintain the feeling that it was the designer and not industry and its available options, that decided, is one essential ingredient of seeking a tactile traces de la main *solution.*[4]

Among other things, Rice strove to achieve an element of surprise, in which traditional materials such as stone would be used in a totally new way thanks to digital precision in both calculation and manufacture. At the same time many highly functional structures owe their form to digital iteration – which, as in the case of the Kansai Airport Terminal in Japan, constructed to the designs of Rice and Renzo Piano, permitted a serial variation in the roof-truss profiles that make up the 1.6 km long torus form of the airside terminal. At the same time, it is equally evident that the same capacity may be used for formal iterations that have no other aim than the generation of exotic form as an end in itself. Perhaps the most balanced position in this regard, in terms of both conception and realization, is that advocated by the American architect Steven Holl, who insists that in order to maintain its multi-semantic character the design of architectural work should be constantly cycled through three different modes of studio representation: manual drafting, digital plotting and the physical modelling of form.

Dystopia

The past 50 years have radically transformed the metropolitan centres of the developed world. What were still essentially nineteenth-century cities in the early Fifties have since become surrounded and partially penetrated by megalopolitan development; that is to say, by the techno-commercial infrastructure of the autoroute, the strip and the shopping mall, together with the random distribution of high-rise structures, set amid a seemingly endless proliferation of free-standing suburban dwellings. In this way, traditional city form, capable of combining many different uses within its continuous, densely woven urban fabric, has found itself superceded by an economically optimizing 'motopia'.[5]

The suburbanization of the American continent and the simultaneous dissolution of the American provincial city, aided after 1945 by the not so benign neglect of public transport in all its aspects, seems to have directly arisen as a result of the political pressure exerted by the maximizing concerns of the oil and automotive industries. While these environmentally negative processes are to be found at their most extreme in the United States, the same tendency may be encountered almost everywhere today: so much so that one is tempted to argue that if there is a single environmentally negative invention in the modern world, it is surely the internal combustion engine. Apart from the overall pollution of the earth's atmosphere, the depletion of the world's rain forests would have been virtually impossible had it not been for the automobile's capacity to penetrate every corner of the globe – not to mention the largely disfiguring impact that this vehicle has had on the landscape as a whole.

Meanwhile, migrating rural populations continue to implode upon major cities across the world, particularly in developing countries. Most of this expansion occurs in the form of spontaneous housing, where land is appropriated overnight and shacks are hastily erected without the essential infrastructures of water, sewage and power. Despite greatly increased densities, such land settlement patterns are comparable in their random character to the sprawling *megalopoli* of the developed world, a term coined by the French geographer Jean Gottman in 1961.[6] Gottman had in mind conglomerations like the Boston–Washington corridor, the Randstad in northwest Europe or the Hokkaido–Osaka continuously urbanized region in Japan. It is symptomatic of the maldistribution of wealth that much of this regional urbanization has been accompanied by uneven economic development – to such an extent that we are now witness to the spontaneous generation of 'Third Worlds' within the interstices of so-called 'First Worlds' and vice versa.

It is disingenuous to suggest that we are devoid of any effective strategies with which to mediate these imploding socio-cultural transformations. Two examples taken from the Third World come immediately to mind in this regard. The first of these dates from 1964 when Charles Correa, Pravina Mehta and Sherish Patel conceived their plan for decanting some two million people out of Bombay's overloaded urban fabric into the extension known as New Bombay. Today this settlement has finally become viable through the implementation of appropriate forms of public and private transit linking it to the capital city. The second example, dating from the late Seventies is that of Curitiba in Brazil where, due to the initiative of the architect-mayor Jaime Lerner, advantage was taken of the existing grid of the city to introduce an economic system of public transport, utilizing articulated buses especially designed for the occasion by Volvo. These buses, running in designated lanes, afford diverse high-speed connections between the labour force living in the hills surrounding the city and the sources of employment variously distributed throughout the urban fabric. What is especially intriguing about the success of the Curitiba infrastructure and its current expansion is the multi-faceted character of the complementary urban policy pursued by Lerner, which from the very outset extended beyond what we normally consider to be the province of infrastructural design. Many social factors were involved in the overall success of Lerner's policy, from the municipal exchange of basic foodstuffs in return for bringing garbage to collection points, to the provision of an efficient means of public transport without entailing the prohibitive levels of investment that are required for the installation of fixed-rail systems.

If we are ever to come to terms with the current proliferation of the megalopolis in both a socio-cultural and ecological sense, then we shall only be able to do so in a post-facto compensatory way, that is to say by adopting denser patterns of land settlement and by providing adequate infrastructures for public transport, operating at differentiated speeds – from fast inter-city trains to slower intra-city light-rail transit systems, augmented by buses. As far as the first is concerned I have in mind the high-speed train that has been an ongoing development project in Europe and Japan for the last 35 years, with the result that today for inter-city journeys of up to 500 kilometres, rail has become preferable to air travel in terms of trip time, reliability, energy consumption and environmental pollution. As far as the intra-city option is concerned I am thinking of the current revival of the tram as an increasingly viable mode of inner urban transit due to its moderate speed, its frequency and its capacity for stopping at frequent intervals. The fact is that all forms of public transport require a minimum residential density of 100 persons per acre in order to be economic.

The issue of urban residential density returns us to the challenge of land settlement in relation to global urbanization, and thus to the concept of low-rise, high-density housing, which has been available as a general model for residential development ever since the early Sixties – particularly in the so-called developed world – following the realization of Siedlung Halen outside Bern in 1960 and the publication in 1963 of Serge Chermayeff and Christopher Alexander's seminal study *Community and Privacy*.[7] To these two models, the one specific and built and the other generic and unrealized, we may add Roland Rainer's Puchenau Garden City, built on the Danube near Linz between 1960 and 1980, together with his proto-ecological thesis *Livable Environments* published in 1972.[8]

Such models are certainly applicable to the general dilemma we face at a megalopolitan scale. What we lack, however, is the political and cultural will to establish these or similar patterns of low-rise, high-density settlement as a new and necessary form of development. Successful one-off demonstrations of low-rise, high-density housing have been realized in many parts of the world over the past 30 years, but for such patterns to become the norm we need to introduce legislation that would outlaw contemporary forms of dispersed suburban development. While low-rise, high-density is by no means incompatible with the automobile, it is clear, as we noted above, that such an increase in density favours the introduction of auxiliary mass transit. That these issues are ecological and political in nature rather than architectural tends to be supported by the fact that only a very small proportion of the built environment is subject to the intervention of an architect. It is the real estate and home-building industries – aided by banks, bureaucracies and our laissez-faire planning policies – that are jointly responsible for the dispersed and totally chaotic disaggregation of the environment. This sobering fact returns us to the importance of education, because until society becomes more enlightened, little in this regard will fundamentally change.

Sustainability

The optimization of technology is far from synonymous with the neutral application of techno-science, for it often brings with it a concatenation of side effects that are neither liberative nor beneficial. Countless everyday examples come to mind, from the profligate use of electrical energy in the smelting of aluminum, to the clear-cutting of forests; from the depletion of the ozone layer through industrial pollution, to the emergence of resistant bacteria that no longer respond to antibiotics. This negative feedback is equally pertinent to the field of environmental design, where one should use the term *appropriate* rather than *high* technology in qualifying the application of sophisticated techniques to built form. Appropriate technique presupposes a hybrid approach to environmental culture, wherein buildings are not only harmoniously integrated into the landscape but also rendered climatically responsive by virtue of the way they are oriented, insulated, heated, ventilated and constructed. Favourable orientation to wind, sun and topography; the use of double glazing and the partial recycling of warm air in winter; the induction of air movement through low-speed fans; the application of servo-mechanisms for the control of louvres and vents; the provision of manually operated windows and screens; and, finally, the use of solar walls and photovoltaic cells, are nothing but so many devices for the modification of a structure's internal climate in response to changes in environmental conditions.

However, the project of pursuing a sustainable architecture assumes a more intractable character when one turns to consider the energy incorporated within the building materials themselves. As Peter Buchanan has written:

The common building material with the least embodied energy is wood, with about 640 kilowatt-hours per ton ... Hence the greenest building material is wood from sustainably-managed forests. Brick is the material with the next lowest amount of embodied energy, 4 times (4x) that of wood, then concrete (5x), plastic (6x), glass (14x), steel (24x) and aluminum (126x). A building with a high proportion of aluminum components can hardly be green when considered from the perspective of total life cycle costing, no matter how much energy it might save.[9]

The built environment accounts for about half to two-thirds of our current energy use; this alarming statistic is exacerbated by our present attitudes towards impermanence, commodification and the rapid amortization of building stock. Buchanan goes on to show that historic buildings are inherently more adaptable to re-use than modern structures, first because they were built to more generous standards and second because they were constructed of more durable natural material. Moreover, from the point of view of function they tended to be 'long life, loose fit' structures; that is to say they may be much more readily adapted to re-use than more modern, ergonomically optimized building forms.

In relation to the potential for the adaptive re-use of pre-existing structures we should surely restrict our current habit of exploiting ex-agricultural *greenfield* sites in favour of re-using ex-industrial *brownfield* sites. Rather than continuing to proliferate urban sprawl we should either re-use obsolete buildings or demolish them and re-use their sites once they have been cleared. Only provisions of this order will save us from the continual consumption of fertile land and along with this, the ultimate depletion of the planet's non-renewable resources.

The emerging shortage of water on a worldwide basis points in a similar direction. Three other factors invariably come to the fore once one entertains the project of an ecologically responsible architecture: among them the use of solar- and wind-powered energy, the harvesting of rainwater and the re-use of 'grey' water, that is to say the discharge from handbasins, baths, etc., which may be purified by being passed through reed beds.

Contrary to the contention that sustainable design must of necessity be unaesthetic, the legacy of vernacular building suggests that architecture stands only to be enriched through the incorporation and elaboration of mediating bioclimatic elements. A great deal of contemporary work points in this direction, from the relative eco-sensitivity of hi-tech architecture to the current resurgence of timber construction in Europe, Australia, Canada and Japan. There is perhaps no single work that points more towards the possibility of synthesizing these two trends than Renzo Piano's Tjibaou Cultural Centre, realized in Nouméa, New Caledonia in 1999. Here the steel-reinforced timber public volumes, called 'cases' by the architect, were designed not only to evoke the form and woven fabric of the traditional kanak dwelling, but also to induce and modify natural ventilation in response to varying wind speed and direction.

Topography

As far as the future of British urban development is concerned, it has been projected that 90 per cent of that which will exist in 20 years' time has already been built.[10] If this is indeed the case, then it follows that there are not so many options available for improving the existing socio-cultural character of the average megalopolis. Other than introducing environmentally friendly, complementary systems of public transport, only one possible form of generic intervention seems to remain as a way of ameliorating existing regional urbanization, namely the re-design of the intersticial landscape. The ubiquitous asphalt parking lot is a case in point, for clearly all such lots could be transformed into *'parterres'* through planting and other landscape modifications. Apart from the provision of coordinated rows of shade trees in order to prevent parked automobiles from overheating in summer, the ecological long-term benefits of such planting would help to offset the current effects of global warming since parking lots substantially contribute to the creation of 'heat islands' in high summer. Instead of asphalt, parking lots can be covered with perforated concrete paving. This surfacing system, as well as helping to absorb rainwater, may also be seeded to provide for a softer, more sympathetic environment.[11] Other topographic modifications to parking lots, such as enclosing them with low-rise berms planted with turf, would yield benefits of a more cultural nature, helping to reintegrate otherwise environmentally barren and ill-defined areas of black top into the urban fabric as a whole.

The contemporary environment is now so overwhelmed by automotive technology as to seriously limit the possibility of creating significant urban form. The interests of land speculation restrict the scope of urban design to such a degree that any kind of master planning, other than the provision of mass transit, largely remains an academic exercise. As a result, urban designers have attempted to evolve alternative strategies for the piecemeal development of the modern city. Among them are the architects Henri Ciriani and Fumihiko Maki: the former with his concept of the urban piece (*la pièce urbaine),* and the latter with his idea of *megaform* (first developed with Masato Ohtaka in 1965). To such models we may now add the notion of 'urban acupuncture' as evoked by the Barcelona urbanist Manuel de Solà Morales.[12] This concept refers to the reparative potential of compact, catalytic urban interventions, with the proviso that these should be realizable within a fairly short period of time and be capable of spontaneously restructuring their immediate surroundings. A corollary to such interventions is the urban *megaform*, a predominantly horizontal complex capable of creating an identifiable landmark in what is otherwise a 'space-endless' condition. Unlike the technological rhetoric of the megastructure, the megaform tends not to indulge in ostentatious structural or mechanical display (cf. the Centre Pompidou in Paris). Instead it favours the kind of calm articulation that we find in the L'Illa block, realized in the Avenida

Diagonal, Barcelona in 1997 to the designs of Rafael Moneo and Manuel de Solà Morales. This multi-use structure serves as a hybrid civic microcosm, capable of uniting into a single whole many different functions: shopping galleria, commercial frontage, offices, hotel, etc. Beyond the confines of traditional urban form, where such a dense fabric still prevails, the megaform possesses the potential of serving both as a landmark and as a city-in-miniature, thereby compensating, both topographically and socially, for the 'non-place urban realm' of the average megalopolis.[13]

Tradition and Innovation

Aside from the familiar dialectic between *form* and *function*, which has played such a prominent role in the evolution of twentieth-century architecture, one may argue that the generation of form invariably involves an interplay between a further series of polarities, beginning with the fundamental opposition between *tradition* and *innovation*. As the philosopher Hans Georg Gadamer instructs us, this opposition implies a continuous discourse between the two, in which the prejudice of a given cultural legacy has to be continually reassessed against a critique that stems from another 'mode of beholding'. As Georgia Warnke put it in her 1987 study of Gadamer's philosophy:

. . . we understand history not simply because we make it but also because it has made us; we belong to it in the sense that we inherit its experience, project a future on the basis of the situation that the past has created for us and act in the light of our understanding of this past, whether such understanding is explicit or not.[14]

What Gadamer has in mind is that which he refers to as a 'fusion of horizons', in which one tradition or received mode comes to be gradually modified in the light of an 'other'. This stance has been recently echoed by the British architect David Chipperfield in an essay entitled 'Tradition and Invention', wherein he writes:

. . . We must resolve the possibilities of a shapeless future with the significance and meaning of established forms and experience. That which has been with that which could be, memory and imagination. Architecture inherits the consequence of general technological advance, occasionally encouraging, rarely determining. In fact we may say that despite the rhetoric, materials and construction methods have charted a relatively slow path of change compared with other technologies.[15]

Chipperfield envisages the architect as standing both *in front of and behind* the constraints and opportunities proferred by contemporary reality. For him the process of modernization is a project that today benefits as much from resistance as encouragement.

Many factors come together in this vision of contemporary practice, above all perhaps the recognition that advanced techno-science has an independent existence, one that does not necessarily implicate architecture, and indeed does not need the practice of architecture in order to demonstrate its power and assert its dominance. At the same time any significant exchange between *tradition* and *innovation* presupposes a relatively slow process of mediation, something that is hard to sustain in a society that is relentlessly impelled by global commodification and by the ever escalating speed of digitalized information.

As I attempt to indicate at the beginning of this essay after my citation of Enzensberger's Olympian overview, the only balanced option that is available to architecture today is one that is critically creative rather than wilfully neo-avant gardist. And yet as Enzensberger indicates the renunciation of technological modernization is not any kind of historical option. We are stuck with the ameliorative challenge of the unfinished modern project whether we like it or not, even though this project can only be significantly continued in terms of architecture through the reinterpretation and reformulation of the new, in light of specific means and conditions obtaining in a particular place and at a particular time. One might say our key critical role now turns on discriminating between mediation and maximization when it comes to the application of technology to environmental form. Since any kind of *tabula rasa* overcoming is categorically denied us we now have no choice but to address ourselves not only to the living needs and wishes of the client and the body politic, but also to the specificity of the context as this may be defined in terms of topography, technology and tradition. As Alvaro Siza put it with characteristic irony, 'architects don't invent anything, they transform reality'. An act of transformation must also anticipate its own subsequent metamorphosis, by virtue of embodying within the poetic of its form the trace of the historical moment that produces it. In other words it must not only provide for the living but also for the dead, that is to say for the mortality of the future as well as for that of the past.

In this deeper sense, architecture is by definition anachronistic or let us say, it pertains to its own time and to moments that project beyond it, both forwards and backwards. It is this dichotomous condition that constitutes both its weakness and its strength: weak partly because of its marginality in relation to the dominance of maximizing technology, and strong because at its best it not only testifies to its time against the commodified never-ending newness of fashion but also because it is the built guarantor of the public realm as a symbolic and political arena. Such will surely remain its prerogative providing it is not seduced by either the populism of kitsch or the experimentation of empty avant-gardism: the twin avatars of Enzensberger's consciousness industry. In short, architecture can only survive as a form of critical culture, as a resistant 'otherness'; all of which returns us to the etymology of the word *tradition* and to the fact that this term is closely allied to other terms having an equally ambivalent significance, such as trade, treason, translation and betrayal. This possibly goes some way towards explaining the paradoxical aphorism of the Catalan philosopher Eugénio d'Ors, who according to Luis Bunuel was in the habit of saying something to the effect that 'all that is not tradition is plagiarism'.[16]

theory
history
criticism

Introduction

The first theoretical piece initially came into being as a result of two formative experiences: (1) my first visit to the United States in 1964, when I was overawed by the aerial prospect of the post-industrial society at the height of its nocturnal consumption of energy; and (2), a reading at the same time of Hannah Arendt's *The Human Condition* (1958), which had been recommended to me by Thomas Stevens just prior to my departure for New York. Serving as a primary influence on Colin Rowe when he was a student at the Liverpool School of Architecture at the end of World War II, Sam Stevens was the generic intellectual of my generation, as at home with the architecture of Luigi Moretti as he was an expert on Baroque organs and small-bore heating systems. Arendt's 1958 study prompted me, a decade after its publication, to write an essay entitled 'Labour, Work and Architecture', which was included in George Baird and Charles Jencks's anthology *Meaning in Architecture* of 1969. This piece was to be reworked, exactly a decade later, into the essay featured here, under the title 'The Status of Man and the Status of his Objects'. This subsequent version is placed at the head of the theory section because of the seminal influence of Arendt's thought on all my writing after 1965.

At Princeton University, where I taught in the second half of the Sixties, I had as a close colleague the Argentine painter and design theorist Tomás Maldonado who had just resigned from the faculty of the Höchschule für Gestaltung in Ulm. Maldonado's lasting influence on me, both politically and otherwise, is evident from the second essay 'Apropos Ulm' that appeared in *Oppositions 3*, May 1974. It is included here under the rubric of theory because it recapitulates the auto-critical debate that took place in HfG in the Sixties as to the problematic status of architecture and industrial design in a consumerist society.

The third theory essay, 'The Volvo Case', of 1976, also came about as the result of a personal encounter, this time with Pehr Gyllenhammar, who was then director of AB Volvo in Gothenburg, Sweden. Gyllenhammar's Columbia University lecture of 1973, featuring Volvo's Kalmar system of modified on-line production, impressed me for its potential to mediate the crisis attending the division of labour in late modern society. While it is no doubt unusual to include such a topic in an anthology on architecture, the Kalmar system brought together many of the factors that are discussed in this volume, including the impact of education and feminism on the conditions that attend industrial production, together with the role to be played by the welfare state in mediating the contradictions of capitalism. Kalmar also highlights other issues that are touched on in this anthology, above all, perhaps, the potential of democracy to affect not only the manner of production but also the nature of what is produced. (Such considerations recall the ornamental interventions of John Ruskin in the realization of the Natural History Museum in Oxford in

1847.) The title of this piece alludes to Francesco Rossi's film *Il Caso Mattei*, wherein Rossi speculates that Enrico Mattei, the director of the Italian state-owned oil and natural gas corporation, ENI, was assassinated in a contrived aircraft accident, largely because he challenged the pre-OPEC Anglo–American monopoly over the production and distribution of oil. It seems that this speculation has subsequently been confirmed by figures who have confessed to tampering with the aircraft.

'Towards a Critical Regionalism', which first appeared in Hal Foster's anthology *The Anti-Aesthetic: Essays on Post-Modern Culture* of 1983, also had its origin in a personal encounter. This time it was the Czech architect Dalibor Vesely, who introduced me to Paul Ricoeur's seminal essay of 1961, 'Universal Civilization and National Cultures'. It seemed to me that this distinction between civilization and culture was still manifest in continental European architecture during the early Sixties, the period when I served as Technical Editor of the British magazine *Architectural Design*. I recall thinking at the time that the then still vital city-state cultures of Europe had an inherently greater capacity for patronage and cultivation of local culture than did their British equivalent. With 'Rappel à l'Ordre' of 1990, my earlier efforts to ground the practice of architecture in critical regionalism were redirected to 'the poetics of construction'. Departing from the hypothesis that as far as the relative autonomy of architecture was concerned, built form was as much about structure and construction as it was about the creation and articulation of space, I attempted to recover the nineteenth-century notion of the tectonic in an effort to resist the contemporary tendency to reduce architecture to scenographic effects.

The Status of Man and the Status of his Objects

The only philosophy which can be responsibly practised in the face of despair is the attempt to contemplate all things as they would present themselves from the standpoint of redemption; all else is reconstruction, mere technique. Perspectives must be fashioned that displace and estrange the world, reveal it to be, with its rifts and crevices, as indigent and distorted as it will appear one day in the messianic light.
Theodor Adorno, *Minima Moralia*, 1947

The architectural corollaries of labour and work

In her book *The Human Condition*, significantly subtitled 'a study of the central dilemmas facing modern man', Hannah Arendt designated three activities – *labour*, *work* and *action* – as being fundamental to the *vita activa*. She established at the beginning of her argument the particular meaning that she would consistently assign to each of these terms. Of *labour* she wrote:

Labor is the activity which corresponds to the biological process of the human body, whose spontaneous growth, metabolism, and eventual decay are bound to the vital necessities produced and fed into the life process by labor. The human condition of labor is life itself.[1]

Of *work* she wrote:

Work is the activity which corresponds to the unnaturalness of human existence, which is not embedded in, and whose mortality is not compensated by, the species' ever-recurring life cycle. Work provides an 'artificial' world of things, distinctly different from all natural surroundings. Within its borders each individual life is housed, while this world itself is meant to outlast and transcend them all. The human condition of work is worldliness.[2]

In her definition of the public and private attributes of the *vita activa* – the former having a dependency on the latter – Arendt amplified further her unusual distinction between *work* and *labour*. She argued that labour by being a constantly transforming but repetitive procedure – akin to the cycle of biological survival – is inherently *processal*, *private* and *impermanent*, whereas work, by virtue of being the precondition for the reification of the world as the space of human appearance, is by definition *static*, *public* and *permanent*.

An architect could hardly fail to remark on the correspondence between these distinctions and the fundamental ambiguity of the term 'architecture'; an ambiguity that finds reflection in the Oxford English Dictionary in two significantly different definitions – first, 'the art or science of construction edifices for human use' and second, 'the action and process of building'.[3] These definitions with their potential hierarchy latent even in the etymology of the Greek term *architekton* – meaning chief constructor – proffer themselves as paralleling the distinction that Arendt draws between work and labour.[4]

The designation 'for human use' imparts a specifically human, if not humanist, connotation to the whole of the first definition, alluding to the creation of a specifically human world, whereas the phrase 'the action and process of building' in the second definition clearly implies a continuous act of building forever incomplete, comparable to the unending process of biological labour. The fact that the dictionary asserts that the word 'edifice' may be used to refer to 'a large and stately building such as a church, a palace, or a fortress' serves to support the work connotation of the first definition, since these building types, as the 'representations' of spiritual and temporal power, have always been, at least until recent times, both public and permanent. Furthermore, the word 'edifice' relates directly to the verb 'to edify', which not only carries within itself the meaning 'to build' but also 'to educate', 'to strengthen' and 'to instruct' – connotations that allude directly to the didactic character of the public realm. Again the Latin root of this verb – *aedificare*, from *aedes*, a 'building', or, even more originally, a 'hearth', and *ficare*, 'to make' – has latent within it the public connotation of the hearth as the aboriginal 'public' space of appearance. This aspect persists even today in the domestic realm, where surely no place is more of a forum in the contemporary home than the hearth or its surrogate, the television set, which as an illusory public substitute tends to inhibit or usurp the spontaneous emergence of 'public' discourse within the private domain.

Within the corpus of modern architectural theory, no text is more aware of the respective statuses of architecture and building than Adolf Loos's essay 'Architecture 1910', wherein he characterizes the eminently biological, innate and repetitive nature of vernacular construction in the following terms:

The peasant cuts out the spot on the green grass where the house is to be built and digs out the earth for the foundation walls. Then the mason appears. If there is loamy soil in the vicinity, then there will also be a brickworks to provide the bricks. If not, then stone from the river-banks can be used for the same purpose. And while the mason places brick upon brick and stone upon stone, the carpenter has established himself nearby. The strokes of the axe ring out merrily. He makes the roof. What kind of roof? One that is beautiful or ugly? He does not know. The roof . . . His aim was to build a house for himself, his family and his livestock and in this he has succeeded. Just as his neighbours and ancestors succeeded. As every animal which allows itself to be led by its instincts, succeeds.[5]

Loos was aware that, like the pure instrumentality of engineering, this rooted vernacular had nothing whatsoever to do with the traditionally representative role of architecture. Later in the same text he wrote:

Only a very small part of architecture belongs to art: the tomb and the monument. Everything else, everything which serves a purpose should be excluded from the realms of art . . . If we find a mound in the forest, six feet long and three feet wide, formed into a pyramid, shaped by a shovel, we become serious and something within us says, someone lies buried here. This is architecture.

The public realm and the human artifice

While the representative scope of architecture had already become severely curtailed by the turn of the century, the space of public appearance could still serve not only to house the public realm, but also to represent its reality. Where in the nineteenth century the public institution was exploited as an occasion on which to reify the permanent values of the society, the disintegration of such values in the twentieth century has had the effect of atomizing the public building into a network of abstract institutions. This dissipation of the *agora* reflects that mass society whose alienating force stems not from the number of people but from 'the fact that the world between them has lost its power to gather them together, to relate and to separate them'.[6]

While the political life of the Greek polis did not directly stem from the physical presence and representation of the city state, Arendt emphasizes, in contrast to our present proliferation of urban sprawl, the spontaneous 'cantonal' attributes of concentration:

The only indispensable material factor in the generation of power is the living together of people. Only where men live so close together that the potentialities of action are always present can power remain with them, and the foundation of cities, which as city-states have remained paradigmatic for all Western political organization, is therefore indeed the most important material prerequisite for power.[7]

Nothing could be further from this than our present generation of motopia and our evident incapacity to create new cities that are physically and politically identifiable as such. By the same token, nothing could be more removed from the political essence of the city state than the exclusively economic categories of rationalistic planning theory; that theory espoused by planners such as Melvin Webber, whose ideological conceptions of *community without propinquity* and the *non-place urban realm* are nothing if not slogans devised to rationalize the absence of any adequate realm of public appearance within modern suburbia.[8] The manipulative and 'apolitical' bias of such ideologies has never been more openly expressed than in Robert Venturi's *Complexity and Contradiction in Architecture*, wherein the author asserts that the Americans don't need piazzas, since they should be at home watching television.[9] These and similar reactionary modes of beholding seem to emphasize the impotence of an urbanized populace who have paradoxically lost the object of their urbanization. That their power grew initially out of the city finds corroboration in Arendt's conception of the relations obtaining between politics and built form:

Power preserves the public realm and the space of appearance, and as such it is also the life-blood of the human artifice, which, unless it is the scene of action and speech, of the web of human affairs and relationships and the stories engendered by them, lacks its ultimate raison d'être. *Without being talked about by men and without housing them, the world would not be a human artifice but a heap of unrelated things to which each isolated individual was at liberty to add one more object; without the human artifice to house them, human affairs would be as floating, as futile and vain, as the wanderings of nomad tribes.*[10]

It was a similar realization that the monuments of the Ringstrasse, built around Vienna during the second half of the nineteenth century, were nothing but a sequence of 'unrelated things', that caused Camillo Sitte to demonstrate that each of these isolated public structures could be restored to being a *res publica* in itself. In his *City Planning According to Artistic Principles* (1889), he revealed how the fabric of the medieval town had had the capacity of enclosing as a single 'political' entity both the monument and its civic piazza.[11]

The private realm and the rise of the social

While Arendt acknowledges that the rise of modern intimacy and individualism has largely eliminated the aspect of privation from the term 'privacy', she nonetheless remains aware that a life excluded from the public realm is still 'deprived' by virtue of its being confined to the shadowy domestic interior of the *megaron* – that traditional single-cell volume of the Greek peninsular, whose very etymology reveals the household as the domain of darkness.[12] Unlike the Greeks, who despised the individual domain or *idion* as the province of idiocy,[13] but like the Romans, who valued the interdependence of both realms, Arendt conceives of the private as the essential 'darker' ground that not only nourishes the public realm but also establishes its experiential depth. At the same time she recognizes that the rise of the social – to which the intimate is of course related – has had the ultimate effect of impoverishing both the public and private spheres and with this the mediatory capacity of built form to articulate one from the other. Arendt argues that the flowering of the social art form, the novel, after 1750 effectively coincided with the progressive decline of all the public arts, especially architecture.[14] The ultimate triumph of the social in collectivized life has, as Arendt puts it, given rise to a 'mass society [that] not only destroys the public realm but the private as well, [and] deprives men not only of their place in the world but of their private home, where they once felt sheltered against the world and where, at any rate, even those excluded from the world could find a substitute in the warmth of the hearth and the limited reality of family life.'[15]

This thesis, as to the loss of the private realm at the hands of the social, finds some corroboration in the fragmentary writings of the Mexican architect, Luis Barragán, who has criticized the overexposed landscape of the contemporary suburb in the following terms: 'Everyday life is becoming much too public. Radio, TV, the telephone all invade privacy. Gardens should therefore be enclosed, not open to public gaze.' Elsewhere, Barragán continues:

Architects are forgetting the need of human beings for half-light, the sort of light that imposes a tranquillity, in their living rooms as well as in their bedrooms. About half the glass that is used in so many buildings – homes as well as offices – would have to be removed in order to obtain the quality of light that enables one to live and work in a more concentrated manner.[16]

Arendt's insight that the triumph of labouring society has condemned man to perpetual movement[17] finds a further echo in Barragán's text wherein he asserts:

Before the machine age, even in the middle of cities, Nature was everybody's trusted companion ... Nowadays, the situation is reversed. Man does not meet with Nature, even when he leaves the city to commune with her. Enclosed in his shiny automobile, his spirit stamped with the mark of the world whence the automobile emerged, he is, within Nature, a foreign body. A billboard is sufficient to stifle the voice of Nature. Nature becomes a scrap of Nature and man a scrap of man.[18]

This tendency towards global reduction, not to say of a total fusion, between man, machine and Nature – latent in the processal triumph of industrial production – finds its ideological corollary in the behavioural sciences, of which Arendt has written:

To gauge the extent of society's victory in the modern age, its early substitution of behaviour for action and its eventual substitution of bureaucracy, the rule of nobody, for personal rulership, it may be well to recall that its initial science of economics, which substitutes patterns of behaviour only in this rather limited field of human activity, was finally followed by the all-comprehensive pretension of the social sciences which, as 'behavioural sciences', aim to reduce man as a whole, in all his activities, to the level of a conditioned and behaving animal.[19]

The duality of the *homo faber*: artifice versus instrumentality

The dependency of the human artifice on the work of *homo faber* stems from the intrinsic durability of objects and their capacity to withstand (*Gegenstand*) both the erosions of nature and the processes of use. As Arendt has written:

The man-made world of things, the human artifice erected by homo faber, *becomes a home for mortal men, whose stability will endure and outlast the ever-changing movement of their lives and actions, only insomuch as it transcends both the sheer functionalism of things produced for consumption and the sheer utility of objects produced for use. Life in its non-biological sense, the span of time each man has between birth and death, manifests itself in action and speech, both of which share with life its essential futility . . . If the* animal laborans *needs the help of* homo faber *to ease his labour and remove his pain, and if mortals need his help to erect a home on earth, acting and speaking men need the help of* homo faber *in his highest capacity, that is, the help of the artist, of poets and historiographers, of monument-builders or writers, because without them the only product of their activity, the story they enact and tell, would not survive at all. In order to be what the world is always meant to be, a home for men during their life on earth, the human artifice must be a place fit for action and speech, for activities not entirely useless for the necessities of life but of an entirely different nature from the manifold activities of fabrication by which the world itself and all things in it are produced.*[20]

No other passage in *The Human Condition* formulates the essential duality of the *homo faber* so succinctly as this – man as the maker split between the fabrication of useless things, such as works of art, which are ends in themselves, and the invention and production of useful objects, which serve as various predetermined means to a given set of ends. For Arendt, *homo faber* is at once both artificer and tool-maker; the builder of the world and the maker of the instruments with which it is built. Where the one addresses itself to the 'what' of representation and reification – that is to say, to that object of commemoration which Loos was to consign to the province of art – the other concerns itself with the 'how' of utility and process, in which tools tend, at least in the modern world, to be the sole things to survive the occasion of their use. Nothing reveals this second condition of production more than the machine fabrication of goods for consumption, nor the first than the cyclical history of built monuments which, from inception to demolition, testify to a continual transference of value from the past into the future.

The ambiguity of architecture – its status as 'edification' or as 'building' and often as different aspects within the same physical entity – reflects the parallel ambiguity of the *homo faber*, who is neither pure artist nor pure technician. In a similar manner, representation and commemoration can never be entirely prised apart and the present embodiment of past value already assures its availability for the future. All signification in built form thus embodies a sense of immortality. This much Arendt attempts to make clear in her discussion of art:

In this permanence, the very stability of the human artifice, which, being inhabited and used by mortals, can never be absolute, achieves a representation of its own. Nowhere else does the sheer durability of the world of things appear in such purity and clarity, nowhere else therefore does this thing-world reveal itself so spectacularly as the non-mortal home for mortal beings. It is as though worldly stability had become transparent in the permanence of art, so that a premonition of immortality, not the immortality of the soul or of life but of something immortal achieved by mortal hands, has become tangibly present, to shine and to be seen, to sound and to be heard, to speak and to be read.[21]

While fabrication invariably terminated in the ancient world in either an instrument of use or an art object, it came with the emergence of empirical science to insinuate its process into the methodology of research and, with this deviation, to remove itself from the traditional teleology of artifice in favour of achieving the abstract instruments of cognition. The Renaissance, split between the liberal and the mechanical arts – already anticipatory of the industrial division of labour – led to the rise of the *homo faber* as a man of invention and speculation; of which the architect and *uomo universale*, Filippo Brunelleschi, was one of the earliest examples. As G C Argan has shown, this rise of the *homo faber* as architect resulted in widening the incipient division between invention and fabrication and led to the degradation of the traditional craftsmen into the status of the *animal laborans*:

Brunelleschi thought that a new technique could not be derived from the past, but must come from a different cultural experience, from history. In this way he refuted the old 'mechanical' technique and created a new 'liberal' technique based on those typically individualistic actions which are historical research and inventiveness. He abolished the traditional hierarchical form of the mason's lodge where the head was the co-ordinator of the specialized work of the various groups of skilled workers who made up the lodge of the masters. Now, there was only one planner or inventor; the others were merely manual laborers. When the master mason rose to the status of sole planner, whose activity was on a par with the other humanistic disciplines, the other members of the team of masons fell from the rank of maestri *in charge of various aspects of the job to that of simple working men. This explains the impatience of the masons and their rebellion against the master mason who had become 'architect' or 'engineer'.*[22]

This wilful creation of distance between conceiving and building pervades the entire Renaissance. It was as much present in Brunelleschi's invention of perspective or in his machines for the building of the cupola over Santa Maria del Fiore in Florence in 1420, as it was in Galileo Galilei's invention of the telescope in 1610, with which men first established the proof of the Copernican universe. The effective split of appearance and being that was the consequence of this proof, served to institute Cartesian doubt as the fundamental basis of the new scientific perspective. As Arendt has written:

The Cartesian method of securing certainty against universal doubt corresponded most precisely to the most obvious conclusion to be drawn from the new physical science: though one cannot know truth as something given and disclosed, man can at least know what he makes himself. This, indeed, became the most general and most generally accepted attitude of the modern age, and it is this conviction, rather than the doubt underlying it, that propelled one generation after another for more than three hundred years into an ever-quickening pace of discovery and development.[23]

Just as the shift to a heliocentric model of the universe was developed with the aid of an optical tool – the telescope – so the *homo faber* came to his place in the modern world through a re-evaluation of his traditional role. From Galileo on, he was not so much valued for his product as an end result but for his process as a means to an end. As Arendt shows, fabrication, which had hitherto disappeared into the product, now became an end in itself since pure science was not interested in the appearance of objects, but in the capacity of objects to reveal the intrinsic structure lying behind all appearance. It abandoned the passive contemplation of objects *per se* for the instrumental penetration of the laws of nature. This effectively reversed the traditional hierarchy of contemplation and action – a shift which, as Arendt shows, had profound consequences for the object of architecture:

As far as homo faber *was concerned, the modern shift of emphasis from the 'what' to the 'how', from the thing itself to its fabrication process, was by no means an unmixed blessing. It deprived man as maker and builder of those fixed and permanent standards and measurements which, prior to the modern age, have always served him as guides for his doing and criteria for his judgment. It is not only and perhaps not even primarily the development of the commercial society that, with the triumphal victory of exchange value over use value, first introduced the principle of interchangeability, then the relativization, and finally the devaluation, of all values ... It was at least as decisive that man began to consider himself part and parcel of the two superhuman, all-encompass-*

ing processes of nature and history, both of which seemed doomed to an infinite progress without ever reaching any inherent telos or approaching any preordained idea.[24]

This shift from the 'what' to the 'how' found its reflection in the division of engineering from architecture during the Enlightenment; first in Colbert's categorically anti-guild creation of the various royal academies for the arts and sciences including the Académie Royale d'Architecture (1677), whose 'architectural' graduates were to dedicate themselves solely to the 'what', that is, to the reification of public structures commissioned by the State; and then in 1747, with Perronet's creation of the Ecole des Ponts et Chaussées, whose 'engineering' graduates were to concern themselves largely with the 'how', namely, with the processal means of gaining permanent access to the realm. That these two aspects of the *homo faber* had already become professionally divided over the defence and siege of the walled city may be gauged from the fact that according to Michel Parent and Jacques Verroust, 'In the sixteenth century the defence of towns and castles was the work of *architects*. The word *engineer* remained reserved for those who not only built the siege machines but also handled them.'[25] The progressive invasion of the city of artifice by the machine – first the siege engine and later the locomotive, and then of course the electric tram and the automobile – accompanied the ultimate dissolution of the walled city in the middle of the nineteenth century. Aside from its monumental rhetoric and its simultaneous reduction of honorific built form to the status of being a rentable commodity, the Ringstrasse that came to replace Vienna's fortification in the second half of the century was coincidentally the initial proving ground for the horse-drawn tram.[26]

Deprived by Cartesian doubt of its faith in the received culture of the Renaissance, architectural theory was compelled to search for its authority in the knowledge of an objective archaeology. At the same time it began to look for its creative principle in the all-encompassing processes of nature. Thus while architects began to record and emulate the surviving models of antiquity, natural law came to be asserted as the prime universal principle. Our modern concepts of archaeology and history were both the outcomes of developments such as these. Stripped by science of its magical coalescence, the modern world began to fragment. Since appearance now belied truth, it became necessary to regard form as being separate from content and to this end the modern science of esthetica came into being with Baumgarten's *Aesthetica* (1750). At the same time architectural theoreticians, such as the Abbé Laugier in his *Essai sur l'architecture* (1753), began to advocate 'natural' primitive structures of self-evident lucidity. Pure reduced structure became the paradigm of architecture, and light came to be regarded as a metaphor for the illumination of reason itself.

The ascendance of the bourgeoisie, the rise of the social and the intimate, the rediscovery of antiquity, the duality of light and nature as the sublime emanence of the Supreme Being, and above all the influence of Rousseau and Newton combined to distract architecture from the task of realization and to project it into either an archaeologically remote past or an unattainable utopian future. This ideological distraction is prominently displayed in the works of Etienne Boullée, who imagined spectacular masses of masonry, at the scale of natural escarpments – vast megaliths of prohibitive size, penetrated by endless galleries of often inaccessible space. Is it not just such a figure that Arendt had in mind when she wrote of the *homo faber* renouncing his traditional calling in favour of the *vita contemplativa*? 'All he had to do was let his arms drop and prolong indefinitely the act of beholding the *eidos*, the eternal shape and model he had formerly wanted to imitate and whose excellence and beauty he now knew he could only spoil through any attempt at reification.'[27]

While architectural theory tended toward total dematerialization, as in the writings of Laugier, or toward the surreality of sublime, unrealizable form, as in the images of Boullée, engineering proceeded to work upon nature and to subject its untamed wastes to a measured infrastructure of metalled roads and embanked canals. Its province was now no longer the bastions and counterscarps of the fortified city, but the viaducts, bridges and dams of a universal system of distribution. Its technique not only outstripped the performance of traditional materials and methods but also afforded a more explicit form of structural expression – one in which structure was transparently penetrated by process. From now on architecture looked to such structure for much of its symbolic substance – and we find a late neo-classical architect such as Karl Friedrich Schinkel totally ignoring contemporary architecture on his first visit to England in 1826 and recording instead the distributive and productive achievements of the time: the Menai Straits suspension bridge and the 'processal' mill buildings of Manchester.

The *animal laborans* and the fungibility of the world

The brute concentration of natural labour-power, as though it were akin to water power, preceded, as Robin Evans has attempted to show, the late eighteenth-century development of industrial production as it is now generally understood. The workhouse as a place of production, secrecy and moral improvement (this last being nothing more than forcibly obtaining 'desirable' behaviour from the human animal) was fully instituted long before the invention of such important productive instruments as Newcomen's engine or Arkwright's spinning jenny. That this workplace was invariably a closed world only served to emphasize the essential *worldlessness* of labour for all that the privacy arose primarily out of a need for industrial secrecy. It was in any event a hermetic domain, where deprivation in the original sense was coupled with the work ethic and placed at the disposal of the machine. In the earliest workhouse the imprisoned vagrants, who had hitherto only been subjected to pillory, were punished for their nomadic idleness, after the mid-sixteenth century, by being forced to engage in both useful and useless production. Useful in the sense that Jeremy Bentham's Panopticon project of 1797 – to cite a highly developed workhouse type – was a machine for the extraction of improving labour from those 'on whose part neither dexterity nor good will were to be depended'.[28] Useless in the sense that William Cubitt's treadmill installed in the Brixton House of Correction in 1821 powered a rotating windsail on top of the mill house that indicated only too well the inutility of the prisoners' efforts.

The fundamental worldlessness of the *animal laborans* that manifested itself in the eighteenth century with the 'blind' mechanical production of the workhouse and the mill was paralleled in the twentieth century by the equally blind processes of mass consumption. As Arendt has written:

In our need for more and more rapid replacement of the worldly things around us, we can no longer afford to use them, to respect and preserve their inherent durability; we must consume, devour, as it were, our houses and furniture and cars as though they were the 'good things' of nature which spoil uselessly if they are not drawn swiftly into the never-ending cycle of man's metabolism with nature. It is as though we had forced open the distinguishing boundaries which protected the world, the human artifice, from nature, the biological process which goes on in its very midst as well as the natural cyclical processes which surround it, delivering and abandoning to them the always threatened stability of a human world.[29]

Arendt goes on to argue that the modern age has increasingly sacrificed the ideas of permanence and durability to the abundance ideal of the *animal laborans*, and that we live in a society of labourers inasmuch as the labour-power has been divided in order to eliminate from the thrust of its natural metabolism the 'unnatural' and conscious obstacle of the human artifice – the original object of the *homo faber*.

That the *animal laborans* cannot construct a human world out of its own values is borne out by the accelerating tendency of mass production and consumption to undermine not only the durability of the world but also the possibility of establishing a permanent place within it. The science fiction forms projected by the utopian urbanists of the twentieth century have arisen out of either elitist or populist attempts to reify industrial process as though it were some 'ideal' manifestation of a new nature. From the futurist architect Antonio Sant'Elia's Città Nuova (1914), of which, to quote from the *Manifesto of Futurist Architecture*, he stated that 'our houses will last less time than we do and every generation will have to make its own',[30] to Constant Nieuwenhuys's spontaneously dynamic New Babylon (1960), where urban change would be so accelerated as to render it pointless to return home – in each instance we are presented with equally kinetic images that project through prophetic exaggeration the fundamental placeless tendency of our present urban reality. Nieuwenhuys wrote:

There would be no question of any fixed life pattern since life itself would be as creative material ... In New Babylon people would be constantly travelling. There would be no need for them to return to their point of departure as this in any case would be transformed. Therefore each sector would contain private rooms (a hotel) where people would spend the night and rest for a while.[31]

From the point of view of machine or rationalized production, architecture has been as much affected as urbanism by the substitution of productive or processal norms for the more traditional criteria of worldliness and use. Increasingly buildings come to be designed in response to the mechanics of their erection or, alternatively, processal elements such as tower cranes, elevators, escalators, stairs, refuse chutes, gangways, service cores and automobiles determine the configuration of built form to a far greater extent than the hierarchic and more public criteria of *place*. And while the space of public appearance comes to be increasingly overrun by circulation or inundated at the urban scale by restricted high-speed access, the free-standing, high-rise megaliths of the modern city maintain their potential status as 'consumer goods' by virtue of their isolated form. At the same time the prefabricated elements from which such forms are increasingly assembled guarantee the optimization of their production and consumption within the overall industrial economy. Their potential for rapid amortization, convenient demolition and replacement begins to invalidate the traditional distinction of *meubles* from *immeubles*, a diffusion of meaning that was first announced in the nineteenth century, with the wholesale 'removal' of structures intact.[32] In a related but more immediate way automation imposes equally processal conditions on all industrial design, for it tends towards the servo-mechanization of consumption, wherein machine rhythms amplify the fundamental tendency of life to destroy the durability of the world.[33] In this manner even the worldly category of use is to be absorbed by consumption inasmuch as use objects – in this instance, tools – become transformed by abundance into disposable 'throwaway' goods; a subtle shift whose real significance resides in the intrinsic destructiveness of consumption as opposed to use.

The consequence of all this for contemporary architecture is as distressing as it is universal. Elevated on freeways or pedestrian decks or alternatively sequestered behind security fences, we are caused to traverse large areas of abstract, inaccessible urban space that can be neither appropriated nor adequately maintained. In a similar way we are confronted by piazzas whose hypothetical public status is vitiated by the vacuousness of the context, or alternatively we are conducted down streets evacuated of all public life by the circulatory demands of traffic. We pass across thresholds whose public-representative nature has been suppressed or we enter foyers which have been arranged or lit in such a manner as to defeat the act of public promenade. Alternatively we are caused to depart from airports whose processal function defies the ritual of leave-taking. In each instance our value-free commodity culture engenders an equivalency wherein museums are rendered as oil refineries and laboratories acquire a monumental form. By a similar token public restaurants come to be rudely incarcerated in basements, while schools find themselves arbitrarily encased within the perimeters of windowless warehouses. In each case a ruthless cultural reduction masks itself by the rhetoric of *kitsch* or by the celebration of technique as an end in itself.[34]

The identity of consumption and the worldlessness of play

The earliest concentrations of labour-power, beginning first with the workhouse and then with the mill, brought about the uprooting of agrarian populations who then became as alienated from their traditional culture as they were from the objects of industrial production. This loss of 'vernacular' was to return to haunt the descendants of these populations as soon as they became the 'emancipated' consumers of their own output. While the specific form of 'worldlessness' that resulted from this induced consumption varied with successive generations and from class to class, the initial loss of identity enforced by the conditions of industrial production was eventually sublimated, irrespective of class, by an identity to be instantly acquired through consumption. The phenomena of *kitsch* – from *Verkitschen*, 'to fake' – appears with the advent of the department store, around the middle of the nineteenth century, when bourgeois civilization achieves for the first time an excessive productive capacity and is brought to create a widespread culture of its own – a culture that was to remain strangely suspended between the useful and the useless, between the sheer utility of its own puritan work ethic and a compulsive desire to mimic the licentiousness of artistocratic taste.[35]

While Marx, writing just before mass consumption began in earnest, projected the eventual liberation of all mankind from the necessity of remorseless labour, he failed to account for the latent potential of machine production to promote a voracious consumer society wherein, to quote Arendt, 'nearly all human "labor power" is spent in consuming, with the concomitant serious social problem of leisure'.[36] In such a society the basic problem is no longer production but rather the creation of sufficient daily waste to sustain the inexhaustible capacity for consumption. Arendt's subsequent observation that this supposedly painless consumption only augments the devouring capacity of life, finds its corroboration in a world where shorter working hours, suburbanization and the mass ownership of the automobile have together secured for the realm of consumption the ever-accelerating rate of daily commutation within the megalopolis, a situation in which the hours saved from production are precisely 'compensated' by the hours wasted in the consumptive journey to work.

The victory of the *animal laborans* with which Arendt concludes her study of the dilemmas facing modern man turns not only on the reduction of art to the problematic 'worldlessness' of free play, but also on the substitution of social gratification for the fabricating standards of function and use. For, as Arendt has argued:

Nothing perhaps indicates clearer the ultimate failure of homo faber *to assert himself than the rapidity with which the principle of utility, the very quintessence of his world view, was found wanting and was superseded by the principle of 'the greatest happiness of the greatest number'.*[37]

While utility originally presupposed a world of use objects by which man was significantly surrounded, this world began to disintegrate along with the 'tool-making' tendency of each object not to be an end in itself but rather a means to other objects and other ends. As Arendt has put it, at this juncture 'the "in order to" has become the content of the "for the sake of", ... utility established as meaning generates meaninglessness.'[38]

Art, on the other hand, as the essence of inutility – and this of course includes the non-functional aspect of architecture – is rendered worldless in such a society, insofar as it is reduced to introspective abstraction or vulgarized in the idiosyncratic vagaries of *kitsch*. In the first instance it cannot be easily shared and in the second it is reduced to an illusory commodity. If, as Arendt insists, the world must be constructed with thought rather than cognition,[39] then insomuch as it is not essential to the life processes of a labouring society, art loses its original worldliness and comes to be subsumed under play. This, of course, raises the problematic question as to the conditions under which play may be considered to be worldly. Be this as it may, freedom in labouring society is perceived solely as release from labour, namely, as play, and it is Arendt's recognition of this fact that makes her text such a perceptive, if partial, critique of Marx.

Marx predicted correctly, though with an unjustified glee, 'the withering away' of the public realm under conditions of unhampered development of the 'productive forces of society', and he was equally right, that is, consistent with his conception of man as an animal laborans, *when he foresaw that 'socialized men' would spend their freedom from laboring in those strictly private and essentially worldless activites that we now call 'hobbies'.*[40]

The human condition and critical theory: a postscript

Given Hannah Arendt's scepticism as to the redemption promised by the Marxist prognosis it will no doubt appear extraneous to compare her discourse to the critical theory of the Frankfurt School.[41] The reserve which Arendt publicly exercised in respect to this school of Marxist criticism should be sufficient caution against making such a comparison. Yet despite the disdain she seems to have felt for those whom she regarded as renegade Marxists, a common concern and even method may be found to relate the arguments developed in *The Human Condition* to the socio-cultural analyses of the Frankfurt School. It is clear that both Arendt and the Frankfurt School were equally obsessed with the interaction of structure and superstructure in advanced industrial society, even if such terms were entirely foreign to her thought.

These qualifications accepted, one may argue that the succession of the Frankfurt School, specifically the theoretical progression that links the later thought of Herbert Marcuse to the writings of Jürgen Habermas, takes up a number of themes that were either suppressed or suspended at the conclusion of *The Human Condition*. Amongst these issues one may arguably posit two. First, the problematic cultural status of play and pleasure in a future labouring society after its hypothetical liberation from the compulsion of consumption (Marcuse) and, second, the problematic possibility for mediating the autonomous rationality of science and technique through the reconstruction of the space of public appearance as an effective political realm (Habermas).

If one derives from *The Human Condition* the implication that a highly secular, labouring and industrialized order must inevitably prevail in either state-capitalist, capitalist or socialist societies, and if one posits some future state in which the 'fatality' of an ever-accelerating consumption is, in some measure, redeemed, then the question arises as to what are the minimum environmental priorities that such a transformed state could realistically envisage?

While the *vita activa* in the ancient sense would no doubt initially remain in abeyance, some upgrading of the private habitat, essential to the quality of domestic life, would surely assert itself as a priority once this life was no longer subject to either rapacious consumption or optimized production. For while it is true, as Arendt asserts, that from the point of view of nature it is *work* rather than *labour* that is destructive, this observation overlooks that qualitative dimension of consumption beyond which 'man's metabolism with nature' becomes even more destructive of nature than *work*, beyond that frontier that we have already crossed, where non-renewable resources such as water and oxygen begin to become permanently contaminated or destroyed.[42] At this juncture, labour, as optimized consumption, stands opposed to its own Benthamite cult of life as the highest good, just as privacy *per se*, as the quintessence of labour and life, is undermined by the productive reduction of all built objects to the status of 'consumer goods'; a threshold that has again been reached in the mobile home industry of the United States.

Human adaptability notwithstanding, the basic criterion of privacy asserted by Barragán, posits itself not only as the necessary 'figure' to the public ground but also as the only standard by which a *balanced and rhythmic* life for the species could eventually be maintained. The urban consequences of applying such criteria as economic densities would be to spontaneously create the boundaries of a 'negative' urban form – namely, some kind of public realm, even if this would not immediately constitute a 'world' in the Arendtian sense. That the public space of the medieval city was the physical counterform of the private fabric Arendt herself has recognized in her assertion that it is the exterior perimeter of the private realm that effectively shapes the space of the city.

As to art, that is to say, as to the symbolization of common values and the manner in which they might be represented, this immediately introduces the cultural dilemma of 'play' and the extent to which communal expression may or may not be reified. Permanence is not the absolute precondition for reification, music being an obvious exception, as Arendt herself acknowledges: 'In music and poetry, the least "materialistic" of the arts because their "material" consists of sounds and words, reification and the workmanship it demands are kept to a minimum.'[43]

Twentieth-century avant-garde art has frequently resorted to collective play or at least to aleatory forms of art as the necessary expression of an essentially 'social' and dynamic future, although in many instances innate 'labouring' values have assured that nothing could be achieved save the tautology of production itself.[44] While this strategy may capitalize on the indisputable authority of instrumentality, the parallel tendency of art to survive through the reductive assertion of its own autonomy is yet a further illustration of the general tendency of a labouring society to move toward privatization. It is hardly an accident that both of these avant-garde strategies first emerged in the early years of the Soviet Union; the former, the *productivist sensibility*, being typified at its most extreme in the self-referential films of Dziga Vertov where the production of films about production exemplified production itself;[45] and the latter, the cult of *autonomous structure*, being reflected in the general artistic formalism of the period. The failure of this avant-garde to find its ostensible public led to the familiar withdrawal of the Soviet state into the *kitsch* of social realism. Only the repressed Proletcult with its political theatre and its programme for the 'theatricalization of everyday life' retained some lucid potential for a collective realization of an alternative culture.

Whether architecture, as opposed to building, will ever be able to return to the representation of collective value is a moot point. At all events its representative role would have to be contingent on the establishment of a public realm in the political sense. Otherwise limited by definition to the act of commemoration it would remain exactly where Adolf Loos left it in 1910. That this commemorative impulse would remain alive even in a labouring society became manifest after World War I in the numerous memorials to the 'unknown soldier', those testaments to an unidentifiable somebody whom four years of mass slaughter should have revealed.[46]

Nothing less is outlined in *The Human Condition* than the teleological abyss that has progressively opened up before the path of industrialized man. That Arendt and the Frankfurt School perceived the same void but drew different conclusions from it may be sensed in the following passage from Herbert Marcuse's *Eros and Civilization*:

The argument that makes liberation conditional upon an ever higher standard of living all too easily serves to justify the perpetuation of repression. The definition of the standard of living in terms of automobiles, television sets, airplanes, and tractors is that of the performance principle itself. Beyond the rule of this principle, the level of living would be measured by other criteria: the universal gratification of the basic human needs and the freedom from guilt and fear – internalized as well as external, instinctual as well as 'rational'... Under optimum conditions, the prevalence, in mature civilization, of material and intellectual wealth would be such as to allow the painless gratification of needs, while domination would no longer systematically forestall such gratification. In this case, the quantum of instinctual energy still to be diverted into necessary labor... would be so small that a large area of repressive constraints and modifications no longer sustained by external forces would collapse. Consequently the antagonistic relation between pleasure principle and reality principle would be altered in favor of the former. Eros, the life instincts, would be released to an unprecedented degree.[47]

While this utopian projection of a future where 'the elimination of surplus repression would *per se* eliminate if not labor, then the organization of human existence into an instrument of labor' does nothing if not stress the life-bound values of the *animal laborans*, Marcuse's recognition that the cult of *productivity* as an end in itself is the primary impasse of industrial society brings him surprisingly close to Arendt:

Efficiency and repression converge: raising the productivity of labor is the sacrosanct ideal of both capitalist and Stalinist Stakhanovism. The notion of productivity has its historical limits: they are those of the performance principle. Beyond its domain, productivity has another content and another relation to the pleasure principle: they are anticipated in the processes of imagination which preserve freedom from the performance principle while maintaining the claim of a new *reality principle.*[48]

That one day such a reality might still be achieved seems to be anticipated to an equal degree by Arendt's appraisal of the earliest Russian Soviets and Jürgen Habermas's prognostications for the future of the *vita activa*. The two relevant passages are given below, the former from Arendt's study of revolutionary politics entitled *On Revolution* and the latter from Habermas's essay, dedicated to Marcuse on his seventieth birthday, bearing the title 'Technology and Science as Ideology'. Of the Soviets, Arendt was to write:

The councils, obviously, were spaces of freedom. As such, they invariably refused to regard themselves as temporary organs of revolution and, on the contrary, made all attempts at establishing themselves as permanent organs of government. Far from wishing to make the revolution permanent, their explicitly expressed goal was 'to lay the foundations of a republic acclaimed in all its consequences, the only government which will close forever the era of invasions and civil wars'; no paradise on earth, no classless society, no dream of socialist or communist fraternity, but the establishment of 'the true Republic' was the 'reward' hoped for as the end of the struggle. And what had been true in Paris in 1871 remained true for Russia in 1905, when the 'not merely destructive but constructive' intentions of the first soviets *were so manifest that contemporary witnesses 'could sense the emergence and the formation of a force which one day might be able to effect the transformation of the State'.*[49]

And was it not just such a transformation that Habermas had in mind when he attempted to establish the following necessary limits for the emergence of a truly scientific rationality?

Above all, it becomes clear against this background that two concepts of rationalization must be distinguished. At the level of subsystems of purposive-rational action, scientific-technical progress has already compelled the reorganization of social institutions and sectors, and necessitates it on an even larger scale than heretofore. But this process of the development of the productive forces can be a potential for liberation if and only if it does not replace rationalization on another level.

Rationalization at the level of the institutional framework can only occur in the medium of symbolic interaction itself, that is through removing restrictions on all communication. Public, unrestricted discussion, free from domination, of the suitability and desirability of action-ordering principles and norms in the light of the socio-cultural repercussions of developing subsystems of purposive-rational action – such as communication at all levels of political and repoliticized decision making processes – is the only medium in which anything like 'rationalization' is possible.[50]

We are confronted in this complex passage with an existential political perspective that for Arendt and Habermas alike is the only possible vehicle for the rational determination of human ends. Such a decentralized 'cantonal' conception tends, I would submit, to return us to the dependency of political power on its social and physical constitution, that is to say, on its derivation from the living proximity of men and from the physical manifestation of their public being in built form. For architecture at least, the relevance of *The Human Condition* resides in this – in its formation of that political reciprocity that must of necessity obtain, for good or ill, between the status of men and the status of their objects.

First published in Melvyn A Hill, ed., *Hannah Arendt and Recovery of the Public World*, New York: St Martin's Press, 1979, pp.101–30. Subsequently published as 'The Status of Man and the Status of his Objects: A Reading of *The Human Condition*', *Modern Architecture and the Critical Present* (special issue of *Architectural Design*), no.7/8, 1982, pp.6–19.

Apropos Ulm: Curriculum and Critical Theory

The technical rationalism advocated whole-heartedly by the HfG constituted a progressive element particularly during the earlier years of its existence. Previously opposed, it has now gained acceptance everywhere. The socio-political factor associated with this rationalism is, however, less welcome; for it cannot be fitted snugly into the productive and reproductive process of society. Industrial societies need intelligence to remain alive. One brand of intelligence is favoured. Instrumental intelligence is taken into service but critical intelligence is desired to a lesser degree or not at all.
Gui Bonsiepe, *Ulm 21*, 1968

The fundamental thing in judging the work of a bourgeois intellectual is not to determine whether it includes reactionary elements or not; rather one must ascertain whether these elements constitute a universe in expansion or in contraction. In my intellectual work, there is a constant attempt to reduce the reactionary components that could 'invade' the theory it formulates.
Tomás Maldonado[1]

Introduction

There is little doubt that the Hochschule für Gestaltung, Ulm, has been the most significant school of design to come into existence since the end of World War II, not so much for what it achieved in terms of actual production, nor for the large number of designers it effectively educated, but for the extraordinary high level of critical consciousness that it managed to sustain in its daily work. In many respects the Hochschule was a pioneer, not only in terms of its evolution of design methods and the quality of the designs it achieved with these methods, but also because of the crisis of identity it suffered as a consequence of its dialectical rationality. The questions that the Hochschule began to ask a decade ago are now being asked, consciously or unconsciously, by every design and architecture school throughout the country, and the crisis of identity that befell the Hochschule has now become a universal malaise. For, over the past ten years it has become increasingly clear that certain lines of rational inquiry lead very promptly to an abyss where the relation between the design product and the society becomes extremely problematic; or, put in other terms, to a situation where the impossibility of an overall rational projection, under present circumstances, becomes clearly manifest.

Once design has reached this level of consciousness, it is inevitably confronted with a dilemma in which, in the broadest terms, it is usually faced with two choices. Either, as in the case of the famous Bertrand Russell paradox, it may choose to exclude a certain area of enquiry – a gesture which, although it sufficed to sustain mathematics, is difficult to maintain without rupture in the social world – or it may choose to continue to confront the immanent contradictions of the projection of rational human goals in relation to the dominant processes of the society. Should it choose the latter course, there is little doubt but that, as in the experience of the Hochschule, the liberal consensus of pluralism would be placed in jeopardy and relations with the establishment would become increasingly strained. This much is evident from the accounts of the development of the Hochschule given in the journal *Ulm*, nos 1 to 21, which have been the main source for the study that follows here. It is clear even from a most cursory reading of this publication that, contrary to popular myth, there was never any monolithic position obtaining at the Hochschule, for the discourse that was carried on in its journal came into being solely through interchange of individual opinion. In this respect, by virtue of quoting extensively, I have largely let the protagonists speak for themselves, although, as always, the choice of text for excerption must inevitably support one interpretation rather than another.

Nick Roedich, Thomas China, HfG student diploma work, Industrial Design Department, 1959.

In my treatment of the curriculum and the pedagogical method employed, I have only been able to outline the circumstances of a very complex development, partly because the material published in the journal is insufficient for an exhaustive analysis, and partly because this has not been my main intention. My aim has been to trace the evolution of the general ideology of the curriculum rather than to reveal the multiple vicissitudes of the teaching method, and in this, I should add, I have used throughout the term 'ideology' in the non-perjorative sense, to mean, as in the Oxford English Dictionary, 'a system of ideas concerning phenomena, especially those of social life ...'. I have also deliberately adopted the term 'critical theory' to suggest that there was something more than just a casual connection between the critical consciousness of the Hochschule and the critical theory developed by the Frankfurt School of Social Research.

It is not generally realized that the Hochschule survived as an institution for a comparatively long time, at least as long as the Bauhaus, if one counts the terminal date for that institution as being 1932; and although the Hochschule did not have so convoluted a history as the Bauhaus, with its cryptic men of genius and enforced migrations, it nonetheless had its own complexity and richness, which only an archivist, with ample time and space at his or her disposal, will ever be able to master. Such a researcher would certainly have to meet as many of the survivors of the institution as possible, and this I have not even attempted. Thus, many figures and incidents that no doubt featured prominently in the history of the school do not appear in this account, not only because of the limitations outlined above, but also because this was not my aim. In this context the extensive use of footnotes is meant as a primer for further research. In the light of that familiar and in many ways false opposition between 'thinkers' and 'doers', I have certainly placed the emphasis on the former, although it should be noted that all those quoted herein, with the exception of the philosopher Anatol Rapoport, not only taught regularly in the Hochschule but also practised as designers. The exception to this last is the sociologist Abraham Moles who, although he taught for quite some time at the Hochschule, never practised as a designer.

Finally I have not attempted to deal with the complex events leading up to the closure of the school, since, despite the fact that this was surely the crystallization of the conflict with the establishment, it still largely remains the stuff of national, if not local, history, rather than the substance of the conceptual confrontation.

The ideology of a curriculum

In an indirect way, the Hochschule für Gestaltung was a product of the German resistance to the Nazi regime, for the Hochschule was created, in principle, in 1950 by the Geschwister-Scholl Foundation, in memory of two young members of the Scholl family, Hans and Sophie Scholl, who had been executed by the Nazis some seven years before. It was the purpose of the foundation to establish a school which would, in the words of the constitution, combine 'as one entity, professional ability, cultural design and political responsibility'.

According to Konrad Wachsmann, the Hochschule had its origins in a move on the part of the American High Commissioner for Germany, John J McCloy, to sponsor, with considerable American aid, the foundation of a school of social research and political science as part of the American programme for the postwar reconstruction of Germany.[2] It would seem, if Wachsmann is correct, that this initiative was officially channelled through the Geschwister-Scholl Foundation and that it was Max Bill who, on being commissioned to design the building, persuaded Inge Aicher Scholl, and presumably the American High Commission, to found not a school of politics but rather a school of design. Nonetheless, a vestige of this initial political intent remained in the curriculum of the school, and this element contributed significantly to the shaping of its destiny.

Apart from this political legacy, the Hochschule was a conscious continuation of the German Applied Art School reform movement,[3] begun in the last decade of the nineteenth century, out of which the Bauhaus emerged in all its various incarnations. Even the name *Hochschule für Gestaltung* derives directly from the Bauhaus, since this was already a subtitle for the Dessau Bauhaus before Walter Gropius's resignation in 1928.[4] In any event the connection was made explicit in Max Bill's first public statement as the director of the Hochschule in 1953, wherein he wrote:

The founders of the Ulm School believe art to be the highest expression of human life and their aim is therefore to help in turning life into a work of art. In the words of that memorable challenge thrown down by Henry Van de Velde over 50 years ago, we mean 'to wage war on ugliness', and ugliness can only be combated with what is intrinsically good ... 'good' because at once seemly and practical. As the direct heir to Van de Velde's School at Weimar, the Dessau Bauhaus had set itself precisely the same objects. If we intend to go further at Ulm than they did at Dessau this is because postwar requirements clearly postulate the necessity for certain additions to the curriculum. For instance, we mean to give still greater prominence to the design of ordinary things in everyday use; to foster the widest possible development of town and regional planning; and to bring visual design up to the standard which the latest technical advances have not made possible. There will also be an entirely new department for the collection and dissemination of useful information.[5]

So much for Bill's rather idealistic initial statement of intent. But was this formulation still the intent by 1955, at the time of the formal opening, or by 1958, when the first issue of the Hochschule quarterly journal, *Ulm 1*, was published? There is a decided shift in both the language and the emphasis of this journal, as we may clearly appreciate from the following opening statement:

The Hochschule für Gestaltung educates specialists for two different tasks of our technical civilization: the design of industrial products (industrial design and building departments); the design of visual and verbal means of communication (visual communication and information departments) ... The school thus educates designers for the production and consumer goods industries as well as for present-day means of communication: press, films, broadcasting, television and advertising. These designers must have at their disposal the technological and scientific knowledge necessary for collaboration in industry today. At the same time they must grasp and bear in mind the cultural and sociological consequences of their work.[6]

The resignation of Bill in 1956 and his replacement by a triumvirate found its reflection in these discreetly formulated goals from which any reference to city and regional planning had been eliminated. It also found reflection in the four-year curriculum outline that followed, above all in the foundation course which was mandatory for all first-year students. This course, which was established as a *Grundlehre* by the Argentinian painter/designer Tomás Maldonado,[7] ostensibly comprised the following subjects: visual method, workshop practice, presentation methods, design methodology, sociology, perception theory, twentieth-century cultural history and a remedial course in mathematics, physics and chemistry. Judging from the highly schematic exposition given in *Ulm 1*, this course attempted to place a distinct and unusual emphasis on mathematics; first, on the creative and manipulative use of mathematical constructs in pragmatic design training, and second, on mathematical logic as the conceptual basis of design method. At the same time, the sociological and cultural aspects of the course emphasized Western superstructural transformations since the Industrial Revolution. One should note in passing that the workshop practice was markedly different from that of the Bauhaus, its emphasis being entirely away from any kind of craft production and towards the photo-reproduction of material and the making of prototypes. In fact, training was only given in wood, metal, plaster and photography.[8]

That there had been a major shift in orientation between Bill's brief tenure and the triumvirate rule of 1958 is also reflected in the curricula of the four departmental courses of industrial design, building, visual communication and information. If the heritage of the Bauhaus, initially acclaimed by Bill, still manifested itself in the recreation of a common foundation course and in the importance attached to some form of workshop practice, the departure from the Bauhaus tradition found clear expression in three sets of academic courses that were common to all four departments. First, in the return to *socio-cultural history*, a subject which had never been regarded as having any kind of validity within the millennial perspective of the Bauhaus; second, in a course known as *operational research*, comprising group theory, set theory, statistics and linear programming; and finally in courses dealing with the theory and *epistemology of science*, branching out into behaviour theory and the theory of machines.

Irrespective of the level initially attained in this ambitious programme, there is no reason to doubt but that this curriculum served not only to structure the pedagogic programme but also to publicly proclaim the ideology of the school; and, lest there should be any doubt as to the changed nature of the school, this schematic statement of intent was followed in the same month by the second issue of the journal, *Ulm 2*, which was largely devoted to a transcript of Tomás Maldonado's address to the

Brussels World Fair, given in September 1958, under the title, 'New Developments in Industry and the Training of the Designer'. This, as far as I know, was Maldonado's first public declaration; the range and complexity of the argument warrants a brief analysis of its salient points, particularly as this discourse clearly exerted a major influence on the formation of school policy. In retrospect, one cannot see that either of the other members of the triumvirate – neither the graphic designer Otl Aicher, who in any event betrayed little taste for intellectual discourse at this time, nor the sociologist Hanno Kesting, whose critical sociological position could not have been very far removed from that of Maldonado, and whose studies into the nature of industrial society had been published in the previous year[9] – would have much cause for disagreement with Maldonado's position.

Given the inescapable, almost fatal orientation of the Hochschule towards an updating of the Bauhaus, the initial point of interest in Maldonado's 1958 address lies in his measured critique of that legendary institution, and in particular for the distance he took in placing this legend in its proper historical context. Thus, of its dependence on the Arts and Crafts heritage, Maldonado observed that:

The inaugural manifesto of the Bauhaus in 1919 at Weimar, announced – not without declamatory élan – the union of the arts and the crafts and their future integration in a higher entity: architecture. It is a typical 'arts and crafts' manifesto, which Ruskin and Morris could have signed without contradicting themselves . . .

Of its problematic influence in the period that followed its demise, he argued, with unusual insight into the ambiguities of its achievement, that:

The American economic crisis of 1930 gave the day to styling – a new variation of industrial design whose influence has in fact extended up to the present day. The Bauhaus, its followers and its sympathizers, denounced from the start the commercial opportunism of styling, its indifference to artistic and cultural values. But the problem was no easy one: from time to time the stylists created products which could not but have been approved by the partisans of the Bauhaus. Stylists such as Henry Dreyfuss and Walter Dorwin Teague were sometimes damned, at other times, deified.[10]

That American styling since the Thirties had stolen much of the Bauhaus thunder and that, in any event, a good deal of Bauhaus and post-Bauhaus design could be regarded justly as some form of neo-academic formalism, that is, as the substitution of one aesthetic formula for another, was a position equally shared at that time by both Maldonado and Reyner Banham. At the same time, Maldonado could not accept Banham's acclaim of Fifties' industrial styling as the manifestation of legitimate folk culture. In refutation of such 'consensus' populism he stated: 'I am not convinced that the aerodynamic fantasies of vice-president Virgil Exner, responsible for the design of Chrysler automobiles, coincide with the artistic needs of the man in the street.'[11] Maldonado was to dismiss as irrelevant Banham's analogous characterization of the difference between elite design and pop art as a distinction between 'rare' and 'wild' flowers, arguing that:

Neo-academism is a right wing aestheticism, an aesthetic for but a few people, 'rare flowers'; styling is a left wing aestheticism, an aesthetic for many people, 'wild flowers'. The metaphor is doubtless pleasing, but I hold that the new tasks of the designer will have nothing to do with artistic horticulture, be it from the left or from the right . . . The aesthetic factor merely constitutes one factor among others with which the designer can operate, but it is neither the principal nor the predominant one. The productive, constructive, economic factors – perhaps, too, the symbolic factors – also exist. Industrial design is not an art nor is the designer necessarily an artist. The majority of objects exhibited in the museums, and in the exhibitions of 'good design', are anonymous and often executed in technical offices by subordinate employees who never imagined they were producing art.[12]

Donau Zeitung
Diplomatische Beziehungen zu Israel — Bruch mit Irak
Vietnam-Politik in Sackgasse
Kurz gemeldet
Deutschland-Erklärung des Westens zurückhaltend
Kommuniqué der Kompromisse
Koalition in Niedersachsen
Mehr Rente für Kriegsopfer
Deutschland - England 0:1

Gerd Zimmermann, Donau Zeitung *newspaper design, HfG Visual Communication Department, 1964–5.*

Maldonado followed this dismissal of liberal populism with an equally critical rejection of radical idealism as represented by Gregor Paulson's position on styling of some ten years earlier. Paulson had argued that the proper task for the industrial designer was one whereby the aesthetic factor becomes integrated into the *use value* of the product, rather than being assimilated by virtue of the function of style in the marketing process, into the *exchange value* of the product. Maldonado's refusal to be persuaded either by liberalism or by this latter-day *Neue Sachlichkeit*[13] formula gave him the opportunity to pose the interrelated issues of his later criticism: firstly, under what circumstances will industrial production be capable of freeing itself from the rhetorical demands of neo-kitsch marketing? And secondly, how may we rationally determine the phenomenon of consumption in relation to need? In 1958 he was to state:

Neither the psychoanalysts nor the professional critics of our civilization can give us a comprehensive explanation of all the phenomena of the world of consumption. The Marxists themselves do not succeed. One of them, the French philosopher Henri Lefebvre, recently wrote: 'By the side of the scientific study of the productive relations which effect political economy, there is . . . room for a concrete study of appropriation: for a theory of needs.[14]

Aside from these complex issues turning on the nature of industrial production and consumption, Maldonado praised the progressive aspects of the Bauhaus for its commitment to the 'learning through doing' approach of Hildebrandt, Kerchensteiner, Montessori and Dewey, and for its pragmatic opposition to the verbal emphasis of the humanist tradition. Nevertheless, it was clear that this particular pedagogical approach had now outlived its usefulness and that a new philosophy of praxis was needed. To this end, Maldonado proposed scientific operationalism, of which he remarked, '… it is no longer a question … of knowledge, but of operational, manipulable knowledge'.[15]

By 'operationalism' Maldonado seems to have been referring to that philosophical system developed in the early Fifties by Anatol Rapoport and published by him, in 1953, under the title *Operational Philosophy*. Given the persistence of the Bauhaus heritage, it is hardly surprising to find that Rapoport's philosophy was really a methodological updating of John Dewey's pragmatic-instrumentalism. The appeal of Rapoport's method lay in his attempt to provide a precise system for the evaluation of alternative courses of action. It is a measure of his discretion that, despite his dependence on mathematical logic, Rapoport was at pains to distinguish both his and Dewey's system from that of the logical positivists, with their belief that philosophy should become a purely analytic discipline, akin to mathematics. Instead, Rapoport thought of his operationalism as being a synthetic action-oriented discipline. In 1953 he wrote that operationalism '… is the philosophy of action-directed goals. It starts with logical analysis but transcends it by relating this analysis to society.'[16] At the time this seems to have been relatively close to Maldonado's own notion of scientific operationalism, of which he has since written, 'By scientific operationalism I intended then a model of action oriented towards overcoming the dichotomy between theory and practice. Later on, following Kotarbinski, I preferred to call it "praxiology" – and even more recently, "the philosophy of praxis", as seen in Gramsci.'[17]

Rejecting its Arts and Crafts origins and ever conscious of the perspectives of Marxist analysis, the Hochschule, bound to the service of neo-capitalism, had little choice in the Fifties but to look beyond the limits of these traditions for a mediatory ideology from which to develop not only a satisfactory heuristic method, but also a theory of design. A theoretical basis seems to have been proferred by Rapoport's operationalism, save for its incapacity to deal in an adequate manner with the intrinsic significance of form itself. For this the Hochschule seems to have turned first to Max Bense, whose communications approach to the determination of aesthetic need was first outlined in his book *Aesthetica*, published in 1954;[18] and then to the writings of Charles Morris, whose first semiotic works had appeared in the Unified Science publications of the late Thirties.[19] *Operation* and *communication*: these are the two 'poles' that are to play major roles in the evolution of Hochschule theory.

One cannot complete an outline of the ideology of the Hochschule without some reference to its teaching methodology. It is evident that with the change in the directorship in 1957, the school began to take a more rigorous approach to the problem of both design and design training. That is to say, it encouraged a logical approach to the organization and generation of basic form, with the intent of applying such procedures to actual design problems. These operations varied from simple projections to three-dimensional transformations, from matrices to the manipulations of lattices, from the progressive deformation of regular grids to the rotation of ellipses centred on such grids, from the application of graph theory to topological studies, from exercises in solid geometry to the development of three-dimensional modular components which were capable of being combined in alternative sequences. Whereas in the visual communications department these exercises were often decisive in determining the general approach to an informational problem, such as the design of a subway map, in the building department a modular method was invariably adopted as a way to approach a variety of problems, from the design of a diaphragm for a building panel to the combinatorial range of a set of prefabricated elements.

But the pursuit of a mathematical methodology did not restrict itself to this rational yet free manipulation of formal propositions. In the field of design programming, where initial criteria and alternative solutions have first to be established and evaluated, the rigour rapidly developed into a form of heuristic determinism and into a logical positivism of design that would often tend to forego a solution rather than arrive at a synthesis that could not be entirely determined algorithmically. In these instances, design method rapidly degenerated into that which Maldonado has since characterized as 'method-idolatry'.[20] That Maldonado's own attitude to the positivistic approach was at first somewhat ambivalent seems to be reflected in the endless controversies that arose inside the Hochschule during the early Sixties, which amounted to a long drawn out confrontation between the pragmatic designers on the one side – epitomized in such brilliant figures as the late Hans Gugelot – and the methodologists on the other, the most extreme faction, according to Maldonado, being led by a guest professor at the Hochschule, the Swiss political economist and art historian, Lucius Burckhardt.

Although little mention of this conflict emerged in the quarterly journal, it is quite clear that it nonetheless took place. This much is evident from Gunter Schmitz's paper on the Hochschule, read before the AIA/ACSA Teachers' Seminar of 1968, wherein he stated:

From 1960 to 1962 a controversy over the evaluation of the theoretical courses in relation to practical design work engaged the school. At the base of this lay the question of the exact role that analytical methods should play in the design process. The tendency towards an objectification of creative activities had nourished the dangerous yearning for a methodology which would automatically lead to original and perfect results.[21]

Schmitz then went on to briefly characterize the development of design teaching and practice within the school, from the beginning of Otl Aicher's directorship to its closure in 1968:

Since 1962 the Hochschule has tried to balance the results and methods of the different scientific disciplines with the practical requirements of the design process, or, to put it another way, the Hochschule tries to avoid a

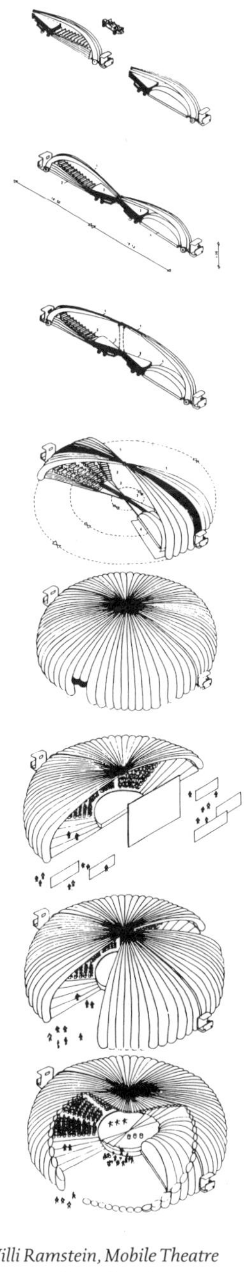

Willi Ramstein, Mobile Theatre Design, HfG student thesis project, Building Department, 1960–1.

mere accumulation of theoretical courses indigestible to the student. The concept since that time has involved an accentuation of the instrumental character of theory and the performance of practical design work on an experimental basis. As a consequence the number of general theoretical courses is reduced in favour of lectures which are more directly connected with design problems. On the other side the design problems stimulate prospective investigations, where theory plays an important role.[22]

An idea of the Hochschule curriculum and educational policy at the time of its stability, so to speak, that is, just prior to its enforced closure in February 1968, may be best gained from the tables that Schmitz made available to the Montreal seminar, wherein the number of hours spent in various subjects and tasks during a four-year course in the building department was made quite explicit. Since this breakdown reveals the pedagogical emphasis in its prime, it seems fitting here to make a brief summation of the academic balance achieved at the Hochschule prior to its closure. By then it should be noted that the foundation course, or *Grundlehre*, had been discontinued, after Maldonado had been appointed as head of the industrial design department with the reorganization of 1962. After this year, students were channelled into one of three departments from the very beginning; that is, from the first year they entered directly into their chosen speciality, be it building, product design or visual communication. The department of information had been eliminated in Aicher's reorganization. A certain communality of approach was now assured by common theoretical courses taken primarily over the first two years by students of all three departments. Very roughly speaking, for a student of industrialized building (and it needs to be emphasized that this was the sole orientation under Herbert Ohl), the breakdown would have been as follows: in the first year, some 45 per cent of the student's time would have been spent in basic design, some 20 per cent in theoretical lectures and some 35 per cent in technical courses – 15 per cent of the latter being devoted to workshop practice. In the second year, some 65 per cent would go to studio work with some 23 per cent to technical courses other than workshop, while the remaining 12 per cent would be spent in theoretical lectures. During the third and fourth years studio work occupied nearly 70 per cent of the time available, the remainder being devoted to technical courses other than the workshop. From this we can see that workshop training was over by the end of the first year, and theory was largely covered by the end of the second.

It is clear from this that the highly ambitious educational programme projected in *Ulm 1* in 1958 had been heavily trimmed in the Aicher reorganization of 1962, yet something of the unusual initial orientation remained in the curtailed curriculum, for all that the term and even the topic 'operational research' had been discreetly dropped. Thus we find the first year theory courses, taken by students of all three departments, with roughly

27 per cent of their time devoted to mathematical techniques applicable to design, some 37 per cent of their time to sociology, economics, political economy, psychology and ergonomics, and the remainder of their time to a very brief survey of twentieth-century cultural history, including architecture, industrial design, film, literature, painting, music and visual communication. In other words, the mathematical, political and socio-cultural emphases of 1958 remained largely intact, although by the end of the first year, cultural history was abruptly concluded, with the remainder of the courses then being broadly divided between systems theory on the one hand and political economy on the other.

Whether it was economically enforced from without or ideologically determined from within, this curtailment of the course work seems to be indicative of some kind of theoretical containment within the school. This contraction of the programme seems to have been accompanied by a loss of conviction in the efficacy of positivistic design methods, along with a good deal of scepticism as to the relevance of Rapoport's liberal pragmatism for the solution of socio-cultural problems. Whatever the repercussions of Aicher's reorganization, there was a discernible shift in the nature of the discourse appearing in the journal thereafter, a shift which seems to have reflected a retrenchment on the part of the theoreticians to a more radical position. In any event, after 1962 any hope of reconciliation between the Hochschule and the promise of postwar neo-capitalism, decidedly began to fade.

The development of a critical theory

Despite the reorientation of the school under Aicher's stewardship, the socio-cultural criticism emanating from the Hochschule continued to grow over the next five years, most particularly through the contribution of Maldonado, Claude Schnaidt and Gui Bonsiepe. These three happened to announce their common critical attitude in the review section of *Ulm 7*, published in 1963, wherein their notes were respectively addressed; first, to a criticism of the intrusion of neo-Dada into the field of industrial design;[23] second, to an appraisal of Leonardo Benevolo's *History of Modern Architecture*;[24] and finally, to a review of Georg Klaus's critique of Norbert Weiner's information theory, which had then just appeared in Klaus's book *Cybernetics in the Light of Philosophy*. The aim of the Klaus study was to refute the Weiner reduction of information to a mere quantifiable assessment of its relative density and predictability. Rejecting the implicit Weiner split of *sign* from *import* and his classification of information as a mere quantum, akin to energy, Klaus argued that 'All information must rather have a definite meaning, must be a carrier of some significance.'[25]

This apparently banal but nonetheless anti-positivist statement had of course been the basic assumption behind the Maldonado seminars in semiotics, given as a regular course in the Hochschule from 1957 to 1960, the first fruits of which were the Maldonado essay 'Communication and Semiotics' that appeared in *Ulm 5* in 1959, and the Bonsiepe text 'Uber formale und informale Sprachanalyse: Carnap und Ryle' that was written in 1960.[26] Strangely enough the only adequate publication of the work of these seminars did not appear in the journal *Ulm*, but in a little-known publication entitled *Uppercase*, edited by Theo Crosby. Thus, *Uppercase 5* of 1963, dedicated in the main to work of the Hochschule, featured texts by Maldonado and Bonsiepe, a design case study by Walter Muller and a semiotic glossary.[27]

In retrospect, the most significant aspect of this approach was the distance it implicitly took from a positivistic design approach and the corresponding stress it placed on form as a necessary communicative element. In his 'Notes on Communication' Maldonado refused the positivistic split of operation from communication in a text that is remarkable for its perception of *function* as being an integral part of *culture*, and vice versa:

Fallen or existing civilizations document themselves primarily by their material products, i.e. by the objects which they create and which under appropriate conditions succeed in surviving. The ethnologists and anthropologists usually classify these products in the following manner:

1. *those which man has created with the aim to extend, strengthen or to consolidate his physical power over nature;*
2. *those which man has created with the aim of communicating with other men.*

The first ones are called artifacts, i.e. objects made by man, as distinguished from natural objects (artifacts, e.g. tools, utensils, apparatus, machines, etc.), the second ones are signs or sign structures (e.g. pictographic inscriptions, writings, emblems, musical scores, traffic signs, publications and prints of any kind, discs, photographs, films, etc.). The classification of the products of a culture – operative world of the artifacts and communicative world of the signs – becomes less and less convincing. In reality, all these products of a culture belong to one common system. The artifacts are operable in the extension – and only in the extension, are they capable of communicating a definite meaning unit to the operator; the signs of their part are communicative in the extension – and only in the extension can they directly or indirectly influence behaviour in an operative way.[28]

Maldonado extended this argument to embrace the field of ergonomics and in particular the province of machine design, where the *operative* and *communicative* aspects become dramatically intermeshed and where the critical 'man–machine' relationship of advanced industrialization acquires an undeniably concrete dimension. In this respect, the advanced ergonomic theories of Chapanis, Fitts and Taylor[29] were welcomed by Maldonado for the stress they placed on the redesign of the machine and for their mutual intent to resolve the 'man–machine' couple in such a way as to liberate a man as much as possible from the tyranny of the machine.

This measured critique was extended in the Maldonado/Bonsiepe essay 'Science and Design', which appeared in 1964 in *Ulm 10/11*. Broadly speaking, this paper was an attack on the simplistic borrowing of design methods from the field of 'human engineering', beginning with a critique of the established methods of experimental psychology for their untenable lineality of approach and going on to upbraid that aspect of ergonomics which grounded itself in a servo-mechanical model of the human being – a schema whereby the complexity of man becomes reduced (usually under conditions of *extremis*) to the so-called H-factor. The authors concluded their survey of heuristic methods, derived from the margins of applied science, with a highly sceptical appraisal of the procedures of market and motivational research and for the propensity of such research to convert 'undifferentiated needs into definite demands'. The concluding paragraphs of 'Science and Design' convey the irony of their attack. Referring to the categories used in motivational research, they argued that:

The latter hardly appears convincing when one calls to mind that the clients of both market and motivational research are, in all cases, the very interest groups who influence on a large scale – on a far larger scale than psychological categories – the taste, wants and even dreams of the consumer. The motivational researcher sometimes reminds us of a detective with a two-sided commission: to seduce the wife on the one hand and to find out who is her lover on the other. To produce the motives and at the same time to find out what they are . . . In our society neither the world of merchandise can be easily penetrated nor, in many cases, can product design which influences this world of merchandise. Despite all these unfavourable circumstances one thing emerges: in the future, the function of the product designer should not consist of designing products according to an outline demand, as is still the custom in our free economy. Rather, the product designer should be the one who contributes to the creation of demand; otherwise he will be able to play only a subordinate role and preserve the existing products with only superficial modification. The product designer should not consider his function to keep quiet but to promote disquiet.[30]

Maldonado and Bonsiepe clearly felt they had no choice but to promote disquiet. Not for its own sake, since there is little enough anarchy in their thought, but as a direct consequence of their analysis. While simultaneously practising and teaching industrial design, they could not fail to become aware of the overall predicament of the designer in a neo-capitalist economy. Unlike the Pre-Raphaelites or the artists of the Weimar Bauhaus, they were neither romantic iconoclasts nor Spenglerian critics of science. On the contrary, they sought, in accordance with the initial orientation of the

Hochschule, to come to terms with the realities of industrial production and distribution. But it was precisely this determination to comprehend reality that led them into the uncomfortable lucidity of their analyses. In collaboration with their colleague, Claude Schnaidt, in the HfG building department, they saw all too clearly the present highly problematic situation of the architect and the industrial designer.

Maldonado's own views on the teaching and practice of industrial design have never perhaps been more clearly articulated than in the article he wrote (presumably late in 1963) for the education volume of Gyorgy Kepas's *Vision and Value*. In this text Maldonado defined the métier of industrial design in the following terms: 'Industrial design is an activity whose ultimate aim is to determine the formal properties of the objects produced by industry. By "formal properties" is not meant the external features, but rather those structural and functional relations which convert an object into a coherent unity from the point of view of both the producer and the user.'[31] This definition, which was and still is distinguished by its precise qualification of the term 'formal' and by its insistence on the need to satisfy the user as well as the producer, appeared as the fulcrum of Maldonado's argument, which, while it exposed the commercial limitations of industrial design in a competitive society, could not bring itself to condone the pathetic mimicry of neo-capitalist products in non-competitive societies such as the Soviet Union. Disturbed by the complacent claims made for Soviet design by Yuri Soloviev, at the Aspen Design Conference of 1961, Maldonado wrote:

Curiously enough, the industrial designer in the Socialist countries is not fully conscious of the new possibilities that his economic and social system – at least in theory – offers to his profession. If this were not so, how can we explain that the frankly pathological manifestations of American and European industrial design are adopted by the Soviet designers as models worthy of imitation and perfection? One does not expect from the Soviet designers the imitation of our weaknesses, but rather the full exploitation of their own, specific possibilities. One expects them to tackle problems we are not allowed to tackle. For instance, technical products themselves require an urgent revision as far as their structural and functional properties are concerned, but in the framework of our competitive society, initiative in this direction cannot be imagined, because the main activity of our society is to merchandise these products . . . The designers of a non-competitive society are in a favourable position for attacking this new kind of task, but until now not very much has happened. One can only hope that this cannot be traced to the same reason which in the past caused Soviet architects and urbanists to commit such mistakes as maintaining naive confidence in a tradition in which no one any longer believes.[32]

Thereafter, in the same text, Maldonado added to his definition of industrial design the rider that its interpretation and application would be differentiated according to the following variables: '... (1) the social and economic context, i.e. whether the profession is exercised in a competitive or non-competitive society; (2) the degree of the structural and functional complexity of the objects to be designed; (3) the degree of dependence of the particular object to be designed on the traditions of craft and the traditions of taste.'[33]

For Maldonado, *design* in general, after a dialectical overcoming of both the 'degeneracies' of admass populism and the paradoxical 'alienations' of bureaucratic socialism, has to be returned to a strict distinction in practice between puristic formalism on the one hand and formal order in its broadest sense on the other. In the last analysis, for Maldonado, this distinction can only be made in the context of preserving human values, an issue with which the second half of the twentieth century has yet to come to terms. Given the economic and highly abstract imperatives of our present society, this is understandable, since the reintegration of such values ultimately presupposes a dialectical definition of 'needs' which would have to transcend, without excluding them, the primary demands of production and use. Such a definition would have to assimilate these basic criteria into a perspective that takes cognizance of the fundamental limitations of human life – *eros* and *thanatos*, hedonism and mortality.

The position taken by Schnaidt and Maldonado with regard to the particular predicament of architecture, as it was then being practised and taught in the Sixties, remains remarkably timely. Their views, now almost ten years old and strongly influenced by the conditions of the time, retain nonetheless a certain general validity that makes them as applicable today as when they were first written. In fact, in a decade, little has changed except that the opportunities for the architect to make significant contribution to the society are possibly even more limited now than they were in the early Sixties. In his essay 'Prefabricated Hope', which appeared in *Ulm 10/11*, Schnaidt attempted a comprehensive analysis of the failure of industrialized building. He then argued against the by now familiar sterility of treating this prospect from a purely technical standpoint, writing:

It is difficult to apply profitably industrial production methods in the building of housing estates containing less than 500 dwellings. Given the current density of population, 500 dwellings require at least 2.5 hectares of land ... To create such sites one must acquire many small lots, paying the owners a surplus value estimated according to the expected value of the lot after mains supplies and sewerage pipes have been laid. This is where speculation is let loose. The sale and resale of building sites to the profit of the few is a curse which is becoming increasingly ruinous to the community. On the outskirts of numerous major European cities, the price of real estate has increased ten-fold in the last ten years; in 1950, the ground rates represented about ten per cent of the selling price of a house; by 1960, it had risen to 45 per cent. The reduction in the cost of housing which can be achieved by industrializing building seems ridiculously small in comparison with the increase caused by land-speculation . . . The future of the industrialization of building will depend on the solution found to all these problems. This is why it is erroneous, if not dishonest, to speak solely of technical matters when evoking decisions that affect this future. The choice is not, as they would have us believe, between so-called traditional building and prefabrication. It is between a disordered, slow and precarious development of technical progress in building as a whole and a coherent, rapid and planned industrialization for the benefit of the community.[34]

One need hardly add that this critique was, in many respects, an implicit attack on the work of the Hochschule building department in which Schnaidt himself functioned as a teacher. In a parallel criticism of architectural education given as the Lethaby Lecture at the Royal College of Art, in 1965, under the title 'The Emergent World: A Challenge to Architectural and Industrial Design Training', Maldonado was to argue that the upgrading of architectural school curricula had largely resulted in a shifting of the academic scenery, in which the fundamental pedagogical orientation had remained unchanged. A primary aspect of this apparent transformation had clearly been the universal adoption of basic design courses, along the lines of the Bauhaus, while the most common secondary change, largely unrelated to the first, had been the wholesale acceptance of modern architecture. Of this Maldonado remarked, 'On the altar where Palladio was worshipped, Wright, Le Corbusier, Gropius, Mies van der Rohe, Fuller, Louis Kahn or Kenzo Tange are now being honoured. The idols have changed but not the doctrines.'[35] Yet for Maldonado not even those schools which had attempted to restructure their curricula along scientific lines were entirely free from criticism, for he could see all too clearly, after his own experiences at the Hochschule, how a naive worship of scientific method could lead to designs even more abstracted from any legitimate form of socio-cultural reality than before.

It would seem that by 1966 the 'critical theory' of the Hochschule had already reached the threshold of disputing by implication the viability of design schools *per se*, and there is little reason to doubt but that Otl Aicher's essay 'Planning All Awry?', which appeared in *Ulm 17/18* of that year, was nothing but an oblique attempt to counter the auto-criticism of his 'left wing' faculty; Aicher urging all designers, not only planners, to accommodate themselves to the power constraints of neo-capitalism. It is interesting to note that the anti-monumentalism of his position would have been shared by Schnaidt, but not the ultimately apolitical, mystifying scientism of his conclusions, wherein Aicher stated:

Viewed in this way, conventional architects still form the professional category which is best suited to satisfying the demands of a planner. Only the days are past when the proximity of art shed some of the glory of genius on the architectural profession. The specific skills of the architect are today just adequate to enable him to elicit from the facts assembled by science *a tangible plan tailored to* political objectives *[my emphasis], and then he must again leave it to the politicians to make the final decision as to its implementation. The planner loses nothing by recognizing in the development director a figure of political power who is set above him as regards both the definition of objectives and the assessment of feasibility. The planner loses nothing if he tolerates the presence of scientists who can make forecasts in respect of an applied development theory. He will undoubtedly be forfeiting his chance of a niche in cultural history because he will have surrendered his sole authority. But in return he will enjoy a special advantage: the prospect of seeing what he plans actually being realized. The prospect, that is, of gradually narrowing the gap between plan and reality which today condemns the plan to impotence.*[36]

Aicher was apparently unable to realize the inadequacy of this position, wherein, irrespective of the 'forecasts of science', the contradictions of society as they impinge on design are incapable of resolution through the 'mythical' aggregation of power on the part of the designer. The *Neue Sachlichkeit* architects of the Weimar Republic certainly had no taste for the 'glory of genius', but this had little evident effect on the realization of their plans; particularly after 1933, when the figures of power chose to define the overall objectives in entirely different terms.

In any event Aicher did not go unanswered, first inadvertently by Maldonado, in the same issue of the journal, *Ulm 17/18*, in a text with the provocative title, 'How to Fight Complacency in Design Education', and then in the penultimate issue of the journal, *Ulm 19/20*, in 1967, in a seminar report by Abraham Moles addressed to 'Functionalism in Crisis', and in an essay by Claude Schnaidt entitled 'Architecture and Political Commitment'.

Where Maldonado, while pleading the case for C S Peirce's 'university of methods',[37] stressed conflict and disorder and the reciprocal link that existed in the Third World between violence and necessity, Moles went straight to the *raison d'être* of the Hochschule and argued in effect that its basis had been overtaken by the success of the 'economic miracle', since the pure functionalism it professed was no longer required by the economic system it was pledged to serve. While diplomatically evading the ultimate consequences of this argument, Moles presented his case with characteristic irreverence:

Affluent society as an economical theory purports that the machinery of production has to run permanently; therefore the consumer has to be stipulated to consume at any price. Consumption and production are linked into a combined system which runs at an ever increasing speed. Functionalism necessarily contradicts the doctrine of affluent society which is forced to produce and to sell relentlessly. Finally functionalism tends to reduce the number of objects and to realize an optimal fit between products and needs, whereas the production machinery of an affluent society follows the opposite direction. It creates a system of neo-kitsch by accumulating objects in the human environment. At this point the crisis of functionalism becomes manifest. It is torn between the neo-kitsch of the supermarket on the one side and ascetic fulfillment of function on the other side.[38]

It was left to Schnaidt to articulate in unequivocal terms the consequences of this crisis in its wider ramifications, and in many respects his text was to be the last major contribution to the critical theory of the Hochschule before its self-dissolution in February 1968. His indirect response to the Aicher model of planning reality requires little comment, save that his arguments led him to advocate regional decentralization:

While architects take refuge in aestheticism, fantasy and technocracy, man's environment and everyday life are steadily deteriorating. The megalopolises which are taking shape are stricken at the least failure of their over-burdened infrastructures. They call for prodigious amounts of money to function at all ... The annual subsidy received by the Paris Passenger Transport Board is four times larger than all the allocations made to help the industrialization in Brittany during the past ten years ...

The concentration of industries and their head offices in and around the metropolis and the continuous increase in rents which compels those working there to put up their homes far afield have made certain reductions in working hours a purely illusory gain. After all, a cut of six to eight hours a week means very little when two to three hours a day are lost travelling to and from work. And all this lost time comes off the leisure which people are forever talking about ...

Apart from the loss of time, money and lives, the problem of home-to-job distance causes another kind of trouble, this time of a social nature with repercussions on both the individual citizen and the urban region. The latter has gone onto 'half-time' and its inhabitants have followed suit. Thus a man sets off at dawn from his village, his suburb, his satellite town which provides the labour needed for the big city. He is away the whole day and he comes home in the evening depleted of energy and longing for nothing else but peace and quiet. And for this reason it is rare for him to contribute anything to the community in which he lives; he has no ideas, no criticism, no impetus to give it. As far as his environment is concerned he might just as well be dead ... What is the basic cause of concentration? When a manufacturer sets up in a developed area he can use the existing infrastructure and equipment. And these – water, gas, electricity, telephones, sewage, communications, public transport services, public buildings – are paid for by the community. Thus the manufacturer is enabled to avoid the expenditure involved in setting up, renewing and adapting this infrastructure ... He is thus able to increase his profit margin. Put differently, the community has to bear what has been called the 'social cost of private enterprise'. Political commitment requires one to demand that the brunt of the social cost of private enterprise should no longer be borne by the community. .[39]

The unequivocal and sometimes simplistic remedies that Schnaidt prescribes in 'Planning All Awry?' categorically reveal the radical nature of his own political affiliations, but this in no way detracts from the general accuracy of his analysis nor from the pertinence of his revolutionary perspective.

The critical theory of Bonsiepe, Maldonado and Schnaidt was fated to return the Hochschule to its point of departure. Having started its existence as a school of design, in lieu of a school of politics, it was paradoxically returned to its political destiny by men whose lives were dedicated to design. The vicissitudes that their respective theories passed through, over a decade, tend to confirm that this development arose naturally out of adopting a certain attitude towards design. For design as the self-determination of man on earth, through the exercise of his collective *consciousness*, still remains with us as a positive legacy of the Enlightenment. Despite the admass absorption of the Modern Movement, the fundamental frustration of its *genuine* realization in every domain of life still testifies to the present containment of its liberating force. This much was stated by Schnaidt when he wrote of the historical co-option of the movement that 'Modern architecture which wanted to play its part in the liberation of mankind by creating a new environment to live in, was transformed into a giant enterprise for the degradation of the human habit ...',[40] and by Bonsiepe when he wrote in the last issue of the journal, *Ulm 21*, the following text of resignation:

Admittedly there is little evidence of realization in training institutions that the communications industry is a consciousness industry, whether it is concerned with the engendering of truth or untruth in consciousness, with enlightenment or ideology. The more visual designers concentrated on the aesthetic perfection of the designs, the more the communications industry was able to keep its power out of sight. The insistence on the aesthetic as one aspect of design is undoubtedly warranted and was capable of retaining its validity over the years. But the aesthetic cannot be maintained in unsullied and apolitical detachment from the social. Formerly, the aesthetic figured as the anticipation of a state of affairs which implied liberation from the constraints of necessity. But the aesthetic met with a fate which could not have been foreseen. It was found that it could very readily be pressed into the service of repression. The forms of power have been sublimated. In the course of this sublimation the aesthetic – which was and still is a promise of the state of liberation of mankind – has been harnessed by the agencies of power and thus used to acquire and maintain power. No consequences have as yet been drawn from this change in the role of the aesthetic insofar as it affects either the theory or practice of training in visual communication.[41]

First published in *Oppositions*, no.3, 1974, pp.17–36.

Student poster announcing the dissolution of the HfG in February 1968. It alludes to a similar level of political reaction as was responsible for the closure of the Weimar Bauhaus.

The influence of changes in the structure of Swedish society

By 1970 Volvo had been made forcibly aware, through a heavy increase in absenteeism, of the intrinsically negative aspects of repetitive 'on-line' production. Above all else the company had become sensitive not only to days lost through absenteeism but also to the general decline in the quality of the product. The 1968 student revolt had the effect of bringing the half-repressed discontent of the labour force into the open and Volvo, like many other Swedish industries, experienced a series of wildcat strikes. Naturally Swedish industrial management became extremely concerned and new parameters such as working hours, work rhythm, social facilities and the quality of the working environment were at once admitted into the field of labour relations. A delegation from Volvo was dispatched to the Norwegian Works Research Centre at Oslo[1] and at the end of 1969 a decision was made to delegate a certain range of decisions to the individual productive unit.

On succeeding to the directorship of the company in May 1971, the present Managing Director, Pehr Gyllenhammar, began to participate in these productive reforms, at once commissioning an inter-disciplinary research team with the task of devising a totally new procedure. The intensive research of this team led eventually to the development of the Volvo carrier and to the layout of the new plants at Kalmar and Skövde. Since 1970, innovations have occurred within the whole of AB Volvo in many diverse forms, ranging from work organization to automation and from ergonomic refinement to environmental improvement. Throughout these developments, a regard for the idiosyncrasies of local conditions has always proved to be essential, for what might well succeed in one instance has often proved to be disastrous when applied to another.

In 1966 the Federation of Swedish Trade Unions (LO) brought out a report entitled *The Trade Union Movement and Technological Development*, in which it began to examine the impact of advanced technological methods and the resultant working environment on the life of the average employee. While this report acknowledged the necessity for organizing modern production along rational lines – namely in accordance with Tayloristic principles – it went on to note the growing reluctance of the labour force to accept monotonous work and to endure unsatisfactory working environments. A subsequent parliamentary commission, established for the purposes of enquiring into the overall living standard of the population, noted that while certain jobs brought about physical and mental exhaustion, others enabled the employee to continue to develop his productive capacity, without any detriment to his general well-being.

In the late Sixties the LO, as the main body of Swedish organized labour, began to play a decisive role in the development of the Swedish economy. Taking its initiative from the political unrest of 1968, the LO was able to establish certain principles for the evolution of an industrial democracy. For all its achievements to date, however, this aggressive reformism has yet to be pushed to its ultimate limits; namely, the taxing of profits for the purposes of establishing employees' funds, for the gradual union acquisition of industrial capital.

The unsatisfactory conditions prevailing in the engineering environment have been frequently cited by trade unions and researchers alike as the reason for high employee turnover and absenteeism. Recently, however, other structural changes in society have begun to exert an influence on the tendency of the labour force to remain excessively mobile. Amongst these factors, three have already had direct impact on the calibre of those working in the automobile industry: first, the 1969 education act, which increased the minimum period of education from seven to nine years; second, a policy decision to reduce the dependency of Swedish industry on foreign labour; and third, the changing status of women in society, which effectively began to encourage them to participate in industrial production.

The entry of large numbers of women into industry is bound to have an impact not only on the quality of the working environment (particularly in respect of its cleanliness, noise, etc.) but also on the determination of working hours – namely the reduction of the working shift to six hours so that household management can be sustained in conjunction with industrial production. Ironically, at least in the case of Volvo, a further reason for the introduction of the six-hour shift arises out of the production of the car itself, which has had the effect of extending the time spent in commuting to and from work. Should travelling time also come to be regarded as 'working' time, as the unions argue it should, then only a reduction in the 'shift length' would be able to compensate for the loss of 'free time'. At the same time the general high level of education in a society which realizes that without an adequate education one has little chance of adjusting to future changes in the economy, has led to a state of affairs where 60 per cent of the Volvo labour force has spent 13 years in formal education, whereas in 1969, 70 per cent of the same labour force had only seven years of education or less. It is hardly surprising that this raising of the educational level should impose conditions on the nature of the production, and it is becoming clear that one cannot expect the members of a highly educated society to suffer the indignities of authoritarian control and the repetitively moronic procedures of 'on-line' production. Thus the spontaneous extinction of Frederick Taylor's 'trained gorilla'[2] seems to be a precondition for the present aim of both the unions and the management to involve the individual worker in the continual reorganization of work. The corollary to this is not lost on those delegations of American automobile workers who have visited the Kalmar plant, namely that without an adequate education such participation becomes invidious and that the ill-educated worker is at once placed at a disadvantage in respect of such a sophisticated system of production. It says something for the efficacy of the Taft Act, and the so-called capitalization of the unions that was its outcome, that American car manufacturers and workers alike should regard Kalmar with the deepest suspicion and declare themselves in favour of optimizing their earning capacity at the expense, if necessary, of modifying the work organization or transforming the quality of the working environment. By a similar token there is little doubt that the Volvo experiment would hardly have been developed as far as it has had not Swedish industry been encouraged, by all the forces cited above, to operate at overall lower rates of profit than is the norm in American industry.[3]

The development of new productive procedures

One of the major incentives for the invention of new productive procedures in the Volvo concern was not only absenteeism but also a gradual decline in the overall quality of the product. Pehr Gyllenhammar, the decisive force behind the effort to restructure the Volvo work organization, was convinced from the outset that high quality could only be maintained by people who found their work to be of significance. In giving the managerial brief to the interdisciplinary research team for the Kalmar project he established the following general goal: 'In Kalmar,' he declared, 'we must produce a factory which, without sacrificing efficiency and economic results, provides the possibility for the employees to work in groups, to communicate freely, to carry out job rotation, to vary their rate of work, feel identification with the products, to be aware of quality responsibility and also be in a position to influence their working environment.'[4]

In addition to these criteria, which coincided with the basic union objectives, the following additional specifications were imposed by the management: 1) that the plant should have an initial capacity of 30,000 units annually, on a single day shift, with the potential for doubling this output should two shifts be introduced; 2) that the plant should be sufficiently flexible to accommodate unforeseen technical and social developments over the next 20 years; 3) that the plant should be restricted to the final assembly of painted bodies from the Torslanda plant and engines from the Skövde works; 4) that the plant should commence production by the spring of 1974; 5) that the project should involve, including the development and testing of new machine tools, an investment around 110,000.000 Swedish kronor, that is some ten per cent over and above what it would have cost to build a traditional on-line plant of comparable quality; finally, that all these criteria shoud be met in such a way as to assure reasonable levels of efficiency and profit.

Both the initial research team and the second 'brainstorming' interdisciplinary team, the Ultra Group, were asked to work in direct consultation with a reference group comprising a supervisor, a foreman and two permanent workers' representatives. While the two successive research teams seem to have been comprised of equal numbers of technicians, production engineers, economists, psychologists, doctors and architects, Gyllenhammar was compelled to reject the findings of the initial team as being too conservative. Within a month a somewhat reconstituted group, the Ultra Group, arrived at a solution, basing the bias of its findings on interviews with ex-Volvo workers who, above all else, declared that what they would have liked most was to have worked in teams. Two fundamental design propositions were crucial to the final development of the Kalmar system of team production; one was the tripartite hexagonal block formation, first sketched out by production engineer Torgny Karlsson and architect Gerhard Goehle as a 'butterfly' factory plan; and the other was the invention of the cybernetically controlled Volvo carrier which was, to a large degree, the contribution of Bertil Ahlsen, who is now in charge of the further development of this system.

General layout and sequence of assembly

Within its tripartite organization of three hexagonal blocks grouped about a triangular central core, with a complementary hexagonal block located to one side, Kalmar is organized on two levels, as a 'broken-line' some one and a half miles in length. This line, which is structured into a sequence of regular, faceted work stations, reflects the breaking down of the assembly process into 25 separate procedures.

After having been washed and inspected, the painted body, delivered by rail from Torslanda, is lifted onto a mobile flat carrier where it at once comes under the control of the central computer, which will monitor its progress throughout the 25 workshop sequences. Once registered the body is elevated to the first floor, where its doors are removed, and then passes through the various assembly teams in an anti-clockwise direction.

As the body proceeds through its first-floor assembly, with one team being responsible for the fitting of the electronics and another for the installation of the upholstery and so on, the engine, gearbox, axles and exhaust systems are assembled into a complete chassis mounted on a high-level carrier at the ground floor. Once the body has completed its first-floor circuit it is lowered by lift to the ground floor and 'married' to the completed chassis. At this juncture brakes and wheels are added, and then the total car is returned to a low-level carrier. All that now remains is a ground-floor clockwise circuit, wherein the supplementary parts are fitted and the car passes through the final stages of adjustment, inspection, testing and sealing.

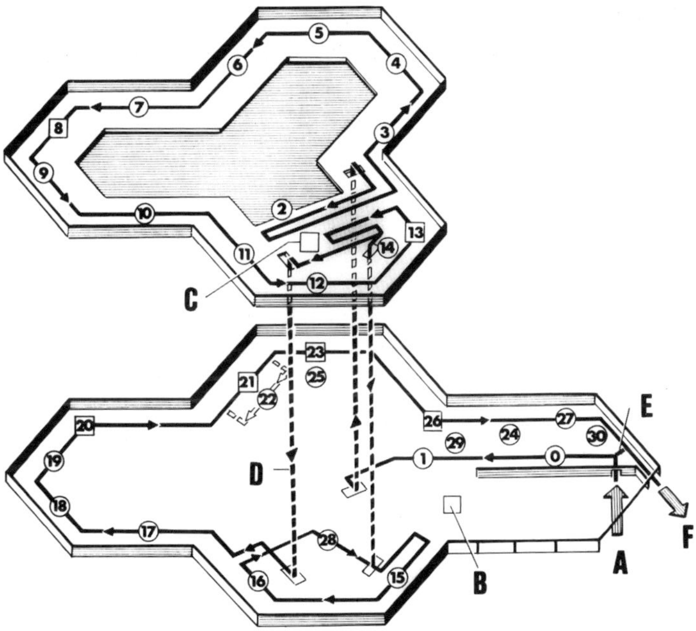

Axonometric of the Kalmar plant showing the production sequence (1–30) taking place on two separate levels: a) delivery of car bodies; b) check point; c) clearing point; d) loaders for empty carriers; e) return of empty carriers into the production line; and f) exit of finished cars.

An essential feature in this system of production at two levels is the central 'Y'-shaped, 10 metre high storage hall, housing crated components stacked in steel storage racks for the full height of the space. Large fork-lifts (capable of a 10 metre lift) remove these crates as required and deposit them against the respective working zones. These components are then withdrawn by smaller fork-lifts which belong to each of the workshop zones and are redeposited by them at the precise points of assembly within each shop.

The complement of each workshop zone will vary from 15 to 20 people. It is further broken down into a potentially ever-changing pattern of work organization, which may assign, say, three men to assuring the continual provision and distribution of supplies, while the remaining number will be assigned to work in pairs, in a system of 'straight assembly', at six different carrier stations. In the case of 'straight assembly' the carrier moves from station to station at the rate set by the working team through its terminal computer. In the system of 'dock assembly' the working carrier is 'docked' to one side of the straight sequence and here a team of, say, three people will complete the entire fabrication task on one car for that particular zone, and then move on to the next.

Service elements – exits leading to access stairs, locker rooms, shower rooms, coffee lounges and offices – form a bridge between adjacent workshops at every other corner. At these points are also located offices for the technicians and foremen, whose supervisory responsibilities include coordination of the 'flow' between the two adjacent zones.

The Volvo carrier in the Kalmar plant, 1974. The movement of the platform carrying the car is cybernetically controlled through movable tracks laid into the floor.

The Kalmar carrier is aluminium faced and steel framed; it runs on four rubber wheels and is driven by an integral electric motor fed by a battery. Its overall dimensions – approximately 6 by 2 metres – permit it not only to transport the unit under fabrication but also to provide a base on which to work while the unit is in motion, at speeds varying from 3 to 30 metres per minute. The speed, timing and movement of the carrier is pre-set and then electromagnetically controlled by a central computer, via signals transmitted through tracks set in the concrete floor. The configuration and hence the encoded movements embedded in the placing of these elements may be easily altered by drilling out the tracks and re-setting their position and pattern. The carrier is equipped with automatic safety devices which interrupt the functioning of servo-mechanism once the bumper of the carrier encounters an obstruction. The carrier, which may be disconnected from the automatic control and manually steered, comes in two basic types: low and high, depending on the jig mechanisms that are built into the base. The lower-level carrier has a tilting frame capable of rotating the body of the car through 90 degrees. This device, which Volvo was the first to introduce, permits assembly work to be carried out on the underside of the car in a correct and comfortable working position. The control unit of each carrier is equipped with illuminated diodes which indicate not only whether the carrier is standing exactly over a cable but also whether the cable is in operation and whether the setting is manual or automatic. The same system also signals the moment at which the battery requires recharging. Aside from all the variations that may be encoded into its movement, one of the most flexible aspects of the carrier is that basically the same flat bed could be used for the assembly of any object that would roughly fit within its overall dimensions. Thus Kalmar is by no means committed for the rest of its working life to the manufacture of cars.

Quality feedback and control

Within the whole one and a half mile broken-line there are four control points where the cars are checked at their respective stages against the monitored data of the central computer. As the body proceeds through the production circuit, the central memory bank of the computer compiles the statistical errors most recently encountered in each of the sectors of the line, governed by each of the four control points. At each of these points the controller checks for the most recently recorded errors of that particular sector and searches at the same time for others. Where other faults are found these are fed back into the computer, to contribute to the ever-changing statistical compilation of the error pattern at any particular point. Errors involving the security of the finished vehicle are given special emphasis by the computer, and instant efforts are made to check this error in the production at source. In general errors are either rectified on the spot or returned to the team; alternatively they are stored in the computer and rectified at the end. As far as possible every effort is made through this system of control – known by the initials KVIK (KValitets Information, Kalmar) – to eliminate 'built-in' faults. Workshop teams may obtain feedback information, at any time, in the form of a printout on any given car in the line. This data not only affords information as to the quality of the product at the particular stage but also monitors the current performance of the team in relation to the agreed speed of production.

Variation in the rhythm and organization of the work

The mean hourly rate of car production and hence the speed of the carrier is controlled by two variable factors: 1) the current order for automobiles in relation to the stocks available; and 2) an agreed MTM (Method Time Measurement) rate of pay per productive unit per hour, established through negotiation between the management and the local union. The current speed at Kalmar is set at around 15.5 cars per hour, with the carrier remaining on average some five minutes at each work station or some 25 to 30 minutes in each shop. This rate may be increased within a particular shop from, say, 15.5 to 17 cars per hour in order to create a 'buffer' of completed cars for that stage, at the 'threshold' to the next shop. Through the creation of a buffer any team may achieve a longer coffee break or, for that matter, a more varied rhythm of such 'breaks' within its daily work schedule. No bonuses are paid over the basic MTM rate, other than the extended rest periods achieved through buffer production, or an incremental addition paid for a person's consistent presence within the team – an inducement clearly designed to consolidate work teams and reduce the level of absenteeism. The nature and pace of the specific task within the team may be varied by the work team itself, acting collectively in the following four ways: 1) the speed and rhythm of the work may be changed by mutual agreement; 2) an operative may change the nature of his specific task within the assembly team; 3) rather than work individually an operative may choose to work in a group of, say, three, on a single car – the so-called 'dock' assembly system – in order to complete a significant section of the car and then move on, as a group, to the next car; 4) an operative may transfer from one workshop team to the next, thereby changing not only the specific task but also the assembly category; an example would be a move from the installation of electrical equipment to the fitting of upholstery.

The last of these alternatives points towards the perpetual education of the worker in the Dewey sense of the term. Theoretically, an operative could pass from workshop to workshop until he has in effect completed the entire assembly cycle and, in a certain sense, 'built a whole car'. Aside from affording an obvious route to promotion within a technical hierarchy, and apart from approaching in an elliptical way the Gyllenhammar ideal of a team of workers being able to build an entire machine, this capacity for training and retraining within the Kalmar plant seems to be nothing other than a reflection of a general awareness present throughout society: namely, that in a highly volatile techno-economy, workers must be prepared for continual retraining. It is now generally accepted in Swedish society that at least once within his or her lifetime the average professional or technician will need to be partially or wholly reeducated from a professional standpoint, due primarily to internal restructuring or the obsolescence of his or her initial métier.

Environmental quality

The main body of the Kalmar plant consists of three hexagonal units, and for the most part the process of assembly is carried out against the external perimeter of these forms. By virtue of this location the assembly bays are extremely well lit through continual strip windows, a system which also affords immediate views over the surrounding landscape. In general every effort has been made to keep the working area as unobstructed, light, quiet and well ventilated as possible. To this end the concrete factory floor has been kept flat and well illuminated by shadow-free artificial light. By the same token all the pneumatic power tools are suspended on retractable arms from the ceiling. The sound generated by these tools has been reduced as much as possible, first by running them at the lowest feasible speed and second by hanging absorbent acoustic bafflers from the ceilings in almost all of the shops. While the noise level can still at times attain 85 decibels, the normal level throughout the plant is 65 and these levels make the use of hearing protection unnecessary. Even though the air is changed at the rate of 20 cubic metres per hour per square metre (that is around six air changes per hour) all tools producing a polluting by-product – such as sanders or gasoline feeds – are fitted with an instantaneous vacuum return that immediately evacuates the pollutant from the working area. Exhaust gases from cars or heavily polluting processes such as underbody sealing and surface finishing are immediately eliminated by powerful fans. Most of the more polluting processes are carried out in specially sealed and ventilated chambers. The standard of hygiene both within and without the working area is scrupulously maintained by a team of continuously circulating cleaners. These same standards of hygiene and environmental control naturally extend into the three-storey personnel areas clustered at the corners around the perimeter of the building.

Architectural representation

Kalmar's most representative gesture, the prominent display of the Volvo logo and a cluster of five national flags which seems to be the ubiquituous symbol of the Swedish state, serves to dramatize the bland anonymity of the factory building itself. And while this may be all that is required in this age of objective production and social welfare, the fact remains that a feeling of almost deliberate isolation, in the physical and psychological sense, pervades the entire structure and site. The bleakness of the general approach to the works can hardly be overlooked, and it is difficult to dispel the sense that one is trespassing on an arena in which the human species *per se* is unwelcome. The associations that such an expression gives rise to are no doubt subjective, but while we may reject as extravagant an impulse to compare Kalmar to the literally lifeless landscape of the fully automated oil refinery, by the same token we are reminded of those windowless, introspective structures that have since become the typical building form of the North American megalopolis: the factories, bowling alleys, supermarkets and stores that flank the average freeway. Flags and logo notwithstanding, the approaches to Kalmar approximate all too closely to Melvin Webber's paradigm of the 'non-place urban realm'[5] and this is distressing when one realizes that this is the landscape in which some 600 men regularly spend the best part of their working day.

The barely inflected, sandwich-like elevations are sufficient to affirm that we could not be further from Peter Behrens's reification, in 1910, of the AEG Turbinenfabrik in Berlin as a 'temple' of industrial power, or from the transcendental value attached to glass, as the lucid revelation of the production process itself, that we witness in Brinkman and Van der Vlugt's Van Nelle Factory, Rotterdam of 1929.

The poverty of the external environment at Kalmar is evident from the general blandness of the views obtained from the shop floors and from the coffee-break rooms – the latter being not only burdened with the bleakness of the aspect but also with the physical and psychological inaccessibility of the immediate exterior space. The fact that neither these rooms nor the main dining space give on to terraces that are significantly related to the surrounding landscape, points to the strict limits within which the restructuring of the environment has been conceived. The hold of functionalism is so great that hedonism and production are still seen as incompatible. An equally ironic observation might also be made with regard to the 'individual' workshop entries distributed around the perimeter, which due to their relative inaccessibility, seem rarely to be used. Indeed they appear to be almost a 'kitsch' system of access whose 'sign value' is meant to indicate the presence of an individual shop. The employees are not deceived, however, since naturally they all enter and leave by the main entry situated in close proximity to the road.

Thus, for all the remarkable achievements of Kalmar, three fundamental doubts remain: 1) that the whole installation is only schematically related to its location and site; 2) that the amenities in both visual and physical terms fail to extend beyond the hermetic skin of the production space; and 3) that the building fails to represent itself in adequate terms to the society at large. Since current Volvo planning policy is moving towards the creation of further plants comprising free-standing workshops, these problems look set to continue.

It is surely no accident that the new Volvo factories at Kalmar and Skövde contain at least in embryonic form those distinctly separate political arenas, whose discourse is divided between the two principles of rationalization identified by Jürgen Habermas in his 1968 essay 'Technology and Science as Ideology', wherein he wrote:

Above all it becomes clear against this background that two concepts of rationalization must be distinguished. At the level of sub-systems of purposive-rational action, scientific-technical progress has already compelled the reorganization of social institutions and sectors and necessitates it on an even larger scale than heretofore. But this process of the development of the productive forces can be a potential for liberation only if it does not replace rationalization at another level. Rationalization at the level of the institutional framework can occur only in the medium of symbolic interaction itself, that is through removing restrictions on communication.[6]

The disproportion of emphasis accorded to these two forms of rationalization in advanced industrial society seems to find its direct reflection in the built environment, and while at Kalmar the team workshop areas function only too well for free discourse within the terms of the technostructure, the somewhat restricted personnel or coffee-break rooms on the perimeter of the building, far from serving as adequate areas for 'symbolic interaction', are clearly only intended to function, like the saunas in the washrooms, for the instant restoration of the will to work. And it is surely no accident that these rooms are inadequately represented and that they open not so much to a social prospect as to a landscape of amnesia – that empty terrain of communication that serves to separate the worker from the pleasure of his family life. This clinical separation of the reality of work from the pleasure of life – so much of an anathema to Charles Fourier – speaks for itself. The preoccupation of modern industry with abstract linkages, rather than concrete adjacencies, seems at this juncture to be far from accidental, for only through their being masked by the opportunism of their dislocation may the so-called value-free abstractions of exploitation be kept open and intact. As Habermas has written:

The question is not whether we completely utilize an available or creatable potential but whether we choose what we want for the purpose of the pacification and gratification of existence. But it must be immediately noted that we are only posing this question and cannot answer it in advance. For the solution demands precisely that unrestricted communication about the goals of life activity and conduct against which advanced capitalism, structurally dependent on a depoliticized public realm, puts up a strong resistance.[7]

This is an edited version of an essay first published as 'Il Caso Volvo' in *Lotus*, no.12, 1976, pp.16–41.

Towards a Critical Regionalism:
Six Points for an Architecture of Resistance

The phenomenon of universalization, while being an advancement of mankind, at the same time constitutes a sort of subtle destruction, not only of traditional cultures, which might not be an irreparable wrong, but also of what I shall call for the time being the creative nucleus of great cultures, that nucleus on the basis of which we interpret life, what I shall call in advance the ethical and mythical nucleus of mankind. The conflict springs up from there. We have the feeling that this single world civilization at the same time exerts a sort of attrition or wearing away at the expense of the cultural resources which have made the great civilizations of the past. This threat is expressed, among other disturbing effects, by the spreading before our eyes of a mediocre civilization which is the absurd counterpart of what I was just calling elementary culture. Everywhere throughout the world, one finds the same bad movie, the same slot machines, the same plastic or aluminum atrocities, the same twisting of language by propaganda, etc. It seems as if mankind, by approaching en masse a basic consumer culture, were also stopped en masse at a subcultural level. Thus we come to the crucial problem confronting nations just rising from underdevelopment. In order to get on to the road toward modernization, is it necessary to jettison the old cultural past which has been the raison d'être of a nation? ... Whence the paradox: on the one hand, it has to root itself in the soil of its past, forge a national spirit, and unfurl this spiritual and cultural revindication before the colonialist's personality. But in order to take part in modern civilization, it is necessary at the same time to take part in scientific, technical, and political rationality, something which very often requires the pure and simple abandon of a whole cultural past. It is a fact: every culture cannot sustain and absorb the shock of modern civilization. There is the paradox: how to become modern and to return to sources; how to revive an old, dormant civilization and take part in universal civilization.

Paul Ricoeur, 'Universal Civilization and National Cultures', 1961[1]

1. Culture and civilization

Modern building is now so universally conditioned by optimized technology that the possibility of creating significant urban form has become extremely limited. The restrictions jointly imposed by automotive distribution and the volatile play of land speculation serve to limit the scope of urban design to such a degree that any intervention tends to be reduced either to the manipulation of elements predetermined by the imperatives of production, or to a kind of superficial masking which modern development requires for the facilitation of marketing and the maintenance of social control. Today the practice of architecture seems to be increasingly polarized between, on the one hand, a so-called 'high-tech' approach predicated exclusively upon production and, on the other, the provision of a 'compensatory facade' to cover up the harsh realities of this universal system.[2]

Twenty years ago the dialectical interplay between civilization and culture still afforded the possibility of maintaining some general control over the shape and significance of the urban fabric. The last two decades, however, have radically transformed the metropolitan centres of the developed world. What were still essentially nineteenth-century city fabrics in the early Sixties have since become progressively overlaid by the two symbiotic instruments of megalopolitan development: the free-standing high-rise and the serpentine freeway. The former has finally come into its own as the prime device for realizing the increased land value brought into being by the latter. The typical downtown which, up to 20 years ago, still presented a mixture of residential stock with tertiary and secondary industry has now become little more than a *burolandschaft* cityscape: the victory of universal civilization over locally inflected culture. The predicament posed by Ricoeur – namely, 'how to become modern and to return to sources'[3] – now seems to be circumvented by the apocalyptic thrust of modernization, while the ground in which the mytho-ethical nucleus of a society might take root has become eroded by the rapacity of development.

Ever since the beginning of the Enlightenment, *civilization* has been primarily concerned with instrumental reason, while *culture* has addressed itself to the specifics of expression – to the realization of the being and the evolution of its *collective* psycho-social reality.[4] Today civilization tends to be increasingly embroiled in a never-ending chain of 'means and ends' wherein, according to Hannah Arendt, 'The "in order to" has become the content of the "for the sake of"; utility established as meaning generates meaninglessness.'[5]

2. The rise and fall of the avant-garde

The emergence of the avant-garde is inseparable from the modernization of both society and architecture. Over the past century-and-a-half avant-garde culture has assumed different roles, at times facilitating the process of modernization and thereby acting, in part, as a progressive, liberative form, at times being virulently opposed to the positivism of bourgeois culture. By and large, avant-garde architecture has played a positive role with regard to the progressive trajectory of the Enlightenment. Exemplary of this is the role played by Neoclassicism: from the mid-eighteenth century onwards it serves as both a symbol of and an instrument for the propagation of universal civilization. The mid-nineteenth century, however, saw the historical avant-garde assume an adversary stance towards both industrial process and neoclassical form. This is the first concerted reaction on the part of 'tradition' to the process of modernization, as the Gothic Revival and the Arts and Crafts movements take up a categorically negative attitude towards both utilitarianism and the division of labour. Despite this critique, modernization continues unabated, and throughout the last half of the nineteenth century bourgeois art distances itself progressively from the harsh realities of colonialism and palaeo-technological exploitation. Thus at the end of the century the avant-gardist Art Nouveau takes refuge in the compensatory thesis of 'art for art's sake', retreating to nostalgic or phantasmagoric dream worlds inspired by the cathartic hermeticism of Wagner's music–drama.

The progressive avant-garde emerges in full force, however, soon after the turn of the century with the advent of Futurism. This unequivocal critique of the *ancien régime* gives rise to the primary positive cultural formations of the 1920s: to Purism, Neoplasticism and Constructivism. These movements are the last occasion on which radical avant-gardism is able to identify itself wholeheartedly with the process of modernization. In the immediate aftermath of World War I – 'the war to end all wars' – the triumphs of science, medicine and industry seemed to confirm the liberative promise of the modern project. In the 1930s, however, the prevailing backwardness and chronic insecurity of the newly urbanized masses, the upheavals caused by war, revolution and economic depression, followed by a sudden and crucial need for psycho-social stability in the face of global political and economic crises, all induce a state of affairs in which the interests of both monopoly and state capitalism are, for the first time in modern history, divorced from the liberative drives of cultural modernization. Universal civilization and world culture cannot be drawn upon to sustain 'the myth of the State', and one reaction-formation succeeds another as the historical avant-garde founders on the rocks of the Spanish Civil War.

Not least among these reactions is the reassertion of neo-Kantian aesthetics as a substitute for the culturally liberative modern project. Confused by the political and cultural politics of Stalinism, former left-wing protagonists of socio-cultural modernization now recommend a strategic withdrawal from the project of totally transforming the existing reality. This renunciation is predicated on the belief that as long as the struggle between socialism and capitalism persists (with the manipulative mass-culture politics that this conflict necessarily entails) the modern world cannot continue to entertain the prospect of evolving a marginal, liberative, avant-gardist culture which would break (or speak of the break) with the history of bourgeois repression. Close to *l'art pour l'art*, this position was first advanced as a 'holding pattern' in Clement Greenberg's 'Avant-Garde and Kitsch' of 1939; this essay concludes somewhat ambiguously with the words: 'Today we look to socialism *simply* for the preservation of whatever living culture we have right now.'[6] Greenberg reformulated this position in specifically formalist terms in his essay 'Modernist Painting' of 1965, wherein he wrote:

Having been denied by the Enlightenment of all tasks they could take seriously, they [the arts] looked as though they were going to be assimilated to entertainment pure and simple, and entertainment itself looked as though it was going to be assimilated, like religion, to therapy. The arts could save themselves from this leveling down only by demonstrating that the kind of experience they provided was valuable in its own right, and not to be obtained from any other kind of activity.[7]

Despite this defensive intellectual stance, the arts have nonetheless continued to gravitate, if not towards entertainment, then certainly towards commodity and – in the case of that which Charles Jencks has since classified as Post-Modern Architecture[8] – towards pure technique or pure scenography. In the latter case, the so-called Post-Modern architects are merely feeding the media-society with gratuitous, quietistic images rather than proffering, as they claim, a creative *rappel à l'ordre* after the supposedly proven bankruptcy of the liberative modern project. In this regard, as Andreas Huyssen has written, 'The American Post-modernist avant-garde, therefore, is not only the end game of avant-gardism. It also represents the fragmentation and decline of critical adversary culture.'[9]

Nevertheless, it is true that modernization can no longer be simplistically identified as liberative *in se*, in part because of the domination of mass culture by the media industry (above all television which, as Jerry Mander reminds us, expanded its persuasive power a thousandfold between 1945 and 1975[10]) and in part because the trajectory of modernization has brought us to the threshold of nuclear war and the annihilation of the entire species. So too, avant-gardism can no longer be sustained as a liberative moment, in part because its initial utopian promise has been overrun by the internal rationality of instrumental reason. This 'closure' was perhaps best formulated by Herbert Marcuse when he wrote:

The technological apriori *is a political* apriori *inasmuch as the transformation of nature involves that of man, and inasmuch as the 'man-made creations' issue from and re-enter the societal ensemble. One may still insist that the machinery of the technological universe is 'as such' indifferent towards political ends – it can revolutionize or retard society . . . However, when technics becomes the universal form of material production, it circumscribes an entire culture, it projects a historical totality – a 'world'.*[11]

3. Critical Regionalism and world culture

Architecture can only be sustained today as a critical practice if it assumes an *arrière-garde* position, that is to say, one which distances itself equally from the Enlightenment myth of progress and from a reactionary, unrealistic impulse to return to the architectonic forms of the pre-industrial past. A critical *arrière-garde* has to remove itself from both the optimization of advanced technology and the ever-present tendency to regress into nostalgic historicism or the glibly decorative. It is my contention that only an *arrière-garde* has the capacity to cultivate a resistant, identity-giving culture while at the same time having discreet recourse to universal technique.

It is necessary to qualify the term *arrière-garde* so as to diminish its critical scope from such conservative policies as Populism or sentimental Regionalism with which it has often been associated. In order to ground arrière-gardism in a rooted yet critical strategy, it is helpful to appropriate the term Critical Regionalism as coined by Alex Tzonis and Liane Lefaivre in 'The Grid and the Pathway' (1981); in this essay they caution against the ambiguity of regional reformism, as this has become occasionally manifest since the last quarter of the nineteenth century:

Regionalism has dominated architecture in almost all countries at some time during the past two centuries and a half. By way of general definition we can say that it upholds the individual and local architectonic features against more universal and abstract ones. In addition, however, regionalism bears the hallmark of ambiguity. On the one hand, it has been associated with movements of reform and liberation; . . . on the other, it has proved a powerful tool of repression and chauvinism . . . Certainly, critical regionalism has its limitations. The upheaval of the populist movement – a more developed form of regionalism – has brought to light these weak points. No new architecture can emerge without a new kind of relations between designer and user, without new kinds of programmes . . . Despite these limitations critical regionalism is a bridge over which any humanistic architecture of the future must pass.[12]

The fundamental strategy of Critical Regionalism is to mediate the impact of universal civilization with elements derived *indirectly* from the peculiarities of a particular place. It is clear from the above that Critical Regionalism depends upon maintaining a high level of critical self-consciousness. It may find its governing inspiration in such things as the range and quality of the local light, or in a *tectonic* derived from a peculiar structural mode, or in the topography of a given site.

But it is necessary, as I have already suggested, to distinguish between Critical Regionalism and simple-minded attempts to revive the hypothetical forms of a lost vernacular. In contradistinction to Critical Regionalism, the primary vehicle of Populism is the *communicative* or *instrumental* sign. Such a sign seeks to evoke not a critical perception of reality, but rather the sublimation of a desire for direct experience through the provision of information. Its tactical aim is to attain, as economically as possible, a preconceived level of gratification in behaviouristic terms. In this respect, the strong affinity of Populism for the rhetorical techniques and imagery of advertising is hardly accidental. Unless one guards against such a convergence, one will confuse the resistant capacity of a critical practice with the demagogic tendencies of Populism.

The case can be made that Critical Regionalism as a cultural strategy is as much a bearer of *world culture* as it is a vehicle of *universal civilization*. And while it is obviously misleading to conceive of our inheriting world culture to the same degree as we are all heirs to universal civilization, it is nonetheless evident that since we are, in principle, subject to the impact of both, we have no choice but to take cognizance today of their interaction. In this regard the practice of Critical Regionalism is contingent upon a process of double mediation. In the first place, it has to 'deconstruct' the overall spectrum of world culture which it inevitably inherits; in the second place, it has to achieve, through synthetic contradiction, a manifest critique of universal civilization. To deconstruct world culture is to remove oneself from that eclecticism of the *fin de siècle* which appropriated alien, exotic forms in order to revitalize the expressivity of an enervated society. (One thinks of the 'form-force' aesthetics of Henry Van de Velde or the 'whiplash-Arabesques' of Victor Horta.) On the other hand, the mediation of universal technique involves imposing limits on the optimization of industrial and post-industrial technology. The future necessity for re-synthesizing principles and elements drawn from diverse origins and quite different ideological sets seems to be alluded to by Ricoeur when he writes:

No one can say what will become of our civilization when it has really met different civilizations by means other than the shock of conquest and domination. But we have to admit that this encounter has not yet taken place at the level of an authentic dialogue. That is why we are in a kind of lull or interregnum in which we can no longer practice the dogmatism of a single truth and in which we are not yet capable of conquering the scepticism into which we have stepped.[13]

A parallel and complementary sentiment was expressed by the Dutch architect Aldo van Eyck who, quite coincidentally, wrote at the same time:

Western civilization habitually identifies itself with civilization as such on the pontificial assumption that what is not like it is a deviation, less advanced, primitive, or, at best, exotically interesting at a safe distance.[14]

That Critical Regionalism cannot be simply based on the autochthonous forms of a specific region alone was well put by the Californian architect Harwell Hamilton Harris when he wrote, now nearly 30 years ago:

Opposed to the Regionalism of Restriction is another type of regionalism, the Regionalism of Liberation. This is the manifestation of a region that is especially in tune with the emerging thought of the time. We call such a manifestation 'regional' only because it has not yet emerged elsewhere ... A region may develop ideas. A region may accept ideas. Imagination and intelligence are necessary for both. In California in the late Twenties and Thirties modern European ideas met a still-developing regionalism. In New England, on the other hand, European Modernism met a rigid and restrictive regionalism that at first resisted and then surrendered. New England accepted European Modernism whole because its own regionalism had been reduced to a collection of restrictions.[15]

The scope for achieving a self-conscious synthesis between universal civilization and world culture may be specifically illustrated by Jørn Utzon's Bagsvaerd Church, built near Copenhagen in 1976, a work whose complex meaning stems directly from a revealed conjunction between, on the one hand, the *rationality* of normative technique and, on the other, the *arationality* of idiosyncratic form. Inasmuch as this building is organized around a regular grid and is comprised of repetitive, in-fill modules – concrete blocks in the first instance and precast concrete wall units in the second – we may justly regard it as the outcome of universal civilization. Such a building system, comprising an *in situ* concrete frame with prefabricated concrete in-fill elements, has indeed been applied countless times all over the developed world. However, the universality of this productive method – which includes, in this instance, patent glazing on the roof – is abruptly mediated when one passes from the optimal modular skin of the exterior to the far less optimal reinforced concrete shell vault spanning the nave. This last is obviously a relatively uneconomic mode of construction, selected and manipulated first for its direct associative capacity – that is to say, the vault signifies sacred space – and second for its multiple cross-cultural references. While the reinforced concrete shell vault has long since held an established place within the received tectonic canon of Western modern architecture, the highly configurated section adopted in this instance is hardly familiar, and the only precedent for such a form, in a sacred context, is Eastern rather than Western – namely, the Chinese pagoda roof, cited by Utzon in his seminal essay of 1963, 'Platforms and Plateaus'.[16] Although the main Bagsvaerd vault spontaneously signifies its religious nature, it does so in such a way as to preclude an exclusively Occidental or Oriental reading of the code by which the public and sacred space is constituted. The intent of this expression is, of course, to secularize the sacred form by precluding the usual set of semantic religious references and thereby the corresponding range of automatic responses that usually accompany them. This is arguably a more appropriate way of rendering a church in a highly secular age, where any symbolic allusion to the ecclesiastic usually degenerates immediately into the vagaries of kitsch. And yet paradoxically, this desacralization at Bagsvaerd subtly reconstitutes a renewed basis for the spiritual, one founded, I would argue, in a regional reaffirmation – grounds, at least for some form of collective spirituality.

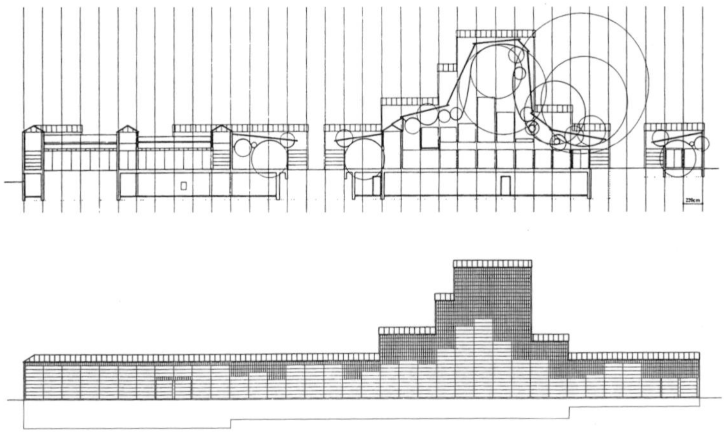

Jørn Utzon, Bagsvaerd Church, Copenhagen, 1973–6, geometrical section (above right) showing the generation of vault profiles, plus the north elevation representing their presence on the exterior (below right).

4. The resistance of the place-form

The megalopolis, recognized as such in 1961 by the geographer Jean Gottman,[17] continues to proliferate throughout the developed world to such an extent that, with the exception of cities that were laid in place before the turn of the century, we are no longer able to maintain defined urban forms. The last quarter of a century has seen the so-called field of urban design degenerate into a theoretical subject whose discourse bears little relation to the processal realities of modern development. Today even the super-managerial discipline of urban planning has entered into a state of crisis. The ultimate fate of the plan which was officially promulgated for the rebuilding of Rotterdam after World War II is symptomatic in this regard, since it testifies, in terms of its own recently changed status, to the current tendency to reduce all planning to little more than the allocation of land use and the logistics of distribution. Until relatively recently, the Rotterdam masterplan was revised and upgraded every decade in the light of buildings which had been realized in the interim. In 1975, however, this progressive urban cultural procedure was unexpectedly abandoned in favour of publishing a non-physical, infrastructure plan conceived at a regional scale. Such a plan concerns itself almost exclusively with the logistical projection of changes in land use and with the augmentation of existing distribution systems.

In his essay of 1954, 'Building, Dwelling, Thinking', Martin Heidegger provides us with a critical vantage point from which to behold this phenomenon of universal placelessness. Against the Latin or, rather, the antique *abstract* concept of space as a more or less endless continuum of evenly subdivided spatial components or integers – what he terms *spatium* and *extensio* – Heidegger opposes the German word for space (or, rather, place), which is the term *Raum*. Heidegger argues that the phenomenological essence of such a space/place depends upon the *concrete*, clearly defined nature of its boundary, for, as he puts it, 'A boundary is not that at which something stops, but, as the Greeks recognized, the boundary is that from which something begins its presencing.'[18] Apart from confirming that Western abstract reason has its origins in the antique culture of the Mediterranean, Heidegger shows that etymologically the German gerund *building* is closely linked with the archaic forms of *being*, *cultivating* and *dwelling*, and goes on to state that the condition of 'dwelling' and hence ultimately of 'being' can only take place in a domain that is clearly bounded.

While we may well remain sceptical as to the merit of grounding critical practice in a concept so hermetically metaphysical as Being, we are, when confronted with the ubiquitous placelessness of our modern environment, nonetheless brought to posit, after Heidegger, the absolute precondition of a bounded domain in order to create an architecture of resistance. Only such a defined boundary will permit the built form to stand against – and hence literally to withstand in an institutional sense – the endless processal flux of the megalopolis.

The bounded place-form, in its public mode, is also essential to what Hannah Arendt has termed 'the space of human appearance', since the evolution of legitimate power has always been predicated upon the existence of the 'polis' and upon comparable units of institutional and physical form. While the political life of the Greek polis did not stem directly from the physical presence and representation of the city state, it displayed in contrast to the megalopolis the cantonal attributes of urban density. Thus Arendt writes in *The Human Condition*:

The only indispensable material factor in the generation of power is the living together of people. Only where men live so close together that the potentialities for action are always present will power remain with them and the foundation of cities, which as city states have remained paradigmatic for all Western political organization, is therefore the most important material prerequisite for power.[19]

Nothing could be more removed from the political essence of the city state than the rationalizations of positivistic urban planners such as Melvin Webber, whose ideological concepts of *community without propinquity* and the *non-place urban realm* are nothing if not slogans devised to rationalize the absence of any true public realm in the modern motopia.[20] The manipulative bias of such ideologies has never been more openly expressed than in Robert Venturi's *Complexity and Contradiction in Architecture* (1966) wherein the author asserts that Americans do not need piazzas, since they should be at home watching television.[21] Such reactionary attitudes emphasize the impotence of an urbanized populace which has paradoxically lost the object of its urbanization.

While the strategy of Critical Regionalism as outlined above addresses itself mainly to the maintenance of an *expressive density and resonance* in an architecture of resistance (a cultural density which under today's conditions could be said to be potentially liberative in and of itself since it opens the user to manifold *experiences*), the provision of a place-form is equally essential to critical practice, inasmuch as a resistant architecture, in an institutional sense, is necessarily dependent on a clearly defined domain. Perhaps the most generic example of such an urban form is the perimeter block, although other related, introspective types may be evoked, such as the galleria, the atrium, the forecourt and the labyrinth. And while these types have in many instances today simply become the vehicles for accommodating pseudo-public realms (one thinks of recent megastructures in housing, hotels, shopping centres, etc.), one cannot even in these instances entirely discount the latent political and resistant potential of the place-form.

5. Culture versus nature: topography, context, climate, light and tectonic form

Critical Regionalism necessarily involves a more directly dialectical relation with nature than the more abstract, formal traditions of modern avant-garde architecture allow. It is evident that modern development favours the optimum use of earth-moving machinery so as to achieve a totally flat site which is almost regarded a precondition for the rationalization of construction. Here again, one touches in concrete terms the fundamental opposition between universal civilization and autochthonous culture. The bulldozing of an irregular topography into a flat site is clearly a technocratic gesture which aspires to a condition of absolute *placelessness*, whereas the terracing of the same site to receive the stepped form of a building is an engagement in the act of 'cultivating' the site.

Clearly such a mode of beholding and acting brings one close once again to Heidegger's etymology; at the same time, it evokes the method alluded to by the Swiss architect Mario Botta as 'building the site'. It is possible to argue that in this last instance the specific culture of the region – that is to say, its history in both a geological and agricultural sense – becomes inscribed into the form and realization of the work. This inscription, which arises out of 'in-laying' the building into the site, has many levels of significance, for it has a capacity to embody, in built form, the prehistory of the place, its archaeological past and its subsequent cultivation and transformation across time. Through this layering into the site the idiosyncrasies of place find their expression without falling into sentimentality.

What is evident in the case of topography applies to a similar degree in the case of an existing urban fabric, and the same can be claimed for the contingencies of climate and the temporally inflected qualities of local light. Once again, the sensitive modulation and incorporation of such factors must almost by definition be fundamentally opposed to the optimum use of universal technique. This is perhaps most clear in the case of light and climate control. The generic window is obviously the most delicate point at which these two natural forces impinge upon the outer membrane of the building, fenestration having an innate capacity to inscribe architecture with the character of a region and hence to express the place in which the work is situated.

Until recently, the received precepts of modern curatorial practice favoured the exclusive use of artificial light in all art galleries. It has perhaps been insufficiently recognized how this encapsulation tends to reduce the artwork to a commodity, since such an environment must conspire to render the work placeless. This is because the local light spectrum is never permitted to play across its surface: here, then, we see how the loss of aura, attributed by Walter Benjamin to the processes of mechanical reproduction, also arises from a relatively static application of universal technology. The converse of this 'placeless' practice would be to provide that art galleries be top-lit through carefully contrived monitors so that, while the injurious effects of direct sunlight are avoided, the ambient light of the exhibition volume changes under the impact of time, season, humidity, etc. Such conditions guarantee the appearance of a place-conscious poetic – a form of filtration compounded out of an interaction between culture and nature, between art and light. Clearly this principle applies to all fenestration, irrespective of size and location. A constant 'regional inflection' of the form arises directly from the fact that in certain climates the glazed aperture is advanced, while in others it is recessed behind the masonry facade (or, alternatively, shielded by adjustable sun breakers).

The way in which such openings provide for appropriate ventilation also constitutes an unsentimental element reflecting the nature of local culture. Here, clearly, the main antagonist of rooted culture is the ubiquitous air conditioner, applied in all times and in all places, irrespective of the local climatic conditions which have a capacity to express the specific place and the seasonal variations of its climate. Wherever they occur, the fixed window and the remote-controlled air-conditioning system are mutually indicative of domination by universal technique.

Despite the critical importance of topography and light, the primary principle of architectural autonomy resides in the *tectonic* rather than the *scenographic*: that is to say, this autonomy is embodied in the revealed ligaments of the construction and in the way in which the syntactical form of the structure explicitly resists the action of gravity. It is obvious that this discourse of the load borne (the beam) and the load-bearing (the column) cannot be brought into being where the structure is masked or otherwise concealed. On the other hand, the tectonic is not to be confused with the purely technical, for it is more than the simple revelation of stereotomy or the expression of skeletal framework. Its essence was first defined by the German aesthetician Karl Bötticher in his book *Die Tektonik der Hellenen* (1852); and it was perhaps best summarized by the architectural historian Stanford Anderson when he wrote:

'Tektonik' *referred not just to the activity of making the materially requisite construction ... but rather to the activity that raises this construction to an art form ... The functionally adequate form must be adapted so as to give expression to its function. The sense of bearing provided by the entasis of Greek columns became the touchstone of this concept of* Tektonik.[22]

6. The visual versus the tactile

The tactile resilience of the place-form and the capacity of the body to read the environment in terms other than those of sight alone suggest a potential strategy for resisting the domination of universal technology. It is symptomatic of the priority given to sight that we find it necessary to remind ourselves that the tactile is an important dimension in the perception of built form. One has in mind a whole range of complementary sensory perceptions which are registered by the labile body: the intensity of light, darkness, heat and cold; the feeling of humidity; the aroma of material; the almost palpable presence of masonry as the body senses its own confinement; the momentum of an induced gait and the relative inertia of the body as it traverses the floor; the echoing resonance of our own footfall. Luchino Visconti was well aware of these factors when making the film *The Damned*, for he insisted that the main set of the Altona mansion should be paved in real wooden parquet. It was his belief that without a solid floor underfoot the actors would be incapable of assuming appropriate and convincing postures.

Alvar Aalto, Säynätsalo Town Hall, Säynätsalo, 1949–52, access stair leading to council chamber.

A similar tactile sensitivity is evident in the finishing of the public circulation in Alvar Aalto's Säynätsalo Town Hall of 1952. The main route leading to the second-floor council chamber is ultimately orchestrated in terms which are as much tactile as they are visual. Not only is the principal access stair lined in raked brickwork, but the treads and risers are also finished in brick. The kinetic impetus of the body in climbing the stair is thus checked by the friction of the steps, which are 'read' soon after in

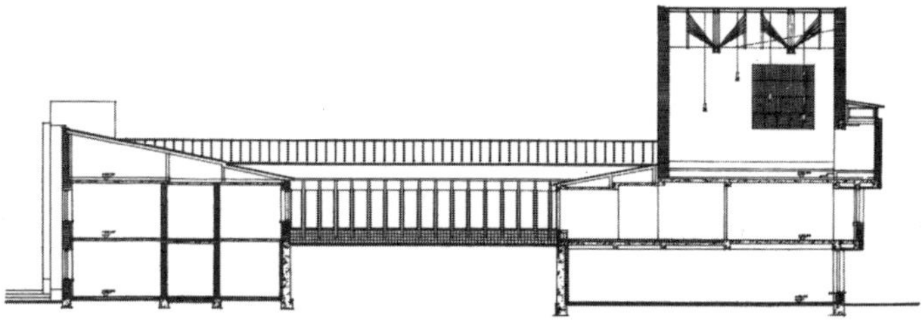

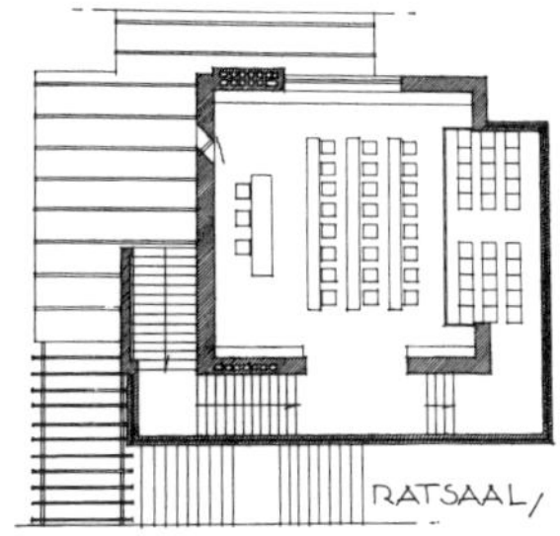

Alvar Aalto, Säynätsalo Town Hall, longitudinal section (left) showing honorific trusses over the council chamber plus plan (above) indicating the route of the access stair.

contrast to the timber floor of the council chamber itself. This chamber asserts its honorific status through sound, smell and texture, not to mention the springy deflection of the floor underfoot (and a noticeable tendency to lose one's balance on its polished surface). From this example it is clear that the liberative importance of the tactile resides in the fact that it can only be decoded in terms of *experience* itself: it cannot be reduced to mere information, to representation or to the simple evocation of a simulacrum substituting for absent presences.

In this way, Critical Regionalism seeks to complement our normative visual experience by readdressing the tactile range of human perceptions. In so doing, it endeavours to balance the priority accorded to the image and to counter the Western tendency to interpret the environment in exclusively perspectival terms. According to its etymology, perspective means rationalized sight or clear seeing, and as such it presupposes a conscious suppression of the senses of smell, hearing and taste, and a consequent distancing from a more direct experience of the environment. This self-imposed limitation relates to that which Heidegger has called a 'loss of nearness'. In attempting to counter this loss, the tactile opposes itself to the scenographic and the drawing of veils over the surface of reality. Its capacity to arouse the impulse to touch returns the architect to the poetics of construction and to the erection of works in which the tectonic value of each component depends upon the density of its objecthood. The tactile and the tectonic jointly have the capacity to transcend the mere appearance of the technical in much the same way as the place-form has the potential to withstand the relentless onslaught of global modernization.

First published in Hal Foster, ed., *The Anti-Aesthetic: Essays on Post-Modern Culture*, Port Townsend, WA: Bay Press, 1983, pp.16–30.

Rappel à l'Ordre: The Case for the Tectonic

I have elected to address the issue of tectonic form for a number of reasons, not least of which is the current tendency to reduce architecture to scenography. This reaction arises in response to the universal triumph of Robert Venturi's decorated shed; that all too prevalent syndrome in which shelter is packaged like a giant commodity. Among the advantages of the scenographic approach is the fact that the results are eminently amortizable, with all the consequences that this entails for the future of the environment. We have in mind, of course, not the pleasing decay of nineteenth-century Romanticism but the total destitution of commodity culture. Along with this sobering prospect goes the general dissolution of stable references in the late-modern world; the fact that the precepts governing almost every discourse, save for the seemingly autonomous realm of techno-science, have now become extremely tenuous. Much of this was already foreseen half a century ago by Hans Sedlmayr, when he wrote, in 1941:

The shift of man's spiritual centre of gravity towards the inorganic, his feeling of his way into the inorganic world, may indeed legitimately be called a cosmic disturbance in the microcosm of man, who now begins to show a one-sided development of his faculties. At the other extreme there is a disturbance of macrocosmic relationships, a result of the especial favour and protection which the inorganic now enjoys – almost always at the expense, not to say ruin, of the organic. The raping and destruction of the earth, the nourisher of man, is an obvious example and one which in its turn reflects the distortion of the human microcosm from the spiritual.[1]

Against this prospect of cultural degeneration, we may turn to certain rear-guard positions, in order to recover a basis from which to resist. Today we find ourselves in a similar position to that of the critic Clement

Greenberg who, in his 1965 essay 'Modernist Painting', attempted to reformulate a ground for painting in the following terms:

Having been denied by the Enlightenment of all tasks they could take seriously, they [the arts] looked as though they were going to be assimilated to entertainment pure and simple, and entertainment itself looked as though it was going to be assimilated, like religion, to therapy. The arts could save themselves from this leveling down only by demonstrating that the kind of experience they provided was valuable in its own right, and not to be obtained from any other kind of activity.[2]

If one poses the question as to what might be a comparable ground for architecture, then one must turn to a similar material base, namely that architecture must of necessity be embodied in structural and constructional form. My present stress on the latter rather than the prerequisite of spatial enclosure, stems from an attempt to evaluate twentieth-century architecture in terms of continuity and inflection rather than in terms of originality as an end in itself.

In his 1980 essay 'Avant-Garde and Continuity', the Italian architect Giorgio Grassi had the following comment to make about the impact of avant-gardist art on architecture:

. . . as far as the vanguards of the Modern Movement are concerned, they invariably follow in the wake of the figurative arts . . . Cubism, Suprematism, Neoplasticism, etc., are all forms of investigation born and developed in the realm of the figurative arts, and only as a second thought carried over into architecture as well. It is actually pathetic to see the architects of that 'heroic' period and the best among them, trying with difficulty to accommodate themselves to these 'isms'; experimenting in a perplexed manner because of their fascination with the new doctrines, measuring them, only later to realize their ineffectuality . . .[3]

While it is disconcerting to have to recognize that there may well be a fundamental break between the figurative origins of abstract art and the constructional basis of tectonic form, it is, at the same time, liberating to the extent that it affords a point from which to challenge spatial invention as an end in itself: a pressure to which modern architecture has been unduly subject. Rather than join in a recapitulation of avant-gardist tropes or enter into historicist pastiche or into the superfluous proliferation of sculptural gestures – all of which have an arbitrary dimension to the degree that they are based in neither structure nor in construction – we may return instead to the structural unit as the irreducible essence of architectural form.

Needless to say, we are not alluding here to mechanical revelation of construction but rather to a potentially poetic manifestation of structure in the original Greek sense of *poesis* as an act of making and revealing. While I am well aware of the conservative connotations that may be ascribed to Grassi's polemic, his critical perceptions none the less cause us to question the very idea of the new, in a moment that oscillates between the cultivation of a resistant culture and a descent into value-free aestheticism. Perhaps the most balanced assessment of Grassi has been made by the Catalan critic Ignasi Solà Morales, when he wrote:

Architecture is posited as a craft, that is to say, as the practical application of established knowledge through rules of the different levels of intervention. Thus, no notion of architecture as problem-solving, as innovation, or as invention ex novo, *is present in Grassi's thinking, since he is interested in showing the permanent, the evident, and the given character of knowledge in the making of architecture.*

... The work of Grassi is born of a reflection upon the essential resources of discipline, and it focuses upon specific media which determine not only aesthetic choices but also the ethical content of its cultural contribution. Through these channels of ethical and political will, the concern of the Enlightenment ... becomes enriched in its most critical tone. It is not solely the superiority of reason and the analysis of form which are indicated, but rather, the critical role (in the Kantian sense of the term) that is, the judgement of values, the very lack of which is felt in society today ... In the sense that his architecture is a meta-language, a reflection on the contradictions of its own practice, his work acquires the appeal of something that is both frustrating and noble...[4]

The dictionary definition of the term 'tectonic' to mean 'pertaining to building or construction in general; constructional, constructive used especially in reference to architecture and the kindred arts', is a little reductive to the extent that we intend not only the structural component *in se* but also the formal amplification of its presence in relation to the assembly of which it is a part. From its conscious emergence in the middle of the nineteenth century with the writings of Karl Bötticher and Gottfried Semper, the term not only indicates a structural and material probity but also a poetics of construction, as this may be practised in architecture and the related arts.

The beginnings of the Modern, dating back at least two centuries, and the much more recent advent of the Post-modern, are inextricably bound up with the ambiguities introduced into Western architecture by the primacy given to the scenographic in the evolution of the bourgeois world. However, building remains essentially *tectonic* rather than scenographic in character and it may be argued that it is first and foremost an act of construction rather than a discourse predicated on the surface, volume and plan, to cite Le Corbusier's 'Three Reminders to Architects'. Thus one may assert that building is *ontological* rather than *representational* in character and that built form is a presence rather than something standing for an absence. In Martin Heidegger's terminology we may think of it as a 'thing' rather than a 'sign'.

I have chosen to engage with this theme because I believe it is necessary for architects to reposition themselves given that the predominant tendency today is to reduce all architectural expression to the status of commodity culture. In as much as such resistance has little chance of being widely accepted, a 'rear-guard' posture would seem to be an appropriate stance to adopt rather than the dubious assumption that it is possible to continue with the perpetuation of avant-gardism. Despite its concern for structure, an emphasis on tectonic form does not necessarily favour either Constructivism or Deconstructivism. In this sense it is astylistic. Moreover it does not seek its legitimacy in science, literature or art.

Greek in origin, the term *tectonic* derives from the term *tekton*, signifying carpenter or builder. This in turn stems from the Sanskrit *taksan*, referring to the craft of carpentry and to the use of the axe. Remnants of a similar term can also be found in Vedic, where it refers to carpentry. In Greek it appears in Homer, where it again alludes to carpentry and to the art of construction in general. The poetic connotation of the term first appears in Sappho where the *tekton*, the carpenter, assumes the role of the poet. This meaning undergoes further evolution as the term passes from being something specific and physical, such as carpentry, to the more generic notion of construction and later to becoming an aspect of poetry. In Aristophanes we even find the idea that it is associated with machination and the creation of false things. This etymological evolution would suggest a gradual passage from the ontological to the representational. Finally, the Latin term *architectus* derives from the Greek *archi* (a person of authority) and *tekton* (a craftsman or builder).

The earliest appearance of the term 'tectonic' in English dates from 1656 where it appears in a glossary meaning 'belonging to building', and this is almost a century after the first English use of the term *architect* in 1563. In 1850 the German oriental scholar K O Muller was to define the term rather rudely, as 'A series of arts which form and perfect vessels, implements, dwellings and places of assembly'. The term is first elaborated in a modern sense with Karl Bötticher's *The Tectonic of the Hellenes* of 1843–52 and with Gottfried Semper's essay 'The Four Elements of Architecture' of the same year. It is further developed in Semper's unfinished study, *Style in the Technical and Tectonic Arts or Practical Aesthetic*, published between 1863 and 1868.

The term 'tectonic' cannot be divorced from the technological, and it is this that gives it a certain ambivalence. In this regard it is possible to identify three distinct conditions: 1) the *technological object*, which arises directly out of meeting an instrumental need; 2) the *scenographic object*, which may be used equally to allude to an absent or hidden element; and 3) the *tectonic object*, which appears in two modes. We may refer to these modes as the *ontological* and *representational* tectonic. The first involves a constructional element that is shaped so as to emphasize its static role and cultural status. This is the tectonic as it appears in Bötticher's interpretation of the Doric column. The second mode involves the representation of a constructional element which is present, but hidden. These two modes can be seen as paralleling the distinction that Semper made between the *structural-technical* and the *structural-symbolic*.

Aside from these distinctions, Semper was to divide built form into two separate material procedures: into the *tectonics* of the frame, in which members of varying lengths are conjoined to encompass a spatial field; and the *stereotomics* of compressive mass that, while it may embody space, is constructed through the piling up of identical units (the term *stereotomics* deriving from the Greek term for solid, *stereos* and cutting, *-tomia*). In the first case, the most common material throughout history has been wood or its textual equivalents such as bamboo, wattle and basketwork. In the second case, one of the most common materials has been brick, or the compressive equivalent of brick such as rock, stone or rammed earth and later, reinforced concrete. There have been significant exceptions to this division, particularly where, in the interest of permanence, stone has been cut, dressed and erected in such a way as to assume the form and function of a frame.

While these facts are so familiar as to hardly need repetition, we tend to be unaware of the ontological consequences of these differences; that is to say, of the way in which framework tends towards the aerial and the dematerialization of mass, whereas the mass form is telluric, embedding itself ever deeper into the earth. The one tends towards light and the other towards dark. These gravitational opposites, the immateriality of the frame and the materiality of the mass, may be said to symbolize the two cosmological opposites to which they aspire: the sky and the earth. Despite our highly secularized techno-scientific age, these polarities still largely constitute the experiential limits of our lives. It is arguable that the practice of architecture is impoverished to the extent that we fail to recognize these transcultural values and the way in which they are latent in all structural form. Indeed, these forms may serve to remind us, after Heidegger, that inanimate objects may also evoke 'being', and that through this analogy to our own corpus, the body of a building may be perceived as though it were literally a physique. This brings us back to Semper's privileging of the joint as the primordial tectonic element, as the fundamental nexus around which building comes into being, that is to say, comes to be articulated as a presence in itself.

Semper's emphasis on the joint implies that fundamental syntactical transition may be expressed as one passes from the *stereotomic* base to the *tectonic* frame, and that such transitions constitute the very essence of architecture. They are the dominant constituents whereby one culture of building differentiates itself from the next.

There is a spiritual value residing in the 'thingness' of the constructed object, so much so that the generic joint becomes a point of ontological condensation rather than a mere connection. The work of Carlo Scarpa would seem to exemplify this attribute.

The first volume of the fourth edition of Karl Bötticher's *Tektonik der Hellenen* appeared in 1843, two years after Schinkel's death in 1841. This publication was followed by three subsequent volumes which appeared at intervals over the next decade, the last appearing in 1852, the year of Semper's 'Four Elements of Architecture'. Bötticher elaborated the concept of the tectonic in a number of significant ways. At one level he envisaged a conceptual *juncture*, which came into being through the appropriate interlocking of constructional elements. Simultaneously articulated and integrated, these conjunctions were seen as constituting the body-form, the *Korperbilden* of the building that not only guaranteed its material finish, but also enabled this function to be recognized as a symbolic form. At another level, Bötticher distinguished between the *Kernform* or nucleus and the *Kunstform* or decorative cladding, the latter having the purpose of representing and symbolizing the institutional status of the work. According to Bötticher, this shell or revetment had to be capable of revealing the inner essence of the tectonic nucleus. At the same time Bötticher insisted that one must always try to distinguish between the indispensable structural form and its enrichment, irrespective of whether the latter is merely the shaping of the technical elements – as in the case of the Doric column, or the cladding of its basic form with revetment. Semper will later adapt this notion of *Kunstform* to the idea of *Bekleidung*, that is to say, to the concept of literally 'dressing' the fabric of a structure.

Bötticher was greatly influenced by the philosopher Josef von Schelling's view that architecture transcends the mere pragmatism of building by virtue of assuming symbolic significance. For Schelling and Bötticher alike, the inorganic had no symbolic meaning, hence structural form could only acquire symbolic value by virtue of its capacity to engender analogies between tectonic and organic form. However, any kind of direct imitation of natural form was to be avoided since both men held the view that architecture was an imitative art only in so far as it imitated itself. This view tends to corroborate Grassi's contention that architecture has always been distanced from the figurative arts, even if its form can be seen as paralleling nature. In this capacity architecture simultaneously serves both as a metaphor of, and as a foil to, the naturally organic. In tracing this thought retrospectively, one may cite Semper's 'Theory of Formal Beauty' of 1856 in which he no longer grouped architecture with painting and sculpture as a plastic art, but with dance and music as a cosmic art, as an ontological world-making art rather than as representational form. Semper regarded such arts as paramount not only because they were symbolic but also because they embodied man's underlying erotic-ludic urge to strike a beat, to string a necklace, to weave a pattern, and thus to decorate according to rhythmic law.

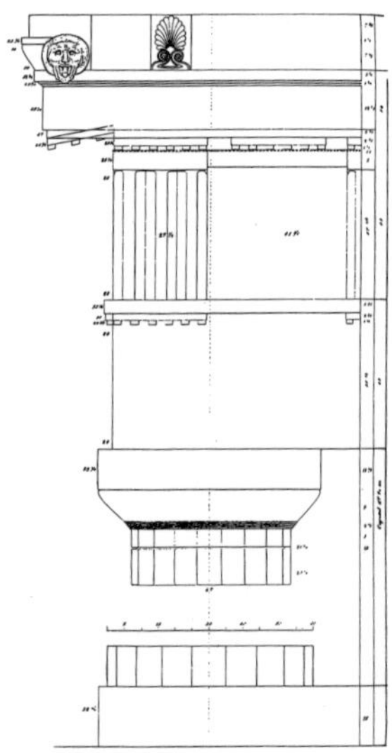

The Doric Order from Lafever's The Modern Builder's Guide, *1883. According to Karl Bötticher's theory the* Kunstform *is the fluting and the* Kernform *is the body of the column.*

Semper's 'Four Elements of Architecture' brings the discussion full circle in as much as Semper added a specific anthropological dimension to the idea of tectonic form. Semper's theoretical schema constitutes a fundamental break with the 400-year-old humanist formula of *utilitas, firmitas, venustas* that first served as the intentional triad of Roman architecture and then as the underpinning of post-Vitruvian architectural theory. Semper's radical reformulation stemmed from his seeing a model of a Caribbean hut in the Great Exhibition of 1851. The empirical reality of this simple shelter caused Semper to reject Laugier's primitive hut, adduced in 1753 as the primordial form of shelter with which to substantiate the pedimented paradigm of Neoclassical architecture. Semper's 'four elements' countermanded this hypothetical assumption and asserted instead an anthropological construct comprising: 1) a hearth, 2) an earthwork, 3) a framework and a roof, and 4) an enclosing membrane.

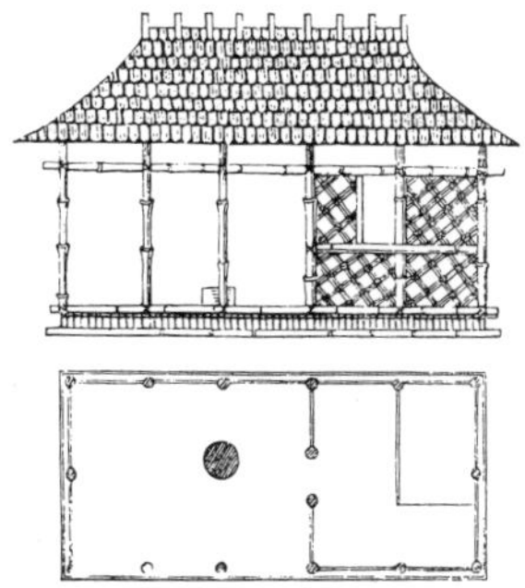

Gottfried Semper, drawing of a Caribbean hut exemplifying the 'four elements': structure and roof, podium, hearth, and infill wall, 1851.

While Semper's elemental model repudiated Neoclassical authority it none the less gave primacy to the frame over the load-bearing mass. At the same time, Semper's four-part thesis recognized the primary importance of the earthwork, that is to say, of a telluric mass that serves in one way or another to anchor the frame or the wall, or *Mauer*, into the site.

This marking, shaping and preparing of ground by means of an earthwork had a number of theoretical ramifications. On the one hand, it isolated the enclosing membrane as a differentiating act, so that the *textual* could be literally identified with the proto-linguistic nature of textile production that Semper regarded as the basis of all civilization. On the other hand, as Rosemary Bletter has pointed out, by stressing the earthwork as the fundamental basic form, Semper gave symbolic import to a non-spatial element, namely, the hearth, which was invariably an inseparable part of the earthwork. The term 'breaking ground' and the metaphorical use of the word 'foundation' are both obviously related to the primacy of the earthwork and the hearth.

In more ways that one Semper grounded his theory of architecture in a phenomenal element having strong social and spiritual connotations. For Semper the hearth's origin was linked to that of the altar, and as such it was the spiritual nexus of architectural form. The hearth bears within itself connotations in this regard. It derives from the Latin verb *aedisficare* which in its turn is the origin of the English word *edifice*, meaning literally 'to make a hearth'. The latent institutional connotations of both hearth and edifice are further suggested by the verb *to edify*, which means to educate, strengthen and instruct.

Influenced by the linguistic and anthropological insights of his age, Semper was concerned with the etymology of building. Thus he distinguished the massivity of a fortified stone wall, as indicated by the term *Mauer*, from the light frame and in-fill – wattle and daub, say – of medieval domestic building, for which the term *Wand* is used. This fundamental distinction has been nowhere more graphically expressed than in Karl Gruber's reconstruction of a medieval German town. Both *Mauer* and *Wand* reduce to the word 'wall' in

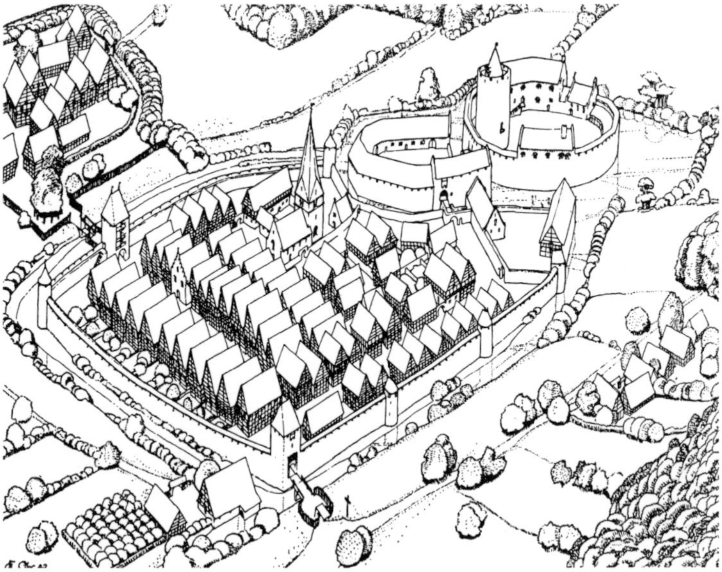

Reconstruction of a typical medieval town from Karl Gruber's Die Gestalt der Deutschen Stadt, *1937. The image shows the difference between the heavyweight monumental architecture and the lightweight residential fabric.*

English, but the latter in German is related to the word for dress, *Gewand*, and to the term *Winden*, which means to embroider. In accordance with the primacy that he gave to textiles, Semper maintained that the earliest basic structural artefact was the knot, which predominates in nomadic building form – especially in the Bedouin tent and its textile interior. There are etymological connotations residing here of which Semper was fully aware, above all, the connection between *knot* and *joint*, the former being in German *die Knofen* and the latter *die Verbindung*, which may be literally translated as 'the binding'. All this evidence tends to support Semper's contention that the ultimate constituent of the art of building is the joint.

The primacy that Semper accorded to the knot seems to be supported by Gunter Nitschke's research into Japanese binding and unbinding rituals as set forth in his seminal essay 'Shime' of 1974.[5] In Shinto culture these proto-tectonic binding rituals constitute agrarian renewal rites. They point at once to that close association between building, dwelling, cultivating and being that was remarked on by Martin Heidegger in his essay 'Building, Dwelling, Thinking' of 1954.

Semper's distinction between *tectonic* and *stereotomic* returns us to theoretical arguments recently advanced by the Italian architect Vittorio Gregotti, who proposes that the marking of ground, rather than the primitive hut, is the primordial tectonic act. In his 1983 address to the New York Architectural League, Gregotti stated:

... The worst enemy of modern architecture is the idea of space considered solely in terms of its economic and technical exigencies indifferent to the idea of the site.

The built environment that surrounds us is, we believe, the physical representation of its history, and the way in which it has accumulated different levels of meaning to form the specific quality of the site, not *just for what it appears to be, in perceptual terms, but for what it is in structural terms.*

Geography is the description of how the signs of history have become forms, therefore the architectural project is charged with the task of revealing the essence of the geo-environmental context through the transformation of form. The environment is therefore not a system in which to dissolve architecture. On the contrary, it is the most important material from which to develop the project.

Indeed, through the concept of the site and the principle of settlement, the environment becomes the essence of architectural production. From this vantage point, new principles and methods can be seen for design. Principles and methods that give precedence to the siting in a specific area [sic]. This is an act of knowledge of the context that comes out of its architectural modification *[my emphasis]. The origin of architecture is not the primitive hut, the cave or the mythical 'Adam's House in Paradise'. Before transforming a support into a column, a roof into a tympanum, before placing stone on stone, man placed a stone on the ground to recognize a site in the midst of an unknown universe, in order to take account of it and modify it. As with every act of assessment, this one required radical moves and apparent simplicity. From this point of view, there are only two important attitudes to the context. The tools of the first are mimesis, organic imitation and the display of complexity. The tools of the second are the assessment of physical relations, formal definition and the interiorization of complexity.*[6]

With the tectonic in mind it is possible to posit a revised account of the history of modern architecture, for when the entire trajectory is reinterpreted through the lens of *techne* certain patterns emerge and others recede. Seen in this light a tectonic impulse may be traced across the century, uniting diverse works irrespective of their different origins. In this process well-known affinities are further reinforced, while others recede and hitherto unremarked connections emerge asserting the importance of criteria that lie beyond superficial stylistic differences. Thus for all their stylistic idiosyncrasies a very similar level of tectonic articulation patently links Hendrik Petrus Berlage's Stock Exchange of 1897–1904 to Frank Lloyd Wright's Larkin Building of 1904 and Herman Hertzberger's Centraal Beheer office complex of 1968–72. In each instance there is a similar concatenation of span and support that amounts to a tectonic syntax in which gravitational force passes from purlin to truss, to pad stone, to corbel, to arch, to pier and abutment. The technical transfer of this load passes through a series of appropriately articulated transitions and joints. In each of these works the constructional articulation engenders the spatial subdivision and vice versa, and this same principle may be found in other works of this century possessing quite different stylistic aspirations. Thus we find a comparable

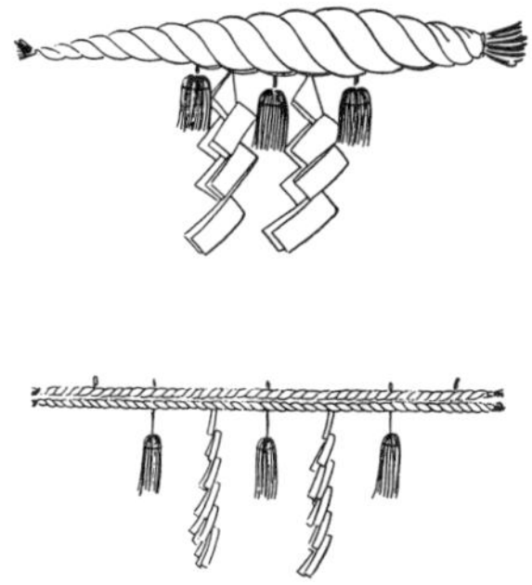

'Shime-nawa', traditional apotropaic Shinto signs in bound rice straw and paper.

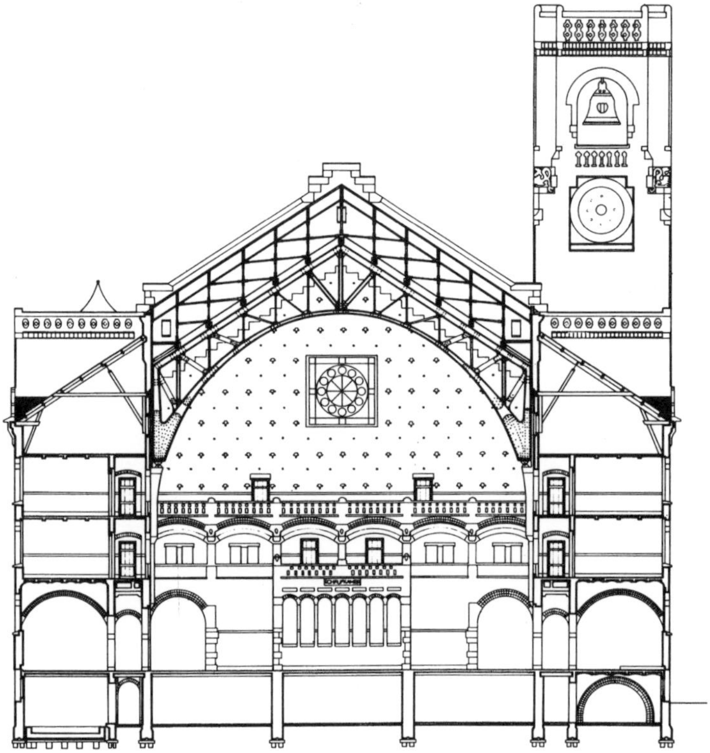

Hendrik Petrus Berlage, Stock Exchange, Amsterdam, 1897–1904, cross-section.

concern for the revealed joint in the architecture of both Auguste Perret and Louis Kahn. In each instance the joint guarantees the probity and presence of the overall form while alluding to distinct different ideological and referential antecedents. Thus, where Perret looks back to the structurally rationalized classicism of the Greco–Gothic ideal, dating back in France to the beginning of the eighteenth century, Kahn evokes a 'timeless archaism', at once technologically advanced but spiritually antique.

The case can be made that the prime inspiration behind all this work stemmed as much from Eugène Viollet-le-Duc as from Semper, although clearly Wright's conception of built form as a petrified fabric writ large, most evident in his textile block houses of the Twenties, derives directly from the cultural priority that Semper gave to textile production and to the knot as the primordial tectonic unit. It is arguable that Kahn was as much influenced by Wright as by the Franco–American Beaux-Arts line, stemming from Viollet-le-Duc and the Ecole des Beaux-Arts. This particular genealogy enables us to recognize the links tying Kahn's Richards' Laboratories of 1961 back to Wright's Larkin Building. In each instance there is a similar 'tartan', textile-like preoccupation with dividing the enclosed volume and its various appointments into *servant* and *served* spaces. In addition to this there is a very similar concern for the *expressive rendering of mechanical services* as though they were of the same hierarchic importance as the structural frame. Thus the monumental brick ventilation shafts of the Richards' Laboratories are anticipated, as it were, in the hollow, ducted, brick bastions that establish the four-square monumental corners of the Larkin Building. However dematerialized, there is a comparable discrimination between servant and served spaces in Norman Foster's Sainsbury Centre of 1978, combined with a similar penchant for the expressive potential of mechanical services. And here again we encounter further proof that the *tectonic* in the twentieth century cannot concern itself only with structural form.

Wright's highly tectonic approach and the influence of this on the later phases of the Modern Movement have been underestimated, for Wright is surely the primary influence behind such diverse European figures as Carlo Scarpa, Franco Albini, Leonardo Ricci, Gino Valle and Umberto Riva, to cite only the Italian Wrightian line. A similar Wrightian connection runs through Scandinavia and Spain, serving to connect such diverse figures as Jørn Utzon, Javier Saénz de Oíza and most recently Rafael Moneo, who as it happens was a pupil of both.

Something has to be said of the crucial role played by the joint in the work of Scarpa and to note the syntactically tectonic nature of this architecture. This dimension has been brilliantly characterized by Marco Frascari in his essay on the mutual reciprocity of 'constructing' and 'construing':

Technology is a strange word. It has always been difficult to define its semantic realm. Through the changes in meaning, at different times and in different places, of the word 'technology' into its original components of techne *and* logos, *it is possible to set up a mirror-like relationship between the* techne *of* logos *and the* logos *of* techne. *At the time of the Enlightenment the rhetorical* techne *of* logos *was replaced by the scientific* logos *of* techne. *However, in Scarpa's architecture this replacement did not take place. Technology is present with both the forms in a chiastic quality. Translating this chiastic presence into a language proper to architecture is like saying that there is no construction without a construing, and no construing without a construction.*[7]

Elsewhere Frascari writes of the irreducible importance of the joint not only for the work of Scarpa but for all tectonic endeavours. Thus we read in a further essay entitled 'The Tell-the-Tale Detail':

Architecture is an art because it is interested not only in the original need for shelter but also in putting together spaces and materials, in the meaningful manner. This occurs through formal and actual joints. The joint, that is the fertile detail, is the place where both the construction and the construing of architecture takes place. Furthermore, it is useful to complete our understanding of this essential role of the joint as the place of the process of signification to recall that the meaning of the original Indo-European root of the word art *is joint. . .*[8]

If the work of Scarpa assumes paramount importance for stress on the joint, the seminal value of Utzon's contribution to the evolution of modern tectonic form resides in his reinterpretation of Semper's 'four elements'. This is particularly evident in all his 'pagoda/podium' pieces, which invariably break down into the earthwork and the surrogate hearth, embodied in the podium, and into the roof and the textile-like in-fill, to be found in the form of the 'pagoda' – irrespective of whether this crowning roof element comprises a shell vault or a folded slab (as in the Sydney Opera House of 1973 and the Bagsvaerd Church of 1976). It says something for Moneo's apprenticeship under Utzon that a similar articulation of earthwork and roof is evident in his Roman archaeological museum completed in Merida, Spain in 1986.

As we have already indicated, the tectonic lies suspended between a series of opposites, above all between the *ontological* and the *representational*. However, other dialogical conditions are involved in the articulation of tectonic form, particularly the contrast between the culture of the heavy-*stereotomics*, and the culture of the light-*tectonics*. The first implies load-bearing masonry and tends towards the earth and opacity. The second implies the dematerialized A-frame and tends towards the sky and translucence. At one end of this scale we have Semper's earthwork reduced in primordial times, as Gregotti reminds us, to the marking of ground. At the other end we have the ethereal, dematerialized aspirations of Joseph Paxton's Crystal Palace, that which Le Corbusier once described as the victory of light over gravity. Since few works are absolutely the one thing or the other, it can be claimed that the poetics of construction arise, in part, out of the inflection and positionings of the tectonic object. Thus the earthwork extends itself upwards to become an arch or a vault, or alternatively withdraws first to become the cross-wall support for a simple lightweight span and then to become a podium, elevated from the earth, on which an entire framework takes its anchorage. Other contrasts serve to articulate this dialogical movement further – such as *smooth* versus *rough* at the level of material (see Adrian Stokes's study *Smooth and Rough*, 1951), or *dark* versus *light* at the level of illumination.

Finally, something has to be said about the signification of the 'break' or the 'dis-joint' as opposed to the signification of the joint. I am alluding to that point at which things break against each other rather than connect: that significant fulcrum at which one system, surface or material abruptly ends to give way to another. Meaning may be thus encoded through the interplay between 'joint' and 'break', and in this regard rupture may have just as much meaning as connection. Such considerations sensitize the architecture to the semantic risks that attend all forms of articulation, ranging from the over-articulation of joints to the under-articulation of form.

Postscript: tectonic form and critical culture

As Sigfried Giedion was to remark in the introduction to his two-volume study *The Eternal Present* (1962), among the deeper impulses of modern culture in the first half of this century was a 'transavantgardist' desire to return to the timelessness of a pre-historic past; to recover in a literal sense some dimension of an eternal present, lying outside the nightmare of history and beyond the processal compulsions of instrumental progress. This drive insinuates itself again today as a potential ground from which to resist the commodification of culture. Within architecture the tectonic suggests itself as a mythical category with which to acquire entry to an anti-processal world wherein the 'presencing' of things will once again facilitate the appearance and experience of men. Beyond the aporias of history and progress and outside the reactionary closures of historicism and the neo-avant-garde lies the potential for a *marginal* counter-history. This is the primeval history of the logos to which Vico addressed himself, in his *Nuova Scienza*, in an attempt to adduce the poetic logic of the institution.[9] It is a mark of the radical nature of Vico's thought that he insisted that knowledge is not just the province of objective fact but also a consequence of the subjective, 'collective' elaboration of archetypal myth, that is to say, an assembly of those existential symbolic truths residing in the human experience. The critical myth of the tectonic joint points to just this timeless, time-bound moment, excised from the continuity of time.

First published in *Architectural Design*, vol.60, no.3/4, 1990, pp.19–25.

theory

history

criticism

Introduction

The essays assembled under the rubric of history begin with two pieces originally published in 1968. The first of these 'The Humanist versus the Utilitarian Ideal' was based on the comparative critical analysis of two categorically opposed designs for the canonical Société des Nations Competition of 1927, namely, the entries by Le Corbusier and Pierre Jeanneret on the one hand, and by Hannes Meyer and Hans Wittwer on the other. This essay enabled me to instruct readers as to the implicit values embodied in the different ways in which these two projects had been conceived, organized and detailed.

The second essay is a piece dedicated to the work of the Soviet avant-gardist El Lissitzky, written as a delayed response to one of the earliest postwar retrospectives of his work, staged in the Powers Gallery, London, in 1965. This essay was subsequently published in *Architects' Year Book 12* of 1968. Influenced by Camilla Gray's seminal study of 1962, *The Great Experiment: Russian Art 1863–1922*, this essay announces the beginning of my involvement with the Soviet avant-garde, leading to a series of essays with a similar focus during the second half of the Sixties, including a piece in Thomas Hess's *The Art News Annual* of 1967 and a contribution to Norbert Lynton's British Arts Council catalogue for the exhibition 'Art and Revolution' of 1971. Justifiably characterized by Reyner Banham in his *Theory and Design in the First Machine Age* (1960) as the great ideas man of the modern movement, El Lissitzky surely remains one of the artists of the twentieth century with the widest conceivable range of activity: architect, painter, exhibition designer, photographer, polemicist, culture diplomat and, above all, along with Herbert Bayer and Jan Tschichold, one of the principal pioneers of modern graphic design.

In 1975, following the publication of the *Team 10 Primer* edited by Alison Smithson in 1968, I wrote a piece entitled 'Team 10, Plus 20: The Vicissitudes of Ideology', an overview of the work of Team 10 that was published in *L'Architecture d'aujourd'hui*. This was a partially analytical account of the 'turn' from modernism to postmodernism on the part of the postwar European neo-avant garde in architecture.

My preoccupation with the politically radical wing of the modern movement then turned to a deeper consideration of the term constructivism that had been defensively dismissed by Le Corbusier as a vague term that attempted to signify too much. This was the essay 'Constructivism: The Pursuit of an Elusive Sensibility' which appeared in *Oppositions 6* in the autumn of 1976. This last led me to suggest that film was perhaps the ultimate manifestation of constructivism, particularly as we find this in Dziga Vertov's masterpiece *The Man with the Movie Camera* of 1929.

In this constant oscillation between the prewar avant-garde and the architecture of the present I then attempted a retrospective assessment of the work of Louis Kahn entitled 'Louis Kahn and the French Connection', published in *Oppositions 22* in 1980; the connection in question is as much Italian as French however, to the extent that the entire essay was greatly inspired by the exceptionally perceptive work of Italian scholars, who were among the first to point out the influence of French Neoclassicism and Structural Rationalism on the work of Kahn.

The essay entitled 'The Maison de Verre as Bachelor Machine' is the reworking of a section of my essay 'Pierre Chareau: An Eclectic Architect' which appeared in *Pierre Chareau: Architect and Craftsman 1883–1950*, first published in French by Editions du Regard in 1984. To a certain extent this essay is based on my measured drawing and photographic documentation of the Maison de Verre, made in collaboration with Michael Carepetian and Robert Vickery in 1965. It is nothing short of perverse that I should fail to mention the Maison de Verre in my *Modern Architecture: A Critical History* of 1980; an omission that can only be explained by the anomalous, unclassifiable character of this work.

There follows an essay on the work of Adolf Loos written shortly after the 1985 British Arts Council exhibition *The Architecture of Adolf Loos*, curated by Yehuda Safran and Wilfried Wang. The introspective, sub-aqueous character of the Maison de Verre may be said to find something of an antecedent in the 'negative' critical attitude adopted by Loos, which is as evident in his architecture as in his sardonic writing.

'The Other Le Corbusier: Primitive Form and the Linear City, 1929–52' was written for the 1987 British Arts Council catalogue, *Le Corbusier: Architect of the Century*, issued for the centennial of Le Corbusier's birth. The essay focuses on Le Corbusier's break with his earlier ideal notions of equipping the machine-age civilization, leading to his subsequent adoption of a more realistic attitude towards both architecture and urbanism.

The next essay, 'The Usonian Legacy', deals with the southern Californian modern domestic tradition, extending from the pioneering works of the Austrian émigré architects Rudolph Schindler and Richard Neutra, through Frank Lloyd Wright's own Usonian houses of the late Thirties and on, via John Entenza's so-called Case Study Houses, into the last quarter of the century. The work of the Finnish master Alvar Aalto also assumes an equally organic, socially accessible character, particularly after World War II, as the last essay in this set attempts to make evident. It is an extract from my contribution to the 1998 Museum of Modern Art catalogue, *Alvar Aalto: Between Humanism and Materialism*.

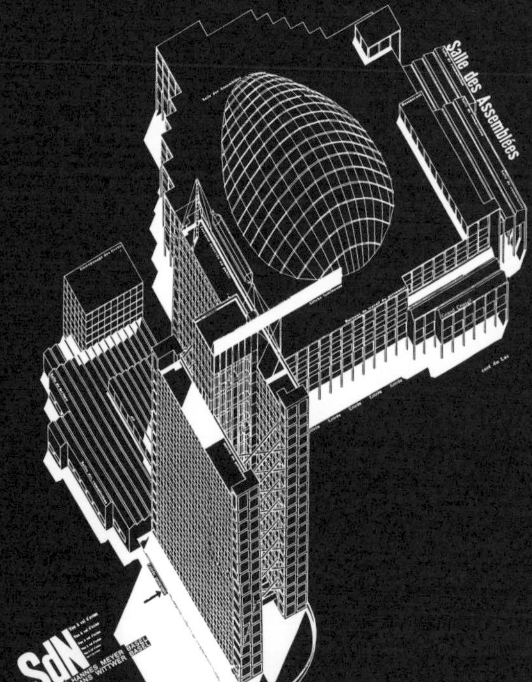
Salle des Assemblées
SdN
ARCHITEKT HANNES MEYER BASEL
ARCHITEKT HANS WITTWER BASEL

The Humanist versus the Utilitarian Ideal

Half a century ago the nations of the world held a competition for the building of the League of Nations. The judging of this competition was something of a major scandal. Modern architecture was effectively excluded in a decision that, it may be argued, seriously retarded the development of modern architecture. However, it was the signal for a bitter debate that vitally stirred the theorists of the Modern Movement. Two of the most significant entries – those of Le Corbusier and Hannes Meyer – so crystallized the opposed approaches of the visionary idealists and the strict utilitarians that one may assess the subsequent development of modern architecture by an analysis of these works.[1]

This refers, of course, to the year 1927 and to Le Corbusier's initial success and subsequent disqualification, on a technicality, as the author of the premiated design for the Palais des Nations, Geneva. It is possible to see this event and its aftermath as symptomatic of a profounder schism between humanism and utilitarianism. Paradoxically, Le Corbusier's entry, while as idealistic as most of the competition entries, was regarded by reactionaries as being unduly utilitarian. For Neoclassicism was considered the ideal style of authority. This style, however debased, manifested itself increasingly after 1927 as a reaction on the part of all nationalistic governments. Thus the post-1918, utilitarian-oriented architecture of the Soviet Union suffered a sudden eclipse in the early Thirties. The 1931 Palace of the Soviets competition, consciously conceived as an international Communist counterpart to the League of Nations, was to result in a triumph for so-called 'left classicism', and Le Corbusier was to suffer in this the agonies of rejection all over again.

In spite of differences in architectonic development between the projects submitted by Le Corbusier and Meyer, both reveal a functional commitment to the accommodation of the programme. They are both concerned with the direct expression of these requirements in the derivation of their forms and in the arrangements of the complex as a whole. The two projects have in very general terms a similar *parti*, arising directly out of the competition brief, and comprising in each case a distorted H-plan secretariat block, linked by *passerelles* to a large, free-standing auditorium building. Apart from this, the projects differ in the following respects: in their siting and the attitude taken by their authors to landscape and nature in general; in the manipulation and ordering of space; in the selection and application of structural modules and their relations to space; in the selection and application of circulation systems and service devices; in the selection and application of materials; and in iconography and prototype.

Both projects are partially lifted off the site on a system of *pilotis*, accommodating cars under their elevated sections in much the same manner

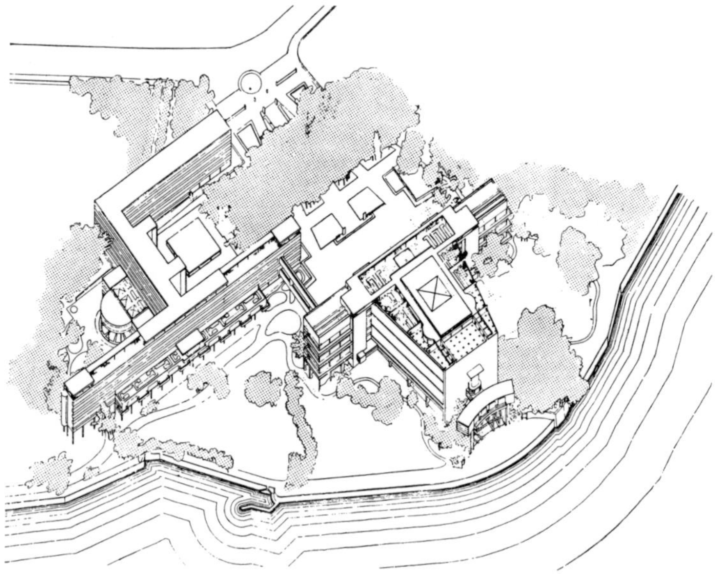

Le Corbusier and Pierre Jeanneret, competition project for the League of Nations, Geneva, 1927, axonometric.

as pile dwellings accommodate boats. The car set-down points in Le Corbusier's plans are marked *Quai de la grande salle* and *Quai du secrétariat*, thereby emphasizing the nautical metaphor by direct reference to the *quais* that border the shores of Lake Geneva. In spite of Le Corbusier's highly developed car consciousness, it is Meyer who makes, in excess of the competition requirements, an altogether larger and more realistic provision for future car access. In Le Corbusier's project one senses the car to be an unavoidable, almost embarrassing necessity, compromising pedestrian movement across the site by its presence. In Meyer's, on the other hand, pedestrian movement on the site is totally discouraged, and the car becomes essential to the building's workability. Both projects pay surprisingly little attention to the need to separate pedestrian and vehicular movement. Meyer idealizes the car and inundates the site with vehicles,

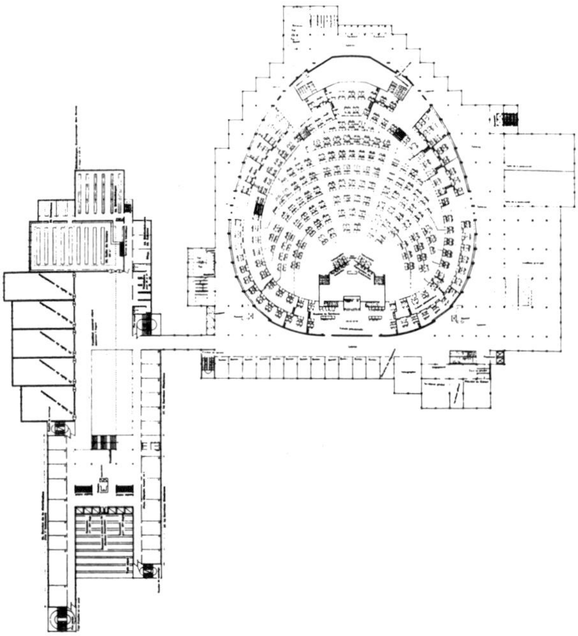

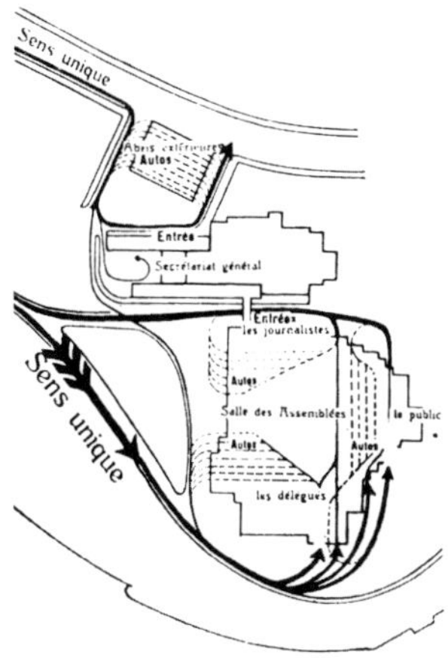

Hannes Meyer and Hans Wittwer, League of Nations, 1927, first floor plan (left) and car flow diagram (above).

cars flowing around the lowered belly of the auditorium and its related entry points like whirlpools of water around a large, obstructive rock. In this respect, Meyer's project is far in advance of its time, providing six times the amount of parking space required by the brief. This extended system of mechanical access is deliberately utilized by Meyer to classify the various types of people arriving at the building. Personnel, journalists, public and delegates are separated out through the vehicular medium into their respective parking lots before entering the building as pedestrians. Thus they may enter the secretariat from the uncovered secretariat park or the auditorium building by way of three different parking lots, all located under the *pilotis*, and adjacent to their appropriate entry foyers located on three separate sides of the auditorium. While Meyer uses the car for not only distribution but also classification, Le Corbusier simply diverts his vehicular traffic to two main entry points – the secretariat and the *grande salle*. The mechanics of classification occur inside the building, through an ingenious system of interlocking staircases, which lead from classified entrances providing restricted access to the various levels within the auditorium. Thus, while Meyer uses the dynamic agency of the machine, Le Corbusier uses a more static one for the same purpose.

Both Meyer and Le Corbusier oriented their secretariat blocks east–west, but thereafter their separate attitudes to the context and to the *genius loci* of the site could not have been more different. Meyer, with doctrinaire vehemence, declares that the siting of his building depends solely on traffic flow and on natural and artificial lighting diagrams. He categorically proscribes any artificial landscape link between his building and its park-like environment. 'As a deliberately contrived work of man,' he writes, 'it stands in legitimate contrast to nature.' This sentiment is echoed in the writings of Le Corbusier, but whereas Meyer ignored the nature of the site and stressed the divorce of his deterministic structure from its existential locale, Le Corbusier is concerned deeply – as always – to relate the artefact to the site. The axonometrics of the two schemes are testament enough. Meyer allows no vestige of the site whatsoever to show. In Le Corbusier's drawings, a bucolic landscape impinges upon the representation of the man-made structure.

It is typical of the early design work of Meyer that he failed to respond to the special characteristics of the site, even though these were outlined at some length in the competition conditions. The latter included a special appendix of ten photographs that showed not only the magnificence and grandeur of the site's macro-environment but also the idyllic pastoralism of its micro-scale. Meyer's Peterschule project for Basel, of the previous year, had displayed a similar unconcern for the peculiarities of its urban location. He appears always to have been preoccupied with the internal organization of the programme itself. This may explain why his League of Nations entry did not make any provision for the eventual extension of the institution northwards as far as the then existing Bureau International du Travail. This omission appears to reflect his indifference to certain aspects of the competition brief.

For Le Corbusier the site was of the utmost importance. He not only adhered to the competition brief in this respect, but also interpreted the nuances of its implied intentions. He provided, as Meyer did not, an alternative processional route leading into the complex from the south in addition to the main entrance from the route Lausanne. The horizontality of his complex was a deliberate attempt to layer the building into the site so as to parallel the macro-scale of both the lake and the Alps. This entailed much greater internal horizontal circulation in the secretariat than was the case in the Meyer project, where a 21- to 24-storey secretariat yielded circulation economies at the price of producing a strong formal vertical contrast to the natural environment. It was apparently out of deference to the nature of the site and out of the need to provide for extension that Le Corbusier relegated to second choice his *parti* in its most ideal form. The small drawing appended on the right of the main site plan, illustrated in *Une Maison, un palais*, demonstrates clearly the ideal arrangement of the elements.

In this version, captioned '*proposition de variante avec emploi des mêmes éléments de composition*', the symmetrical system of traffic access, distorted in the actual entry, is implicit in a prime, workable form. Its implementation would have depended upon Le Corbusier's proposal to extend the quai Wilson as a straight line into the route Lausanne. The operational benefit would have been a more coherent system of pedestrian and vehicular access at all levels. The library foyer adjacent to the covered garage would also have been established on the axis of the extended quai Wilson. In this manner the somewhat unconvincing location of secretariat entrances in the project submitted would automatically have been obviated.

Similarly, horizontal high-level circulation between the secretariat and the assembly building would have been greatly improved through the duplication of the *passerelle* links and the symmetrical disposition. Clearly Le Corbusier rearranged the elements of his ideal solution in order to provide for a 'mirror' extension to his secretariat wing in the form of a large future secretariat expansion to the north on the axis of the *bureau de travail*. This distortion of the ideal type through the manipulation of its elements in response to the empirical demands of site and programme was detrimental to the elegance and efficiency of the basic idea that is shown in the '*proposition de variante*'. However, it was to result in a product of great aesthetic richness, relatively independent of notions of an ideal.

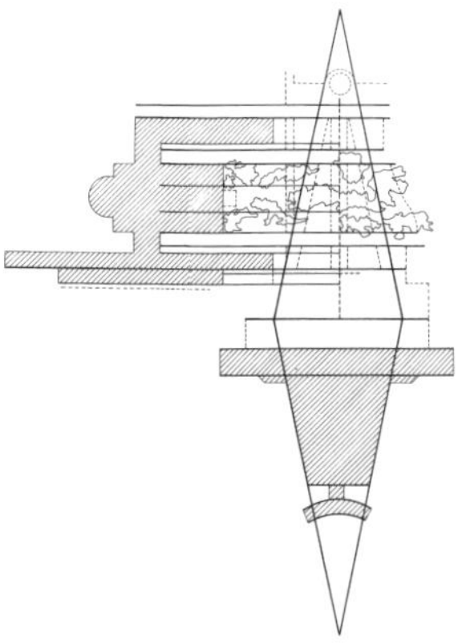

Colin Rowe and Robert Slutzky, analysis of planar organization of Le Corbusier's League of Nations site plan.

Le Corbusier described the disposition of his buildings on the site as a *conception paysagiste*, a phrase suggestive of Romantic Classicism. The devices involved in the development of this conception, however, are complex and sufficiently removed from traditional notions of relating a building to its site. As Colin Rowe and Robert Slutzky have pointed out, Le Corbusier's League of Nations entry comprises a series of parallel longitudinal spaces running perpendicular to the main east–west access of approach.[2] Hypothetically, a visitor approaching the assembly building along this axis, through the *cour d'honneur*, passes through a series of shallow striated spaces, defined by planes that, either planted or built – that is, either green or granite – deflect visual attention to the lateral views of the lake and the surrounding foliage. The centre of vision, however, would naturally remain focused on the assembly hall, and the space before the advancing visitor would alternately compress frontally and expand laterally and diagonally, creating a perceptual ambiguity as to the position of the frontalized planes suspended in space.

The siting of the Le Corbusier and Meyer projects leads naturally to a consideration of their different attitudes to the ordering of space and structure. As before, essential differences are to be found in Meyer's description: 'Our League symbolized nothing. Its size is automatically determined by the dimensions and conditions of the programme. As an organic building it expresses unfeignedly that it is intended to be a building for work and cooperation.'[3] The key words in this passage are 'organic' and 'automatically determined'. Meyer's aim is the automatic determination of an empirical programme and the expression of this random empiricism. If we compare the arrangement of the eleven *salles des commissions* in the two projects – five small and private, six large with public access – we find that each designer has reacted consistently with those differences in attitude already noted in their respective handling of the site.

Meyer does manage to achieve an automatically determined assembly of spatial elements. The asymmetrical plan forms of his two structures are, at least in part, a result of the agglomeration of commission rooms adjacent to the two main foyers of the secretariat and the auditorium. These rooms have opaque walls and are top-lit by east–west saw-tooth roof lights. The stepped plan profile of the perimeters of these two structures arises largely out of the automatic superimposition of the scheduled room areas on a regular planning grid. The resultant plastic effect appears random and inconsequential. One questions whether such high levels of natural top-lighting were necessary or even desirable.

It would seem that Meyer was seeking to express his egalitarian idea through the repetition of a standard structural module, part of an infinite field of coordinates. On this field his structural arrangement would arise in much the same manner as the 'image' came into being on a Mondrian canvas. The Platonic element for Meyer was the structural grid; for Le Corbusier, it was the resultant volume and mass. To this end Le Corbusier assigned to the smaller commission rooms the same minimum depth, so that they might be conveniently assembled as side-lit rectangular spaces arranged *en série*, parallel to the eastern facade of the secretariat. In a similar manner his larger commission rooms were stacked into the wings of the assembly building. Paradoxically, this gave a far clearer expression to the commission rooms than did Meyer's top-lighting.

Le Corbusier's basic notion of spatial order is hierarchical. The cross-section of his assembly building comprises a complex architectural promenade, which is best described in his own words. 'I attach major

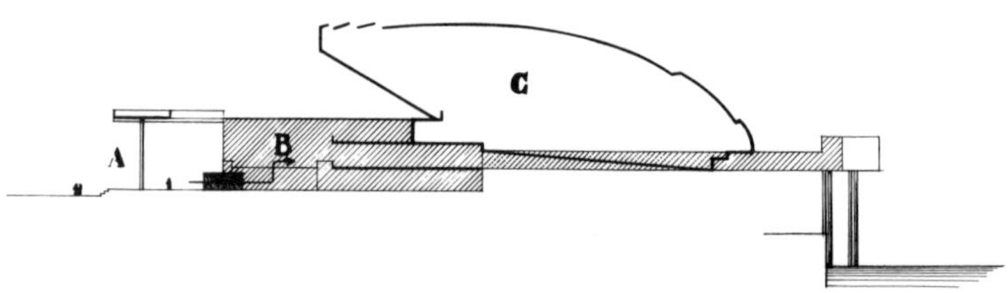

Le Corbusier and Pierre Jeanneret, League of Nations, cross-section through the assembly building showing the 'promenade architecturale' *that passes for the portico (a) through the main stair hall (b) and into the auditorium (c) and on to the secretary general's suite overlooking the lake.*

architectural importance to this little schematic section,' he writes. 'It shows, from A to C, the various architectural sensations experienced by the visitor; the rhythm of successive architectural volumes, of the *quai*, and of the canopy which projects it, of the entry drum, of the vestibule, of the Pas-Perdus, of the Pavillon du Président and finally of the Grande Salle.'[4] This promenade was envisaged by Le Corbusier as the orchestration of a series of psychological states, to be induced by successive changes in volume, light and view.

In his project Meyer resists as far as possible the creation of processional space. The idea of an architectural promenade seems anathema. The classification of people by parking pattern at ground level allows him thereafter to rely primarily on a vertical mode of access. The interjection of various banks of elevators at strategic points in the plan affords him

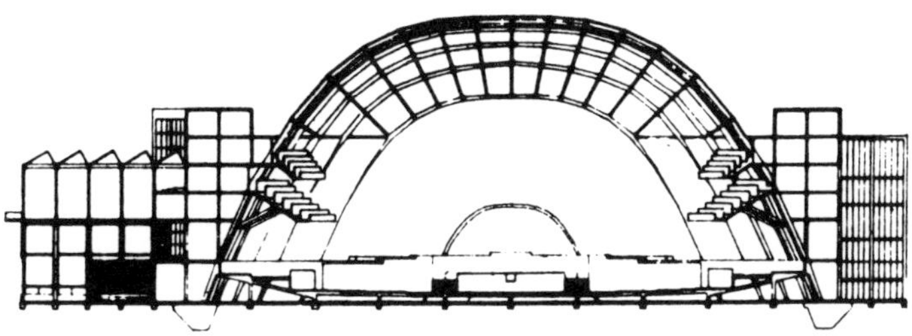

Hannes Meyer and Hans Wittwer, League of Nations, cross-section of assembly hall.

direct vertical access to the irregular foyers located between the wings of the secretariat or around the periphery of his egg-shaped auditorium. He endeavours as best he can to accommodate the inherent spatial hierarchy without increasing the structural scale. Most of his spaces, irrespective of their size, are ordered by the 9 by 4.5 metre structural grid. Only the top-lit meeting rooms are an exception. Even the large roof of Meyer's egg-shaped auditorium is carried on 'hyperbolic' concrete ribs located at every 4.5 metres on grid. Eccentric in shape and location and structured by the standard grid, the principal vestibule to this auditorium at mezzanine level precludes its interpretation as a *res publica* in the traditional sense.

Le Corbusier's 'Five Points of a New Architecture'[5] afforded him a freedom of movement denied to Meyer, whose design was an architecture of building method rather than one of volume, mass and space. As a doctrinaire constructivist, Meyer was dedicated to building method as the very basis of creation. For Le Corbusier, the means, as construction photographs of his villa at Garches testify, were rather less important than the ends. He varied the structural grid of his *palais* according to the different volumetric demands of the programme; thus the secretariat and library were based on a 7.5 by 3.5 metre bay, and the assembly hall undercroft on a 7.5 metre square bay increasing to 15 metres or larger where the scale of adjoining public spaces demanded a longer span. The free facade and free plan permitted further modulations of these basic variations. The ultimate contrast between the two schemes is to be found in the roof structure of the respective auditoria, Meyer proposing a two-way, ribbed, semi-hyperbolic structure based on his standard grid, and Le Corbusier, two 70 metre half-arch lattice spans carrying three cross-girders simply supported at their ends. Meyer's homogeneous approach is, once again, in contrast to Le Corbusier's hierarchical one.

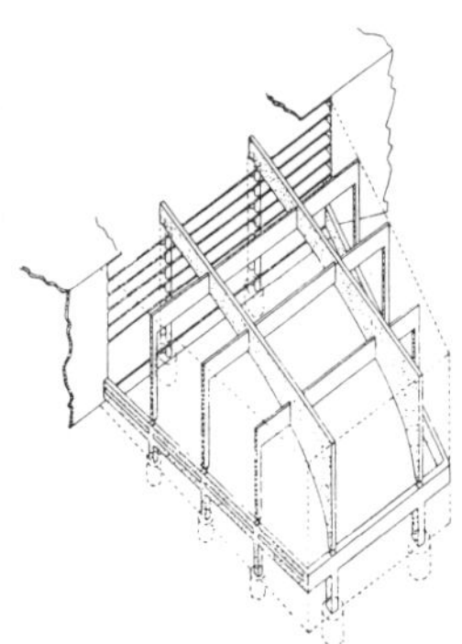

Le Corbusier and Pierre Jeanneret, League of Nations, auditorium roof structure, axonometric.

As we have seen, Meyer's project depends on mechanical circulation – that is, on cars, elevators and also escalators. In his secretariat there are six elevators, and two paternosters, rising 27 floors to the level of the radio station and observation deck. This is in addition to two service hoists and two sets of escalators that rise through the first 20 floors of the secretariat itself, and two book lifts serving the 11-storey book stack. In his assembly building there are another 16 elevators rising a height of six floors – ten for the public, four for the journalists and two for the delegates. From this analysis one can see that only the delegates were expected to use a staircase. For once Meyer made some concession to hierarchy, introducing a *scala regia* between the delegates' ground-floor foyer and the foyer of the auditorium. Curiously enough, Meyer displays little understanding of the economics of elevators. In his assembly building we find ten elevators assigned primarily to connect the public foyers at ground level with the public tribune of the hall situated four floors above. Meyer rationalizes this provision by assigning the upper floors of his assembly to a concourse for 3,000.

Le Corbusier's use of mechanical circulation is extremely economical by comparison. Five passenger elevators and two service hoists serve the eight floors of his secretariat, while four passenger lifts and two service hoists (*monte-charges*) carry all the traffic for the eight floors of his assembly building. He relies on staircase access for all other distribution.

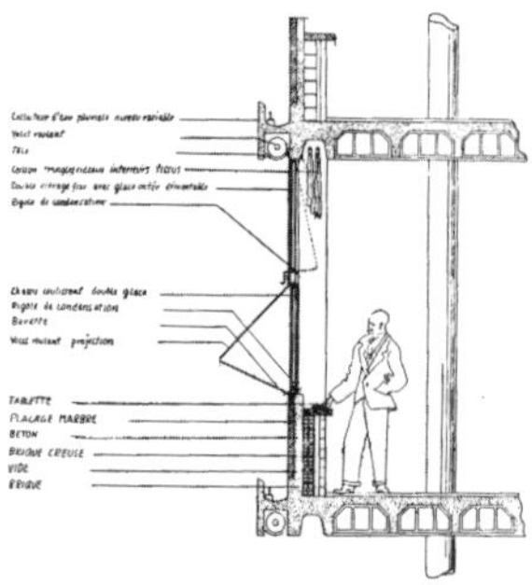

It is surprising that the utilitarian Meyer should make such an inept provision for servicing his structure. No provision, for instance, is made for cleaning the extensive glazed area of his *palais*; Le Corbusier, on the other hand, supplements his invention of the continuous window with an equally integrated mechanical device for cleaning its glazed surface. Similarly, Meyer makes no provision for air conditioning or even for adequate ventilation of his assembly hall, while Le Corbusier, with great zest and in considerable detail, provides for the complete environmental control of his major volume. Both architects pay adequate consideration to the acoustic performance of their respective auditoria, although Meyer's elliptical plan is hardly the profile on which one traditionally relies for acoustic perfection.

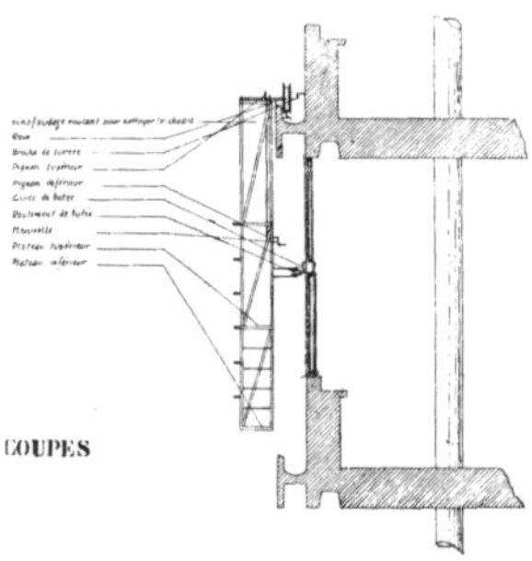

The complex relations that exist between the relative utility of an artefact and its iconography tend to be insufficiently acknowledged. A utilitarian iconography may be as detrimental to the relative utility of an object as the vestiges of an ideal or religious iconography. That is to say, a utilitarian iconography does not assure optimum utility. Conversely, an ideal iconography does not preclude an effective operational solution. The iconography of Meyer's League of Nations clearly derives from the early utilitarian socialist architecture that evolved in Russia immediately after the Revolution. The glazed elevator shafts of the secretariat block are evidence enough, not to mention the radio aerial and sky sign, which echo the imagery of the Pravda project designed by the Vesnin brothers in 1923.

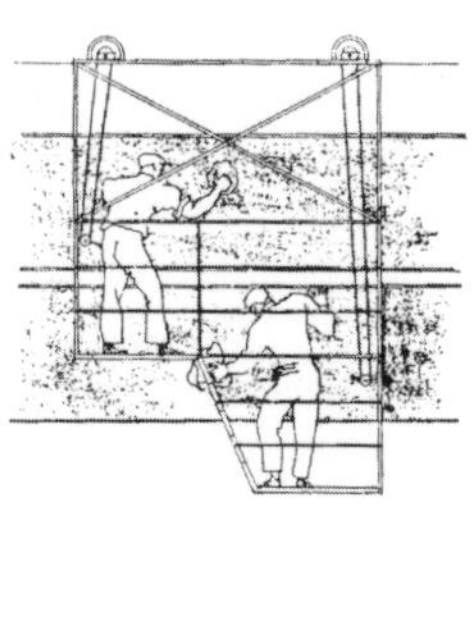

In 1928 Le Corbusier found 'constructivism' to be an optimistic but vague term. 'It is vague,' he wrote, 'because it contains too much. It neither limits an aesthetic, nor a category of human production.'[6] For his part, he was prepared to confine his elaborate spatial aesthetic within the limits of an architectural typology substantiated by the past. 'I have one master,' he wrote, 'it is the past.' Elsewhere, opposite an axonometric of Les Terrasses at Garches – which he regarded as a prototype for his League of Nations – he wrote, 'we are strengthened by the past because the past has proven to us that under conditions of clarity and

Le Corbusier and Pierre Jeanneret, League of Nations, cross-sections of secretariat block facade and elevation of the cleaning cradle.

lasting equilibrium, the house becomes typified and that when the type is pure, it possesses an architectural potential ... it is able to elevate itself to the dignity of a palace.' Conversely, he referred to his League of Nations as 'the administration house of the nations'. 'It is an organism,' he continued, 'a mechanism of precise ends. It is a machine for living in.' Under an elevation of his palace he shows a schematic elevation of Garches to the same scale, accompanied by the caption, 'The disposition of the windows is the same as at the Villa Garches.'

This transposition of the house into the palace and vice versa is one of those basic cultural insights that illuminate the whole of Le Corbusier's work. The elaborate metaphorical edifice that is the content of his work is incomprehensible if we do not understand that it is built on this fundamental hierarchy. The primal universal myth of sacred and profane space, since expounded upon at length by Mircea Eliade,[7] is the essential corollary of this concept. Enclosure itself is sufficient to render a space sacred, as Le Corbusier's sketch of a nomadic temple illustrates, but the approach route and the act of entry are critical. Hence the peristyle and the related architectural promenade of Le Corbusier's 'high palace' create a context in which the rite of passage from profane to sacred space may be enacted. This act of entry initiates a progression that culminates both literally and metaphorically in the ideal centre of the world – the chamber of the international assembly.

The prototype of Meyer's 'building' for the League of Nations – he scrupulously avoids referring to it as a 'palace' in his text – is, ironically enough, the Crystal Palace, the industrialized reification of a structural invention with no content other than itself. The prototype for Le Corbusier's *palais* is a Renaissance palace, and its form is an expression of a clear hierarchy of values. It is significant in this context that Meyer faces his building in Eternit, an essentially modern material, implying a non-hierarchical structure, while Le Corbusier faces his palace in polished granite, the traditional material of monumental architecture.

The house/temple/palace is seen by Le Corbusier as the ultimate archetype of the human world. On this ancient ideal, inherited via utopian socialism from a classical past, Le Corbusier superimposes a rich metaphorical culture, a mythology compounded from the ancient past and the major technological innovations of the nineteenth and twentieth centuries. To this end, in a sequence of sketches he pairs – after Victor Considerant – a classical palace with an ocean liner, and then draws parallels between the liner, his League of Nations secretariat, and the skyscraper.

This drive to fuse the dichotomy between idealism and utilitarianism was to bring Le Corbusier into conflict with the young utilitarian socialist designers of the twentieth century. The Cité Mondiale, or Mundaneum, which Le Corbusier designed for Geneva in 1929 as a centre of world thought, prompted a reaction from his young Czech admirer, the archi-

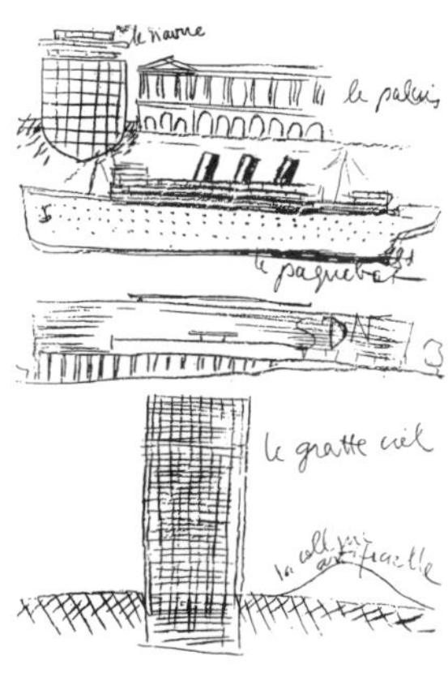

Le Corbusier, Les Techniques sont l'assiette même du lyrisme, *1930. In this sketch he draws a parallel between his League of Nations design and other 'palatial' forms including a neoclassical palace and an ocean-going liner.*

tect–writer Karel Tiege. The Cité was intended as a supplement to the League of Nations and was therefore located close to the site of the *palais*. It was not the content but the forms of the Cité to which Tiege objected, in particular the helicoidal ziggurat of the Musée Mondial. Tiege, who had championed Le Corbusier in 1927, savagely attacked him two years later for the formalism of the Cité Mondiale. Such was the vehemence of his attack that Le Corbusier decided to take up his own defence, and in an essay entitled 'Défense de l'architecture', written for the Czech paper *Stavba*, he replied to Tiege's challenge. In his attack Tiege had quoted from Hannes Meyer's essay 'Bauen', of 1928:

All things in the world are a product of the formula, function × economics, so none of these things are works of art; all art is composition and hence unsuited to a particular end. All life is function and therefore not artistic, the idea of the composition of a dock is enough to make a cat laugh. But how is a town plan designed or a plan of a house? Composition or Function? Art or Life?[8]

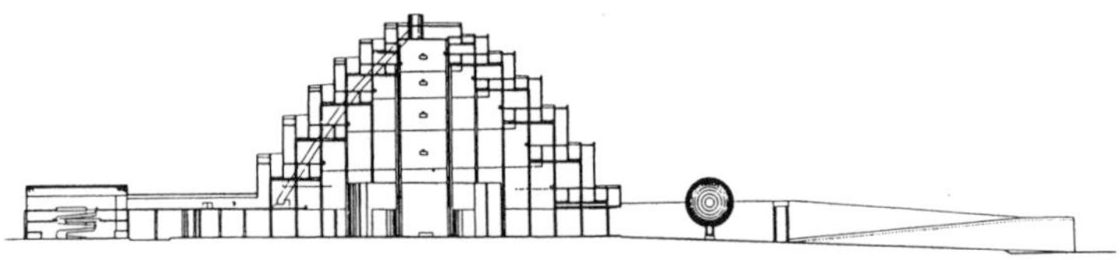

Le Corbusier and Pierre Jeanneret, Musée Mondial, Geneva, 1929, section.

Le Corbusier placed this quotation at the head of his essay and made it clear that his riposte was directed as much against Meyer as against Tiege.[9] He was to mount a similar defence in his book *Précisions*, written in the same year as Tiege's attack. He wrote, 'The plans of the Cité Mondiale have drawn violent attack from the extreme architectural left of the Germanic countries. I have been accused of academicism.' He then went on to protest that 'The buildings projected are strictly utilitarian, in particular this helicoidal Musée Mondial so violently incriminated.' Yet later he gives a denial verging on an admission. 'The plans of the Cité Mondiale bring to buildings, which are true machines, a certain magnificence wherein one wishes to discover, at any cost, some archaeological inspiration. But from my point of view this harmonious quality arises from another thing, from a simple response to a problem well stated.'[10] Yet he could not deny that his much-proclaimed use of regulating lines and ordering geometry imparted to his Cité Mondiale a monumental architectural quality usually reserved in the past for sacred cities or high towns. Peking and Angkor Wat are obvious models that, although he refused to acknowledge them on this occasion, are clearly present as images elsewhere in his published work.

The Mundaneum was the ultimate polarization of Le Corbusier's utopian idealism. It was to be varied formally, yet essentially repeated, in the many city centre projects that he designed throughout his life. It was the sacred enclosure *par excellence*. Thus it is hardly surprising to find that his subsequent proposals for the Ville Radieuse found little response in the Soviet Union. Clearly Marxist urbanism could not be served by such a hierarchical model.

The 1931 Palace of the Soviets competition terminated all ideological conflict through the official imposition of a synthetic architectural style, effectively declaring a moratorium on architectural thought. Under the circumstances, it is ironic that Le Corbusier's Palais des Soviets should have been such a tour de force of constructivist style. Yet its formal organization remained symmetrical, Baroque and, as preliminary sketches indicate, elementarist in composition. Its eventual rejection, in spite of the lucidity of its solution, was an act of propaganda.

To deny the existence of a conflict by totalitarian edict is one matter; to keep thought alive under such restrictions is another. Today the problem of idealism versus utilitarianism re-emerges not only in the capitalist West, but also in the socialist East, under conditions that are even less propitious for its resolution than they were 40 years ago. Then the millennium was a distant possibility; today, at least technically, it is within our grasp.

The utilitarianism of Hannes Meyer leads to the idealization of the appearance of utility. The idealism of Le Corbusier leads to the idealization of the appearance of man. His Palais des Soviets was rejected for its functionalism – yet it was he who provided the ideal space of public assembly, his open-air tribune or agora for 50,000 people. As Hannah Arendt says, 'What makes mass society so difficult to bear is not the number of people involved, at least not primarily, but the fact that the world between them has lost its power to gather them together, to relate and to separate them.'[11] Le Corbusier's Palais des Soviets was the representation of such a world, a realm designed both to unify and to differentiate men. Such realms by definition imply hierarchy; they demand a system of values and the creation and maintenance of a mythology.

First published in *Architectural Design*, vol.38, no.3, March 1968, pp.134–6.

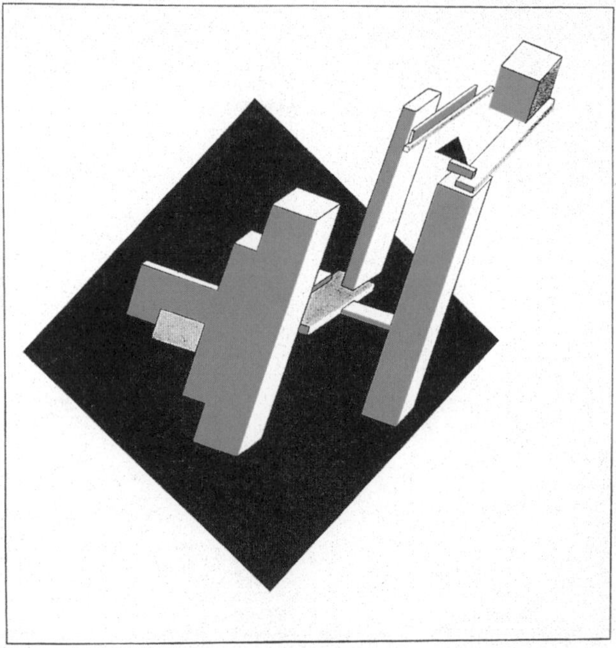

и По ЧЕРНОМУ

установилось

Кра
Я
сно

The Work and Influence of El Lissitzky

The seminal role that El Lissitzky played in the evolution of twentieth-century applied art and architecture has been obscured by time, politics and contemporary history. The Soviet social realist line effectively isolated his later life in the East, so that it is now difficult for us in the West to appreciate to what degree his work suffered official eclipse after 1933. As Chimen Abramsky has recently pointed out, no Lissitzky exhibition was held in Moscow between 1933 and 1962.[1]

For our recent awareness and knowledge of Lissitzky, and for that matter of Russian twentieth-century avant-garde art as a whole, the English-speaking world is clearly indebted to Camilla Gray, who in 1960 revealed a forgotten 'seam', as it were, with her article on Lissitzky that appeared in *Typographica 16*. Prior to this publication, Lissitzky had remained a mere reference point in the received accounts of twentieth-century art and architecture – his name recurring unexpectedly at apparently unrelated junctures, making one sense the presence of a relatively unknown artist of considerable calibre.

The various forces of political action and reaction that isolated Lissitzky and terminated the international socialist movement in European culture also closed the Bauhaus and caused it to migrate in a decimated form to the United States, where it emerged as a total if diverse concept, apparently without any antecedents other than the European Arts and Crafts movement. It is perhaps natural in the climate of the late Thirties that the Bauhaus masters should not feel themselves obliged to stress unduly their debt to Lissitzky. In all justice they did acknowledge him, and to have done more under the circumstances would probably have been untimely and impolitic. Today the record is in need of redress as the evidence begins to amass that Lissitzky was an artist of major stature and of great polemical and conceptual import to the overall development of European art and architecture. There is little doubt now, for instance, that he was the major initiator of the so-called new typography, an innovation that, until now, was commonly credited to the Bauhaus alone. Similarly, there is now no doubt at all that the brilliant international phase of Constructivism in European architecture and applied art would not have occurred had it not been for Lissitzky's unbounded initiative, energy and enthusiasm and his outstanding ability as a designer and thinker.

Lazar, or Eleazar, Lissitzky, later to denominate himself 'El', was born in the town of Polschinok near Smolensk in 1890. Following his education in Smolensk he made an attempt in 1909 to enter St Petersburg Academy of Arts but was excluded owing to the restricted number of places then available to those of Jewish birth. As a result, he left at once for Germany, where he entered in the same year the school of architecture and engineering at Darmstadt. He remained there as a student of engineering from 1909 to the outbreak of World War I. In Darmstadt Lissitzky would have come in contact with the milieu of the artist's colony, then of declining importance, that had been founded under the patronage of the Grand Duke of Hesse in 1899. By the time of Lissitzky's arrival in Darmstadt, Olbrich's expressionism had already reached its limits and the Werkbund movement, centred in Berlin, was in the ascendant. Of Lissitzky's development while a student at Darmstadt we have no knowledge. At all events, in addition to his professional training, he must have become proficient in German and familiar with the latest cultural developments in Europe. In 1915 he returned to Russia to conclude his diploma studies as an architect. After his return, he exhibited paintings with the 'World of Art' and other avant-garde groups in Moscow.[2] Two years later, Chagall, who was then commissar of the Vitebsk School of Art, invited him to join the faculty in Vitebsk to work on a series of Jewish book illustrations.

It was essentially as a book illustrator under Chagall's supervision that Lissitzky began his initial development as a typographer. Between 1917 and 1922, he devoted most of his time to illustrating Yiddish books for children. It was during this period that he produced his famous set of ten illustrations for the Jewish Passover story, the *Chad Gadya*, or 'Story of a Goat'. In style, these illustrations are much more crisp and sardonic than Chagall's own peculiar brand of ethnic mysticism. The Hebrew script suggested to Lissitzky, by now also under the influence of Suprematism, a new typographic structure in which the geometric characteristics of the letters could be utilized to create a structural order over the entire page. This concept found an ultimate statement in Hebrew characters in his title page to *Four Tales from the Ukraine*, published by Vostok in Berlin in 1922, his last work in Yiddish.

The master–pupil relationship between Chagall and Lissitzky at Vitebsk was soon interrupted by the arrival of Kasimir Malevich, again at

Chagall's invitation. Malevich gained control of the Vitebsk school from Chagall shortly after his arrival, and Lissitzky, in turn, became subjected to a totally different influence. By then Malevich had developed fully his Suprematist concept, and Lissitzky immediately grasped its potential for a broader application, in spite of Malevich's lifelong ambivalence and indifference toward applied art. Although Lissitzky continued to paint, his intellectual environment inspired him to the creation of a new Suprematist–Elementarist world, comparable to the early formulations of the De Stijl movement in Holland, a world in which all fine art would eventually be superseded by the art of the environment as a whole.

In 1919, when the *Chad Gadya* was published, Lissitzky produced his first political street poster, influenced both by 1914 Futurist typography and by Suprematism; it bore the slogan 'Beat the Whites with the Red Wedge'. In the same year he painted his first 'Proun', a name that he had coined for his innovative polemical artwork, which he provocatively subtitled 'the changing trains (or the interchange) between painting and architecture'.[3] Thus, by the early Twenties, Lissitzky had evolved his mature position both as a polemical graphic artist and as an architect. Around 1922 he designed a symbolically transitional work that presaged the effective end of his activity as an illustrator and typographer to the Jewish press. It was his title collage for Ilya Ehrenburg's *A Journey to America*. In this work, a fragmented star of David is combined with sections from a shipping timetable and various other material symbolic of ethnic origin and suggestive of the state of being in transit, including the fragment of a cabbalistic text, overprinted in ink with the silhouette of a hand (probably Lissitzky's), upon which is stencilled in white the Hebraic letters *peh* and *noon*, spelling the Hebrew gravestone inscription, 'here lies buried'. This is a typical Lissitzkian play on words; *peh* and *noon* are the first and last letters of the made-up word *Proun*. In 1920 Lissitzky designed, as a Proun, his famous project for a Lenin Tribune, which immediately suggested a wholly new and subtle attitude toward total environment, an attitude that he would make continuous attempts to amplify and clarify throughout his professional life.

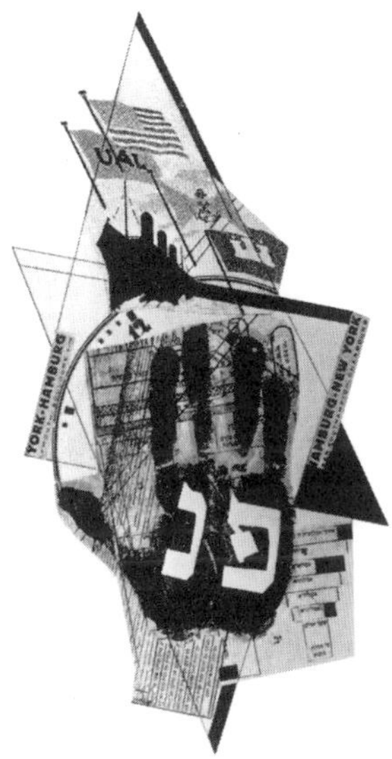

El Lissitzky, collage for Ilya Ehrenburg's book A Journey to America, *c.* 1922.

The years 1920 to 1923 were crucial for Lissitzky's future development and for the influence that he was to exert upon European art and architecture. By 1921, he had already reacted as an architect and a designer against the extreme utilitarianism proclaimed late in 1920 by the Productivist wing of the Constructivists, led by Rodchenko and Tatlin. However, although he maintained an allegiance to the Elementarism that he and his Suprematist colleagues had developed in Vitebsk, at the same time he recognized the validity of the utilitarian claim that engineering mechanisms and structures possessed an inherent morphology of their own. His Lenin Tribune project of 1920 epitomizes this dichotomy, for whereas the whole tribune is elevated on an inclined lattice girder with Lenin photomontaged into position at its crown, the rostrum itself and the girder base are Elementarist forms, miraculously secured in space. In this project Lissitzky combined in one work the innovations that were to preoccupy him throughout the rest of his life – the direct use of photomontage, the overall Proun concept with its dynamic imagery and inherent typographical implications, and finally the precarious compound of statically determinable real structures with 'elemental' *metaphysical* forms.

From 1920 onwards Lissitzky's career advanced on a number of levels at once, first as a graphic artist, second as a polemical Suprematist–Elementarist theoretician, and finally as an architect–designer. Above all else, it was the children's book *The Story of Two Squares* that marked the beginning of Lissitzky's pre-eminence as an international typographer and graphic designer. First published in Vitebsk in 1920, it was republished in 1922 by Skythen Verlag in Germany and by the Dutch magazine *De Stijl* in Holland. To this one work may be attributed the marked change that occurred in European typography during the early Twenties, in which the so-called new typography was invented.

The story is an allegorical account of the cryptic adventures of two squares (i.e. two Suprematist elements) in the cosmos; these adventures are apparently attendant upon the millennialistic creation of order out of chaos as the result of an apocalyptic revolution. As in the *Chad Gadya* illustrations, there are ten plates, a number seemingly favoured by Lissitzky for such works. Each plate, as in the *Chad Gadya*, illustrates a sequence in the story; the plate texts, as translated by Camilla Gray, read in sequence as follows:

1. About two squares, El Lissitzky
2. To all, to all Young Fellows
3. El Lissitzky: A Suprematist story – about Two Squares in 6 constructions: Berlin, Skythen 1922
4. Do not read: Take-Paper – Fold
Blocks – Colour
Pieces of wood – Construct
5. Here are – Two Squares
6. Flying towards the Earth – from far away – and
7. and – see – Black Chaos
8. Crash – all is scattered
9. and on the Black was established Red clearly
10. Thus it ends – further.

In 1923 Lissitzky further reinforced his position as a graphic designer of world stature and as a theoretician and innovator, first with his book design for Mayakovsky's collection of poems entitled *For Reading Aloud*, and second with his designs for Kruchenykh's Futurist opera play, *Victory over the Sun*. This play was first performed in St Petersburg's Luna Park in 1913, with decor and costumes to the designs of Kasimir Malevich.[4] Malevich later claimed that he was stimulated to create Suprematism out of his designs for this play, thus anticipating not only his own iconic invention but also Oskar Schlemmer's designs for the Bauhaus stage, made some ten years later. Schlemmer's first costume and set designs incorporated geometricized and mechanical distorted figures, and Lissitzky's designs for *Victory over the Sun* are virtually of the same date, 1923. Lissitzky's designs, published under the German title *Sieg über die Sonne* and subtitled *An Electro-Mechanical Spectacle*, were issued as a folio of ten coloured lithographs by the Kestner-Gesellschaft in Hanover in 1923. Lissitzky's subsequent close associations with Hanover appear to date from this time. Included in the folio was a short introductory note explaining the design intention, from which the following is a central extract:

We are constructing a scaffolding in a public square, open and accessible on all sides. It is the SPECTACLE MACHINERY. This scaffolding provides every possibility of movement for objects in play. The individual forms of the scaffolding must therefore be capable of movement in various positions, rotations, extensions and so forth. The different levels must quickly interpenetrate. All is of open ribbed construction, in order not to hide from view the play of objects running through it. Each of the objects themselves is formed according to requirements and intentions. They glide, roll, float in the air, above and inside the scaffolding. All parts of the scaffolding system and all the play objects are activated by means of electrical-mechanical forces and devices, controlled from a central station by one man. He is the SHAPER OF SPECTACLES. His place is the middle point in the scaffolding, in control of all the energies at the switchboard capsule. He directs the movements, the capsule and the lights. He switches on the radio speaker, and over the public square is heard the deafening clamour of a railway station, the thunder of Niagara Falls, the hammering of a boiler factory. When the play objects are in proper position, the SHAPER OF SPECTACLES speaks into a telephone connected to an arc-lamp, or into some other apparatus, which transforms his voice according to the character of his figures of speech. Electrical sentences glow and fade away. Beams of light follow objects, fractured by prisms and mirrors. In this way, the SHAPER OF SPECTACLES brings the elementary prelude to its highest intensity.

The music comes from Matiushin (four-tonal). Malevich painted the decoration (the prelude – a black square). The sun, expressing the old energy of the earth, is ripped out of the heavens by the modern man who creates his own sources of energy through the power of his technical mastery. The idea of the opera is woven together in a simultaneity of happenings. The language is illogical. Individual song sections are sound-poems.

The text of the opera had forced me to preserve in my figures something of human anatomy. The colours in various parts of my drawings, as in my Proun-works, are to be understood as material equivalents. This means: the red, yellow or black parts of the figures do not indicate the colours those parts are to be painted, but rather the appropriate material *they are to be made from, as for example shining copper, dull iron and so forth.*5

In this technocratic prophetic fantasia of Lissitzky's largely unrealizable designs for *Victory over the Sun*, we find that particular combination of empirical elements such as loudspeakers with pure Elementarist forms which we have already encountered in his designs for the Lenin Tribune.

Lissitzky's 1923 thumb-indexed book design for Mayakovsky's collection of 'public' poems, entitled *For Reading Aloud*, established a standard for all his subsequent graphic work throughout the Twenties. For the classically trained German typographer Jan Tschichold this work was the breakthrough that would determine the new European graphic style, a style that was quick to take root in the work of men like Tschichold in Germany and Piet Zwart in Holland. A 1923 business postcard designed by Zwart, for instance, closely resembles in its innovative mixture of typeset and typewritten text a Lissitzky letterhead of approximately the same date. Such a close resemblance suggests the direct influence of the letterhead upon the design for the card, although we have no way to substantiate this; nevertheless a clear date may be deduced for the beginning of a Suprematist influence upon the graphic work of Zwart, who prior to 1923–4 used only Neoplastic systems of ordering in his graphic layouts. Zwart's witty monogram, consisting of a capital 'P' for Piet (but also for 'Proun'), plus a black square for Zwart (meaning 'black' in Dutch), appears to pay a direct double homage to both Lissitzky and Suprematism.

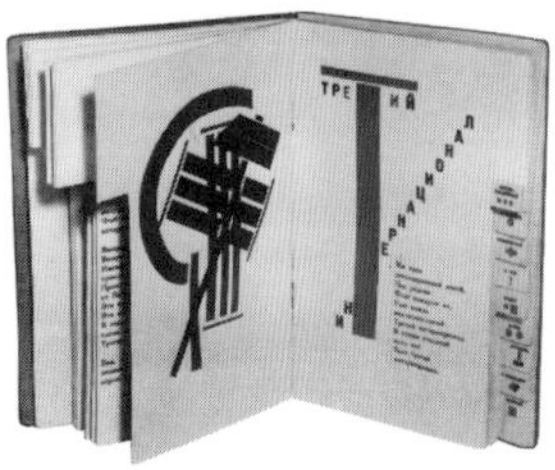

El Lissitzky, book design for Vladimir Mayakovsky's For Reading Aloud *(Dlia Golosa), 1923.*

The direct influence of Lissitzky upon the Bauhaus typographers of the Twenties, men such as Herbert Bayer, Joost Schmidt and László Moholy-Nagy, cannot be so easily determined from the published work. Clearly Neoplasticism continued to maintain a hold on Bauhaus design until after the mid-Twenties. Nonetheless, the first *Bauhausbuch* design, by Farkas Molnar in 1925, is inspired by Suprematism and by Lissitzky in particular. Significant is the predominant use of red, black, grey and white, Lissitzky's preferred colours, in Bauhaus graphics from this date onwards.[6] Suprematist graphics are undoubtedly present in the Bauhaus after 1923 in the work of Schmidt, Moholy-Nagy and even Bayer, finally yielding in the late Twenties to the almost exclusive use of photographic imagery, as in Moholy-Nagy's design for *Bauhausbuch 14*. This move into photography was paralleled by Lissitzky's own development in the late Twenties.

László Moholy-Nagy, Bauhausbuch 14, *1931.*

Typical of Lissitzky's graphic work of 1922–5 are his page layouts for the magazines *Veshch* and *NASCI* or his 1925 design for the book *Die Kunstismen*, in which he introduced the use of strong black vertical printer's rules. At the very end of the Twenties, Lissitzky's style moved away from Elementarism toward a more photographic and kinetic approach. His last essay as a graphic artist in the primitive style of Elementarism is a number of plates, done in 1928, for a children's book on arithmetic. After this work he was to develop his concept of a cinematic book, incorporating both imagery and collage techniques apparently derived directly from Russian avant-garde film. The rudiments of a cinematic book are present in his *All Union Graphic Exhibition* guide of 1927, while a fully cinematographic work, in every sense, is achieved in his design for the report *USSR in Construction* of 1934. One is not surprised to find that the composition of his 1931 cover for the magazine *Brigada Khudozhnikov* resembles a still from a heroic political film of the period.

In 1927 he developed a style involving the combination of typesetting with photographic images, as in his cover for the Vkhutemas publication of that year. In 1928 he began work on several covers for the books published in Vienna under the series title 'Neues Bauen in der Welt'; among these were the covers for Girsberger's *Frankreich* and Neutra's *Amerika* as well as his own *Russland*. In 1929 Lissitzky took his leave of international publicity, using a similar combination of photomontage and type in his poster for the Russian exhibition held in Zurich in 1929. These were Lissitzky's ultimate innovations in typo–photographic montage. From this point on his style acquires an almost classical calm. His 1930 catalogue for a Japanese film exhibition and his layout for *USSR in Construction* of 1933, dedicated to the Red Army, still appear today to be timeless, graphic work of the highest calibre. He was not to surpass this level.

El Lissitzky, poster for Russian exhibition of applied arts, Zurich, 1929.

Lissitzky's own declared typographic principles, somewhat anticipatory of Marshall McLuhan, read almost like a chronological itemized account of his own development as a graphic artist. They are as follows:

1. Printed words are to be seen and not heard.
2. Concepts are communicated by conventional words and shaped in the letters of the alphabet.
3. Concepts should be expressed with the greatest economy – optically but not phonetically.
4. The layout of the text on the page, governed by the laws of typographical mechanics, must reflect the rhythm of the content.
5. Plates must be used in the organization of the page according to the new visual theory.
6. The continuous page – the cinematographical book.
7. The new book demands new writers. The inkwell and quill are outmoded.
8. The printed page is not conditioned by space and time. The printed page and the endless number of books must be done away with. The electro-library.[7]

Lissitzky began a simultaneous second career as a cultural polemicist and thinker in 1922 when together with Ilya Ehrenburg he was sent to Berlin by the Soviet government to design and organize the Russian exhibition of 1922. Upon the lifting of the *cordon sanitaire* by the Western powers in the same year, both men were enabled to become culturally active, as it were, and this activity soon produced results. Late in 1921 and again in 1922 Lissitzky met Theo van Doesburg, to whom he was introduced by Gropius. Later in that year he also met Moholy-Nagy. With the help of these contacts and others Lissitzky was soon able to act at an international level. Thus in 1922, in conjunction with Van Doesburg, he organized two international Constructivist congresses. The first was held in Weimar in the summer of 1922. None of the then Bauhaus faculty attended and the event proved somewhat abortive, turning into a Dadaesque burlesque, Van Doesburg in his I K Bonset persona having invited a number of his Dadaist colleagues. A second congress was held, however, in Düsseldorf in the same year. The Bauhaus this time was represented, and the occasion proved more fruitful, leading to the proclamation of the 'Constructivist Internationale' (i.e. an international manifesto of Constructivism). Lissitzky was in essence the spearhead of this Internationale. Thus in 1922, in conjunction with Ehrenburg, he edited and designed the trilingual magazine *Veshch/ Gegenstand/Objet*, while in 1923, in collaboration with Werner Graaf and Hans Richter, he started the short-lived Berlin magazine *G* (*Gestaltung*). Both the magazines, *G* and *Veshch*, imply by the literal objectivity of their titles a concern for the object *per se*, as opposed to the 'non-objectivity' of Malevich. It was essentially this concern for the product of applied art, that is, for the object, that divided Lissitzky from Malevich. Lissitzky's 1922 designs for *Veshch* were at once to spread his typographic and cultural ideas all over Europe. These ideas clearly influenced the Bauhaus after 1923, through the agency of Moholy-Nagy. Similarly, Van Doesburg's sacrilegious introduction of the diagonal into his painting in 1924, in violation of the Neoplastic canons of Mondrian, occurred soon after Van Doesburg had met with Lissitzky. Lissitzky's ideas may therefore have been indirectly responsible for the crucial rift that occurred between Mondrian and Van Doesburg and that effectively accelerated the disintegration of the De Stijl movement in Holland.

El Lissitzky, cover design for Veshch/Gegenstand/Objet 1, *1922.*

The year 1922 was also that in which Lissitzky first met the Dutch architect Mart Stam, a figure with whom he was to collaborate closely, both as an architect and as an architectural polemicist. Stam accompanied Lissitzky, when the latter fell ill late in 1923, to a tuberculosis sanatorium in Switzerland, where for the next two years they continued intermittently to collaborate on architectural projects and Constructivist–Elementarist propaganda, eventually being jointly responsible for the founding in Basel in 1925 of the Swiss Constructivist group ABC in conjunction with the Swiss architects Hans Schmidt, Hannes Meyer and Hans Wittwer. They thereby completed the German–Swiss–Dutch 'triangle' of international Constructivism, which ranged from the tendency to extreme utilitarianism on the part of the Swiss, German and Dutch factions to the Elementarist preoccupations of Lissitzky.

Lissitzky's final years in Switzerland produced the architectural sketch projects of which his Elementarist yacht club of 1925 is typical. After this period of collaboration with Stam, Lissitzky returned briefly to Russia, where he taught at the Moscow Vkhutemas. In 1925 he returned to Germany at Alexander Dorner's invitation to design a special room for the Landes Museum in Hanover. Yet in spite of his return to Central Europe, the active international phase of his career as a polemicist had begun to draw to a close. In 1926, in collaboration with Nikolai Ladovsky, he managed to help reconstitute the Russian architectural organization ASNOVA as an international architectural group.[8] However, as the chances of an international socialist revolution faded in the late Twenties, indications of political reaction began to appear and Lissitzky decided to return to Russia. In 1928 he entered into the ultimate phase of his public career, in Moscow, as the official exhibition designer to the Soviet government.

The majority of Lissitzky's polemical works were written between 1923 and 1929, the central text of Lissitzky's theoretical thought being the long essay entitled 'K und Pangeometrie', written for the *Europa Almanach of the Arts* and published in Potsdam in 1925. The thesis of this essay leads ultimately to the notion of imaginary space, which Lissitzky explains as follows:

We are now at the beginning of a period in which A. is, on the one hand, degenerating into making pasticci of museum monuments, while, on the other hand, struggling for the creation of a new conception of space. I have demonstrated above that space and objects form a mutually functional relationship. This creates the problem of creating imaginary *space by means of material objects ... the motion of a material line gives the impression of a surface or a volume. That is only one indication of how elementary solids can be used to construct an object while in a state of rest; yet when brought into motion it becomes an entirely new object, i.e., a new space impression that will exist only during the duration of the motion, and is therefore imaginary.*

Elsewhere in the same essay, with regard to monumentality, he writes:

The Eiffel Tower is not monumental, for it was not built for eternity ... no solid masses, but a pierced space needle. We are now producing work which in its overall effect is essentially intangible. For we do not consider a work monumental in the sense that it may last for a year, a century, or a millennium, but rather on the basis of continual expansion of human performance. In the preceding I have traced the variability of our space conceptions and the subsequent F.'s of A., thus arriving at nonmaterial materialism. *This sounds like a paradox. However experience proves that* progress consists of our being compelled to accept and, indeed, to regard as self-evident and essential, views that our forefathers considered incomprehensible and were in fact incapable of comprehending.[9]

It was this conception of an *amaterial materiality* that was to inform the simultaneous third aspect of Lissitzky's career, that is, his work as an architect and designer. This particular immaterial conception is to be distinguished from Futurism in the emphasis that it places upon transformation and movement as revelatory of an ineffable imaginary space, as opposed to the Futurist interest in mechanical movement *per se*.

It was in the Grosse Berliner Kunstausstellung (Berlin Art Exhibition) of 1923 that Lissitzky first formulated his conception of a new environmental space. His own account of the development of this space, which he dubbed a 'Prounen-Raum' and published in the first issue of *G*, makes the overall circumstances of his initial commission very clear. 'Various "rooms"

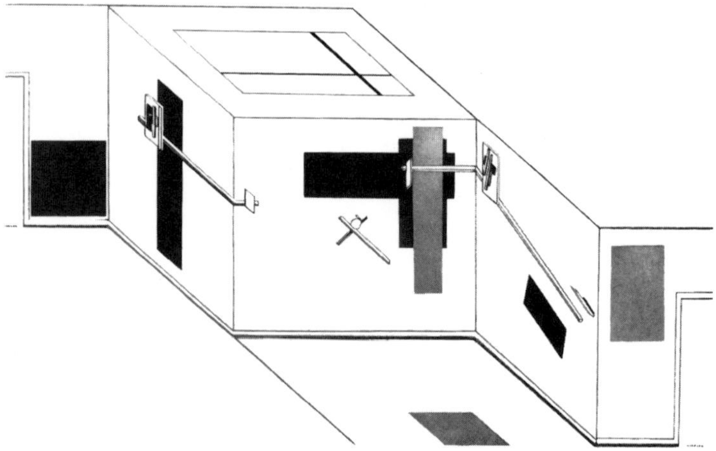

El Lissitzky, design for 'Prounen-Raum', Berlin Art Exhibition, 1923, exploded isometric.

have been built like boxes into the jumble of the exhibition hall at the Lehrter Banhof,' he writes. 'One of these boxes has been kindly put at my disposal. The six surfaces (floor, four walls, ceiling) are the given factors, they are to be designed.' Lissitzky then proceeds to describe in general terms the essential characteristics of his conception of the new Prounen-Raum. He insists that its walls be left 'unstructured' by painting and declares wall painting and hung pictures to be false. Later he was to make an incidental stand against the De Stijl artists, who, he stated in the section on perspective space in 'K und Pangeometrie', 'transposed the Mondrian principle onto three planes in space – thereby becoming decorators'. The new space, he argued in the first issue of *G*, '... is not ... to be conceived in terms of being painted or in terms of pictures'.[10] He then proceeded to describe the new space in a manner anticipatory both of Op and Kinetic art and of 1960s concepts of 'mobile architecture'. He wrote:

When the desire is to obtain the illusion of life within an enclosed space, then this is how I do it: I hang a sheet of glass on the wall; it has no painting behind it, but a periscopic device which shows me what is actually happening at any given moment, in the true colour and with the real movement.

The equilibrium which I seek to attain in the room must be elementary and capable of change, so that it cannot be disturbed by a telephone or a piece of standard office furniture. The room is there for the human being – not the human being for the room. The factors mentioned above, which man requires for rest, work and social life, must be unified; and this unity, through an elementary system of arrangement, must always be capable of change as occasion demands. We no longer want the room to be like a painted coffin for our living body.[11]

It is clear, then, that in this Prounen-Raum Lissitzky attempted optically to destroy, through the agency of suspended relief elements, the constraining walls of the given space and to create out of it a new Suprematist–Elementarist entity. In a sense, under his hand the given space was dematerialized. As Lissitzky was to write of the irrational space of Suprematism in 'K und Pangeometrie', 'We see that Suprematism has swept away the illusions of three-dimensional Perspectival Space and has created the latest illusion of Irrational Space, with infinite extensibility, into the background and into the foreground.'[12]

Two years later Lissitzky received another opportunity to develop further this particular notion of an internal space that was at once mobile, infinitely planar, and in a continual state of transformation. This occurred late in 1925, with Alexander Dorner's invitation to design a room for abstract art in the Landes Museum of Hanover. Lissitzky lined the walls of this room with projecting vertical slats, seven centimetres deep, set at intervals of seven centimetres. These slats were painted black on one side and white on the other and set against a grey background wall. Lissitzky thus at once achieved an optically transformable surface – a device that has since been used extensively by Op artists such as Jacov Agam and others. Depending upon one's position, the walls of Lissitzky's room would have appeared to be grey, black or white, or a compound of any two. Of these transmutable walls, Lissitzky wrote, 'I did not see the four walls as supporting or protecting screens but rather as an optical background for the painting. Therefore I resolved to treat the wall surfaces as such ... with every movement of the spectator in the room the impression of the wall changes – what was white becomes black and vice versa.'[13] In order to accommodate on the available wall space a maximum number of works without incurring the mutual optical interference of one work upon the next, Lissitzky hung certain groups of works in specially designed recesses that were partially covered by vertical sliding screens of perforated metal, the presence of the screened work always being visible through the perforations. Of this device, Lissitzky wrote, 'The play of the walls is complemented by what is visible through the shimmering frames. The open-pattern masking surfaces are pushed up or down by the spectator, who discovers new pictures, or screens what does not interest him. He is physically compelled to come to terms with the exhibited objects.'[14]

During the late Twenties, Lissitzky's growing interest in montage and in a cinematographic approach, coupled with his general aim to involve the viewer psychophysically in both the configuration and manipulation of any exhibition space, led him to his 1928 design for Soviet exhibits at the Cologne Press Exhibition. This was, appropriately enough, a tour de force in the architectural use of montage, employing both type and photographic media. Every available wall surface was covered in graphic material of various kinds, ranging from slogans to statistics to expanses of newsprint to huge blown-up photographs, either real or symbolic, of personalities and events of current import to the young socialist state. Lissitzky's use of media extended from the expressionistic application of montage to destroy and recreate the given wall space around the visitor to the literal use of political symbols such as the hammer and sickle; dynamic elements here appeared in the form of moving factory belts on which were mounted the initial letters USSR cut out of newsprint and other things. Although Lissitzky designed numerous other large scale Soviet exhibitions throughout the Thirties, he was never again to achieve such a heroic and direct use of graphic media. Even his simpler and more architectural Dresden Health Exhibition mounted two years later is lacking in conviction by comparison.

In 1923–4 Lissitzky began to collaborate with Mart Stam on the design of a prototypical office building for the centre of Moscow, the well-known Wolkenbügel, or 'cloud prop' project. It was conceived by Stam and Lissitzky as a series of aerial office structures to be erected over a number of major traffic intersections in the centre of Moscow. Located at intervals along a concentric Moscow boulevard, the Wolkenbügel were in effect dematerialized propylaea, elevated above the main thoroughfares leading into the city centre. As such they are directly comparable to Ledoux's Parisian *barrières* while remaining the very antithesis of monumentality. Each Wolkenbügel consisted of a horizontally layered office complex from three to four storeys in depth and crook-shaped in plan, cantilevered high above the street from three square pylon-support clusters or towers, each cluster accommodating within its structure all necessary elevators and services. The walls of the central access corridors within the offices themselves acted as open-web girders spanning the space between the pylons and beyond, the whole comprising an Elementarist composition to be read from many different aspects. The urbanistic scheme was to locate one such complex over each intersection between the boulevard and the streets radiating from the Kremlin centre point, thereby providing additional central city office space without impeding circulation or disrupting the existing city structure. Lissitzky was well aware of the radical nature of this proposal when he wrote of it in 1929, 'Compared to the prevalent American high-rise system the innovation consists in the fact that the horizontal (the useful) is clearly separated from the vertical (the support, the necessary)'.[15] In this, his most fully developed architectural project, Lissitzky anticipated not only Louis Kahn's thesis of separating servant from served spaces but also propositions by architects such as Yona Friedman and Kenzo Tange to construct additional accommodation, for both the maintenance of

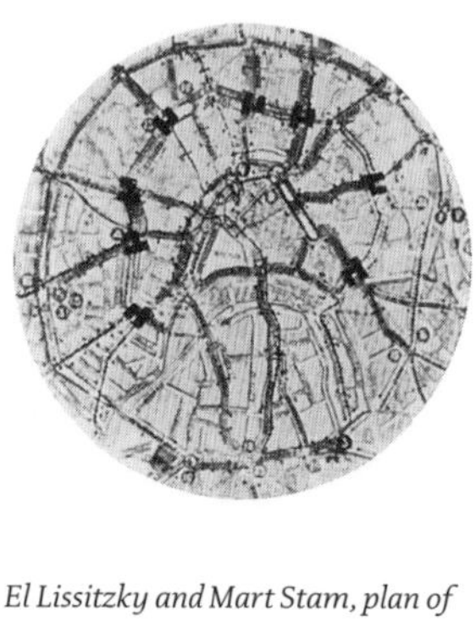

El Lissitzky and Mart Stam, plan of 'anti-skyscraper' gateways over road crossings leading into the centre of Moscow, 1923–4.

density and the alleviation of congestion in urban centres, by means of either space frames or wide-span bridge structures erected on pylons over the pre-existing street system.

In designing the Wolkenbügel, Lissitzky attempted a new building entity that would be capable of automatically transforming the spatial–structural system of the existing great cities of Western capital. In his book *Russland* of 1929, which was in effect a survey of Soviet architecture prior to that date, Lissitzky wrote as follows of reconstituting the old town through a new building entity:

Just as in the past, houses follow a continuous street line, as if the individual lots of private owners still existed. There is no suggestion whatever of the new situation in land ownership. The new houses put up so far give us no indication of the new concept of the open street, or of the city as the expression of a new relationship of new associations as a result of which mass and space may be organized in a different way – even in the old parts of the city. The new social attitude towards all problems suggests a number of new proposals. The introduction of new building types into the old fabric of the city affects the whole by transforming it.[16]

El Lissitzky and Mart Stam, Wolkenbügel anti-skyscraper project design for Moscow, c.1923–4.

At a time when Russian disurbanists were proposing to demolish entirely the legacy of existing capitalistic cities, Lissitzky postulated the gradual transformation of the spatial structures of these cities through the interjection of new building entities. Whereas for Le Corbusier such entities were essentially to be housing accommodations, for Lissitzky they were typically the civic buildings of the new Bolshevik state.

One such typical structure for the new Bolshevik state was Leonidov's project for a Lenin Institute to be erected on a hill outside Moscow. This was the apotheosis of the 'amaterial materiality' to which the Suprematist-oriented Constructivists aspired. Lissitzky's own words convey the intention behind such aspirations. Again in *Russland* he writes:

'One of our utopian ideas is the desire to overcome the limitations of the substructure, the earthbound. We have developed this idea in a series of proposals . . . The design of the Lenin Institute on the Lenin Hills in Moscow is based on this idea. The building complex consists of a tower structure (library of 15 million volumes), low-story buildings with reading rooms and workrooms, and a spherical building (elevated in the air) containing a central reading room for 4,000 users. The latter can be divided up into several sections, and the sphere itself can be used as a planetarium. The institute is connected to the city across the river by means of an aerotrain.

It is the task of technology to make sure that all these elementary volumes that produce new relationships and tensions in space will be structurally safe. The idea of the conquest of the substructure, the earthbound, can be extended even further and calls for the conquest of gravity as such. It demands floating structures, a physical-dynamic architecture.'[17]

In Lissitzky's close collaboration with Mart Stam over the years 1922 to 1926, Stam always tended to take the more rigorous utilitarian attitude. In 1926, for instance, Stam designed the first bent-steel tube chair, a design that has since incorrectly been credited to Marcel Breuer. These early utilitarian furniture designs of Stam appeared in his Weissenhofsiedlung housing of 1927. Throughout this period, Stam also worked in close association with Brinkman and Van der Vlugt on the design of the Van Nelle factory in Rotterdam. This structure approximated fairly closely Lissitzky's ideal of an amaterial materialization incorporating imaginary space; this time, though, it was realized in built form. The imaginary space was here provided by the continuous movement of a conveyor system through the packing floors of the factory. This system crossed the access road to the warehouse by way of glazed bridges. In the architectural play of its curtain wall and its use of aerial bridges, the Van Nelle factory appears to approximate a built section of Lissitzky's own 1925 design for the Pravda printing works. Even in plan form the Van Nelle factory may be said to make Elementarist references, the administration block reflecting, in its curved form, the sweeping movement of cars entering the complex. The immateriality of the factory as realized also clearly derives something from Stam's own 1924 Damrak project for downtown Amsterdam. However, here again the aerial railway is evocative of Lissitzky's concept of imaginary space. Paradoxically enough, Lissitzky was never able to subscribe to the central utilitarian thesis of the international Constructivist group ABC, which called in 1925 for the 'dictatorship of the machine'. In 1924, in an essay that he wrote for the magazine *Merz*, number 8/9, Lissitzky had already made his opposition to such utilitarianism clear. 'The machine,' he wrote, 'is nothing more than a brush and in fact a very primitive brush with which the world canvas is to be designed.'[18] He wrote later, in his essay 'Ideologische Überbau' of 1929, 'To solve the utilitarian need, that is, to construct a volume that will function correctly for the purpose, is only one part of the problem.'[19]

Lissitzky had conceived the Proun metaphorically as a millennialist and synthetic work, simultaneously superseding both fine art and engineering technology. As such it presaged an entirely new, almost science-fiction realm, based on invisible, silent techniques supporting a mobile, planar, controlled environment, miraculously suspended in space. In spatial conception the Proun work thus tended to be homogeneous. Like the Suprematism upon which it was based, its sequential structure could never be ultimately determined. As any function could theoretically be easily accommodated in its shifting volumes, the ever-changing demands of utility were no longer to be considered as formative. Thus for Lissitzky permanent load-bearing walls tied to the earth, whether of the house or the street, were an oppressive anathema, outmoded constraints upon physical and psychic liberty, and thus inherently inappropriate to socialist man. Hence the axial, pyramidal, and gridded layouts of classical urbanism were all to be eschewed, first for being technically inappropriate to current tasks, and second for being symbolic of oppression, imperialism and exploitation. Lissitzky was a utopian visionary inspired by the subtle conceptions of Malevich, who held that form derived from function could be extremely variable. Lissitzky's Elementarism – that is, his environmental Suprematism – demanded the conceptual paradoxes of a 'non-objective object' and an 'amaterial materiality', paradoxes that could only be ultimately conceived as part of a suspended, mobile, 'wall-less' environment. His concept of an urban structure, such as it was, appears to have anticipated such proposals of the 1960s as the programme of mobile architecture by the Groupe d'Etudes d'Architecture Mobile.[20]

Between 1928 and 1932, the whole complex of international Constructivism suffered an eclipse, particularly in Russia. For its protagonists, as the hope of world revolution receded, and as the Soviet government continued to be burdened with unresolved economic and organizational difficulties, a withdrawal came to be expedient. It was necessary to turn back, for survival, to the technocrats of the old system – in a word, politically it was deemed necessary to 'react'. There is no doubt that Lissitzky was a victim of this combination of nationalistic reaction and internal compromise. In April 1932 the party issued its cultural directive and four years of inter-factional struggles, at least in Russia, were over. The voice of Lissitzky was in effect silenced. He was to live and work in comparative seclusion until his death in Moscow in 1941. The party's directive favoured neither the idealists nor the utilitarians with victory, for it was the Neoclassical academicians, the technocrats of the late nineteenth century, who were effectively reinstated.

For Lissitzky the modern world was seamless. He was an international socialist–technocrat. As such, he was as incapable of recognizing the separate traditional provinces of the various arts as he was of acknowledging that national boundaries and difference were consequential. As he wrote of the Vesnins' Pravda building of 1924, 'All of the accessories of a metropolitan street are integrated into this building – the advertising, the clock, the loudspeakers, even the lifts inside. They are treated as equal elements in the design and assembled into an entity. This is the aesthetic of constructivism.' Both through his appreciation of such an aesthetic and through his own work Lissitzky was committed to the culture of a total, integrated environment. The history of the first machine age has yet to recognize the importance of his commitment. It is for us, of the so-called second machine age, to appraise its worth.

First published in *Urban Structure: Architects' Yearbook*, no.12, 1968, pp.253–68.

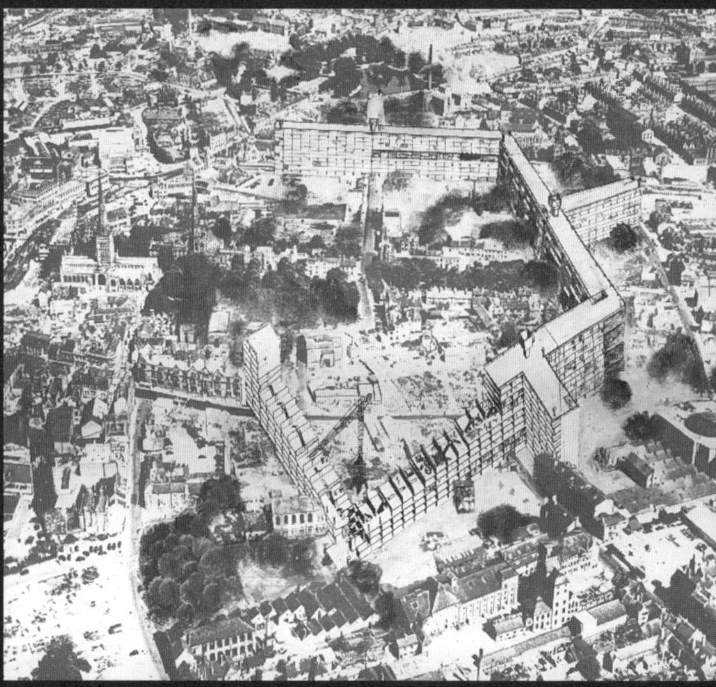

Team 10, Plus 20: The Vicissitudes of Ideology

By now it is rather well known that Team 10 came into being as a reaction to the latter-day ideology of a dispersed and disintegrated CIAM, and that it constituted itself after the 10th CIAM Congress of 1956 as a vehicle by which the younger generation could begin to express and even resolve their deep dissatisfaction with the received paradigms of modern architecture. The complexity of the Team 10 position and its subsequent development defies any simple-minded characterization, and the most one can do by way of an initial approach is to set down a series of critical notes that may hopefully serve as a skeleton for a more comprehensive assessment.

From the very first, Team 10, despite its avant-garde status, was never a polemical movement in the conventional sense. Its ideological foundation in 1954, in the low-key articles of the Doorn Manifesto,[1] gave immediate notice that it had no intention of even matching, as an opposition, the militant stance of the La Sarraz CIAM Declaration of 1928. It was the postwar generation of architects in England, Holland and France – that is, those who had actively experienced World War II – who were to make the initial running in the Team 10 reaction both before and after the Dubrovnik Congress of 1956; namely Alison and Peter Smithson, John Voelcker, Jacob Bakema, Aldo van Eyck, George Candilis and Shadrach Woods. Within this self-constituted avant-garde, the seminal importance of the Smithsons has at once to be recognized since clearly they were among the prime movers of Team 10, and to the extent that the grouping still exists they remain among its more active members. Next in order of influence one would have to place the Dutch: Jacob Bakema, Aldo van Eyck and Herman Haan. These architects had begun to take issue with the materialism of modern architecture well before the liberation of Europe, most notably in

Bakema's 1942 discourse with Kloos, in which he argued that the '"Neue Sachlichkeit" cannot be the stimulating idea for the postwar situation because of its concentration on "things which can be analysed"'.[2] Last but not least one would have to mention Shadrach Woods, whose contribution was central to the basic critique of Team 10 and whose proffered alternatives now seem to be of more universal relevance than the open city 'models' created by the English and the Dutch. George Candilis and the late John Voelcker also clearly played major roles in the earliest meetings of Team 10, but the independent nature of their respective contributions is more difficult to determine.[3]

From Bethnal Green to Golden Lane

Whatever the roles of these various individuals, none of this would have taken place had it not been for the fullness and audacity of the initial English critique at the 9th CIAM Congress held at Aix-en-Provence in 1954. One may also argue that it was the London cultural climate of the period – subject as it was to the influence of Parisian Existentialism – that went a long way towards shaping the ethos of the British Brutalist movement of the early Fifties and of that aspect of the Team 10 polemic that necessarily grew out of it. At this point mention needs to be made of the photographer Nigel Henderson, whose photographs were exhibited by the Smithsons at Aix-en-Provence and whose perception of the social and physical reality of London's East End played a crucial role in shaping the sensibility of the Smithsons. That this sensibility was to be at odds with the tabula rasa rationalizations of Le Corbusier's CIAM Grid, which was still a preoccupation of ASCORAL (Assemblée de constructeurs pour une Rénovation architecturale), the French wing of CIAM, as late as 1952, must in no small part be attributed to Henderson's photographic rendering of spontaneous community life in Bethnal Green. The Smithsons regularly visited the Bethnal Green home of Judith and Nigel Henderson from 1950 onwards. It was from their first-hand experience of the vital street life in this area – now long since obliterated by the admass superblocks of the Welfare State – that the Smithsons drew their first notions of identity and association; while the Bye-Law street itself, however much it may have been distorted by their own 'rationalizations', became the concrete model for their famous Golden Lane project of 1952.[4]

The Smithson proposal for Golden Lane epitomizes in a very succinct and concrete way both the success and failure of the early Team 10 position. Apart from the polemic that accompanied its presentation and which has since entered into the annals of Team 10 history, Golden Lane spoke for itself. In retrospect one can see relatively clearly where it was effectively critical of the received paradigms of modern architecture, just as one can also see with equal clarity where it was nonetheless conditioned by these very same models.

For all its tactical resemblance to Le Corbusier's Ilot Insalubre of 1937,[5] Golden Lane was clearly intended as a critique of Le Corbusier's Ville Radieuse;[6] particularly of its zoning of the generic city into the four functions of *housing*, *work*, *recreation* and *traffic* which were the categories of the CIAM Grid as formulated in the Athens Charter of 1933 (CIAM 4).[7] In 1952 the Smithsons opposed these functions with the more phenomenological categories of *house*, *street*, *district* and *city*, although what they meant by these categories grew deliberately and necessarily vaguer as the scale increased. The 'house' in their Golden Lane project was clearly the family living unit; the 'street' was evidently a system of one-sided gallery access of generous width elevated into the air. The 'district' and the 'city' were consciously and rightly regarded as variable domains that lay outside the bounds of precise definition. So far so good, even although as far as the original model was concerned (i.e. Bethnal Green), both the Bye-Law house and street were already radically transformed by the Smithson proposal. Opposed to the deterministic rationalism of the European Modern Movement, the Smithsons were at once caught in their Golden Lane project by the subliminal presence of a very similar rationalism and, what is worse,

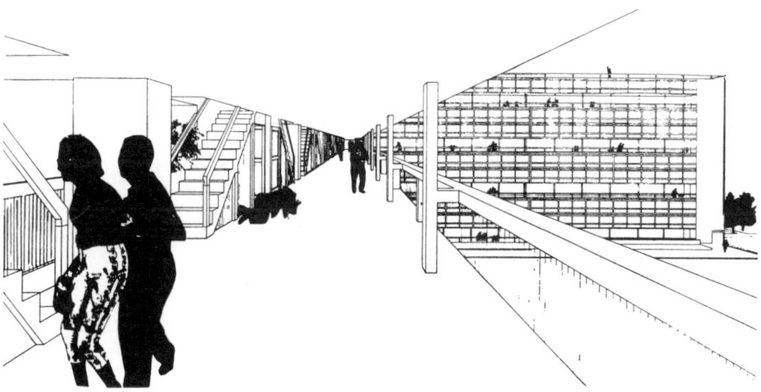

Alison and Peter Smithson, Golden Lane Housing, perspectival rendering of the 'street-in-the-air'.

by an identical rationalizing process; that is, the self-same process as that which had long since been used to vindicate the deterministic projections of CIAM, which were then the ostensible target of their attack. For all that 'yards' were indicated in the Golden Lane plan as adjunct areas to the 'streets',[8] it was nonetheless clear that the 'house in the air' did not have a yard that was in any way comparable to the traditional private yard of the Bye-Law streets and that the street itself, now one-sided and elevated in the air, could clearly no longer perform as a spontaneous agora. Its implacable single-loaded nature only served to stress its linearity as a route rather than its quality of enclosure as a place. The source of 'life' on either side of the Bye-Law street was directly responsible for its public realm, as an early sketch by the Smithsons would indicate. However, the nature of the Golden Lane brief – namely high density on a small site, together with the demands of rationalization – constituted a double predicament that could hardly be overcome.

Yet from the proposed applications of this housing pattern as a prototypical solution one can only conclude that the Smithsons were largely unaware of this dilemma, since they proceeded to show their Golden Lane model, repeated over vast tracts of the metropolitan area, as though it were to be read not only as a critique but also as an alternative to the *à redent* blocks of Le Corbusier's 'radiant city'. And while its random, 'twig-like' distribution could no doubt be taken at the time as a polemic against wholesale demolition and as an argument in favour of piecemeal redevelopment, the now-famous rendering of an extended Golden Lane within the context of bombed-out Coventry exemplifies one of the basic contradictions of the Team 10 critique. As imposed on the ruins of Coventry, Golden Lane appeared to be as much against the continuity of the existing city as were any of the Haussmann-like projections of the Ville Radieuse (such as Le Corbusier's Plan Voisin for Paris of 1925). This never showed itself more clearly than in the Coventry rendering where, aside from the limitations of photomontage, the edge conditions were revealed as a series of inevitable collisions between the old street pattern and the new.

Struggling with the Ville Contemporaine

After the building out of the Golden Lane concept at Parkhill, Sheffield, in 1961,[9] it became obvious that aside from the prewar perimeter block solution, particularly as exemplified by Michiel Brinkman at Spangen in Rotterdam in 1919 (a scheme well known to the Smithsons), there was little possibility of obtaining satisfactory continuity between streets in the air and streets at grade. For all that Team 10 were almost involuntarily committed to the multi-level city (an idea stemming from the source for Le Corbusier's Ville Contemporaine, i.e. Eugène Hénard's Rue Future of 1910) it was to the Smithsons' credit that they remained conscious of its limitations and in consequence produced one of the most critical sketches of their early career: a drawing which demonstrated that above the sixth floor one lost all contact with the ground. Although the Smithsons were using this sketch in the Fifties as a way of rationalizing the megastructure as a generic section, their recognition of tree height as an existential change line was to exert a certain influence on the subsequent development of British housing policy. This, together with their Criteria for Mass Housing of 1959, contributed in the late Sixties to the adoption of 'low-rise high-density' as the official model for family residential development. Such critical awareness was greatly amplified at the time by the Smithsons' still very convincing *close* and *fold* house projects of the mid-Fifties and by their demand, after the ecological thesis of the Doorn Manifesto, that habitat should be integrated into the landscape rather than isolated as an object within it.

Despite an incidental sketch by Bakema featuring a primitive low-rise, self-help housing scheme, nothing could have been generally further from his mind than the creation of an *architecture autre* such as had clearly inspired the Smithsons when, in conjunction with Nigel Henderson and Eduardo Paolozzi, they designed a 'primitive hut' for the 'This is Tomorrow' exhibition of 1956. It was clear that the socio-cultural challenge of Bethnal Green was largely lost on Bakema since, despite the radicalism of his early pronouncements, he was the one member of Team 10 whose practice was always closely affiliated to the site planning principles of the *Neue Sachlichkeit*; that is to the row house principle of open-ended blocks of identical height, set an optimum distance apart. Bakema was an early and active participant in OPBOUW, the prewar Dutch wing of CIAM, and hence more conditioned by the precepts of determinism than the Smithsons (who never worked as members of the English wing of CIAM). His constant point of reference was clearly the Amsterdam South Plan of 1934 and, in particular, the prewar housing work of architects such as Merkelbach, Karsten and Stam. It is clear that in the OPBOUW studies for Pendrecht (1949/51) and for Alexander Polder (1953/56), all of which Bakema participated in, there was a gradual move away from the rigid row house principle, with its uniform height and orientation, to a more modulated layout, comprising swastika formations grouped about a particular centre or about interlocking aggregations of such centres.

The Kennermerland project, designed in collaboration with J M Stokla and submitted to the 'transitional' Otterlo Congress of 1959 (the last congress to be formally associated with CIAM and the first to be organized by Team 10) was, in essence, a culmination of these earlier OPBOUW studies, as Bakema seemed to admit when challenged by Kenzo Tange as to the originality of his 1959 proposal.[10] Yet it says something for the relative naivety of the period that both Tange and Bakema should look for the origins of this work in the urban planning of Le Corbusier, for in many respects Kennermerland seemed to derive more from those abstract 'neighbourhood' planning concepts developed in the Thirties and Forties by German planners such as Ernst May[11] and Arthur Korn. In echoing, whether consciously or not, the kind of planning to be found in Korn's Mars plan for London of 1942,[12] Bakema, in opposition to the Smithsons' notion of district, sought in Kennermerland to give physical definition to a whole hierarchy of different social groups.

At the same time, for all his willingness to acknowledge his debt to Le Corbusier, Bakema did not truly come under the influence of the Ville Radieuse until his Tel Aviv plan of 1963. Here the megastructure corniche form adopted by Le Corbusier for his Algiers scheme of 1931 was used by Bakema as a hypothetical means for giving order to the scattered formation of the existing city. Paradoxically, this use of the continuous superblock in no way served to liberate Bakema from his 'determinist' background. While the fiction of the neighbourhood unit was partially dispensed with, the conceptual void in the Bakema thesis seems to have been largely filled at this time by the projection of urban megaforms that either cascaded down in straight lines over undulating topography, as in the case of Bakema's entry for the University of Bochum of 1962, or appeared in the form of that arabesque superblock projected by Bakema as paralleling his reformulated freeway spine for Tel Aviv.

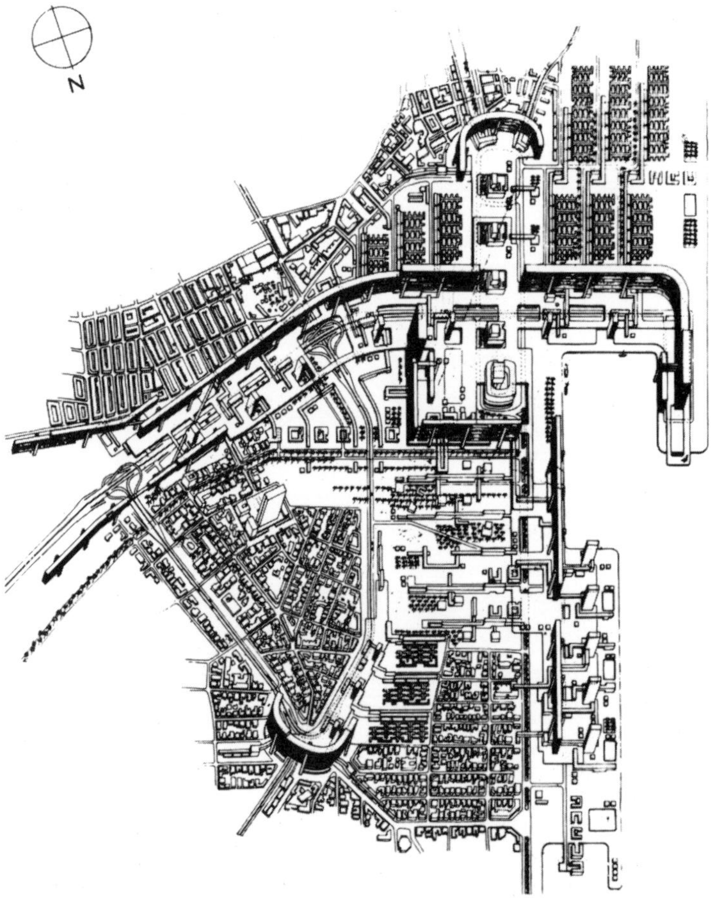

Jacob Bakema, Tel Aviv plan, 1963, isometric of continuous megaforms framing the existing metropolis and giving it a new scalar reading.

It is one of the ironies of the pluralism of Team 10 that Bakema was to propose the continuous superblock as a psychological counterform to the alienating experience of Melvin Webber's 'Non-Place Urban Realm'[13] just at the time when the Smithsons were beginning to have doubts about the viability of such structures. The Smithsons' 'open city' thesis, first broached after their visit to the US in 1958 and projected with Peter Sigmond in their Hauptstadt Berlin competition entry of the same year, argued (like Hans Scharoun's Hauptstadt design) in favour of maintaining a permanently 'ruined' city – ruined in the sense that the scale and speed of twentieth-century movement could no longer be brought to relate to the pattern of the pre-existing urban fabric. And here, once again, their thinking may have exercised some influence on public policy, in as much as their 650 metre superblock, adopted as a hypothetical infrastructure for their Mehringplatz proposal of 1962, seems to have anticipated the adoption of a similar grid in the Milton Keynes masterplan of 1966.

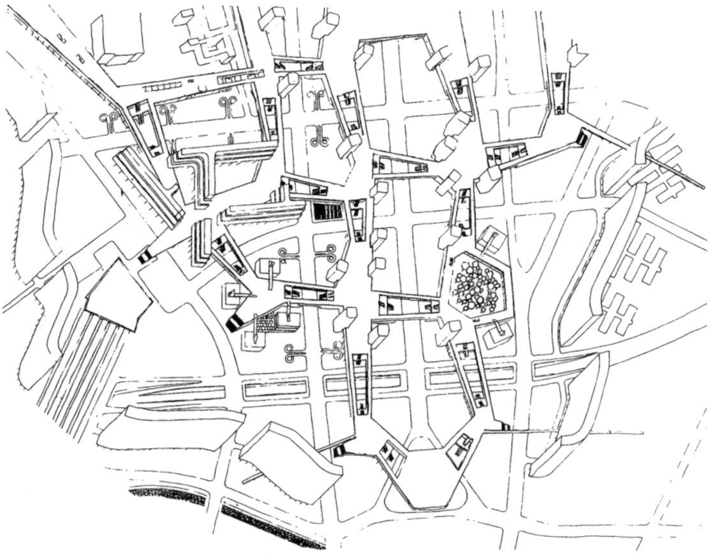

Alison and Peter Smithson and Peter Sigmond, Hauptstadt Berlin competition, 1958, plan of double level pedestrian street system above the existing street grid.

Mehringplatz, designed with Gunter Nitschke, was derived conceptually from the 'landcastle' and 'greenway' postscripts to the Smithsons' London Road Study of 1959, the built form of the platz itself constituting the 'landcastle' while the contingent autoroute irrigated the city-wide system of 'greenway' access (compare with the Merritt Parkway, Connecticut, USA). In their fully developed Mehringplatz report, the Smithsons defined their concept of the open city as a megalopolitan region visually accentuated and 'fixed' by a series of monumental 'landcastles'.[14] They wrote:

We do not build up these 'events' into a unified linear architectural 'composition'... At approximately 650m intervals there are take offs from which the 'events' and the area they serve are reached... The motorway grid forms the macro-structure, and the smaller grid of roads from the take offs form the micro-structure of each area ... Our proposal is closer in spirit to Nancy (calm, urbane and even a little empty) than to most contemporary urban designs. The justification for such an 'aristocratic' use of space for such an ordinary problem is that if lack of crowding, calmness and quiet can be achieved, we have an obligation to use our increased productivity in this direction.[15]

While both Bakema and the Smithsons were to be preoccupied with the notion of 'urban fix', that is, with the monumental contribution to be made by architecture as an 'event' within the 'space endlessness' of 'motopia', the Smithsons, rather than return to the continuous megastructure, were to think in terms of localized traffic-free 'enclaves', be they the high-rise podium towers of their Hauptstadt scheme or the Schinkelesque *paradeplatzen* of their Mehringplatz period. Either way, both Bakema and the Smithsons were, by this date, totally mesmerized by the egalitarian promise of mobility, whose *de facto* presence they thought of exclusively in terms of meeting the situation with appropriate forms of architectural invention.

Of the different models proferred for dealing with this phenomena, those projected by the Smithsons were clearly more feasible. This much is borne out by the subsequent, partial realization of both their Hauptstadt and Mehringplatz prototypes; the one in their Economist Building, London, of 1965,[16] and the other in their Robin Hood Gardens housing scheme of 1969.[17] Yet the kinds of standards and relationships imposed by this a priori monumentality, particularly in the case of the housing, suggest that neither Bakema nor the Smithsons were at the time sufficiently aware of the micro-environmental consequences of such large scale propositions.

Searching for society's counterform

This curious lacuna in the works of otherwise sensitive architects makes one aware once again of the pluralism of Team 10, since one can hardly charge that Van Eyck was ever indifferent to these issues – his entire output having been nothing but a constant witness to the all but impossible task of achieving an architecture in this epoch. From the very beginning Van Eyck was to address himself to a whole set of issues which most of the members of Team 10 were scarcely capable of formulating, and at a time when the movement appeared to ride on a wave of critical optimism, Van Eyck was to be motivated by an impulse that always verged on the pessimistic. No other member seemed to be able to attack the alienating abstraction of modern architecture on such fundamental grounds, presumably because no one else had had Van Eyck's 'anthropological' experience.[18]

Van Eyck's personal preoccupation with 'primitive' culture, and with the timeless aspects of built form that such cultures invariably reveal, dates from the early Forties. By the time he joined Team 10, therefore, he was already in a position to adopt a somewhat singular position. His statement at the Otterloo Congress of 1959 already declared a concern for the 'timelessness' of man, a concern that if it was not beyond the comprehension of Team 10, was certainly beyond that of CIAM:

To discover anew implies discovering something new. Translate this into architecture and you'll get new architecture – real contemporary architecture. Architecture implies a constant rediscovery of constant human qualities translated into space. Man is always and everywhere essentially the same. He has the same mental equipment though he uses it differently according to his cultural or social background, according to the particular life pattern of which he happens to be a part. Modern architects have been harping continually on about what is different in our time to such an extent that even they have lost touch with what is not different, with what is always essentially the same.[19]

Van Eyck's concern for transition, for the amplification of the 'threshold' so as to mediate symbolically between such universal twin phenomena as 'inside' as 'outside' and 'house' as 'city', was to make itself manifest in his work of the late Fifties, most particularly in his orphanage in Amsterdam which was then nearing completion. Here Van Eyck demonstrated his idea of 'labyrinthine clarity' in an interconnected sequence of domed 'family' units, all united under a continuous roof.

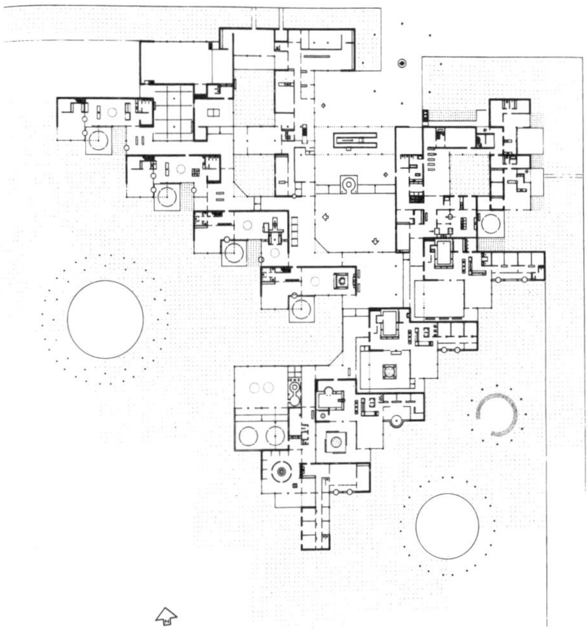

Aldo van Eyck, Orphanage School, Amsterdam, 1955–60, ground floor plan exemplifying his concept of 'labyrinthine clarity'.

Within a few years, however, that which had once been the occasion for his impatience and critical enthusiasm, had become the cause for despair. By 1966 five years of intense urban development had already become more than enough for Van Eyck, so that, in an address given in Australia in that year, he was at once to reveal the full scope of our present predicament. The assessment is as pertinent as it is brief:

What we are after is a new as yet unknown configurative discipline. It's hard to tell anybody about it because nobody in the twentieth century had made it his. The discipline is still not ours – the art of humanizing vast numbers hasn't advanced beyond the first vague preliminaries. We know nothing of vast multiplicity – we cannot come to grips with it – not as architecture, planners or anybody else . . . We have lost touch with what I call harmony in motion, or the aesthetics of number.[20]

Elsewhere Van Eyck was to characterize this predicament in terms of the cultural void left by the loss of the vernacular. In his various writings of the period, he pointed to the role played by modern architecture in the clinical eradication of both style and place. He cited postwar Dutch planning as being largely exemplary of the 'organized nowhere', as being nothing but a proliferation of that *funktionelle Stadt* he had already condemned as uninhabitable in his Otterloo address of 1959.[21] In the end, his doubts as to the capacity of the profession to meet the pluralistic demands of society, without the mediation of a living vernacular, led him to question the authenticity of society itself. In 1966 he was to ask, 'If society has no form – how can architects build its counterform?'[22]

By 1963, Team 10 had already passed beyond the stage of interchange and collaboration, a transformation that was intuitively acknowledged by the Smithsons in their 1968 publication of the *Team 10 Primer*. From now on, Team 10 would primarily continue as a movement only in name, since what there had been to achieve through a creative critique of CIAM had been already largely attained. Little in fact remained to be done in the way of exorcism and reinterpretation, save possibly for the work of two men who had hitherto remained somewhat to one side: Shadrach Woods and Giancarlo de Carlo.

Built infrastructures: paradise found?

The entirely new ground opened up by Woods in his Frankfurt Römerberg competition entry of 1963 seems to have been made in direct response to Van Eyck's appeal for 'labyrinthine clarity' since what was being proferred in the Frankfurt proposal, within the length of a New York city block, was a 'city in miniature'. In the place of the medieval centre destroyed by World War II, Woods proposed an equally labyrinthine (in both plan and section) configuration of shops, public spaces, offices and dwellings, the whole being served by a double-decked underground service level comprising access and parking. If the Frankfurt scheme was an urban 'event', it was certainly conceived in totally different terms from the Smithsonian 'land-castle'. While presenting a precisely articulated three-dimensional counterform in opposition to the form of the existing urban context, it also comprised within itself a three-dimensional gridded 'loft' system served by escalators whose interstices, within the limits imposed by the need for light and air, could be occupied according to demand. That this concept of a 'randomly' occupied infrastructure had already been anticipated in Yona Friedman's *L'Architecture mobile*, published in 1958, in no way detracts from the relevance of the Frankfurt achievement. On the contrary, it says a great deal for the openness of Woods's mind that he was able to build on an idea that had been dismissed out of hand at Dubrovnik in 1956.[23] The continuing validity of the Frankfurt paradigm, even as it was only realized in the Berlin Free University, derives very much from the programmatic resonance that Woods was able to impart to the rather abstract formulations of the initial Friedman scheme; to transpose what was no doubt anathema to Van Eyck into something that he would have been able to accept.

Frankfurt Römerberg, designed with Manfred Schiedhelm, was without question the greatest single achievement of Woods's extensive career. Moreover, it was probably the most important total synthesis ever to be projected by a Team 10 member, since while relating to the strong context of an existing city – that is, while refusing the utopian escapism of both the tabula rasa approach of the Ville Radieuse and the rationalized mobility of the Open City – it endeavoured to put the car in its proper place and to decide in favour of continuing the culture of the existing fabric. For Woods the car was always the subservient element.

Candilis, Josic and Woods, Frankfurt Römerberg, 1963, model.

That the Frankfurt concept, as built out in the Berlin Free University in 1973, was to lose some of its conviction stems in no small part from this 'loss of the city', and this loss has certain ramifications which demand our attention. Firstly, as realized in Thiele Park, Woods's urban microcosm was deprived of the urban form and culture against which it had been initially designed; and secondly, for all that a university may well be a city in miniature, the programme for a self-contained campus is not able to generate anything of the animated diversity of a city proper. Furthermore, an account has to be made in respect of a certain loss of historical 'aura',

Candilis, Josic and Woods with Manfred Schiedhelm, Free University, Berlin, 1973.

whose effect must always be incalculable. In comparison with Frankfurt, the Free University was all too linear and self-contained and the occupation of its infrastructure too exact. Frankfurt's generosity of flexibility in principle was finally replaced by Berlin's idealization of flexibility as an end in itself; but the poetry of Berlin's Free University is undeniable and the promise of Frankfurt remains.

Political responsibility

In 1964, the implicit ideology of Woods's Frankfurt scheme found its complement in Giancarlo de Carlo's plan for Urbino. This plan, which had been preceded by an exhaustive topographical study, was to devote more space to the tactics of rehabilitation than it was to provide for the extensive accommodation of new development. With de Carlo's Urbino, Team 10 finally arrived at the complete antithesis to the prewar tabula rasa projections of the Ville Radieuse. Carlo's basic thesis, namely the re-use of existing stock wherever possible, has recently been borne out by housing studies which have shown conclusively that, despite the higher densities eventually attained, it generally takes about 50 years for the provision of any new housing to compensate for the 'housing loss' incurred through the time spent in demolition and construction. Naturally, this net statistical backlog is invariably achieved at a greater cost than would otherwise be the case were most of the stock rehabilitated. Considerations such as these finally had the effect of precipitating the Team 10 discourse into a realm that it had always strenuously avoided, namely the political. Never was this shift in consciousness more manifest than at the Milan Triennale of 1968 when Woods, in sympathy with the student activists, assisted in the defacement of his own work. Only one year before, he had written from Märkisches Viertel, Berlin, to Alison Smithson, as follows:

What are we waiting for? To read the news about a new armed attack with even more esoteric weapons, news which comes to us through the air captured by our marvellous transistorized instruments somewhere deep in our more and more savaged dwellings? Our weapons become more sophisticated; our houses more and more brutish. Is that the balance sheet for the richest civilization since time began?[24]

The very same theme was taken up by de Carlo in 1968 when he wrote a synoptic analysis of the ideological development of modern architecture under the title *Legitimizing Architecture*. Here he reviewed the consequences of the La Sarraz CIAM Declaration of 1928 and of the Existenzminium Congress of the following year:

Today, 40 years after the Congress, we find that those proposals have become houses and neighbourhoods and suburbs and then entire cities, palpable manifestations of an abuse perpetrated first on the poor and then even on the not-so-poor; cultural alibis for the most ferocious economic speculation and the most obtuse political inefficiency. And yet those 'whys' so nonchalantly forgotten in Frankfurt still have trouble coming openly to the surface. At the same time, we have a right to ask 'why' housing should be as cheap as possible and not, for example, rather expensive; 'why' instead of making every effort to reduce it to minimum levels of surface, of thickness, of materials, we should not try to make it spacious, protected, isolated, comfortable, well equipped, rich in opportunities for privacy, communication, exchange of personal creativity. No one, in fact, can be satisfied by an answer which appeals to the scarcity of available resources, when we all know how much is spent on wars, on the construction of missiles and anti-ballistic systems, on moon projects, on research for the defoliation of forests inhabited by partisans and for the paralysation of the demonstrators emerging from the ghettos, on hidden persuasion, on the invention of artificial needs, etc.[25]

For de Carlo, the students' revolt of 1968 was not only a necessary culmination of the crisis in architectural education, but was also a reflection of the deeper and more significant disfunctions of architectural practice and theory – this last serving to mystify much that would otherwise be obviously reprehensible. As an example of the latter, de Carlo cited the CIAM Hoddesdon Congress of 1951 (CIAM 8), whose sentimental deliberations – published as *The Heart of the City*[26] – were largely responsible for preparing the ideological ground for the subsequent rape of the city core, for that cynical procedure of urban renovation that did not gain its full momentum until about a decade later. As de Carlo reminds us, the Newspeak overtones of this speculative venture were not entirely lost on the critics of American society, who came to regard the process of urban renewal as a euphemism for negro removal.

In the mid-Sixties, however, this cruel point would appear to have been largely lost on Team 10, who chose, it would seem (with the exception of Van Eyck, Woods and de Carlo), not to acknowledge the flagrant destruction of our urban heritage in the name of virulent speculation, rationalized by architecture. That the postulative capacities of Team 10 became bankrupt at this juncture is obvious from what has, and has not, followed since. Their creative force broke itself in the cause of an impossible proof. Paradoxically, what now endures from their work is the power of their initial critique. It remains for the next generation, impassive before the delirious mystifications of our much more recent past, to turn to the roots of this critique and to begin again to search for a valid architecture and to return to the timelessness of man.

First published in *L'Architecture d'aujourd'hui*, no.177, January/February 1975, pp.62–5.

ДА ЗДРАВСТВУЕТ
III-и ИНТЕРНАЦИОНАЛ

Constructivism: The Pursuit of an Elusive Sensibility

> *Where does it begin and end this vague word? It is vague because it contains too much. It admits neither an aesthetic nor a category of production. Truly speaking, it is a word which belongs to the psychology of history, it is a generating word.*
> Le Corbusier, *Une Maison, un palais*, 1928

This somewhat supercilious assessment emphasizes the essential ambivalence of the term 'Constructivism' as it was assimilated in the Twenties into the language of the European avant-garde. Certain left-wing architects, in opposition to Le Corbusier, had borrowed this term from the Soviet Union as a way of characterizing their own particular form of Functionalism, even though no Soviet group had chosen to assert its activity exclusively under this heading. As Naum Gabo was to state, perhaps ingenuously, 'There were no Constructivists until 1920. We all called ourselves Constructivists from the Russian word *postroyenia* meaning construction.'[1] It is a fact that both within and without the Soviet Union artists and architects largely avoided advancing themselves solely as Constructivists. They chose instead to call themselves Realists, Suprematists, Productivists or, later, in Germany where the architectural Left under Soviet influence was concentrated, they worked as functionalist designers, as part of the cultural movement known as *die Neue Sachlichkeit*.[2]

The importance of the term 'Constructivism' seems to have lain not in itself, but rather in the extremely volatile and elusive sensibility it came to evoke. Beyond any doubt, this sensibility played a major role in transforming our way of viewing the world and, if nothing else, it modified our expectancy with regard to the nature of artistic production. The whole question of the boundaries separating art from life was constantly challenged in the Twenties by the Constructivists and other related 'isms', and it is this common synthetic drive that has encouraged us to classify rather diverse positions under the general rubric of 'Constructivism'. Even someone as experienced as Alfred Barr, in his classic text, *Cubism and Abstract Art*, of 1936, could crudely group Tatlin and Rodchenko with Pevsner and Gabo under the category 'Constructivism'. By the same token, and with less excuse, the artist and writer George Rickey has seen reason to include in his recent study of Constructivism artists as diverse as Kandinsky, Albers, Balla, Calder and Gonzalez.[3]

In taking exception to the over-extension of an art historical category, I wish only to emphasize the diversity of intentions that even today are still covered by a term which is incapable, by definition, of distinguishing between them. To this end, my purpose is to isolate certain related movements which from time to time have been conflated under the term 'Constructivism'. The common origin of all these movements seems to lie in the obscurity of the Hylaea movement. This short-lived fountainhead of Russian Futurism led almost directly to the mature works of Kasimir Malevich, Naum Gabo and Vladimir Tatlin; thereby making an understanding of these artists contingent upon an understanding of their roots in Futurism. The title 'Hylaea' (or 'Gileya') was derived from the ancient Greek name for an area on the shores of the Black Sea. Here in the summer of 1911, the painter David Burliuk and the writers Benedict Livshits, Vladimir Mayakovsky, Velimir Khlebnikov and Alexi Kruchenykh mutually dedicated themselves to the creation of a new nationalist and post-Symbolist art form under the name 'Hylaea'. Initially, the Hylaea group stood for a complex brand of Primitivism wherein painting and poetry were to be combined as in the traditional manner of the Russian *lubok* or woodcut. Two years later the very same artists precipitously announced themselves as Futurists. The Hylaea movement seems to have placed great emphasis on the literary component of the *lubok*, and Khlebnikov, Kruchenykh and Mayakovsky carried over into their synthetic art that same sense of infantilism, with its reference to popular, erotic and childish imagery, as had already become a primary component in those Primitivist works of the painters Mikhail Larionov and Natalia Goncharova.

The exceptional thing about the writers of the Hylaea group was the fact that they all had either practised painting or had been initially trained as artists. Kruchenykh, in particular, had been a teacher of art before he met David Burliuk in 1907. By 1911, however, he had abandoned painting for literature and was already moving towards a kind of Primitivist book production; primitive not only in its language and in the alogicality of its textural sense, but also in its graphic presentation and means of production. As Vladimir Markov has remarked of Kruchenykh's poem, 'A Game in Hell', of 1912, with illustrations by Goncharova, 'this long poem about a card game going on between devils and sinners in hell was begun by

Kruchenykh in the style of a folk lithograph [*lubok*] as he himself admitted. Then Khlebnikov added his own stanzas and lines with the result that the text became even more disorganized.'[4]

The years 1912 to 1913 were crucial for the development of the literary aspects of Russian Futurism. They were of equal significance for the initial impact of this movement on the development of twentieth-century art. In the first instance, there was the publication in 1912 by Kruchenykh and Mayakovsky of their manifesto, *A Slap in the Face of Public Taste*, which began with the words, 'Only we are the face of our time. The horn of time trumpets through us the art of the word ...' and continued a few lines later with the injunction to throw Pushkin, Dostoevsky and Tolstoy overboard from the ship of modernity and later to assert the poet's right to enlarge their vocabulary with arbitrary words and 'to feel an insurmountable hatred for all language existing before them'.[5] In the second instance, closely related to the first, there was Kruchenykh's development of his so-called *zaum* poetry which was announced in September 1913 with the publication of the Khlebnikov and Kruchenykh manifesto, *Declaration of the Word as Such*, in which it was asserted that Futurist poetry should appear, 'As if it were written with difficulty, more uncomfortable than black-ened boots in a drawing room.'[6] At this juncture, both men were to enlarge on the freedoms already proclaimed in *A Slap in the Face of Public Taste*, to the effect that, 'Thought and speech cannot catch up with the emotional experience of someone inspired; therefore, the artist is free to express himself not only in common language (concepts) but also in a private one (the creator as individual), as well as in a language that does not have a definite meaning (is not frozen) that is *trans-rational* ... Words die, but the world stays young forever.'

As Kruchenykh had already written in an earlier pamphlet, 'A lily is beautiful but the word "lily" is soiled with fingers and raped. For this reason I call a lily "euy" and the original purity is re-established.'[7]

In 1913 the Hylaea group announced themselves as Futurists, although in so doing they took great care to distinguish themselves from the Italian Futurists to whose influence they had, of course, been subject since the publication of Marinetti's Futurist Manifesto in 1909. The significant culmination of their own intense if short-lived Futurism was their entry into drama, which at once had the effect of uniting their work in a more striking way with the other arts. In the summer of 1913, Kruchenykh, Kasimir Malevich and A V Matyushin announced their decision to organize a Futurist theatre. By then Mayakovsky had already started to write about the cinema, proclaiming the triumph of the kinetic image over the realism of the Moscow Arts Theatre, while David Burliuk and other members of the Hylaea group had made their own foray into film with their proto-dadiast short, *Drama in Cabaret No.13*.[8] Finally, in December 1913, in St Petersburg's Luna Park, there came the first performance of Kruchenykh's opera, *Victory over the Sun*, with sets and costumes by Malevich. In this wild and cacophonous performance the audience was introduced to the so-called strong men (or supermen) of the future, who were destined to survive the messianic destruction of the world. In a final burst of cosmic insanity the sun is first stabbed and then finally captured. They celebrate this victory-cum-apocalyptical disaster with the following chorus:

In smoke and haze
And fatty dust
The blows strengthen
We get stronger like pigs
Our faces are dark
Our light comes from inside
We are warmed by the dead udder
Of the Red Dawn
BRN BRN[9]

The exalted sense imparted by this text is nothing if it is not suggestive of some strange kind of eschatological redemption. Men are to become even more earthy, they are to be illuminated from within and warmed by a new dawn which significantly enough is red. Nothing could be more removed from the conclusion of the Italian Futurist Manifesto of 1909, which celebrated little save the violent banality of a car accident. Given Kruchenykh's mad feeling for apocalyptical fulfilment, we are hardly surprised to learn that *Victory over the Sun* of 1913 was the mainspring for Malevich's creation of Suprematism, despite the fact that Suprematist painting proper did not truly emerge until some two years later. We have Malevich's own testimony, which seems even to paraphrase Kruchenykh, to the effect that his creation of Suprematism was only the desert of the night that he felt within him, epitomized as a black square.

The early development of Russian Futurism fused traditional Russian millennialism with a proto-dadaist sensibility (antedating the Zurich Dada by three years) and united both elements within a Primitivism of folk origin. This strange amalgam seems to have been the basic point of departure for both the Realist and Productivist movements. The most striking connection from the point of view of painting is to be found in the work of the painter Vladimir Burliuk (David Burliuk's brother) whose 1911 portrait of the writer Benedict Livshits seems to anticipate all too directly the first plastic works of the Realist artists Gabo and Pevsner. Despite its superficial stylistic dependence on Picasso's *Les Demoiselles d'Avignon* of 1907, Livshits's portrait is clearly not a Cubistic work in a Parisian sense, just as it is equally clear that its crude faceting of convex and concave planes in space, particularly in the rendering of the neck and head, does nothing if not anticipate Naum Gabo's earliest head construction of 1915.

Vladimir Tatlin, sketch for the stage set of Velimir Khlebnikov's play Zangezi, *1923.*

Along a different line of development, one may posit Vladimir Tatlin's sketches of 1910 as stemming from the Primitivist works of Larionov and Goncharova, and as anticipating that peculiar brand of latent Primitivism that is to pervade his career as an industrial designer after 1920. Nothing confirms these Primitivist–Futurist connections more strongly than Tatlin's stage setting for Khlebnikov's last work, written just before the writer's death in 1922. It would seem that this play, *Zangezi*, was staged by students of the Petrograd Gallery of Artistic Culture under Tatlin's direction in 1923. Tatlin's text describing this work does much by way of explaining not only his own intentions but also those of Khlebnikov:

The Zangezi *production is to be realized on the principle that 'the word is a building unit, a material unit of organized space'. Khlebnikov himself characterized this super narration as an architectural work built of narrations, and each narration as an architectural work built of words. He regards the word as plastic material. The properties of this material make it possible to operate with it to build up 'the linguistic state'.*

This attitude on the part of Khlebnikov gave me an opportunity to do my work in staging it. Parallel with his word-constructions, I decided to make material construction. This method makes it possible to fuse the work of two people into a unity, in spite of their having different specialities, and to make Khlebnikov's work comprehensible to the masses.

Khlebnikov took sounds as elements. They contain the impulse to the birth of the word. The hard 'c' sound, for instance, gives birth to cup, cranium, container. All these words have to do with the concept of sheath. The sound 'p' has to do with a diminishment of energy which stands in relationship to the area in which it is used; as in paddle, position, palm, porringer.[10]

One can only wonder at this obscure text and at the naive literalness of Tatlin's attempt to interpret in plastic form the *zaum*, or trans-rational poetry of Khlebnikov's *Song of Astral Language*, which forms a central feature within the play *Zangezi*. In this play, a god-like being bestows the renewed *trans-rational* cryptic word on the unenlightened mass assembled beneath his feet. Once again, as in the play *Victory over the Sun*, one cannot but fail to notice an almost pathological drive towards the representation of an overwhelming apocalyptic event which first anticipates (in 1913) and then indirectly celebrates (in 1923) the actuality of the Russian Revolution. One is reminded at this juncture of the eschatological tradition in Russian thought emphasized by Nikolai Berdyaev in his book, *The Russian Idea*. This cultural conjunction is confirmed by the very origin of the *zaum* conception in poetry. Of this Vladimir Markov has written: 'The source of Kruchenykh's theories in this instance is an article he never mentioned, "Religious Ecstasy in Russian Mystical Sectarianism", by D G Konovalov; serialized in 1907 and 1908.' According to Markov, Konovalov 'gave many examples of *zaum avant la lettre* produced by sect members in moments of ecstasy. One of them says, "I speak I don't know what and even in languages I don't know."'[11]

This cryptic oracular tradition lying concealed as an impulse beneath much of the Constructivist sensibility is a constituent that has been largely overlooked. It may be characterized in the work of Kruchenykh, Khlebnikov, Malevich and Tatlin as a messianic impulse to reduce and purify both language and form through the largely unconscious crucible of everyday language and life.

Something of Tatlin's own intrinsic primitivism not only as an artist but also as a personality has been captured by George Grosz in a memoire taken from a period in which Tatlin was about to start work on the set for *Zangezi*. Grosz writes of meeting Tatlin, 'I met Tatlin, the great fool, once again. He was living in a small, ancient and decrepit apartment. Some of the hens he kept slept on his bed. In a corner they laid eggs. We drank tea, and Tatlin talked of Berlin, of the Wertheim store and of his performances for the court. Behind him a mattress entirely consumed by rust, was leaning against the wall ...'. Grosz continues, 'When he played his homemade balalaika it was growing dark outside the uncurtained window, the panes of which had been replaced in places by small plates of wood – he gave the impression not of an ultra-modern constructivist but a piece of genuine ancient Russia, as if from a book by Gogol – and there was suddenly a melancholy humour in the room.'[12]

This was Tatlin the *moujik*; a figure which it is difficult for us to reconcile with the undoubtedly more worldly Tatlin who was to be elected in 1918 as head of the IZO School – the Narkompros Department of Fine Arts in Moscow. We have much less difficulty, however, in reconciling this bucolic image with Tatlin's relief and corner relief constructions of the years 1913 to 1915, many of which were displayed for the first time in the exhibition titled '0–10'. Yet despite, or even because of their singular improvised quality, these works are of considerable sophistication. Without question they are a conscious adaption of the *zaum* principle of Khlebnikov and Kruchenykh inasmuch as they are an on-the-spot utilization of the detritus of everyday life. Despite the transformation of this junk into three-dimensional intellectual abstractions of the most severe objectivity, something of a thrown-away 'folk' quality seems to remain. As Troels Andersen has observed, these works were far removed from those aestheticized collages and reliefs produced by Picasso, Gris and Braque at around the same time. For all their latent *bricolage*, these synthetic Cubist pieces remained identifiable as salon objects. Unlike Tatlin's corner relief of 1915 or his large Café Pittoresque relief designed in association with the 'orphist', Georgiy Yakulov, in 1917, Cubism projected itself within the traditional format of the free-standing sculpture or wall-hung painting or relief. Furthermore as Andersen has again remarked, the material itself became Tatlin's 'ready-made' as opposed to Duchamp's bicycle wheel and bottle rack of approximately the same date. Andersen writes of Tatlin, 'The material came to be his "ready-made", the drawing pin holding a piece of paper in place, the string binding together two pieces of metal. One of his reliefs was made of a large piece of parquet flooring which he found when he was out looking for firewood. Any object whatsoever when its situation was changed could be recognized as material.'[13]

This determination to preserve the inherent material quality of the transformed substance and, at the same time, to express directly the nature of its transformation or production, was to become the central precept of Productivism, as set out in *The Programme of the Productivist Group* published in 1921, in response to the more idealistic *Realist Manifesto* published by Naum Gabo and Antoine Pevsner in the previous year.

Materialism, in the broadest sense of that term, was adopted as the basic precept of Productivism by the signatories of the *Programme*, namely by Tatlin and the Inkhuk artists, Alexander Rodchenko and Varvara Stepanova. The Productivists asserted (at least in theory) that the correct relation of form and content was contingent upon the interrelation of three basic precepts. These were (1) the *technique* or *tektonika* which, to quote from the *Programme*, was seen as 'the effective exploitation of industrial matter', in accordance with socialist principles; (2) the *material* or *fakutra* which was seen as being 'deliberately chosen and effectively used without, however, hindering the progress of construction or limiting the *tektonika*'; and finally, (3) the art of construction itself which was largely seen as 'a formal ordering process which should allow for transformation'.[14]

What exactly this cryptic formula meant to the Productivists it is difficult to say, even though Constructivism itself was later defined more clearly by the Constructivist organ LEF as 'the organization of the given material on the principles of tectonics, structure and construction; the form becoming defined in the process of creation by the utilitarian aim of the object.' Despite this Functionalist definition, few were to be finally committed to the principles of structural economy in service of utility and even fewer to Tatlin's own 'culture of materials' which, as Camilla Gray has suggested, came to play such an important part in determining his overall attitude to artistic production.[15]

Tatlin for his part was to draw a precise distinction between the Productivist and Constructivist positions when he wrote in retrospect in 1932 that they, the Constructivists, 'worked in materials but in an abstract fashion, as a formal problem mechanically applying technique to their art. Constructivism did not take into account the organic relation between the material and the tensile capacity, its working character. Essentially it is only as an outcome of the dynamic force resulting from these mutual relations that a vitally inevitable form is born.'[16]

For Tatlin the 'organic' transformation of material through fabrication, in such a manner as to leave its intrinsic nature inviolate and to exploit its unique characteristics, was of far greater consequence than the principle of utility *per se*, despite the fact that Tatlin's projected *Monument to the Third International* of 1920 was intended, to quote the contemporary critic Nikolai Punin, 'to comprise a new type of monumental construction, combining a purely creative form with a utilitarian form'. Punin was to continue:

In agreement with this principle, the monument consists of three great rooms in glass, erected with the help of a complicated system of vertical pillars and spirals. These rooms are placed on top of each other and have different harmonically corresponding forms. They are able to move at different speeds by means of a special mechanism. The lower story, which is cubic in form, rotates around its axis at a rate of one revolution per year. This is intended for legislative assemblies. The next story, which is pyramidal, rotates around its axis at a rate of one revolution per month. Here the executive bodies are to meet . . . Finally, the uppermost cylinder, which rotates one revolution per day, is reserved for centres of an informative character; an information office, a newspaper, the issuing of proclamations, pamphlets and manifestos . . . it will also have a telegraph office and an apparatus that can project onto large screens. These can be fitted around the axes of the hemisphere. Radio masts will rise up over the monument.[17]

Apart from its questionable utility – challenged, indeed, by Trotsky, in a subsequent passage – Punin was to reveal himself as being just as aware of the symbolic aspects of the proposal. Thus of its symbolic form he wrote that:

Just as the triangle, as an image of general equilibrium, is the best expression of the Renaissance, so the spiral is the most effective symbol of the modern spirit of the age . . . while the dynamic line of the bourgeois society, aiming at the possession of the land and the soil, was horizontal, the spiral, which, rising from the earth, detaches itself from all animal, earthly and oppressing interests, forms the purest expression of human-

ity set free by the Revolution. The bourgeois social order developed an animal life on earth, tilled the soil, and there erected shops, arcades and banks; the life of the new humanity rises ever higher and higher above ground.[18]

He wrote, too, of its semiological aspects based on use:

Most of the elements of architecture hitherto in use possessed no practical importance and remained unorganized. Today the principle of organization must rule and penetrate all art. The monument unites legislative initiative with the executive and with information; to each of these functions a position in space has been assigned corresponding to its nature.

And finally, of the latent millennialism of its materials, he wrote:

Just as the product of the number of oscillations and the wavelength is the spatial measure of the sound, so the proportion between glass and iron is the measure of the material rhythm. By the union of these two fundamentally important materials, a compact and imposing simplicity and, at the same time, relationship are expressed since these materials, for both of which fire is the creator of life, form the elements of modern art. By their union, rhythms must be created of a mighty power, as though an ocean were being born.[19]

Punin's excessive rhetoric notwithstanding, this double preoccupation with utility on the one hand and with the culture not to say the cult of materials on the other, pervades the entirety of Tatlin's work after his *Monument to the Third International*. This peculiar dichotomy was to be complemented in Tatlin's later work by an overriding concern with environmental control, with mechanical movement, and with the actual day-to-day mobility of a post-revolutionary, nomadic population. To such interrelated ends we find him designing both a 'dymaxion' stove and workers' clothing at Inkhuk in 1924, where the conscious primitivism of the material testifies to a brutal, almost *zaum* expression of utility. To similar ends we find him designing three years later, with students from the Vkhutemas, a number of moulded ceramic teapots to be held in the hand and, with Rogozin, a Vkhutein student, a bentwood cantilever chair with a rubber moulded seat. All these designs expressively exploited the intrinsic nature of the *substances* from which they were made, together with the nature of the processes by which they had been fabricated into objects. They were in no way determined by a preference for orthogonal order as was the case in the work of Rodchenko of around the same date – such as the aluminium tube and canvas chair that was designed at the Vkhutemas under his direction in 1926.

After the early Twenties, Tatlin's essential contribution becomes increasingly singular even if its precise nature is to remain highly ambiguous. Nothing is able to epitomize this ambiguity more exactly that the last significant work of this career: his *Letatlin* glider, upon which he worked more or less continuously from 1929 to 1932. Even the combination of the name Tatlin with the Russian verb to fly (*let*) recalls the neologistic games of

Khlebnikov. This work, plus his 1944 pamphlet on the construction of a moon for the stage,[20] summed up the essence of his mature sensibility which even his contemporaries characterized as a kind of 'technological Khlebnikovism'. In the pamphlet he stipulated that the 'moon' was not to be painted 'since its greatest value lies precisely in the actual metal as material'. Tatlin's final attempt – with his *Letatlin* – to evolve a new culture of form, whose content was to be as much a metaphor for a possibility, that is for an aspiration, as it was to be an object of rationally determined ends, is best exemplified in an interview he gave in 1932 to Kornely Zelinsky. On this occasion he said, 'I don't want people to take this thing as something utilitarian. I have made it as an artist. Look at the bent wings. We believe them to be aesthetically perfect. Or don't you think *Letatlin* gives an impression of aesthetic perfection? Like a hovering sea gull? Don't you think?' Zelinsky then questioned Tatlin about the working principle of the *Letatlin* and the response was, 'Like a glider. But my wing can produce three sorts of movement like a bird, apart from the tail ...'. Finally, when questioned as to its practical importance, Tatlin replied, 'The same as a glider. Has the proletariat no use for a glider? It is still too early to talk about future air bicycling when the actual apparatus has still not been tested ... But also I really want to emphasize the aesthetic side of the thing. Now art is going out into Technology.'[21]

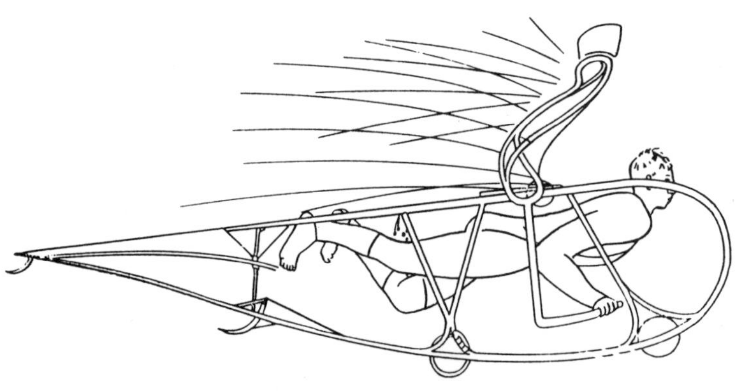

Vladimir Tatlin, design for Letatlin glider, 1929–32.

This all-pervasive notion of art going out into technology had already been formulated some 20 years earlier by one Alexander Malinovsky, otherwise self-styled as Bogdanov (the God-given) who between 1912 and 1932 published his theoretical text on the subject under the title *Tectology: The Universal Organizational Science*. As James Billington has remarked, 'This new super science of *tectology* was designed to provide a harmonious unity between the spiritual culture and the physical experience of the "working collective" in whose interest all science and activity were to be reorganized and all past culture reworked ...'. Billington continues, 'In the manner of Saint Simon rather than Marx, Bogdanov argued that the destructive conflicts of the past would never be resolved without a positive new religion: the undying role once played in society by a central temple of worship and religious faith must now be played by the living temple of the proletariat and a pragmatic, socially oriented philosophy of *empiriomonism*.'[22]

Armed with such a thesis the Bolshevik Bogdanov was to found the Proletcult movement or the Organization for Proletarian Culture as early as 1906, although, as Camilla Gray has pointed out, it was not to become an effective movement until the Revolution of 1917. We have little reason to doubt that Tatlin was as much influenced by this movement as he was by the sensibility of the Futurists, Khlebnikov and Kruchenykh. At all events the *Programme for the Productivist Group* reads like a Proletcult document, particularly in its itemization of future tasks. In ideological terms, it advocated the future application of all intellectual production to the building of a communist culture; in practical terms, it urged agitation and the establishment of contact with those productive centres which would realize 'the communistic forms of life in practice'. It concluded with a set of slogans which could have been derived from the arguments of Bogdanov: 'Down with art which only camouflages humanity's impotence. The collective art of the present is constructive life ...', etc.[23]

Despite this it was the Inkhuk 'Constructivists', namely Rodchenko, Stepanova, Alexi Gan and Liubov Popova, rather than Tatlin himself, who were to contribute directly to the agitatory culture of the Proletcult movement, for there remained something cryptic in Tatlin (the only pure Productivist) – a certain proto-dadaist sense of irony that postulated an all but useless utility. This attitude was fundamentally alien to the propagation of a collective art.

It was to be left to the artists of the '5 x 5 = 25' exhibition of 1921, that is, to the signatories of a declaration,[24] to forego all further easel painting, and to their colleagues Gladkov and Klutsis, to the architect Konstantin Melnikov and, finally, to the film-maker Dziga Vertov, to generate and sustain the agit-prop culture of the Proletcult movement; in the cause of which the purest pieces of Soviet 'production' art were to be achieved. It was these artists who created in accordance with the needs and realities of revolutionary production and who produced the Proletcult pamphlets, posters, kiosks, shelters, propaganda boats and trains of that heroic but relatively short-lived period known as War Communism. Theirs was a collective art of production in the purest sense: transformation of the irrational vitality of Kruchenykh into a new elemental language of form, one in which both the productional context and the societal purpose were self-evident in the forms themselves. We have only to look at the separate works of these artists to recognize the common 'elemental' attitude that they brought to their various productions, from Rodchenko's use of primitive wood-block lettering and printer's rules, linked in black, red and green, to Stepanova's elemental 'packing case' sets for Vesevold Meyerhold's bio-mechanical stage – in particular, her famous 'permutable' pieces for *The Death of Tarelkin* of 1922. These were expressly designed as obstacle devices upon which Meyerhold's actor–acrobats could finally display their dramatic and gymnastic talent.

Where Rodchenko exploited the given elements of the printing process to create the Constructivist mode of symmetrical typography (compare the asymmetry of Lissitzky's Suprematist–Elementarist approach), Stepanova, Popova, Exter, Gladkov and the architect Melnikov used standard timber scantlings as found, namely, the raw material as wrought from the mill, thereafter subjecting it to no further work other than the cross-cutting and fixing necessary to its final assembly. In both instances, minimum use was made of either high craft or advanced industrial technique. It was all run-of-the-mill production; the material components of a ready-made language to be readily converted into an art of the people. Everything depended on the imaginative juxtaposition of standard elements. This much was most simply demonstrated by Rodchenko, in his abstract structural compositions, all employing pieces of wood of exactly the same length. Finally, there lay behind all this agit-prop construction the great Russian vernacular for building out of undressed timber, the famous log cabin technology that rose to such vigorous and dramatic heights in the Carpathians; a mode of building that had been incorporated into Narodnik culture in the Abramtsevo museum built by the artists of the Mamontov colony in the 1880s.

Varvara Stepanova, bio-mechanical stage set for the play The Death of Tarelkin, *1922*.

In architecture the post-revolutionary 'Constructivist' impulse found itself initially restricted to exhibition design where, integrated with the typographic discourse of polemical display, it was able to produce works of exceptional quality; works which from the point of view of achieving the maximum effect with the minimum means have rarely been equalled. The stage designers Exter and Gladkov played a salient role in this development with their open-framed, wood-fretted Isvestia Tower, built for the Moscow Agricultural Exhibition of 1923, this being the first and almost the last occasion on which the 'Productivist–Constructivist' aesthetic was officially acknowledged. The Isvestia Tower was more than well-matched by the angular profiles of Melnikov's Makhorka Pavilion erected for the same occasion. The subtle counterboarded and battened components of this structure at once established Melnikov's unique style. Indeed nothing that Melnikov was to achieve in his later career – his workers' clubs of the late Twenties – was to equal his early structures in wood: his demountable Sukharyovka market erected in Moscow in 1924 and his pavilion and Gostorg annexe built for the USSR in Paris in 1925 for the Exposition des Arts Décoratifs.

Konstantin Melnikov, Makhorka Tobacco Pavilion, Moscow Agricultural Exhibition, 1923.

The part that Alexander Rodchenko played in this exhibition and his subsequent development as an artist serves to establish him as the most typical Productivist–Constructivist of his generation. In his elemental furniture and workers' club interiors for the 1925 exhibition, he revealed himself as a formalist of wood technique. This was never more so than in his red and black chess-playing suite which, given its intrinsic inflexibility, its astructural form and its general inconvenience, was more an elaborate metaphor for a revolutionary dialectic than a piece of utilitarian design. Nothing could be of greater contrast to this than the aluminium tube and canvas chair designed under his direction in the Vkhutemas in the following year, where all reference to formalist metaphor was to be abandoned in an attempt to design in accordance with Tatlin's 'cult of materials'.

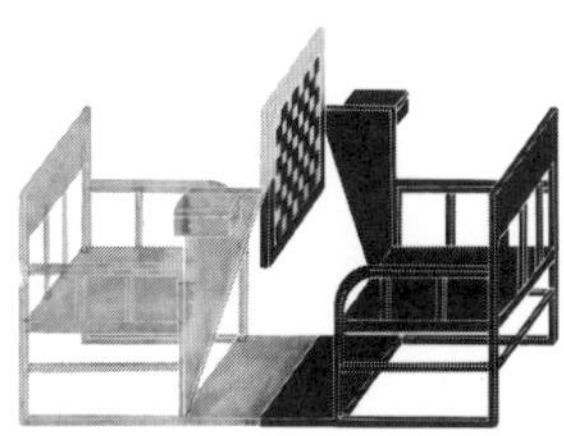

Alexander Rodchenko, chess-playing suite, Exposition des Arts Décoratifs, Paris, 1925.

Rodchenko by the mid-Twenties was already moving away from the abstract formalism of his work as a painter. This much is evident from his graphic designs of 1923 – his covers for *Kino-Fot* and for the Constructivist magazine *Lef*, and from his photomontage illustrations of the same year, to Mayakovsky's poem 'Pro Eto' ('About This'). The same rudimentary shift may also be seen in his titles for Dziga Vertov's documentary film *Kino Pravda*, dating from 1922. As a contemporary critic wrote in the first issue of *Lef*, in March 1923, 'Rodchenko approached these titles in a production spirit, treating them as part of the film itself, guided by its montage and scenario. In this *Kino Pravda* series he used three ideas: a heavy type thrown across the entire width of the screen; an encircling form and a moving title which progressively wrote itself on the film. With these methods the title ceased to be a dead part of the film and became an organic part of it.' The tendency to fuse typographic and cinematographic production at this time can hardly be ignored, and indeed one can see this as part of a more comprehensive impulse to shift all artistic production into either photographic or cinematic media. When it came to the penetration and dissemination of a revolutionary reality and discourse, the camera advanced itself as the natural channel for all forms of informational production. From photomontage to montage was but a step, and vice versa. So that Rodchenko's photomontage work for 'Pro Eto' simulated in a static media the dynamic maelstrom of colliding imagery which was to become the very essence of Vertov's masterpiece of 1929, *The Man with the Movie Camera*.

A more than parallel development took place in the theatre where, despite or even because of the success of the Proletcult stage and of Nikolai Evreinov's mass pageant programme, known as the 'theatricalization of everyday life', the theatre-as-circus or the theatre-as-reenactment began to gravitate towards its representation in film. While the anti-illusionism of Meyerhold's bio-mechanical stage could readily admit a certain injection of abstracted reality – as, for example, in Tretiakov's play *The Earth Uprears* where, to quote from a contemporary description, 'Over the bridge, which leads from the stage to the auditorium, motors and cycles rush continually ... The fury of war rages unfettered on the stage through the auditorium, through the foyer right out to the street ...'[25] – the theatre as a mode of discourse collapsed once it was projected with revolutionary fervour and naive temerity within a workaday proletarian reality. No one has written more frankly of the failure of this projection than Sergei Eisenstein, when of his own attempt to stage Tretiakov's play *Gas Masks* in the actuality of the Moscow gas works in 1924, he wrote:

Alexander Rodchenko, cover design for the magazine Lef, *1923.*

The turbines, the factory background, negated the last remnants of make-up and theatrical costumes, and all elements appeared as independently fused. Theatre accessories in the midst of the real factory plastics appear ridiculous. The element of 'play' was incompatible with the acrid smell of gas. The pitiful platform kept getting lost among the real platforms

Dziga Vertov, The Man with the Movie Camera, *1929; the split screen image implodes the collapsing Bolshoi theatre on itself.*

of labour activity. In short, the production was a failure . . . The cart fell to pieces and the driver dropped into the cinema.[26]

What then was this particular sensibility in its final essence; this 'Productivist' sensibility that gravitated progressively in its expressiveness towards typography, photography and film and in its creation of built form towards the exploitation of the intrinsic nature of material? In each case the old bourgeois media were either to be parodied or abandoned. New, scientific, highly generalized productive media and methods were to be embraced in their stead. Hence the classless and theoretically infinite discourse of the photograph triumphed spontaneously in the early years of the Soviet Union over the old aristocratic-cum-bourgeois media of easel painting, while the total fusion of actor and audience, Meyerhold's anti-illusionist ideal, presupposed an interpenetration of action and intensity in reaction that could only be finally achieved through the use of film.

To this end Dziga Vertov and his fellow film-makers, the so-called *Kinoks*, saw, in their manifesto *We* of 1919, that film was produced out of raw material; that it was in essence both physical and intellectual. It had to come into being through a sequence of conscious reflexes, just as a building or a newspaper is to be forged to comparable ends out of equally fundamental resources. Vertov wrote in the manifesto, 'Almost all art film workers were enemies of the *Kinoks*. This was normal; it meant they would have to reconsider their *métier*. *Kino-Pravda* was made with materials as a house is made of bricks.'

For Vertov, in film, montage was to be as much the imperative of constructive creation as it was for Rodchenko in his graphics and for Melnikov in his architecture. Thus he stated in his lecture 'Kino-Eye':

To make montage is to organize pieces of film, which we call frames, into a cine-thing. It means to write something cinematic with recorded shots. It does not mean to select pieces, to make 'scenes' (deviation of a theatrical character), nor does it mean to arrange pieces according to subtitles (devia-

tions of literary character). Every Kino-Eye *production is mounted on the very day that the subject (theme) is chosen, and this work ends only with the launching of the film into circulation in its definitive form. In other words, montage takes place from the beginning to the end of production.*[27]

For architecture this same principle was viable as long as the techniques involved (as in typography or photography) could be mastered and, more importantly, could be controlled by a limited number of people. As soon as this socio-technical control started to falter, that is, as soon as it ceased to be simple and ingenious, then Soviet architecture, for all its 'projected' brilliance in the Twenties, began to lose its essential orientation. For, by then, with its progressive fantasies about Chicago, and its simulation of the latest Western technique, it was sponsoring a utopian myth of modernity *per se*. It was no longer grounded in a comprehensive and technically comprehensible non-bourgeois culture. Instead, it launched itself into a largely unrealizable rhetoric of advanced technique; all glass facades, transparent bubbles, vast cantilevers and extravagant systems of spun wire suspension; all, at that time, well beyond the general technical and economic capacity of the Soviet Union. While Lissitzky was to write of the translucent Pravda project by the Vesnin brothers that 'All the accessories – which on a typical city street are usually tacked onto the building – such as signs, advertising, clocks, loudspeakers, and even the elevators inside, have been incorporated as integral elements of the design and combined into a unified whole. This is the aesthetic of Constructivism,'[28] he was not in himself interested in Constructivism in the Productivist sense.

Indeed the case could be made that the necessary shift in scale, imposed by the more consequential building tasks then confronting the Soviet Union, such as Dneiperstroi Dam, created circumstances in which it was no longer possible to sustain either the Constructivist–Productivist aesthetic of montage (Rodchenko, Melnikov, Dziga Vertov) or Tatlin's own *zaumny* 'cult of materials'. Advanced reinforced concrete construction on a vast scale was sufficient material cause for the frustration of both these impulses. For how can one reveal the explicit structural process of montage, the final essence of the pure Constructivist aesthetic, if half the material is irredeemably hidden and if the other half is cast as an undifferentiated plastic mass of rapidly coagulating material? By the same token, how can one express the intrinsic nature of a material, if the material itself is no longer natural, and hence in a special sense no longer knowable? Tatlin's bentwood constructions, his *Letatlin* for example, constituted a language inasmuch as they expressively revealed the familiar nature of wood. However, nothing, it seems, can be known, in an immediate sense, about the intrinsic nature of a synthetic material like reinforced concrete.

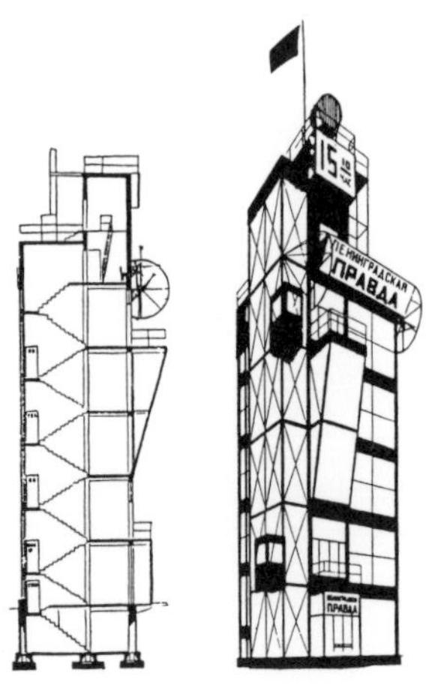

Alexander, Victor and Leonid Vesnin, Pravda Newspaper Building project, Moscow, 1923, section and axonometric.

While neither Rodchenko, Melnikov nor Dziga Vertov were to be solely preoccupied with the intrinsic nature of their materials as such, they were all to be deeply concerned with the revelation of the productive process. Thus

Rodchenko's graphic design reveals the relatively primitive nature of its 'pressed' mechanical reproduction on paper which manifestly is made out of shredded wood pulp. Here the production process was self-evident and became an intrinsic part of the aesthetic. Similarly Melnikov's early timber constructions, despite the fact that they were occasionally painted, were to announce, through their articulated assembly, their initial sawmill origin as standard scantlings of timber. By the same token, it could be argued that, by that date, the standard process of photography was already 'known' and that it now needed only to be handled through anti-illusionist cinematography to reveal both its own process and its relation to the process of life as a whole. Thus, as Annette Michelson has written:

Vertov's disdain of the mimetic, his concern with technique and process, with their extensions and revelation, stamp him as a member of the Constructivist generation. The shared ideological concern with the role of his art as the agent of human perfectibility, of a social transformation which issues in a transformation of consciousness in the most complete and intimate sense, the certainty of accession to the 'world of naked truth' are grounded in the acceptance, the affirmation of, the radically synthetic quality of film-making in the stylistics of montage.[29]

The revelation of the essential socio-cultural nature of productive synthesis through an explicit act of montage: this, perhaps, in the last analysis, was the essence of the 'Productivist–Constructivist' sensibility, a sensibility that depended upon a productive process of relative simplicity. Once this process became too complex then the sensibility could not be recovered. Thus the Dneiperstroi Dam could only be returned to Constructivism through the agency of Rodchenko's acute angled photographs published in the Thirties, in the official government publication entitled *USSR in Construction*. For the rest, as Berthold Lubetkin has written:

Dissarming itself by rejecting the whole of past architectural tradition, the (architectural) profession gradually lost all confidence in itself and in its social purpose. Those architects who were most honest with themselves drew their own conclusion from the worship of the engineer and the denial of all architectural tradition, and actually abandoned their profession to become building technicians, administrators and planners.

The disparity between the vision of a supercharged technique and the reality of a primitive and backward building industry, in which, more and more, idealized technology had to give way to ordinary ingenuity on a low level, led others to a hollow and insincere aestheticism, indistinguishable from that of the formalists they had set out to replace, inasmuch as they were forced to reproduce the adulterated forms of an advanced technique in the absence of its real media.[30]

This essay was originally a lecture presented at the Guggenheim Museum, New York in December 1972. It was first published in *Oppositions*, no.6, Autumn 1976, pp.25–44.

Louis Kahn and the French Connection

Architecture is the masterly, correct and magnificent play of masses brought together in light.
Le Corbusier, *Towards a New Architecture*, 1927[1]

Order is . . .
Design is form-making in order.
Form emerges out of a system of construction.
Louis Kahn, 1955[2]

Cret and French Rationalism

As far as the French 'connections' in Louis Kahn's career are concerned, the obvious point of departure is the French émigré Paul Philippe Cret, who was Kahn's professor in Philadelphia and taught at the University of Pennsylvania from 1903 to 1937. Cret professed the precepts of the Ecole des Beaux-Arts; that is to say, he taught according to the principles on which he himself had been raised in the atelier of Daumet–Esquié–Jaussely. Cret was committed to French Classicism and by and large worked within its constraints throughout his life. He delivered his credo to Dr Fiske-Kimball, director of the Philadelphia Museum of Art, when he wrote that 'classicism is a discipline which requires a certain humility, an abandonment of too much personality or "as we moderns put it" an abandonment of exasperated self-expression.'[3]

While Cret remained committed to the methods of the Ecole, he nonetheless saw Classicism as a tradition that was capable of further development. Above all he was attracted by the precepts of structural rationalism – by the theories of Viollet-le-Duc and the work of Henri Labrouste. This general concern is evident in an essay that he wrote in

Eugène Viollet-le-Duc, design for concert hall in stone, iron and brick, from Entretiens sur l'architecture, *vol. 2, 1872.*

1927, three years after Kahn had graduated, entitled 'The Architect as Collaborator of the Engineer'. Here Cret referred to Henri Labrouste, Anatole de Baudot and Le Corbusier in a text that seems to have been provoked by the English translation of Corbusier's *Vers une architecture*. Cret intimated that he had reservations about the structural rationalism practised by Viollet-le-Duc's acolytes, such as de Baudot, who attempted to derive the entire syntax of a building from structure and construction. Cret quoted the French critic Louis Dimier to the effect that 'the necessities of construction, even supplemented by what M de Baudot calls economic and social necessities, will never suffice to build an edifice. For of course these ideas have only a limiting and corrective value; they are not creative and fruitful. What is fruitful is the conception of form; it is design which emanates neither from geometry, nor from mechanics, but from the imitative arts.'[4]

While entertaining a respect for the syntactical precepts of structural rationalism, Cret was understandably sceptical about the capacity of construction to constitute the sole basis for formal order and cultural significance in architecture. The importance that Cret attached to precedent and imitation clearly had an influence on Kahn's early development. As Vincent Scully has written:

Kahn was trained in the Beaux-Arts manner to regard the buildings of the past as friends rather than as enemies, friends from whom one was expected, perhaps with more intimacy than understanding, to borrow... The young Kahn did not regard himself as a revolutionary. As a dutiful student he traced and adapted forms from archetypal academic books... The spaces of his student schemes are symmetrically made by solid structure and distinguished as to type by changes in structural scale...[5]

Cret's ambivalence toward both Viollet-le-Duc and his prime pupil, de Baudot, is sufficient to indicate that these rival theories were discussed at length by Cret during Kahn's education, and the unique nature of Kahn's mature work suggests that Cret's preoccupation with structural rationalism was to have a lasting impact on his career. For Kahn, as for Cret and Le Corbusier, the engineer was seen as having a unique role to play in the development of architectural form. What remained unclear, for Cret as for others, was the exact nature of this relationship. In the words of the slogan around which the thesis of *Vers une architecture* was organized, Cret was concerned as to the appropriate balance between 'The Engineer's Aesthetic and Architecture'.

In 'The Architect as Collaborator of the Engineer', Cret was to posit his own views about this relationship in terms that were quite close to the spirit of structural rationalism. That Cret's position was close without being identical seems to be evident from the following passage:

The entire mechanical unit must be intensely realized by the architect before he can endow it with character and significance – animate it so that it speaks to the imagination and stirs the emotions. Then he may begin his labors, mindful of the truth that Taine has noted – that strength and dignity of design are attained not by dissembling, but by emphasizing structural purpose. Furthermore, the mechanical restrictions themselves are not wholly inflexible and the mechanical solution is not necessarily arrived at independently of all aesthetic consideration. The mathematician, working to reconcile a number of mechanical conditions, may find not one, but several solutions – all equally adequate to meet the requirements. Obviously there arises a question of choice, which may be guided not by mechanical but by aesthetic considerations. Again, details, such as the shape and thickness of certain beams or the proportions between certain parts of the steel structure, which have no bearing on the mechanical adequacy, can be determined according to their relation to the architectural problem. Details – yes; because a fundamental change is not necessary to render a form significant, *but the knowledge that must be drawn on to effect these minor changes, so vital to the beauty of the whole, is gathered only by long training in aesthetics.*

Thus, the architect, collaborating with the engineer, finds that even in the construction of the framework itself he can exert an influence toward the architectural design that he is to develop. On the other hand, for him to evade the influence of the mechanical design would be a fatal step in the direction of defeating the whole aesthetic purpose. He cannot allow himself to forget, for instance, that the 'spirit' of a steel form is not the spirit of stone. In the middle of the last century Labrouste was among the first to realize this important canon of modern architecture and to experiment in designs peculiarly adapted to the strength and simplicity of the steel frame. The 'beauty of iron' is not the beauty of marble or granite. The cartouches and architectural mouldings of the stone vocabulary lose all meaning as the ornamentation of a metal form.[6]

Soon after his retirement from the university, Cret was to return to this theme, only this time he was to touch on other French connections that were also to be of consequence in Kahn's career. Thus we find him writing of architectural education in 1938:

If, as in some quarters, it is thought that construction methods are generating the forms without the intervention of aesthetic selection, there will be a tendency to increase the construction courses over those dealing with plastics and history. This is by no means a novelty. Functionalism (as we call it today) was the subject of the course given by Viollet-le-Duc to his students around 1865 and later summed up in his Entretiens. *In the same way, the return to simple geometric forms and volumes, the elimination of decoration, is a revival of the theories of Durand around 1803.*[7]

While all of this may appear somewhat incidental, I would like to make the case that Cret not only introduced his students to the work of Viollet-le-Duc, de Baudot, Labrouste and Durand, but that he also involved them in debating the oppositions that existed, at a theoretical level, between on the one hand the structural rationalism of Viollet-le-Duc and de Baudot, with their strong affinity for the Gothic, and on the other hand the classicism of Durand's permutative system, with its rather arbitrary method for combining facades with the modular fabric of the building itself. One may construe from his writing that Cret considered the rational, that is, the structural classicism of Henri Labrouste as the historical mediation between these two extreme aspects of French Rationalism. The Bibliothèque Sainte-Geneviève (1838–50) may be cited as the first demonstration of this mediation.

In any event, these figures appear as the theoretical protagonists to whom Kahn was introduced in his formative years at the University of Pennsylvania, and if one adds to this illustrious company Auguste Choisy, whose majestic *Histoire de l'Architecture* of 1899 Kahn frequently acknowledged as a major influence on his development,[8] one may gain some idea of the full range of French theorists who came to exert an influence on his development.

In this respect primacy must be given to J N L Durand and his *Précis des leçons données à l'école polytechnique*, if only because Durand's elementarist system of composition had become fully incorporated into the teaching the Ecole des Beaux-Arts by the time that Labrouste was a student. For all of Cret's categorization of Durand as a proto-functionalist, it is evident that Durand was not a functionalist in the neo-Gothic sense of the term, for patently he did not subscribe to any kind of 'form follows function' ideology. He posited the grids, enfilades, colonnades and elevations of his *Précis* as essentially empty elements that, if appropriately chosen and combined, could be arranged to accommodate an infinite variety of programmes. His system was open, not only in the sense that a large permutation of elements could be freely combined, but also in the sense that the vacuous generality of the space generated by this system could be brought to accommodate, in a 'loose fit', a wide variety of uses. However much it may have been modified in the interim, traces of this method are still detectable in the mature work of Kahn; his Jewish Community Centre project of 1954 is an early example of such an application.

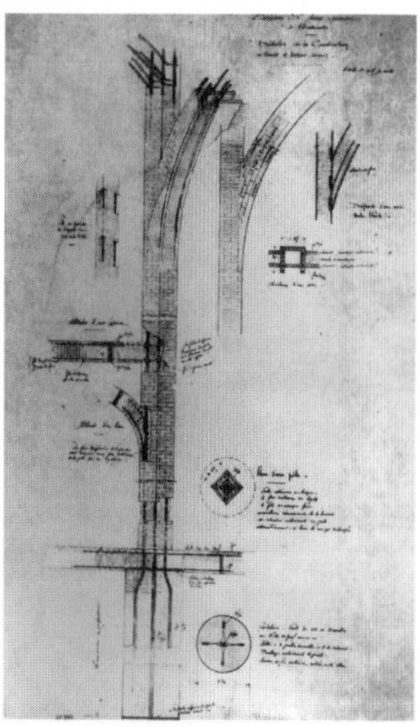

Anatole de Baudot, Saint Jean de Montmartre, Paris, 1894–1904, construction details showing the reinforcement of perforated brickwork with steel wires.

The second major French influence on Kahn was apparently Viollet-le-Duc and, in more specific terms, the work of Viollet-le-Duc's prime pupil, Anatole de Baudot. The main evidence we have for arguing that de Baudot influenced Kahn resides in the invention of *ciment armé* (reinforced concrete), which de Baudot perfected in collaboration with the engineer Paul Cottacin for the purposes of constructing the church Saint Jean de Montmartre, which was finally realized in Paris in 1904. When we look for the sources of Kahn's peculiar approach to structural form, we inevitably return to de Baudot as the sole architect of the turn of the century who anticipated Kahn's approach to the expression of structure.

In sum, there is evidence that, consciously or otherwise, Kahn assumed the full spectrum of the French rational–classical legacy, ranging from the methods of elementarist composition to the sublime preoccupations of the Greco–Gothic ideal. Most of this complex argument had, of course, been assimilated into the Beaux-Arts method, but unlike many other Americans who were educated in the Ecole, Kahn could not accept these complementary and contradictory principles without 'deconstructing' them; that is, he could not use them as a point of departure for his own architecture until he had reduced them to their origins. At the same time, unlike many of his contemporaries who had undergone a comparable training, he did not feel free to abandon the French discourse and simply embrace a modernist functionalism of the kind introduced into North America by Henry-Russell Hitchcock and Philip Johnson in their exhibition 'The International Style' of 1932. It is not that Kahn rejected international Constructivism out of hand, but that he remained dissatisfied with the way in which its elements were constituted. He seems to have sought an architechtonic authenticity that the *Neue Sachlichkeit* could not provide. In order to appreciate the degree to which Kahn launched himself on a life-long quest for architectonic elements of indisputable authority, it is necessary to touch on the French classical debate as this was handed down at the end of the century.

French Neoclassical theory

Cartesian doubt in architecture was first introduced by Claude Perrault,[9] who in his seventeenth-century treatise distinguished between *positive* and *arbitrary* beauty and relegated the Vitruvian orders to the culturally circumstantial. Perrault's controversial consigning of classical elements to the realm of the *arbitrary*, and his insistence that a positive and universal aesthetic could be predicated only on the conditions of *symmetry*, *richness of materials* and *precision of execution*, tended to deprive Classicism of the authority that had hitherto proved essential to its continuity. That this had the effect of throwing French classical culture into disarray is borne out by the strenuous efforts made by Jesuit intellectuals to re-establish the principles of classical architecture on the basis of certain specific elements that could be adduced hypothetically from nature. These intellectuals sought an architecture that would be capable through its constituent elements of bestowing the status of positive beauty on architectural form.

The Abbé de Cordemoy, who was the originator of the Greco–Gothic ideal, tried in his *Nouveau traité de toute l'architecture* of 1706 to combat the excesses of the Baroque by introducing the notion of fitness. He went so far as to argue that certain buildings should be rendered without any ornament whatsoever and warned against the inappropriate application of classical elements to utilitarian structures. At the same time, he insisted that the free-standing column, equally evident in the Greek temple and the Gothic cathedral, was the essence of pure architecture.

The essential element added by Laugier's *Essai sur l'architecture* of 1753 was to advance the authenticity of Greco–Gothic architecture on the grounds that it had been directly derived from nature and from man's interaction with nature. This is the significance of the 'pedimented' primitive hut that serves as the frontispiece to his *Essai*. After Cordemoy, Laugier argued that both Greek trabeated peristylar construction and Gothic freestanding columnar structure should be seen as being tectonically irreducible and hence as attaining the status of *positive beauty* in the sense that Perrault had intended the term. It is ideologically significant that J G Soufflot, in following Laugier's thesis, should attempt to build the pronaos and the peristyle of his Ste Geneviève church with the aid of the same 'reinforced' stone technology that Perrault had pioneered when building his classical peristyle on the east facade of the Louvre. This century-old will to antique form, sceptically embraced in the first instance and affirmatively reasserted in the second, was at variance with the principles of stone construction as these had evolved in Gothic architecture. In both the Louvre east facade and in the Ste Geneviève portico, the trabeated stone structure had to be extensively restrained by iron rods and cramps concealed within the interstices of the fabric. It is clear that this system came close to anticipating the invention of reinforced concrete, and 150 years later such reinforcement techniques were to become part of general concrete practice. In whatever form they appeared, these techniques were resisted by such architects as Viollet-le-Duc and de Baudot; the latter's particular recalcitrance seems to have stemmed from the fact that he not only opposed classical form but also rejected the technical advantages of monolithic building technology, which for him meant reinforced concrete. Instead of the Hennebique system, universally available by 1896, de Baudot employed perforated brick and brick arches and pillars. These delicate filigree elements were held in place by a dense cement in-fill and a thin wire reinforcement, which penetrated the perforated brick fabric like ligaments. In other words, he invented and employed a system that could only result in the production of structurally taut and expressive elements, comparable to those found in Gothic culture. These elements could be perceived as being determined to an equal degree by gravity (i.e. natural force) and the process of fabrication. In analysing the structure of St Jean de Montmartre, one is forced to conclude that something close to de Baudot's precepts was assumed by Kahn, although evidently Kahn did not feel it necessary to reject totally the advantages of reinforced concrete.

Louis Kahn and structural monumentality

Viollet-le-Duc must be held to account for Kahn's early preoccupation with Gothic structure and perhaps above all for his assimilation of the structural and aesthetic concepts of R Buckminster Fuller. Fuller, somewhat like Viollet-le-Duc, clearly intended that a new architecture should be based exclusively on the principles of empirical science and the laws of nature; that is to say, he unconsciously assumed the challenge of Perrault in the most literal way possible. Without ever citing Viollet-le-Duc, Fuller seems to have been equally committed to the precept that 'as to reasoning, we are able to distinguish sophistry from demonstration by verifying the conclusion experimentally and practically. This was the reason of those men in the Middle Ages, the builders of edifices which we in our days sometimes admire, but with which we are so little acquainted.'[10] In this passage, taken from the *Entretiens* of 1872, Viollet-le-Duc approvingly cites Roger Bacon for his advocacy of a system based upon *method*, *examination* and *experiment*.

It is one of the ironies of modern architectural history that the World War II impulse toward monumentality, which arose in part out of the manifesto 'Nine Points on Monumentality' (issued in 1943 by Sigfried Giedion, J L Sert and Fernand Léger) should have brought Kahn to adopt a Baconian stance in his contribution to Paul Zucker's symposium on monumentality held in 1944, given under the misleading title 'New Architecture and City Planning'.[11] Kahn approached the problem of monumentality in an extremely unorthodox way. Above all he seems to have sensed that an authentic monumentality could only be achieved with elements whose tectonic authority was indisputable. Thus we find him writing, 'Monumentality in architecture may be defined as a quality, a spiritual quality inherent in a structure which conveys the feeling of its eternity ...'.[12] While referring in this context to the Parthenon, he nonetheless went on to place the burden of monumentality on the constituent structural elements. Thus in citing the Gothic cathedral he could write, 'Our architectural monuments indicate a striving for structural perfection which has contributed in a great part to their impressiveness, clarity of form, and logical scale.'[13] Immediately afterwards Kahn analysed the decadence of modern engineering in the following terms:

The I-beam is an engineering accomplishment deriving its shape from an analysis of the stresses involved in its use . . . The shape adapted itself to the ease of rolling . . .

Safety factors were adopted to cover possible inconsistencies in the composition of the material of manufacture. Large-scale machinery and equipment needed in its fabrication led to standardization.

The combination of safety factors (ignorance factor, as one engineer termed it) and standardization narrowed the practice of engineering to the selection of members from handbooks recommending sections much heavier than calculations would require and further limited the field of engineering expression, stifling the creation of the more graceful forms which the stress diagrams indicated.[14]

At this juncture Kahn was to follow Cret almost to the letter in recommending that the architect and engineer should collaborate in the evolution of authentic forms, which were to be derived empirically from the scientific principles of statics rather than from the mere convenience of production and fabrication.[15] On the other hand, he was again to follow Cret in taking his distance from any simple-minded determinism. Thus he categorically denied that monumentality can be adduced scientifically or that it should be the only aim of the architectural endeavour.

Kahn clarified his basic thesis in a sequence of illustrations, the first of which was an *esquisse* derived from Auguste Choisy's rendering of the structure of Beauvais Cathedral. This was followed by a series of giant space frames, projected by Kahn as being built out of welded tubular steel. The text explicating these illustrations condensed an attitude that was to remain with Kahn throughout the rest of his career:

Beauvais Cathedral needed the steel we have. It needed the knowledge we have. Glass would have revealed the sky and become a part of the enclosed space framed by an interplay of exposed tubular ribs, plates and columns of a stainless metal formed true and faired into a continuous flow of lines expressive of their stress patterns. Each member would have been welded to the next to create a continuous structural unity worthy of being exposed because its engineering gives no resistance to the laws of beauty having its own aesthetic life.[16]

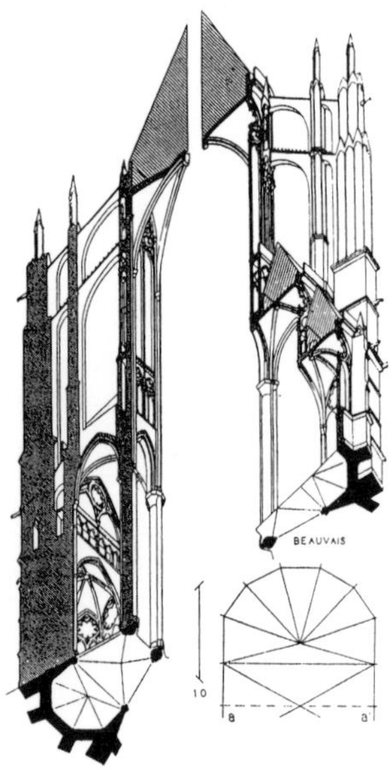

Auguste Choisy, analysis of Beauvais Cathedral, from Histoire de l'Architecture, *1889, axonometric.*

While these concluding words might have even come from Perrault, Kahn's attitude to structure in this illuminating passage is equally close to both Viollet-le-Duc and Fuller. Both men were patently a decisive influence in the remarkable space-frame project for Philadelphia City Hall, which Kahn designed in collaboration with Ann Tyng in 1954. On this occasion he wrote in terms that the French master of neo-Gothic theory would have found decidedly sympathetic:

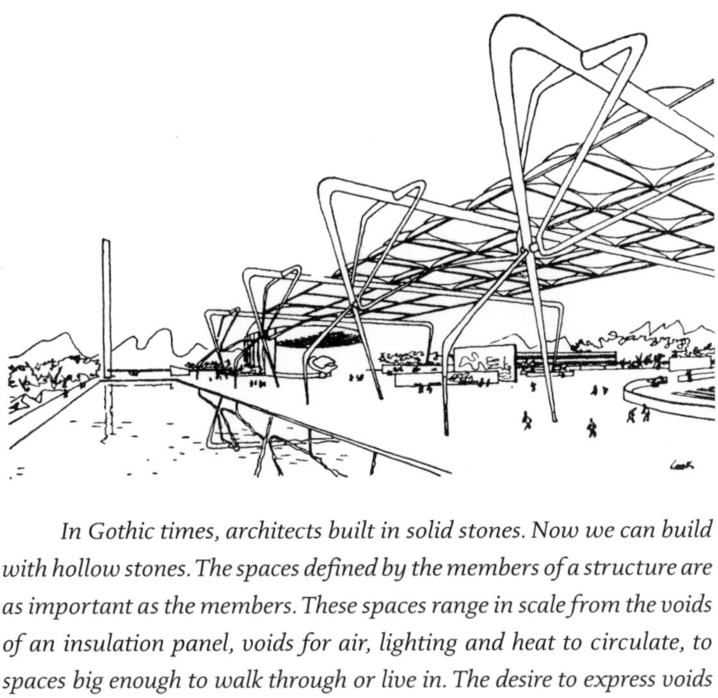

Louis Kahn, space-frame project for an exhibition, 1954.

In Gothic times, architects built in solid stones. Now we can build with hollow stones. The spaces defined by the members of a structure are as important as the members. These spaces range in scale from the voids of an insulation panel, voids for air, lighting and heat to circulate, to spaces big enough to walk through or live in. The desire to express voids positively in the design of structure is evidenced by the growing interest and work in the development of the space frames. The forms being experimented with come from a closer knowledge of nature and the outgrowth of the constant search for order. Design habits leading to the concealment of structure have no place in this implied order. Such habits retard the development of art. I believe that in architecture, as in all art, the artist instinctively keeps the marks which reveal how a thing was done.[17]

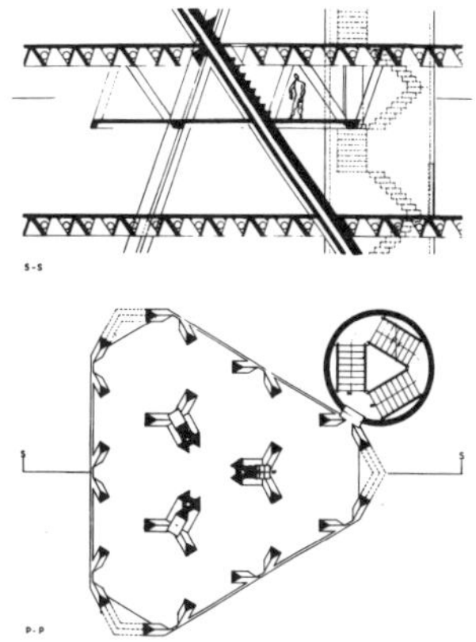

Louis Kahn and Ann Tyng, City Tower Project, Philadelphia, 1957, section and plan detail.

There is yet a third Frenchman whose influence lies behind Kahn's work of the mid-Fifties. This is Robert Le Ricolais, and while he never collaborated with Kahn in his capacity as an engineer, he nonetheless remained a close associate of Kahn's throughout the latter's tenure as professor of the Master's class in the architecture school of the University of Pennsylvania. Like Kahn, Le Ricolais was a structural visionary whose experimental work was close in certain respects to the position expounded by Fuller.

Yet despite his evident affinity with the structural determination of Fuller and Le Ricolais, Kahn clearly believed that a significant architectural culture could not be predicated on this alone, and hence, as Marcello Angrisani has shown in his essay 'Louis Kahn and History',[18] Kahn welcomed the re-emergence of the architectural typologies of the French Enlightenment as these were restored to public attention by Emil Kaufmann's *Three Revolutionary Architects: Boullée, Ledoux, and Lequeu*, conveniently published in Philadelphia in 1952 by the American Philosophical Society.[19] Angrisani argues that three projects from Kahn's hand in the mid-Fifties reveal immediately the extent to which he had been influenced by the Kaufmann publication. These projects are the Yale Art Gallery (1951–3), the

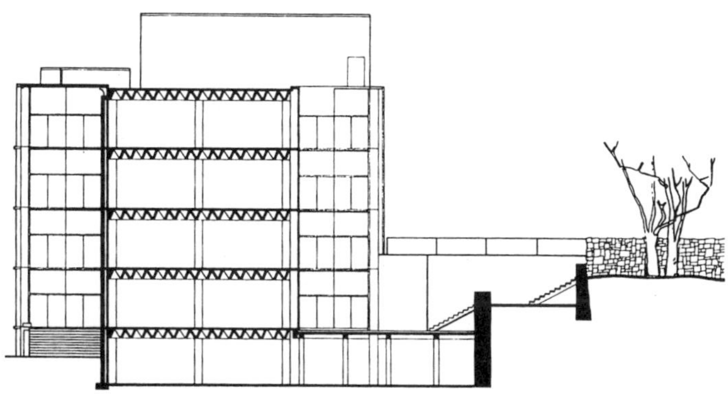

Louis Kahn, Yale Art Gallery, New Haven, Connecticut, 1951–3, cross-section.

Jewish Community Center Bath House in Trenton (1954) and the Adath Jeshurun Synagogue project for Elkins Park (1954). Of the last of these projects Angrisani observes:

The planimetric image of the synagogue is fundamentally embodied by the inscription of an equilateral triangle in a circle . . . and in the two other projects the triangle is an unusual form which draws attention to itself by virtue of the fact that it is largely absent from the figurative conceptions of modern architecture. It is to be found in the entrance hall of

Kahn's Samuel Radbill hospital of 1953 . . . and in the art gallery in one of the two interior staircases, in a cylindrical cage, which encloses three equilateral stair runs. But in these cases the geometric figure does not generate the plan of the entire building, as opposed to the Elkins Park synagogue and the project by C N Ledoux for the Hôtel Saint-Marceau.[20]

Some idea of the method adopted by Ledoux and Kahn may be gained from Laugier's *Essai sur l'architecture*, where he writes:

No doubt at all, it is easy to erect over the plan of an equilateral triangle a church which will look most attractive. This is how I would set about it. I inscribe in the triangle a circle that gives me the outline of a dome which I let rise from the ground. At the three angles I construct three rotundas which give me three sanctuaries where I place three altars. In the center of each of the three facades I make an opening for a door, which produces three entrances each having an altar facing them.[21]

On the typological and liturgical consequences of such a design Laugier is at pains to refrain from comment.

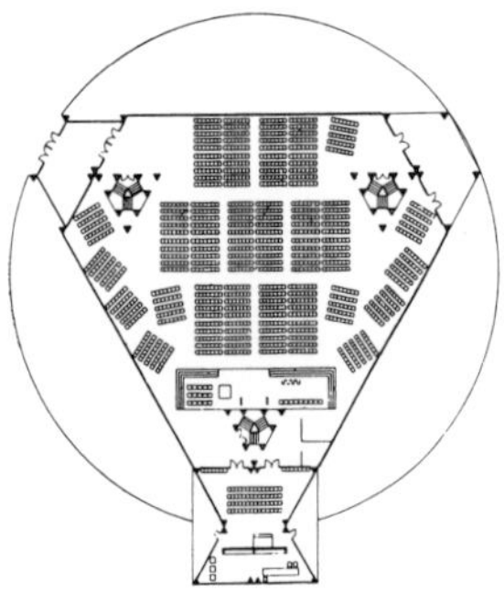

Louis Kahn, Adath Jeshurun Synagogue project, Elkins Park, Pennsylvania, 1954, second floor plan.

It is clear that the Trenton Bath House and the Elkins Park Synagogue were the first of Kahn's projects to display in a striking way that functionally arbitrary play with geometrically absolute form common to both Kahn and Ledoux. In both instances it is as though we are witnessing a procedure repeated through a long trajectory of history in which the initial Cartesian undermining of antique form by Perrault could only be overcome by adducing the positive beauty of Euclidean form. Aside from his 1956 project for a pyramidal library building for Washington University, the Trenton Bath House was surely the most totally *illuministe* work that Kahn was ever to realize. This much is evident from the formal similarity linking this modest shelter to both Ledoux's cannon foundry and Boullée's numerous proposals for pyramidal cenotaphs. A comparable Ledolcian connection is also present in Kahn's initial project for the First Unitarian Church in Rochester of 1959, which was evidently based on the Enlightenment game of enclosing a circle in a square, only to enclose it in another square in its turn. Angrisani cites in this connection Ledoux's De Witt house project, which was prominently illustrated in the Kaufmann study of 1952.

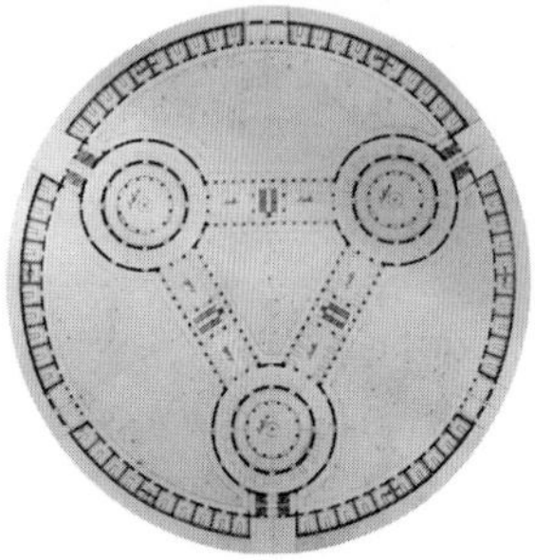

Claude-Nicolas Ledoux, project for Hôtel Saint-Marceau, c.1785, plan.

However, none of this should be regarded as being evidence of any direct imitation of Ledoux, above all because in all of these works Kahn seems to have depended if not on de Baudot then certainly on Viollet-le-Duc for the methods according to which he determined the structural elements that would embody and enrich these lucid but arbitrary geometric schemes. Kahn set about reinterpreting the Ledolcian influence in structurally rationalist terms. At the same time, as Angrisani points out, Kahn took the 'revolutionary' rejection of the classical elements and the Baroque principle of *concatenation* as archetypal points of departure for his own work. What for Ledoux and Boullée had been a daring rejection of the teachings of J F Blondel, by virtue of predicating monumental and institutional form on relatively empty and non-hierarchical Platonic permutations, was for Kahn a necessary stand against the ahistorical 'void' of the modern epoch.

It was this that separated Kahn from the vulgar historicizing and monumental rhetoric of his American contemporaries, that is, from the expression of the New Monumentality as this appeared in the work of Eero Saarinen, Philip Johnson, John Johansen and even Wallace Harrison. For Kahn, 'historicist' monumentally meant an orientation toward the underlying structure of traditional forms. Thus he remained committed to transforming these forms rather than reducing them to the status of being mere references that made rather obvious allusions to historical precedents, and it may well be that it is this subtle distinction that accounts for his eclipse from current discourse.

Both Kahn and Ledoux were brought to confront a situation in which the traditional institutions had not only largely been overrun by unprecedented societal structures, but also the rules for representing such monumental institutions had lost their 'natural' authority. As Angrisani remarks, 'Ledoux's simple geometrical forms were able to assume the social and political problem, providing his egalitarian conception became transcendent and was able to establish itself as a symbol.'[22]

It must be admitted, of course, that the French Enlightenment was by no means the only source of Kahn's characteristic forms. Above all, cognizance has to be taken of the primary importance of Frank Lloyd Wright, who clearly remained a distant but seminal influence on both the First Unitarian Church designed for Rochester and the Richards Laboratories built for the University of Pennsylvania in 1961. It is obvious that Wright's Unity Temple and Larkin Building, both completed in 1904, are fundamental points of departure for these early works of Kahn. Rochester seemingly takes its square theme from the Unity Temple, while the shaft and service structure adopted in the Larkin Building is patently the precedent for formulating the Richards Laboratories as a series of 'served' laboratory towers suspended within a 'servant' latticework of structural piers and masonry service ducts. At this date Kahn had yet to embrace fully the Wrightian strategy of rendering all civic institutions as introspective public realms that, housed in massive structural piers and ducts, establish a more or less hermetic interior, one which is pierced only by architectonic slots for the subtle filtration of both space and light. But the precedent for, say, the Salk Institute or the library at the Phillips Exeter Academy or for the Hurva Synagogue is patently already there in the Larkin Building, and the case can be made, given Wright's evident facility with Beaux-Arts compositional methods (the Durandesque tartan grid, and so forth), that this introspective paradigm also ultimately came, at least in part, from the same source – namely the neoclassicists of the Enlightenment. It has surely been noted before that Ledoux and Boullée projected their public institutions as massive introspective forms.

However, that which Kahn seems to have taken from the Enlightenment – and which Wright strictly left alone – was the possibility of deconstructing classical Roman elements to such a point that they became nothing more than thin tensile screens (empty shells of their origins, so to speak), devices that could be used to simulate the presence of an absent mass and could readily serve to engender a series of buildings within buildings. These manneristic possibilities were perhaps never more evident than in the empty arch screens employed by Ledoux to embody his *Maison destinée à deux artistes*, a ploy that Kahn emulated with far greater subtlety in his community centre projected for the Salk Institute in La Jolla or in many of his works that were finally built in Pakistan.

Louis Kahn, Salk Institute, La Jolla, California, 1959–65, screen wall.

Yet unlike Ledoux, Kahn invariably rendered these empty screens as structural rationalist episodes whose authority resided in the materiality of their tectonic syntax. On the basis of elements such as these Kahn seems to have aspired to an 'order in design' which would rise above the decorative and eclectic historicism of his contemporaries.

The other Enlightenment figure who unquestionably had a lasting impact on Kahn was Piranesi. As Vincent Scully has pointed out, Piranesi's map of Rome was accorded a place of honour above Kahn's desk throughout his mature career, and it seems that Piranesi was the essential catalyst that enabled Kahn to synthesize two otherwise irreconcilable aspects of his art: on the one hand, his constant preoccupation with the technical and tectonic authority of the constituent elements from which building had to be compounded – the ducts and piers of service and support; on the other, the capacity to combine and recombine the ruined fragments of a lost heroic past – ruined both by time and by the delirium of imagination – and to posit these fragments, recomposed *en miettes*, as viable models for a disjunctive future.

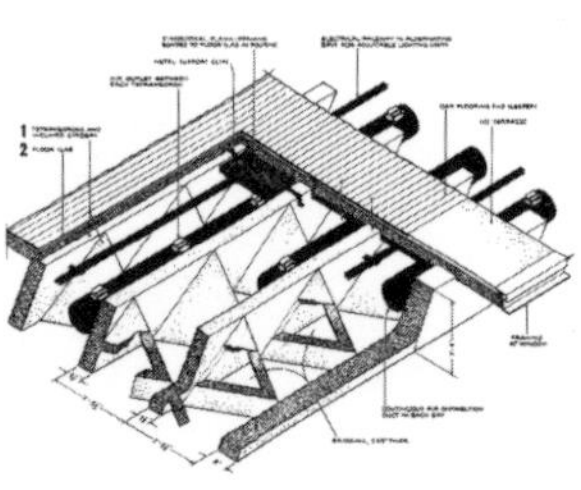

Louis Kahn, Yale Art Gallery, 1951-3, air distribution system woven between the tetrahedral elements of the diagrid floor.

Thus Kahn's work presents us with two complementary yet utterly opposed principles. The first is categorically anti-progressive and asserts the presence of a collective abstract architectural memory in which all valid compositional types are eternally present in their disjunctive purity. The second principle is vehemently progressive and pursues the renovation of architectural form on the basis of advanced technique. It seems that Kahn believed that this second principle, as it responded to new tasks and uses, would be able to lead, when combined with the first, to an appropriate architectural expression, resynthesizing fresh poetic and institutional values in terms of concrete form.

In the last analysis these two principles seem to correspond exactly to Kahn's distinction between *Form* and *Order*, as Francesco Tentori was to point out in his essay 'Order and Form in the Work of Louis Kahn'.[23] Kahn himself made the 'progressive-tectonic' principle explicit when he wrote that 'form comes from the system of construction and the structural elements inherent in them'. Order, on the other hand, he appears to have envisaged as the institutional matrix by which the overall pattern of the work comes into being.[24] In some instances this order could be typologically determined, as in the case of the Hurva Synagogue or the Rochester church. In other cases Kahn resorted to geometrical permutations reminiscent of the compositional strategies of French Neoclassicism.

Apart from these multiple links to the French rationalist line, there remains in all this the perplexing question as to why this unexpected rejection of the functionalist paradigm should make its most abrupt appearance in the United States rather than elsewhere, and the related issue as to why it should be formulated by Kahn in terms of the monumentalization of structure.

It is altogether easier to tackle the second question rather than the first and to speculate as to the reason that Kahn predicated his notion of monumentality in terms of structural form. Clearly Kahn sought to compile his buildings out of well-defined constituent elements whose tectonic authority would be unimpeachable and whose phenomenological presence would be equal to the archetypal building forms of the antique world – to the athletic massiveness of the Roman arch and to the sublimely tapered cylindricality of the Doric column. At the same time, as a post-Cartesian, Kahn sought to reveal these elements in terms of the static forces of nature, as these may be manifested through a syntactic articulation of the constructional process – a 'scientific' verification that would have been impossible in terms of the configuration of the building as a whole. There is, then, a division between *Form* and *Order* in Kahn's work, that is to say, between the constituent elements of a structure (Form) and its 'typological' configuration as an institution (Order). At the same time, the third term in Kahn's exegetic discourse, namely *Design*, is conceived as a mediatory procedure whose role in architectural practice is to reconcile the empirical demands of society with the universal structuring capacity of Form and the specific configuration of Order. While Kahn conceived of Form as being compounded out of structural elements, he also saw it as having a phenomenological presence. Thus he wrote:

Design is a circumstantial act. It is a battle with the nature of man, with the nature of nature, with the laws of nature, with the rules of man, and with principles. One must see all this to put it into being. Design is a material thing. It makes dimensions. It makes sizes. Form is a realization of the difference between one thing and another, a realization of what characterizes it. Form is not design, not a shape, not a dimension. It is not a material thing. In other words, form is really what *and design is* how.[25]

Aside from those subjective issues that rarely respond to enquiry, the reason that this phenomenological and disenchanted 'afunctionality' should make its appearance in America rather than elsewhere is perhaps to be explained by the perennial frontier conditions obtaining in the cultural ethos and socio-psychology of the United States: the fact that North America has always felt itself to be on the frontier, not only because of the progressive thrusts that it has always made into the future (its progressive edge extending from ruthless colonization to technological advance), but also because of its ever-receding frontier of an abandoned culture and history, which by definition was the condition of its foundation. While in the late nineteenth and early twentieth centuries this ontological loss was compensated for by the triumphant academicism of the Ecole des Beaux-Arts and by the innumerable stylistic raids made by the purveyors of high-class kitsch upon traditional European culture – the pastiche Gothic university, convent and cathedral and the endless proliferation of Stockbrokers' Tudor – the more sensitive American architects invariably recognized that this tradition could not be replicated and that the United States would eventually have no choice but to create a transhistorical culture of its own. And while this painful awareness is even detectable in the displaced Palladianism of Thomas Jefferson, it is all the more evident in the heroic programme of H H Richardson's Romanesque style, and it is this oscillating legacy that re-emerges in a transmuted form in the successive careers of Louis Sullivan, Wright and Kahn – oscillating in the sense that Richardson and Wright represent its positive pole and Sullivan and Kahn its negative one. As Maria Bottero has written in her essay 'Organic and Rational Morphology in the Work of Louis Kahn':

I think that the meaning and importance of the architecture and thought of Louis Kahn rises between the two opposite poles of American organicism and European rationalism, like a glowing lamp. The Beaux-Arts aspect which has so long been discussed and accepted as a main element characterizing and determining his work seems to me only secondary and incidental – in any event, in no way central to the real historical meaning that his work has taken on for us.

This meaning lies in the new ambiguous dimension, in the difficult coexistence of past and present, synchronous and diachronic, measurable and immeasurable, that Kahn has managed to achieve, opening a breach in the closed circuits of Wright's organicism and European rationalism. In themselves alone, these two experiences, these two approaches, so coherent and conclusive, to architectural dialectics are no longer fruitful: there is no valid school of Wright, and European rationalism has slipped into the commercialism of the 'International Style.'[26]

The heroic and tragic destiny of Sullivan within this historical trajectory – his ultimately unsuccessful effort to render the tall office building in a manner that would redeem it as a cultural form – is surely the spiritual and historical challenge against which Kahn's own career is to be assessed. It is painfully obvious from the two extant facades of the Guaranty Building in Buffalo that Sullivan sought to turn a commercial exigency into an occasion for a monumental presence, for a form that would be comparable to the finest achievement of Assyrian or Islamic culture. This fact no doubt accounts for the delirious tattoo-like decoration, that is, for Sullivan's determination to impregnate the surface and (by implication) the body of the building with the quintessence of culture. That the speculative and technical forces which determined this building's existence were indifferent to the intentions of culture was not lost on Sullivan, who remained acutely aware of this pathetic suspension, like Herman Melville's heroes, upon a tide of development that was totally oblivious to the destiny of man.

With Kahn, as Bottero suggests, we pass from Sullivan's romantic anguish to Kahn's stoic recognition that the possibility for a 'consequential, temporal participation' does not exist. With great acuity Bottero writes:

Moreover, the Beaux-Arts forms of his architecture have a very precise figurative function, and bear witness to his particular creative process, which disregards actual and legitimate temporal sequences and is always ready for slips of the memory, and that mysterious selection of form, which is all the more mysterious in that the form rises out of a submerged world. This explains the widespread prejudice that Louis Kahn's architecture is academic, monumental, and historically out of context.

In reality the arches, squares, cylinders, skylights, exedrae and symmetrical axes which spring from this architecture in ever richer and more complex ways give rise, once they are realized, to fragile and powerful simulacra of the discontinuous and the non-homogeneous, of what is ours and at the same time what is not. The clean-cut surfaces of the walls are slim diaphragms, the flexible and unconventional use of which creates a continuous interplay of light and shade – highly refined and complex filters of the energy field of light; but the light relayed from these surfaces is an unreal light, une lumière 'autre'. *The more intelligent and pertinent the use of Design and appropriate the choice of materials, perfect the technique of execution and detail, meticulous the expression of all the static forces involved, the more the measurable enters the realm of the immeasurable, and from what is physically and tangibly present, from surfaces, cracks, holes and pools of light, it blows like a metaphysical weightless breeze – without the weight of earthly gravity … but in return, laden with allusions to mnemonic depth and dimension and to everything that this architecture, in its fragile, contingent, physical, and almost miraculous equilibrium 'is not'.*

What it 'is', in fact, one can always define as the product – temporary, fleeting, as limited as you may wish – of everything it 'is not', of this immeasurable and vast force which presses on and continually urges new events. In this sense, and almost reversing the terms of the problem, Kahn's architecture recovers the sense of history and reproposes the basic theme of Sullivan's aesthetics …

But in Kahn, the finite–infinite dichotomy has another meaning which in no way implicates Sullivan's vital dynamism towards a formal–formative end. He, on the contrary, proposes modern cognitive space, in which (after filtering through European rationalism) the subjective and individual can be realized only by limiting, denying, decentralizing itself; but in which … the assumption of subjective finitude … brings up for examination once more the synchronous and logical classifications of rationalism, pointing from behind its fragile, immobile and provisional screen at the dark and blind forces of change in progress and the inevitable erosion of time.[27]

In Kahn a number of strands converge in a transhistorical figure who, subliminally or otherwise, inherits not only the oscillating 'organicism' of the American experience, but also the loss of centre – the *Verlust der Mitte*, to quote the title of Hans Sedlmayr's seminal work – that lies beneath the apparent certainty of European rationalism. This moment of avant-gardist doubt seems to be caught between the delirium of an imagined archaeology (Piranesi) and the arbitrary play of utopian institutional form (Ledoux), or to put it more specifically, by way of Kahn's own terminology, between the Form of a mythic past and the Order of an equally mythic future. Like the Enlightenment architects and like Mies van der Rohe, to whom his work is almost inversely related, Kahn sought refuge from this latent anguish in the transcendental immanence of light, in Mies's *beinähe nichts* or in Boullée's deistic vista of an endlessly cavernous interior irrigated by light – his Métropole of 1783 – or in Ledoux's project for the director's house in his Ville Idéale de Chaux at Arc-et-Senans of 1775. Kahn was patently inspired by Le Corbusier's famous aphorism, with which this text begins, when he wrote in his essay 'Form and Design' of 1960:

Even a space intended to be dark should have just enough light from some mysterious opening to tell us how dark it really is. Each space must be defined by its structure and the character of its natural light. Of course I am not speaking about minor areas which serve the major spaces. An architectural space must reveal the evidence of its making by the space itself. It cannot be a space when carved out of a greater structure meant for a greater space because the choice of a structure is synonymous with the light which gives image to that space. Artificial light is a single tiny static moment in light and is the light of night and never can equal the nuances of mood created by the time of day and wonder of the seasons.[28]

Here we have the fundamental concept that seems to link Kahn to neoclassical rationalism and to permit him to escape the perceptual limits of Platonic form: above all the Greco–Gothic notion of structure as the essential mediator of light. However, for Kahn, as for the Enlightenment architects, the presence of light had deistic connotations. This is evident from the following passage, in which light is seen as having an omnipresent character, as being an essence that is present in the mind even when it is absent from material reality:

When a man says that he believes that natural light is something we are born out of, he cannot accept a school which has no natural light. He cannot even accept a movie house, you might say, which must be in dark-

ness, without sensing that there must be a crack somewhere in the construction which allows enough natural light to come in to tell how dark it is. Now he may not demand it actually, but he demands it in his mind to be that important.[29]

This aphoristic passage would account for the cut that severs the generic vault in his last masterwork – the vault-cum-folded plate that forms the roof of the Kimbell Museum, where a 'silver light' permeates the inner surface of a paraboloid shell in order to indicate how dark it is.

First published in *Oppositions*, no.22, 1980, pp.20–53.

Maison de Verre as Bachelor Machine

In the Maison de Verre, Paris, designed in collaboration with Bernard Bijvoet and under design and construction from 1928 to 1932, Pierre Chareau's penchant for combining 'art deco' furnishings with machinist interiors was brought to a heightened intensity which seemed to reinforce Adolf Loos's earlier insistence that furniture should never be designed by architects but rather created by craftsmen and arranged by the client according to his taste. Loos claimed that the influence of the architect should not extend beyond permanent fixtures. Chareau could accept responsibility for both sides of this argument, because he was, in a sense, at one and the same time, craftsman and architect. Does this account for the way in which the Maison de Verre seems to be capable of adapting to different types of furniture without compromising its technical and architectural syntax in any way? It is as if this house was suffused with some kind of benevolent aura capable of assimilating stylistically different works – an antique dining table with matching chairs, a lounge suite by Chareau, a decorative tapestry by Jean Lurçat – without its overall technical character being compromised or contradicted.

It is necessary to recount the unusual circumstances which prevailed at the time of the house's construction. In 1928, Madame Dalsace's father bought an eighteenth-century *hôtel particulier* in Paris, at 31 rue Saint Guillaume. The site was enclosed on all sides by party walls of varying heights. Besides the three-floor *hôtel particulier* it comprised a forecourt and a garden to the rear. The clients intended to demolish the existing building and build from scratch, but the presence of a protected tenant on the second floor obliged clients and architect to envisage another solution. Out of this came the decision to underpin the second floor with steel and

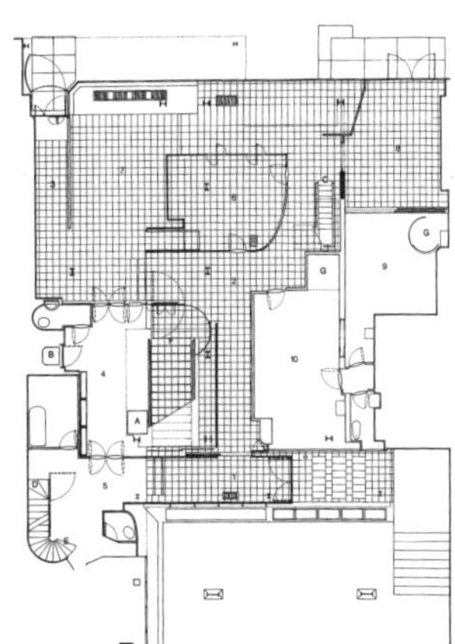

Pierre Chareau and Bernard Bijvoet, Maison de Verre, ground floor plan: 1) entrance; 2) main corridor; 3) corridor to garden; 4) servants' quarters; 5) tradesmen's entrance; 6) reception; 7) waiting room; 8) consulting room; 9) examination room; 10) surgery.

to demolish the unoccupied floors beneath, keeping only the existing access stair. The resulting volume was sufficiently spacious to make room for three new floors of normal height, each level being set aside for a different purpose: the first floor for the practice of medicine; the second floor for daily living; and the third for sleeping quarters. A narrow service wing of three floors was built as an extension on one side of the forecourt to house the kitchen, workroom, maid's room, etc. Once this idea had been perfected and the steel frame erected, all that was needed was to enclose the house in a protective envelope and to furnish the interior. Dr Dalsace was to write of this arrangement on the completion of the house in the following terms:

In order to spare an old lady who didn't want to leave her dingy second-floor apartment, Pierre Chareau has performed the extraordinary feat of building three floors full of light, in the ground and first floor of a small hôtel particulier*...The light circulates freely through this block, the first floor of which is devoted to medicine, the second floor to social life and the third to nighttime privacy. The problem this raised was enormously difficult to resolve. Interconnecting rooms, certain of which occupy two floors, make the problem of soundproofing very difficult...The first floor, the professional section of the building, facilitates work and, with their initial uneasiness, calms the patients down considerably. The whole house has been created under the influence of friendship, in complete affectionate understanding.*[1]

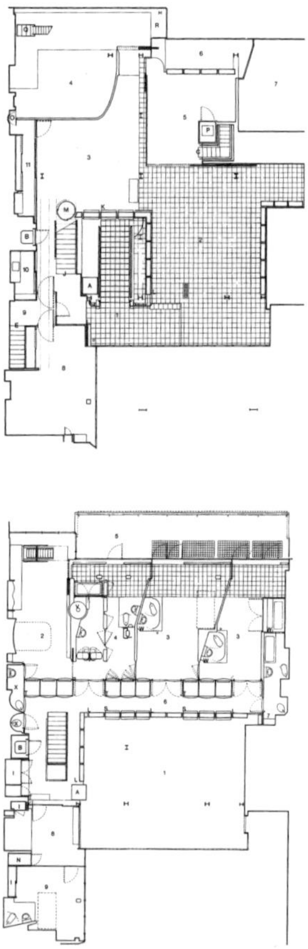

Pierre Chareau and Bernard Bijvoet, Maison de Verre, first floor plan (above): 1) landing; 2) main lounge; 3) dining room; 4) small sun room; 5) study; 6) area above waiting room; 7) area above consulting room; 8) kitchen; 9) entrance to kitchen; 10) pantry; 11) storage room; and second floor plan (below): 1) area of lounge; 2) main bedroom; 3) bedroom; 4) main bathroom; 5) terrace; 6) corridor gallery; 7) guest bathroom; 8) linen room; 9) staff bedroom.

From the initial perspective sketches of the interior one realizes that the subdivisions and fittings were worked out piece by piece, as the work proceeded. These loosely detailed drawings are the only evidence we have of the method of projection and construction. Thus, once the main idea had been laid down, the entire operation unfolded like a montage, bit by bit. In fact, we know that no working drawings in the usual sense of the term were produced.[2] On the contrary, the procedure usually consisted of moving straight from on-site drawings and sketches to fabrication, as the craftsman Louis Dalbet was on hand to build the prototypes and execute the final work. A rather crude model exhibited in 1931 shows the floors in place, together with the glass-block curtain walls which comprised the two facades of the house. Site photographs taken in 1930 show more or less the same state of affairs.

Chareau used this commission to invent and perfect new prototypical components, and in a sense the creator of the Maison de Verre seems to have regarded the work as a laboratory for the development of a hypothetically industrialized architecture. Materials and techniques were either derived from industrial practice or from new technical combinations which possessed an industrial potential. That Chareau had a passion for new materials is evident from the initial perspective sketches. In this respect, it is quite characteristic that bent duraluminum sheeting was the first material considered for the balustrade of the main staircase. Even though this deployment was, in the end, relinquished in favour of a low, psychologically reassuring tubular-steel guard rail, bent duraluminum was to reappear in the cylindrical broom closet placed behind the secondary stair and in the free-standing storage fitting designed for the master bathroom.

Despite the one-off experimental devices which abound throughout, the Maison de Verre is also built along rational lines. Due to this rationalization, it took on a wealth of implications which placed it beyond the confines of a normal bourgeois dwelling. While it is certain that the house could never have been built had it not been for the versatile craft ability of Dalbet, it nonetheless implied, by virtue of its modular nature, a potential for high quality mass-production. Doors, stair rails, bookshelves and cupboards as well as the curtain-wall fenestration are treated like the modular components of a grid which crosses the entire house from back to front and, to a certain extent, from side to side.

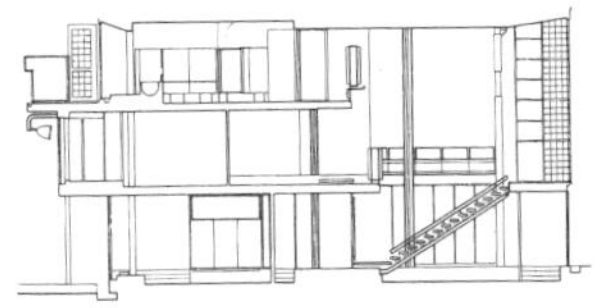

Pierre Chareau and Bernard Bijvoet, Maison de Verre, section.

Apart from this potential for rationalized production, which even today remains largely unexploited in the building industry, the Maison de Verre was machinist object, elegantly conceived and executed with precision. In many instances, in line with the economical tradition of French lightweight construction (exemplified by Jean Prouvé), the resistance of a material or a given component was pushed to its limits, as illustrated by the rolling/sliding mobile library ladder which moves on a carriage made from a single piece of bent tubing. It is equally significant, from a machinist standpoint, that the 'railway carriage' windows of vertically sliding plate glass, together with the remote controlled clerestories and the vertical bank of ventilating shutters, are, aside from a few side-hung doors, the only openings in the outer envelope. From this we can see how the concept of mechanized 'mobility' impregnates nearly all the details of the house, from sliding and pivoting windows to a retractable staircase, from rotating cupboards to pivoting bidets, from sliding partitions to folding screens.

In this respect the Maison de Verre embodies the transformable plan par excellence, although the ultimate motive behind each transformation varies considerably, passing from necessity in one instance to a certain 'poetry of equipment' in the next. Thus, the glass door pivoting on its axis on the ground-floor landing of the main staircase is required in order to separate the social areas from the medical premises, and vice versa. On the other hand, the hinged, perforated zinc 'butterfly' screens which are attached to the same pivoting door may be regarded as a neutral poetic refinement. Similarly, while the service hatch for serving tea in the boudoir may be viewed as a bourgeois convenience, the play between fixed and retractable stairs at the rear of the house may be said to have specific gender connotations to which we will return.

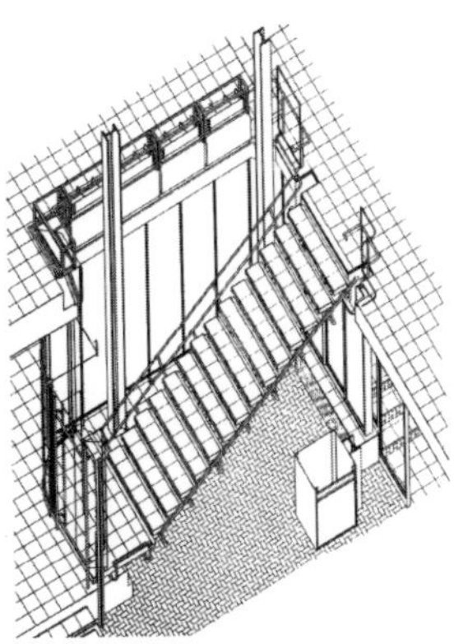

Pierre Chareau and Bernard Bijvoet, Maison de Verre, axonometric of main stairs with pivoting door.

Differences of this sort are clearly presented as psycho-social phenomena throughout the house. In fact, the Maison de Verre appears to be organized homologically, so that paired oppositions and reciprocal relations are found at every turn. This is nowhere more pronounced than in the treatment of light, in which natural light is rhetorically opposed to artificial light – paralleling, as it were, the dialogical filtration of light through the various translucent and transparent surfaces. Thus depending on the hour of day, the light is at times natural, at times artificial, with the house being illuminated at times externally or becoming itself the source of light. In the course of 24 hours, the source, the direction and the character of the light change in a reciprocal fashion. During the day, the house is lit from the outside by natural light penetrating in the main through a translucent enclosure. At night the house is lit from inside by artificial lighting, some of which filters out through the glass block facades, so that the house glows like a Chinese lantern. The interior may also be lit at night by the artificial light that penetrates through these same translucent facades from floodlights mounted on cantilevered brackets at the rear of the house and on free-standing ladders in the forecourt.

Pierre Chareau and Bernard Bijvoet, Maison de Verre, garden facade with modular metal panels, sliding railway carriage windows and glass block curtain wall beneath.

A homology of a similar, though less complex, nature, may be observed in the interior fittings; specifically in the correspondence established between the movement of the library staircase (serving the mind) and the movement of the dumb waiter from the kitchen to the dining area (serving the body). A similar homological structure also appears in the design of all the mechanical services. Thus, throughout the house, most of the electric wiring runs in vertical tubes which rise from one floor to another. At suitable points, these tubes are fitted with chromium-plated consoles on which are located the prerequisite switches and sockets, so that the walls are kept free from such items. While electrical energy and communication lines are conveyed vertically throughout the house in an all but dematerialized grid, heat – in the form of warm air – circulates mainly in horizontal ducts. In the first instance, modern energy is transported vertically; in the second, antique energy (as in the Roman hypocaust system) is conveyed horizontally. Both are kept as self-effacing as possible so that the adjustable polished-metal vents set in black lacquered surrounds are the only signs of the presence of this channelled air.

The Maison de Verre was recognized in its day as a functionalist work and as an integral part of the avant-garde of the Modern Movement, especially by Alberto Sartoris in his book *Gli elementi dell' architettura funzionale* (published in 1931, the year of the house's virtual completion). Otherwise it has been largely omitted from general surveys of the Modern Movement, with the possible exception of the French edition of my own *Modern Architecture: A Critical History*.[3] The reasons for this neglect are not hard to find because, while the Maison de Verre was a machinist work, it was hardly a pure example of utilitarian functionalism. On the one hand, its functionality exceeded the minimum necessary to satisfy material requirements, leading to a certain redundancy in terms of both form and mechanical effectiveness. On the other, it was furnished in such a way as to demonstrate a certain heterogeneity, its capacity, that is, to assimilate different components of varied origin. In this respect, a hardline functionalist would have had more than sufficient reason to mistrust the translucent walls and the curtained domain and upholstery of Dr Dalsace's study, not to mention the extravagant use of black lacquered surfaces throughout. All these ambiguous, luxurious characteristics would surely have been an anathema to the hygienic, functionalist line of the mainstream Modern Movement.[4]

As a result, the Maison de Verre is just as difficult to classify according to accepted genres or received ideological categories as is Marcel Duchamp's equally atypical work, *Le Grande Verre* (*The Large Glass*), his famous construction created during the years 1915–23, more strictly known as *La Marieé mise à nu par ses célibataires, même* (*The Bride Stripped Bare by her Bachelors, Even*). This comparison goes much further than the seemingly trivial fact that the two works were based on an obsessive, superfluous use of glass, since the two objects break the basic taxonomic rules which are spontaneously associated with any traditional understanding of their respective métiers. Should the Maison de Verre be regarded as architecture or as a furnishing on a large scale, and similarly, should *Le Grand Verre* be seen as a painting or as a relief construction? In both cases, the works are unclassifiable in any conventional sense; they are 'other' in the deepest sense of the word, and this 'strangeness' is a consequence of their total understated rupture with the mainstream categories of Western art since the Renaissance. In this respect, both are 'anti-' works, the Maison de Verre being a piece of *anti-architecture* and *Le Grande Verre* being patently an *anti-painting*. The more or less continuous translucent covering of the Maison de Verre does away with the counterpoint between solid and void which one finds in all architecture up to the twentieth century. Something similar takes place with *Le Grand Verre*, which utterly undermines all established ideas on the fundamental nature of painting, that is to say, it is a surface to be looked through rather than an opaque image to be looked at. As Duchamp was to say, '"retained in glass" doesn't mean "painting on glass". It is simply a means no longer regarding the thing in question as a painting.'[5]

This is not to suggest that the conceptual structure of Duchamp's *Le Grand Verre* and Chareau's *La Maison de Verre* have a similar self-conscious origin but rather that they are both homologically structured 'machines' that have more to do with Alfred Jarry's 1893 science-fiction concept of *pataphysics* (the science of imaginary solutions) than with the exclusively rational precepts of a Cartesian civilization. As a result certain common themes become apparent in the two works. In the first place, they display in different ways a sort of excessive and needless mechanization; while in the second, both structures are arranged in ways which, to some extent at least, have erotic or sexual connotations. In the case of *Le Grand Verre*, this much is well established and by now generally accepted; in the case of the Maison de Verre, we have little to go on except that the plan of the house lends itself to a reading which makes it appear as though it were a 'bachelor machine' (*une machine célibataire*), according to the definition that Michel Carrouges has given to these contrivances:

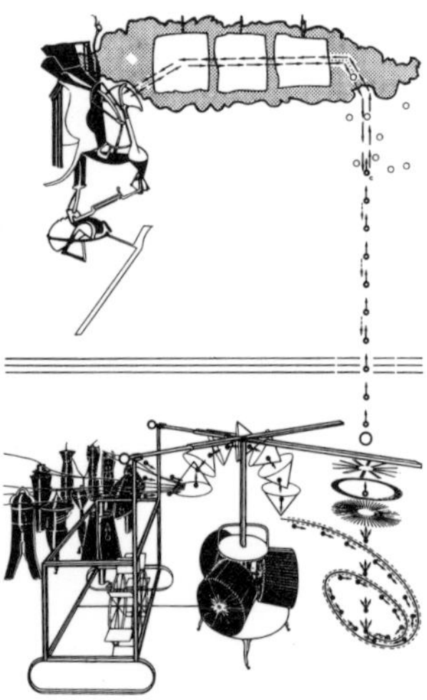

Marcel Duchamp, Le Grand Verre, *1915–23, sketch of the tattered image of the 'bride' above and the nine malic moulds of the 'bachelors' beneath plus other attendant bachelor machinery.*

> *To the contrary of real machines and even the larger part of imaginary but rational and useful machines such as Jules Verne's* Nautilus *or the rockets of science fiction, the bachelor machine appears first and foremost as a machine that is impossible, useless, incomprehensible, delirious . . .*
>
> *Each bachelor machine is a system of images composed of two equal and equivalent* ensembles. *One of these is the* sexual ensemble. *By definition this is comprised of two elements:* masculine *and* feminine . . .
>
> *The other part is the mechanical ensemble, also composed of two* mechanical elements, *which correspond respectively to the two masculine and feminine components of the sexual ensemble.*
>
> *This duality and correspondence appear very distinctly in Duchamp's* Le Grand Verre *which places the 'bride' along at the top, while the masculine 'bachelor machine' is isolated at the bottom.*[6]

With the gynaecological suite entirely occupying the first floor, the scheme of the Maison de Verre corresponds rather surprisingly and only too programmatically with this definition, and not only as far as the first floor is concerned, since the first and second floors follow a similar hierarchical order. In this way, the ground floor.can may be readily recognized as the 'bachelor' or male part of the house, above all because it is Dr Dalsace's professional domain and thus necessarily consecrated to celibacy. By a similar token, the second floor, which is that of the family bedrooms, can be taken naturally as the 'bride's' domain or the feminine area. Between these two floors, of course, lies the complex interface of the *piano nobile* which is in part public and social, and in part private and intimate, and it is a fact that the first floor seems to comply with this complex double coding on more than one level.

This first floor is divided, quite intentionally it would seem, into two sections. The eastern section combines the privacy of the boudoir, the domestic space of the kitchen and the sociability of the dining area and can therefore conventionally be considered as the domain of the bride. The western section combines the privacy of the study and the public status of the double-height salon and, as such, is marginally more subject to the 'worldly' discourse of the bachelor sign. While it is quite reasonable to suggest that this layout was simply a response to functional demands of the programme, the way in which these divisions are coded by the varied floor coverings and by mechanical devices, such as the retractable stair, only go to support my interpretation of the house as a 'bachelor machine'. The rubber tiling of the first-floor gynaecological suite continues via the main staircase to become the floor covering of the salon and is further prolonged along a strip which stops at the threshold to the boudoir. This grey, studded finish to the public domain is complemented by the use of different floor coverings in other areas of the first floor. Both the boudoir (female) and the study (male) are distinguished as intimate spaces by a flooring of matt black ceramic tiles, while the dining room, the service passage which leads to the kitchen and the secondary stair rising to the bedroom level are finished in parquet flooring, the warmth of the wood indicating their character as domestic spaces.

The mechanical aspect of the 'bachelor' syndrome appears in the reciprocal disposition of the auxiliary staircases, which set up discreet but precise relationships between the intimate spaces on the first floor – respectively the male study and the female boudoir – with the bride's domain above and the bachelor's domain below. The specific form of the stairs linking these polarities is not without significance in this regard. The bride's staircase is quite explicitly a mechanical device, an open ladder that can be lowered and retracted into the soffit of the ceiling, thereby serving to connect or separate the boudoir from the main bedroom above. The bachelor's staircase, meanwhile, is fixed, although still of an implicitly mechanical character by virtue of its winding around the first-floor telephone cabin as it descends from the study to the medical suite. This frozen movement, as it were, is emphasized by the way in which the handrail in tubular steel climbs in stepped formation from the ground floor to the *piano nobile*.

The homologous disposition of the private areas in the bride's and bachelor's domains on the first floor reads, then, as follows: the boudoir (the bride) is linked by a retractable 'rising' stair to the main bedroom above, while the study (the bachelor) is linked by a fixed 'descending' stair, to the gynaecologist's consulting room below. A further indication of a similar homology is encountered in virtually the same area in plan, the first and second floors. This coincidence of opposites occurs between the study and the boudoir on the first floor and the bathroom and the main bedroom on the second floor. In the first case, a set of sliding doors set virtually at right angles, creates a 'valvular' passage between the study and the boudoir. In the second, a similarly valvular arrangement is evident in the division of the main bathroom into male and female zones; split between the rectangular bath (female) and the circular shower (male) situated adjacent to each other but entered from opposite sides of the bathroom. The fact that these different arrangements conformed to Madame and Dr Dalsace's respective ablutional preferences reinforces rather than undermines the symbolic organization of the Maison de Verre after the 'myth' of the bachelor machine.

Such a combination is further confirmation of the intimacy which attended the creation of the Maison de Verre. It is clear that, as in all first-rate houses, the client shared the responsibility for the design all but equally with the architect. In fact, there are times when the entire work seems to be an embodiment of the personality of Annie Dalsace, reflected in the perpetual homage that Chareau paid to his client. Subtly, but with a curious insistence, the house appears to be dedicated repeatedly to the generic 'bride', from the gynaecological suite itself to the multiplicity of bidets arranged on the bedroom floor. Moreover, a dominant female figure (which is nevertheless simultaneously servile) is twice placed at the panoptic centre of two spaces: the first panoptical focus occurs in the axis of the entrance hall, which appropriately falls under the eye of the nurse who controls the medical suite; the second is situated on the third floor, where the maid's workroom looks down not only on the entire volume of the salon but also onto the external forecourt of the house. It may be added that these two panoptic roles happen to have been assumed by the servants of the 'bachelor' and 'bride' respectively.

Although the correspondence between *Le Grand Verre* and the Maison de Verre must remain as one of the enigmas of twentieth-century avant-garde culture as a whole, a comparison of this sort cannot overlook the consideration of certain specific idiosyncratic affinities between the two works. For instance, we may ask ourselves whether there is not some justification in comparing the retractable staircase of the Maison de Verre with the *le pendu femelle* ('swinging this way and that') of *Le Grand Verre*, or if it is not correct to see the study staircase or the pivoting, twin shirt cupboard of the main bathroom as unconscious transpositions of Duchamp's *Chocolate Grinder* of 1914, of which he was to write in *La Boîte Verte* of 1934, 'The bachelor grinds his chocolate himself ...'.[7] Whatever credence we may give to these speculations, we surely have to assume that

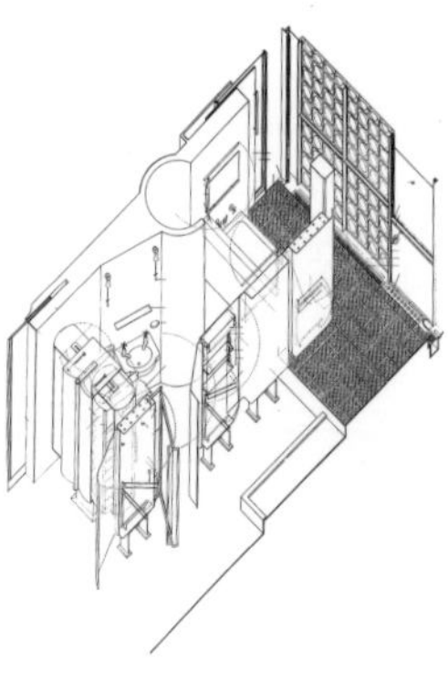

Pierre Chareau and Bernard Bijvoet, Maison de Verre, axonometric of master bathroom.

Chareau was quite cognizant of the vicissitudes of Cubism and Futurism and must therefore without doubt have had some knowledge of Duchamp's *Large Glass* and of the different paintings and other synthetic works from which it was derived. Moreover, it is significant that Chareau resorted to Cubist devices such as collage, particularly in his manipulation of the surface and the different levels of the first floor in order to indicate different sectors of symbolic significance and use. For the rest, the house is perennially suffused, irrespective of the external climate, with a strange, sub-aqueous light imparting to the internal subdivisions and fittings an indeterminable shadowy depth, relieved by the moiré effect of the perforated metal against light, by unexpected scintillating flashes of glass and by the luminous, depthless gleam of black lacquer – a range of 'alchemical' materials comparable to the intaglio, metallic elements laid into the surface of Duchamp's *Le Grande Verre*.

Pierre Chareau and Bernard Bijvoet, Maison de Verre, ground-floor entrance corridor set on the axis of the nurse's office.

Reworked extract, taken from 'Pierre Chareau: An Eclectic Architect', in Marc Vellay and Kenneth Frampton, *Pierre Chareau: Architect and Craftsman, 1883–1950*, London: Thames and Hudson, 1985, pp.233–48. First published in French by Editions du Regard, Paris in 1984.

In Spite of the Void: The Otherness of Adolf Loos

Adolf Loos and I, he in deed and I in words, did nothing more than to show that there is a difference between an urn and a chamber pot, and that that difference is governed by culture. However, the others, the positive ones, are divided into those who use the urn as a chamber pot, and those who use the chamber pot as an urn.
Karl Kraus[1]

Enigma

Adolf Loos remains an enigma;[2] the more we dwell on his motives, the more elusive and paradoxical his achievement appears. In this respect, he may be compared to Marcel Duchamp, although his work and sensibility could not have been more different. As Loos himself was at pains to point out in 1910, the *métier* of building is far removed from that of art: 'Only a very small part of architecture belongs to art – the tomb and the monument. Everything else that fulfils a function is to be excluded from the domain of art.'[3]

Notwithstanding this categorical separation between art and utility, Loos's empirical approach nonetheless remained mediated by the latent presence of a complex ethical critique, so that like Duchamp, who proclaimed the end of painting and celebrated its demise in the ambiguous, part abstract, part figurative images of his *Large Glass* of 1915–23, Loos's œuvre, both written and built, testifies to a historical 'break' that cannot be overcome, let alone understood. One may argue that just as Duchamp created the ultimate 'antipainting/painting', so Loos hypothesized a kind of anti-architecture/architecture, although he never once expressed himself in such terms. For Loos, art, as opposed to either architecture or building, oscillated between *subversion* and *commemoration*. Yet despite the ostensible exclusion of both the iconoclastic and the iconic from his work, his interiors were at once radical and reassuring, so that while they epitomized bourgeois comfort and decorum, they were at the same time permeated throughout with one inexplicable disjunction after another. One may say that these dissonances occurred with sufficient frequency as to constitute the hidden motivation of Loos's *Innenarchitektur* – even more so than his preferred 'palette' of materials and finishes that have been seen as characterizing his *bricolé* style. Prominent among the latter are the overemphatic half-timbered ceilings of Richardsonian inspiration, together with the inevitable brick chimney breast and inglenook as well as the much lighter, white-enamelled wainscoting together with the use of plaster-cast reproductions of historical friezes. There is also his well-known penchant for applying very thin stone revetment, like a kind of permanent wallpaper – the cheapest, in his opinion – and his curious obsession with mirrors and vitrines. Yet although these are indeed the elements out of which the dissonances arise, they are not, in themselves, the source of the alienating effects. Instead these uncanny discords occur through a series of disjunctions, the first of which may be said to appear in Loos's own apartment, dating from 1903, where the absence of soldier courses in the exposed brickwork of the chimney, together with the thickness of the mortar joints, can only be accounted for by two hypotheses. The first of these is that Loos's 'on site', ad hoc method of detailing was in some sense artistically inept, a hypothesis that cannot be generally sustained owing to the high-quality construction and material finish evident in his work as a whole, not to mention his self-proclaimed commitment to the revival and refinement of traditional craft. The second explanation is that Loos wished to make a subtle yet nonetheless subversive statement through, as in this instance, the absence of an appropriate finishing seam or the crudity of the joints themselves.

Adolf Loos, Loos Apartment, Vienna, 1903, interior.

Flashes of courtly ostentation aside, Loos's basic domestic paradigm was the bucolic *heimat* translated through the Anglo-Saxon Arts and Crafts ideal, and yet this received type was always reinterpreted with a certain sense of falsity. Thus, in the living room of his own apartment the black metal hood (of Austrian origin) sweeps down clumsily over the hearth, thereby disrupting the formal unity of the chimney breast. Moreover, the top of this same grotesquely tapering form seems to be wedged awkwardly between the joists of the ceiling, as though it were an afterthought. The maladroit combination is compounded by the coarse structure of the bricks themselves, which contrast violently with the delicately riveted seams of the hood.

Aside from simple ineptness, what other interpretation may be put on Loos's intentions at this juncture? Cannot an indication be found in the essay 'Architecture' of 1910 in which he distinguishes, in ontological terms, between a dwelling and a work of art – above all, the well-known passage in which he argues that the house is conservative and the work of art revolutionary?[4]

Camera obscura

For all his categoric distinction between architecture and art, Loos's domestic interiors were simultaneously both 'houses' and 'works of art', so that while these might well appear to represent the cosy paraphernalia of the typical Anglo-American home, to the initiated or hypersensitive (by whom Loos was surrounded) they signified the opposite, namely the impossibility of returning to traditional culture in an uprooted age. Loos's subtle dissonances served to deny, as in his own apartment, the compensatory illusions of the typical Jugendstil or Arts and Crafts house, as satirized in his parable 'The Story of the Poor Rich Man' of 1900.[5] Consciously or otherwise, Loos seems always to have tried to temper the aura of cosiness and stability with an underlying feeling of alienation and irreality. This must have been what Ludwig Hevesi had in mind when he wrote in 1907, 'in photographs his rooms don't look good'. Loos countered this comment by arguing that: 'The people living in them don't recognize them. That is because space is not drawn but experienced ... What has been conceived in one art does not come out in another.'[6]

This anti-photogenic quality was conceded by Loos himself three years later, although for him the distortions of the camera were more important for what they concealed, namely the three-dimensionality of the space, than for what they revealed about its inherent dissonance. As he put it, 'it is my greatest pride that the interiors which I have created are totally ineffective in photographs. I have to forego the honour of being published in the various architectural magazines. I have denied the satisfaction of my vanity.'[7] Nonetheless, he seems to have remained uncommonly aware of photography as an expressive medium, suspended, as it were, between illusion and reality, as his remarkably early use of photomontage would indicate – above all, his superimposition of Peter Altenberg's portrait over a 'real' representation of the interior of the Kärntner Bar.[8] Loos's distaste for *representational* illusion in both architecture and photography did not prevent him from exploiting the capacity of illusionistic space to challenge the authenticity of the real. That Loos's anti-photogenic approach was conscious seems to be suggested by Tristan Tzara in his appraisal of Loos, which appeared in 1930 as part of a *Festschrift* honouring Loos. Tzara wrote, 'I associate myself with the homage that you address to Adolf Loos, who through uneasiness has seen a human possibility for clarity in the hub of social activity that is closest to the sun, to exterior and interior squalls – this great architect, the only one today whose realizations are not photogenic and whose expression amounts to a profound school and not to a means for attaining illusory beauties ...'.[9]

Speculum

Adolf Loos, Hans Brummel Apartment, Pilsen, 1928–9, interior.

The use of virtual and actual mirrors occupies as strange a place in Loos's interior work as do the dissonances brought about by his penchant for *bricolage*. The virtual mirror first occurs as a conscious intent in Loos's open-planned sleeping–living–music room realized for Willy Hirsch in Pilsen in 1907. A similar illusion is to occur in the Hans Brummel dining room completed in the same town 22 years later. In both instances, Loos uses a system of parallel wall planes and free-standing pilasters entirely faced in polished stone in order to create a virtual or 'false' mirror within the space. He seems to have stumbled on his effect somewhat earlier, in the Schwarzwald Apartment, realized in Vienna in 1905. In this instance, the mirror effect was heightened by real mirrors, which, in reflecting each other through an actual opening, served to engender a continuous oscillation between illusion and reality; that is, the observer was repeatedly misled into thinking that the actual void was a mirror and the real mirror a void.

It is obvious that Loos often used mirrors for the simple purpose of enlarging the *apparent* volume, as in the illusionistic clerestory that helps to extend the visible upper volume of the Kärntner Bar (1907), but this hardly accounts for his handling of real spatial depth as if it were a mirror, as in the first-floor sales room of the Knize men's store in Vienna (1913), where a mezzanine railing extends through two adjacent spaces in such a way as to suggest the presence of a non-existent mirror. Only a vitrine passing through the aperture below the mezzanine serves to establish beyond doubt that the illusionary mirror is, in fact, an opening.

Mirrors in Loos's work also tend to be combined with other subtle disjunctions, as in the Steiner Villa dining room (1910), where a long, square-gridded window, glazed with frosted glass, lies flush on top of a dado-rail capping to the wood panelling of the room. Beneath this rail and centred on the same axis is an almost equally elongated rectangular mirror, which, in partially reflecting the space of the room, sets up a paradoxical opposition between the seeming *transparency* of the mirror and the manifest *opacity* of the frosted glass. This contradiction is heightened by the fact that natural light patently emanates from the window rather than the mirror.

Adolf Loos, Steiner Villa, Vienna, 1910, dining room.

An even more complex and paradoxical assembly of elements occurs in the entrance hall of the Tristan Tzara House, realized by Loos in Paris in 1926. Here a real mirror mediates between two ambiguously scaled and detailed doors, so that while the mirror by virtue of its placement may readily be identified with one of the doors, we are left in doubt as to the door's operability. The result is that the mirror's illusionistic opening seems momentarily to be more real. This contradictory effect is produced by a series of subtle countermanding details, of which the following are the most evident: both the mirror and the doors sit on a baseboard, which serves to deny any potential operability; the shorter and wider of the two doors has a barely concealed surrounding frame, which argues for its status as an actual door; on the other hand, the taller, narrower 'frameless' door, situated in the return wall, insists on its capacity to open inward by virtue of being inset; however, this recession is contradicted by the fact that it too has a baseboard attached to its bottom stile, so that once again the operability is in question. In short, one is left in doubt as to whether either door is an actual opening or merely a cupboard. Aside from all these curious factors affecting the legibility of the space, the varying heights, widths, frames and reveals constantly cause one to question which of the two openings is the more normative. This subtle semantic disturbance is compounded by the placement of wall-mounted tubular lights, at the same height, above the mirror and the wider door, thereby implying once again that a contradictory complementarity obtains between the two. The fact that these lights echo a pair of masks on the return wall and are set at the same datum only serves to exacerbate the ricocheting 'play' of doubt throughout, the constant questioning as to what is real and what is false. This analysis is supported by the fact that, in this instance, both architect and client shared a common preoccupation with the alchemical ambiguity of the mirror, as has been remarked on by Benedetto Gravagnuolo in his study of Loos.[10]

Bricolage

As we have already seen, a range of disjunctive devices was repeatedly deployed by Loos in order to disrupt the potential hermeticism of the 'total' interior. Besides the mirror, among other common Loosian stratagems one may cite the following: a sudden shift in the apparent size of the main spatial focus, as in the deliberately overscaled double doors in the Leopold Goldmann dining room of 1909; an avoidance of expected relationships, as in the living hall of the Strasser House of 1919, where an open stairway passes over the top of a small chimney breast, thereby totally denying the traditional position and function of the chimney (not mention the 'anti-arch' arch that vaults over the hearth itself); interruptions of normally continuous elements, as in the rupturing of plaster-cast ornamental friezes by window openings, exemplified again in the Strasser House; the use of

Adolf Loos, Bellak Apartment, Vienna, 1909–13, interior showing Cipollino marble wall cladding and plastercast Classical frieze.

counterposed marble graining so as to effect either a Rorschach figure, as in the false perspectival picture window of the Steiner Plume and Feather Shop (1907), or a countermanding pattern of strongly veined revetment, as in the violently counter-changing grain of Cipollino marble that lines the walls of the Bellak apartment (1909–13); and the peculiar proportioning adopted in Loos's half-timbered ceilings, where more often than not the main beams seem to have inadequate points of bearing and the depths of the primary and secondary joists are so close as to make one disbelieve in the capacity of the structure to sustain any substantial load. We know that these beams were indeed false in many instances and were simply applied for effect – an operation that is clearly paradoxical in the work of one who was so preoccupied with ethical questions. Last but not least, mention has to be made of the ambiguous, not to say eccentric, lighting elements deployed by Loos in his otherwise *gemütlich* interiors, the dodecahedron glass lampshade (an anti-shade shade in clear glass) that first appears in the Leopold Langer apartment of 1901, the use of bare lightbulbs in the Steiner House of 1910, and curious spring-coiled lighting fixtures employed in the Goldmann and Salatsch accounting office.

Time and the other

Underlying all this there is Loos's strange concept of 'the other', *Das Andere*, which appears overtly as the main title of his short-lived newspaper of 1903. This concept seems to assume concrete form as an 'absent presence' in Loos's penchant for a certain Egyptoid wooden tripod stool, first produced by Liberty in 1884. This so-called Thebes stool crops up as an incidental element in many of Loos's interiors. One cannot entirely discount the possibility that the stools were self-consciously provided by him as 'props' for the publicity shots that make up the photographic record in Heinrich Kulka's standard monograph on Loos published in 1931.[11] Here, one may surmise, is the lost Egyptian 'other', literally returning as a trans-historical figure in Loos's Karma Villa of 1904, where it bears witness to the otherness of the Japanese window fitted within the otherwise occidental panelling of the stair hall. This is the first occasion on which this curious Egyptoid icon appears; thereafter it turns up when one least expects it – in the Steiner Villa *Sitzzimmer*, in the Strasser House, in the Tzara House (this time rendered in a modified form by Loos's favoured furniture-maker, Josef Veillich) and finally in Loos's apartment for Leo Brummel. What this cipher means or meant we shall never finally determine. May we see it as paralleling similar Egyptian preoccupations in both Schönberg's *Moses and Aaron* of 1931 and Freud's *Moses and Monotheism* of 1937? On the other hand, like the 'malic moulds' of Duchamp's *Large Glass*, these stools may be interpreted as the incarnation of ghostly agents. And while their presence or absence may be entirely fortuitous, it is surely more than just another anomaly in what are otherwise seemingly innocuous environments.

Adolf Loos's Thebes Stool (1903), a copy made by Loos's furniture maker Josef Veillich.

Perhaps we may see them as icons of a lost heroic culture sitting in judgment on an age that in Loos's view, was totally deprived of any culture worthy of the name.

If this stool is indeed the embodiment of 'the other', then inasmuch as it is archaic and Oriental, it is also different in meaning from the subtitle of Loos's paper, which was both modern and occidental: *Ein blatt zur Einführung Abendländischer Kultur in Österreich*[12] – a journal for the introduction of Western civilization into Austria. Are we justified in concluding that for Loos the archaically exotic and the historically unprecedented were able to point to the same end; to a sense of time that lies outside time; to the presence, in fact, of an 'other' time? One is reminded of T S Eliot's 'If all time is totally present, all time is unredeemable.'[13]

WIEN, 15. OKTOBER 1903

DAS ANDERE

EIN BLATT ZUR EINFUEHRUNG ABENDLAENDISCHER KULTUR IN OESTERREICH: GESCHRIEBEN VON ADOLF LOOS 1. JAHR

TAILORS AND OUTFITTERS
GOLDMAN & SALATSCH
WIEN, I. GRABEN 20.

Société Franco-Autrichienne
pour les arts industriels
MÖBELSTOFFE
LYONER SEIDEN- UND SAMT-BROKATE
ECHTE UND IMITIERTE GOBELINS
ENGLISCHE UND FRANZÖSISCHE TEPPICHE
STICKEREIEN UND APPLIKATIONEN
SPITZENVORHÄNGE
WIEN, I. Kärntnerstrasse 55, I. Stock
Société Franco-Autrichienne

Adolf Loos, Das Andere, *no. 2, 1903, subtitled* 'a journal for the introduction of western civilization into Austria'.

In one sense, Loos's other is, as he puts it in his essay 'Culture' of 1908, 'the American worker who has conquered the world. The man in overalls',[14] or, more autobiographically, as he wrote in the first article in the inaugural issue of *Das Andere*, it was his émigré watchmaker uncle of Chestnut Street, Philadelphia, with whom he was to stay on his arrival in the United States in 1893. This 'other' for Loos, a new Werther as he calls him, was born on the American frontier, and the Old World had no choice but to accept his destiny, which was to create a new civilization of objective technology and the cult of the everyday. This 'destiny' made itself ironically manifest in the ready-made subject matter presented by Duchamp and Francis Picabia at the famous New York Armory Show of 1913. Perhaps their discourse would have been unduly aestheticized for Loos, but surely a Loosian validation of industrial banality is there in Duchamp's early ready-mades – in his *Bicycle Wheel* of 1913 and *Fountain* of 1915 (the inverted urinal, signed R Mutt) and in Picabia's erotic play on the mirroring effect of the camera, entitled *Ici c'est ici Steiglitz, Foi et Amour*, of 1916.[15]

This sensibility is surely close to that same impulse that will bring Loos to advocate, as Boris Podrecca has put it, 'the same inequality for everyone', although contrary to the Bolsheviks, who seemingly wanted to reduce all men to a proletarian condition, Loos envisaged an aristocratic communism where self-denial and a moral economy would be a matter of nobility and reason – a state of appropriate deportment before the void.[16]

Archimedian Point

May I take you to the shores of a mountain lake? The sky is blue, the water is green, and everything is at peace. The mountains and the clouds are reflected in the lake, as are the houses, farms and chapels. They stand there as if they had never been built by human hands. They look as if they had come from God's own workshop, just like the mountains and trees, the clouds, and the blue sky. And everything radiates beauty and quiet …

What is the discord, that like an unnecessary scream shatters the quiet? Right at the centre of the farmers' houses, which were not built by them, but by God, stands a villa. Is it the product of a good or a bad architect? I do not know. All I know is that beauty, peace and quiet have been dispelled . . .

Thus I ask: Why is it that every architect, whether good or bad, desecrates the lake?

The farmer does not desecrate it. Neither does the engineer who builds a railway on the shore, or he who draws deep grooves in the clear surface of the lake with his ship. They create in a different way . . .

And I ask again: Why does the architect, the good one as well as the bad one, desecrate the lake? The architect, like almost every urban dweller, has no culture. He lacks the certainty of the farmer, who possesses culture. The urban dweller is an uprooted person.[17]

To a greater degree than the more celebrated 'Ornament and Crime' of 1908, Loos's essay 'Architecture', written two years later, from which the above quotation is taken, is the single most comprehensive testament of Loos's life. Written when Loos was 40 years old and in the very year in which two of his most seminal works were finally completed, the Looshaus on the Michaelerplatz and the Steiner Villa, this essay assembles in a most consequential and succinct form the essential precepts of his critical vision. The basic arguments of this cultural critique begin from his affirmation that the historical fate of the vernacular is decided in that very moment when the unconsciously internalized values of traditional folk culture are replaced by the self-conscious aesthetic categories of the urbanized mass. Loos describes the act of building a vernacular roof and then proceeds to interrogate the peasant as to its intrinsic quality. 'What kind of a roof? A beautiful one or an ugly one? He does not know. It is a roof!'[18]

From this point, Loos returns us to a consideration of the alienated and hence 'uncultivated' condition of the deracinated urban middle class, that is to say, exactly that class from which the majority of architects are drawn. Loos describes the consequences of this uprooted condition in the following terms:

By culture I mean that balance of man's inner and outer being which alone guarantees rational thought and action. I am due to give a lecture entitled: 'Why do the Papuans have a culture and why do the Germans lack one?'

Mankind's history has yet to record a period without culture. The creation of such a period was reserved for the urban dweller during the second half of the nineteenth century. Until then the development of our culture had remained in a state of flux. One obeyed the commands of the hour and did not look forwards or backwards.

But then false prophets appeared. They said: 'How ugly and cheerless our life is.' They brought everything together from all cultures, displayed it in the museums and said: 'Behold that is beauty. You, however, have lived in pitiful ugliness.'[19]

Here, in a single insightful passage, the fundamental contradiction of the term *applied art* is ironically exposed. The rest of his argument then follows as a series of corollaries. The first of these returns to the programmatic theme of 'Ornament and Crime', namely that '...cultural evolution is equivalent to the removal of ornament from the object of daily use.'[20] One should note in this regard Loos's awareness of the hierarchical differences separating one object from the next, an insight that led him, in practice, to limit the full thrust of his anti-Jugendstil, purifying drive to the surfaces of daily utensils. He was not so much against all ornament as he was against the *invention* of ornament in modern times. Thus, as he wrote in his rider on ornament of 1924, 'Ornament and Education':

Twenty-six years ago I maintained that the use of ornamentation on objects of practical use would disappear with the development of mankind, a constant and consistent development, which was as natural a process as the atrophy of vowels in final syllables in popular speech. By that I did not mean what some purists have carried ad absurdum, namely that ornament should be systematically and consistently eliminated.[21]

Here, as in 'Ornament and Crime' and 'Architecture', Loos stresses the different ontological conditions obtaining between different men and different objects at different moments in history. Within the spectrum of these differences the advent of modernity is seen as a kind of purifying demiurge, driving constantly toward the 'music of the spheres' as the highest manifestation of the human spirit, toward a condition lying beyond the limits of culture. At the same time, the principle of cultural coexistence – the fact that men live at the same time in different historical periods, has to be consciously accounted for. This partially explains why Loos is at pains in 1924 to distinguish between objects of long and short duration and to admit to the latter – to textiles, wallpaper and female costume – the full play of transitory ornamental fashion. There is in all this a certain sexism characteristic of the Krausian circle during this period. Despite this prejudicial exception Loos remains absolutely opposed to the prospect of an overall return to the culture of ornament. Thus in 1924 he writes, 'What I did mean was that where it had disappeared as a necessary consequence of human development, it could not be restored, just as people will never return to tattooing their faces.'[22] Clearly Loos is close here to Ludwig Wittgenstein's famous aphorism 'What is torn must remain torn', and also to Nietzche's phrase *Alles Entscheidende ensteht trotzdem*, 'That which happens, happens in spite [of everything]', taken from *Also Sprach Zarathustra*, which suggested the laconically cryptic title for Loos's second collection of essays, published in 1930 under the name *Trotzdem*.[23]

In 'Ornament and Crime' Loos distinguishes with disinterested precision between one historical condition and the next. He writes:

My shoes are covered over and over with decoration, the kind made up of pinking and perforations. Work done by the shoemaker but not paid for. I go to the shoemaker and say: 'You want thirty kronen for a pair of shoes. I'll pay you forty.' In this way I have raised the man to a level of happiness which he will repay me for by work and material of a quality absolutely out of proportion to the extra cost. He is happy . . . And then I add: 'But there's one condition. The shoe must be quite plain.' With that I've toppled him from the heights of contentment into Tartarus. He has less work, but I have robbed him of all his pleasure.

I am preaching to aristocrats. I tolerate ornaments on my own body if they afford my fellow men pleasure. Then they are a pleasure to me, too. I put up with the ornaments of the natives, the Persians, the Slovak peasant woman, and my shoemaker's ornaments, for these workers have no other means of reaching the heights of their existence. We have art which has replaced ornament. We go to Beethoven or Tristan after the cares of the day. My shoemaker can't. I must not take away his joy as I have nothing to replace it with. But whoever goes to the Ninth Symphony and then sits down to design a wallpaper pattern is either a rogue or a degenerate.[24]

In what must be one of the most dialectical passages to be found in his entire corpus, Loos opposes the socially liberative potential of simplified production to the sublimated eroticism of ornamental form. He insists that that which is authentic for the vestigial folk culture of his time cannot be condoned in the art of the deracinated metropolitan figure. As he argues, with Joseph Olbrich, Otto Eckmann and Henry Van de Velde in mind, '... Modern ornament has no forebears and no descendants, no past and no future. It is joyfully welcomed by uncultivated people, to whom the true greatness of our time is a closed book and after a short period is rejected.'[25]

Similar categorical distinctions are evident in his essay 'Architecture', where, in a manner that is reminiscent of his attitude towards photography, Loos distinguishes with penetrating exactitude and even a certain envy between the province of the draughtsman and the art of architecture. 'The art of building,' he writes, 'has been degraded by the architect into a graphic art. The greatest number of jobs does not go to the person who is the builder, but to him whose work cuts the best figure on paper. And these two are opposites.'[26] Loos perceives these poles as lying at opposite ends of a spectrum wherein graphic art precedes painting, painting precedes sculpture, and sculpture eventually leads to the threshold of architecture. This discriminatory hierarchical polemic bring Loos to remark that 'The best draughtsman can be a bad architect, the best architect can be a bad draughtsman. The graphic arts are already required as a necessary talent at the beginning of one's choice of a career in architecture ... But we are not, as yet, so cultureless that we teach a young boy poetry by means of calligraphy.'[27]

Although Loos recognized the fundamental inaccessibility of the vernacular, he nonetheless insisted on the latent presence of an authentic contemporary style, neither old nor new, a pattern made manifest through the *slowly* evolving agency of craftwork, through the precise traditions of masonry, joinery, shopfitting, saddlery, shoemaking, tailoring, leather goods manufacture, coachwork and musical instrument making. For Loos, the self-effacement afforded by the well-cut tweed suit and dinner jacket intrinsically embodied the male style of the epoch, so what was needed at the level of architecture was an equally understated sense of deportment – a work of comparable modesty and anonymity, a dinner jacket with black rather than brass buttons.

This appeal to normative sartorial culture led Loos to the most seminal passage of his essay 'Architecture', the one wherein he distinguishes between the relatively *public* realm of the house and the inescapably *private* nature of the work of art:

The house has to please everyone, contrary to the work of art, which does not. The work of art is a private matter for the artist. The house is not. The work of art is brought into the world without there being a need for it. The house satisfies a requirement. The work of art is responsible to none; the house is responsible to everyone. The work of art wants to draw people out of their state of comfort. The house has to serve comfort. The work of art is revolutionary; the house is conservative. The work of art shows people new directions and thinks of the future. The house thinks of the present. Man loves everything that satisfies his comfort. He hates everything that wants to draw him out of his acquired and secured position and that disturbs him. Thus he loves the house and hates art.

Does it follow that the house has nothing in common with art, and is architecture not to be included amongst the arts? This is so. Only a very small part of architecture belongs to art: the tomb and the monument. Everything else that fulfils a function is to be excluded from the domain of art.[28]

Here, in what is perhaps one of the first radical texts to point out the distance separating avant-gardist culture from popular acceptance, Loos causes us to question the fundamental nature of things – not only to distinguish between the private status of art and the public status of commemorative work but also to perceive the gulf that separates the revolutionary or subversive impulse from the conservative instinct. Between these two there appears a third term, which, while never fully articulated, is surely implied by Loos. This unannounced term implicates the culture of building, which is (or rather ought to be) accepted as something apart from either art on the one hand or monumentality on the other. In all this Loos remains categorically opposed to the most popular socio-aesthetic slogans of his time, namely, *arts and crafts* and *applied arts*. He was against the former because of its contamination of craftwork by idealism and against the latter because of the way in which it compromised art through everyday application. All of this is closely linked to the *linguistic* moral philosophy of the Krausian circle, above all to the writings of Ludwig Wittgenstein and

Karl Kraus. Where else in the thought of this time can one find a comparable Nietzschean reflection on the hypocrisy of such terms as 'applied' or 'export' art, the latter being the thesis of Hermann Muthesius's German Werkbund programme of 1914,[29] let alone the sentimental confusion inherent in the post-Pre-Raphaelite slogan of synthesizing art with craft? For Loos, as for Ludwig Mies van der Rohe, who surely followed him in this, culture is the modus vivendi of a period as reflected in the form of the objective world; a collective creation intimately bound up with technique, deportment, quality and convention, the substance, in times of stability, of an *architecture parlante*. As Loos put it with characteristic irony:

> *... The law courts must appear as a threatening gesture toward secret vice. The bank must declare: here your money is secure ... For the Chinese the colour of mourning is white, for us it is black. Consequently, it would be impossible for our architects to produce a happy atmosphere with the colour black.*[30]

Déraciné

Loos concludes his essay 'Architecture' with a laconic appeal to the canon of the classical, an appeal that remains ambiguous by virtue of the distance it takes from the rules of academicism. Like Le Corbusier after him, Loos contrasted the civic instrumentality of Rome with the poetic inventiveness of the Greeks. In this, however, unlike Le Corbusier, he thought of himself as a Roman rather than a Greek; as he put it, 'An architect is a mason who has learned Latin.' This sentiment led him to write in 1910, '... The Greeks could hardly administer their cities; the Romans administered the globe. The Greeks squandered their inventiveness on the orders: the Romans wasted theirs on the plan. And he who can solve the great plan does not think of new mouldings.'[31] In the next paragraph he adds a caveat that implies that the slowly evolving triumph of modern instrumentality has been achieved at the price of cultural disinheritance: 'Ever since humanity sensed the greatness of classical antiquity, one common thought has unified all great architects. They think: the way I build is the same as the way the Romans would have built. We know that they are mistaken. Time, place, function and climate, milieu have upset their calculations.'[32]

For Loos the only inheritance available in his day is the legacy of the classical as it reincarnates itself in the schizophrenia of the modern, the modern that is paradoxically both the triumph of technology and the sentence of silence. As far as architecture is concerned, Loos looks back to the Biedermeier period as the last golden moment and to Schinkel as inspiration for the future. At the same time, he looks within the achievements of modern technology for a recasting of the values of the antique world. Thus he writes, 'Look at the bicycle! Does not the spirit of Periclean Athens waft through its forms?' At the same time, he goes on to reflect that 'classical antiquity was and is the mother of all subsequent periods of culture'.[33] In an equally surprising association he proclaims the English and the engineers to be the quintessential Greeks of the modern world, for as he was to recognize their works cover the entire globe.[34]

Le Corbusier was to claim a similar schismatic legacy in the annotated map of his 'Voyage d'Orient' of 1911, published in his book *L'Art décoratif*

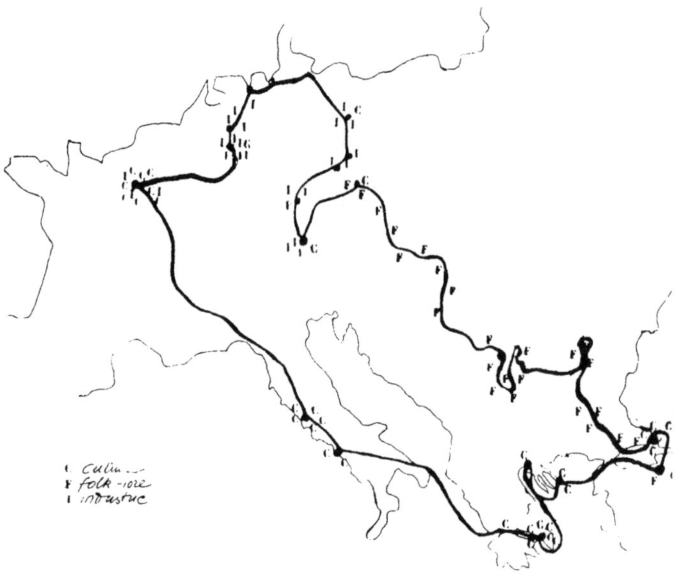

Le Corbusier, map of the Voyage d'Orient (1911), drawn in 1925; C = culture, F = folklore, I = industry.

d'aujourd'hui of 1926. Nothing surely could be more Loosian than this simplistic but nonetheless discriminating analysis of local variations in European culture according to the degree to which these localities manifested aspects of *cultural*, *folkloric* or *industrial* modes of production.[35] In Le Corbusier's cartographic polemic, culture, *C*, indicates the presence of the classical, so that for Le Corbusier, at the turn of the century, classical European culture was mainly restricted to certain capitals – Paris, Rome and Athens – while the *Ruhr Gebiet* was then, as now, largely the province of industry, *I*, as was Berlin, save for the delicate presence of Schinkel, recognized by a modicum of *C*. Needless to say, the primary domain of the folkloric, *F*, was largely perceived by Le Corbusier as lying in the 'Orient', that is, in the Balkans, northern Greece and Asia Minor, although the presence of *C* in Athens was mediated by a touch of *F*. While Schinkel exercised little influence on Le Corbusier, neoclassicism surely did, however much it may have been filtered through Wagner, Perret and Hoffmann.

More important, however, for the subsequent evolution of the Purist culture, was the Loosian concept of contradictory coexistence – above all, perhaps, the prospect of a certain complementarity between industrial production and vernacular craft, between the engineer and the farmer, that is to say, between the two agents who, unlike the architect, did not cause the 'desecration' of the lake. Something akin to this Loosian 'coexistence' seems to have been intended in Le Corbusier's didactic furnishing of the

Pavillon de l'Esprit Nouveau, erected for the Parisian Exposition des Arts Décoratifs of 1925. Here, the industrial and the folkloric, the *I* and the *F*, find their judicious juxtaposition, Le Corbusier following Loos's lead, almost to the letter, in combining standard Thonet bentwood furniture with leather English club armchairs, wrought-iron Parisian park seats, Peruvian pottery and Oriental carpets. All this is encompassed by an 'architecture degree zero', one that is close in its rational negativity to the anti-architectural yet vestigially classical norms embodied in Loos's canonical villas. These ties between Loos and Purism have, surely, been undervalued in the past. The link, however, is never more evident than in the third issue of *L'Esprit nouveau* of 1920, when the Dadaist poet-editor Paul Dermée, together with Amédée Ozenfant and Le Corbusier, republished the 1913 French translation of 'Ornament und Verbrechen'. And while, as Reyner Banham has observed, the roots of Purism lay in the abstract classicizing tendencies of prewar Parisian culture (not to mention the Dada 'ready-made' sensibility of 1913), there is little reason to doubt that the influence of Loos was decisive in refining the typologically *collagiste* approach of Purism. Prior to Le Corbusier one has to look to Loos for that unique formulation of the normative type in conjunction with an anti-hermetic attitude towards the juxtaposition of irreconcilable historical components. This notion corresponds to what Benedetto Gravagnuolo has termed a dilation of history – that assumption of 'the simultaneous coexistence of all historically produced forms', a discourse that comes into being because of the inescapably *collagiste* aspect of all received history.

The Pavillon de l'Esprit Nouveau, like Le Corbusier's Maison Cook of virtually the same date, is uncannily Loosian at yet another level in that it demonstrates to the letter, Loos's anti-*Gesamtkunstwerk* distinction between *meubles* and *immeubles* – that is, his discrimination between the movable furniture that should not be designed by the architect and the built-in storage that legitimately falls within his province. This is the categoric division of labour that Loos sets forth in his essay 'Die Abschaffung der Möbel' of 1924, where he writes:

... The brass bedstead, the wrought-iron bedstead, table and chairs, hassocks and occasional chairs, desk and smoking stand – all items which are made by our craftsmen in the modern idiom (never by architects!) – everyone may buy these for himself according to his own taste and inclination ... The walls of a building belong to the architect. There he rules at will. As with the walls, so with any furniture which is not movable. It must not be treated as furniture. It is part of a wall and does not lead the separate life of the old-fashioned display cabinets.[36]

Raumplan

Loos's recognition of our unavoidably disinherited condition arises from his realization that neither the vernacular nor the classical remains available to the urbanized, industrialized societies of the twentieth century. This is the ultimate meaning of his iconoclastic essay 'Potemkin's Town' of 1898, in which he repudiates the classicizing facades of the Ringstrasse. For Loos, these instrumentally and economically indifferent rent palaces, *Mietspalästen*, must by definition remain a world without qualities. This is the implacable destiny of the modern *Grossstadt* throughout the civilized world, a cultural limbo that prompts Loos to invent the *Raumplan* – plan of volumes – as a way of compensating in *real* terms for the alienating privatization of the triumphant Metropolis. In so doing, he seems to differentiate the 'sayable' from the 'unsayable' and to reconcile, through elision, the asymmetrical irregularities of the vernacular interior with the symmetrical asperities of the stripped but nonetheless classical exterior, although this opposition is hardly made explicit in the first free-standing *Raumplan* structure – the Rufer House, completed in Vienna in 1922. At the same time, the nature of the *Raumplan* reveals itself in the aboriginal dualism of the Loosian interior, as in the Langer apartment of 1901, where Loos attempts to provide, in one continuous volume, for two different bourgeois situations: the *public* formality of the reception space and the *private* intimacy of the inglenook. Irrespective of style, the cultural affinities of this duality are surely obvious – that is to say, the high-ceilinged, 'classical' affinity of the former as opposed to the low-ceilinged, 'vernacular' affinity of the latter. It is only later that Loos begins to articulate this volumetric combination and disjunction, most consciously first in terms of monolithic mass where it manifests itself as an opposition between the formal, regular front and the informal, irregular back exemplified by the Steiner Villa, and then later in terms of changes in floor level as well as ceiling height as we find this in the Strasser House.

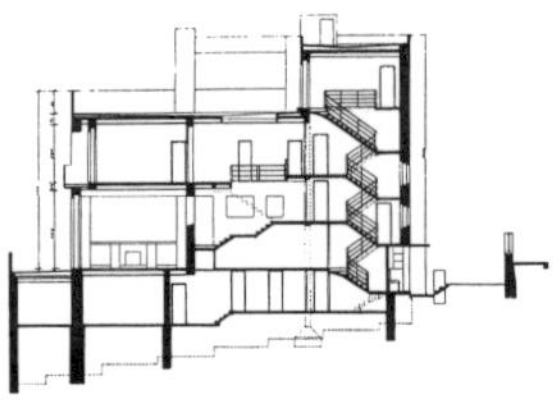

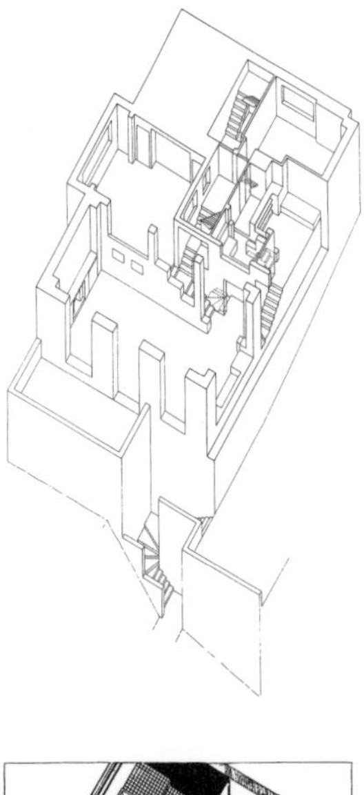

Adolf Loos, Müller House, Prague, 1930, section (top) and axonometric (middle); Le Corbusier, Maison Cook, Paris, 1926, axonometric (below).

While the neoclassical, in a *literal* Schinkelesque or Wagnerian sense, persists as a compositional option for Loos, most notably in the various Viennese villas that he projects in the early Twenties, he gravitates, after his canonical design for Alexander Moissi in 1923, toward a front–versus–back split in his handling of the stripped domestic prism. This is at once evident in his project for a villa at Croissy-sur-Seine (1924), and it is equally present in his compositional treatment of the Tzara House. While this front–back opposition may be less clear in the more cubistically monolithic Moller and Müller houses of the late Twenties, a vestige surely remains even here in the break between the symmetry of the front and the flying beams of the back.

In any event it is clear that Le Corbusier follows this front–back paradigm closely, above all in his villa for Paul Poiret of 1920 and in the Maison Cook and the various projects for the villa at Garches of 1926 and 1927. While Loos's influence is mediated in all three cases, there remains nonetheless an uncanny 'resonance' of something that certainly does not occur in the work of any other architect of this generation. To all intents and purposes, the villa at Garches has an asymmetrical formal front and an asymmetrical eroded rear. The similarity to Loos does not end there, for something of Loos's *Raumplan* is also taken over in the volumetric organization of Le Corbusier's villas. While Le Corbusier does not follow Loos in engendering highly complex, labyrinthine volumes involving multiple displacements in the basic floor levels, he nonetheless organizes his inner volumes as narrative sequences creating *promenades architecturales* of considerable dynamism. Moreover, in the Villa Savoye and above all in the Maison Cook, he goes to great pains to raise the principal living space to the topmost levels of the house, as Loos had already proposed in the Villa Moisi. Thus the L-shaped living room and open terrace of the Moisi project finds its echo in the penultimate volumes of the Maison Cook, where the circulation rises through the living volume to the mezzanine library and roof terrace in a continuous sweep of space. In this respect it is arguable that Le Corbusier attempts to resolve a paradigmatic problem first formulated by Loos, namely how to integrate the asymmetrical, private, vernacular *Raumplan* into the symmetrical public form of the stripped classical prism. The resolution of this problem turns on Le Corbusier's invention of *le plan libre* as a device with which to create a 'gap' between the overall prismatic form of the container and the subdivision of the internal space.

Adolf Loos, Villa Moisi, Venice, 1923, model.

Unlike the Purist Le Corbusier, however, Loos was capable of abandoning the 'cubic–classical' paradigm altogether, so that while the Moller and Müller houses of 1928 and 1930 were still conceived in monolithic terms, the Khuner House, built in Payerback, Austria, at around the same time, allowed vernacular forms to evoke something of their former authenticity. Typologically speaking, the wood-framed Khuner House is a Semmering chalet, although here too there is an 'otherness' that prevents its pitched-roof timber structure from becoming kitsch. Thus while remaining faithful to the logic of the material, Loos nonetheless pushes the craft capacity of the region to its limits, as one may judge from the introduction of novel technical features such as the large picture windows on the lower floors. The few houses that Loos projected for an alpine context are thus misleadingly simple in their appearance, for while distancing themselves from the vernacular they also suggest that the muteness of the 'world without qualities' might be partially redressed in a remote, unspoiled context. Perhaps no two works exemplify this urban–rural opposition more didactically than the Villa Moisi of 1923 and the Haberfeld House designed for Bad Gastein in the previous year. In the Bad Gastein project it is as though the abstract mass of the Villa Moisi has been surmounted by the structural authenticity of Loos's project for a chalet-like house in Semmering of 1913. One's attention thus remains constantly divided between the stereotomy of the former and the tectonic expressivity of the latter.

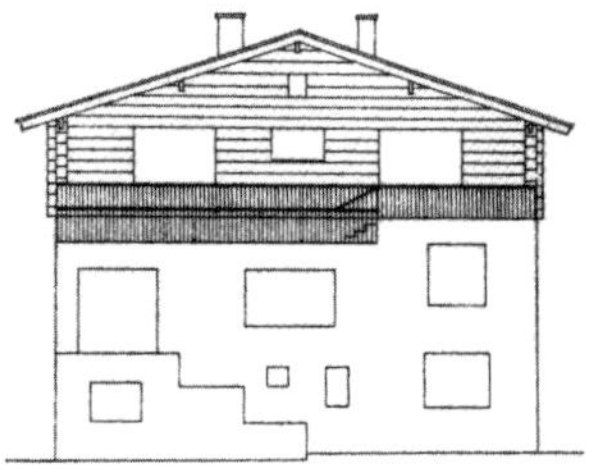

Adolf Loos, Villa Bad Gastein, 1922, front elevation.

Tractatus Architectonicus

Loos's tabula rasa architecture, as Karl Kraus referred to it, came into being out of two complementary but opposed cultural experiences: on the one hand, the hypercritical intelligence of Viennese intellectuals at the turn of the century; on the other, as has already been suggested, the burgeoning empirical reality of the New World, of which Loos had had first-hand experience during his sojourn in America between 1893 and 1896. Where the former gathered its force from an ongoing secular critique of language, science and society, the latter demonstrated the vast and emerging presence of the unreflected 'other' – the democratic and factual indifference of the industrial future. The common ground that linked these otherwise antithetical worlds was the imperative of the real and the epistemological importance accorded to the hypothetical capacity of language to construct an objective description of the world, as variously advanced by such thinkers as Fritz Mauthner, Gottlob Frege, Heinrich Hertz, Ernst Mach and Ludwig Wittgenstein. This *Sprachkritik* led eventually to Wittgenstein's *Tractatus Logico-Philosophicus* (1922), which transposed the thought of Frege and Bertrand Russell into a system for 'modelling' the world wherein the truth of a proposition would depend upon the verifiability of its logical relations with reality. This proto-positivistic propositional theory of language was ultimately achieved at the price of excluding from language the fundamental issue that pursued Wittgenstein throughout his life, namely the question of ethical value. Here the preoccupations of Loos and Wittgenstein, not to mention others from the Krausian circle, appear to converge. Thus, as the architect-philosopher Paul Engelmann has written:

Positivism holds – and this is its essence – that what we can speak about is all that matters in life. Whereas Wittgenstein passionately believes that all that really matters in human life is precisely what, in his view, we must be silent about. When he nevertheless takes immense pains to delimit the unimportant, it is not the coast line of that island which he is bent on surveying with such meticulous accuracy, but the boundary of the ocean.[37]

The closeness of Wittgenstein, philosopher (architect), and Loos, architect (philosopher), resides not only in their momentary role switch, which occurs when Wittgenstein, in collaboration with Engelmann, designs and realizes the Stoneborough House in Vienna in 1926, but also in the virtual correspondence of their respective world views, a correspondence acknowledged by both men. Thus when Wittgenstein remarks in the *Tractatus* that 'Ethics and aesthetics are one and the same' and that 'How things are in the world is a matter of complete indifference for what is higher', the author might well be Loos himself.[38] Indeed, one could go so far as to claim that the ultimate point of the *Tractatus* was exactly the same as the fundamental theme underlying all of Loos's writing, namely to distinguish rigorously between the prosaic realm of logic (building) and the poetic realm of ethics (art). Moreover, the mode of expression was also ultimately the same, namely the paradoxical aphorism – a habit of mind, one might say, that led Wittgenstein to write in the penultimate paragraph of the *Tractatus*:

My propositions serve as elucidations in the following way: anyone who understands me eventually recognizes them as nonsensical, when he has used them – as steps – to climb beyond them. (He must, so to speak, now throw the ladder away after he has climbed up it.)[39]

American Vitruvius

Loos's strangely subtle notion of the classical seems always to have been filtered through the double 'negation' compounded of the intellectual realism of the Old World and the practical realism of the New. In the first instance, he was primed, in architectural terms, by the materialist criticism of Gottfried Semper, to whose writings he would have been introduced in Dresden during his brief education there; in the second, he was indebted to countless American architects and engineers of the pioneering steel-frame period, from William Le Baron Jenny and his First Leiter Building of 1879 to Daniel Burnham and John Root with their Monadnock Block of 1892. What he takes from these buildings, as Roland Schachel has indicated, is what Jean Cocteau took from them when he remarked much later that 'The austerity and size of modern American buildings, stripped by utilitarianism of all superfluity, makes them resemble Greek art.'[40]

From Semper Loos took something of the detached anthropological mode of beholding from which Herman Broch's 'joyous apocalypse' of the modern had to be witnessed. This was virtually the same Archimedian point that Semper had adopted when evaluating the kitsch contents of the Crystal Palace in his famous essay 'Science, Industry and Art' of 1852, a text that ends with the laconic words, 'How will time or science bring order into this until now thoroughly confused state of affairs?'[41] Loos took a more ambiguous, if marginally more optimistic, attitude toward this modern apocalypse when he wrote after Semper in 1898 in his article 'Glass and Clay' that 'All the artefacts of a people ... are informed with this revelatory power. Every implement can tell us something about the customs and character of a people.'[42]

For Loos North America not only was the land of the endless prairie vernacular where the gentleman savages read the newspaper by the light they had invented and likewise took their daily ablutions in hot water (see his essay 'The Plumbers' of 1898), but it was also the land of a somnambulant classicism where the accoutrements and proportions of antique art came and went across the face of gigantic engineering structures in a perennial state of amnesia.

This somnambulism is exactly the property possessed by Loos's own classicism, which comes and goes across the facades of his buildings according to their status, or rather according to the status of their respective parts. Thus the lower two, public floors of the Goldmann and Salatsch store, realized on the Michaelerplatz in Vienna in 1910, are enriched by a two-storey inlaid columnar peristyle, a simplified version, in fact, of that very similar treatment devised by Burnham and Root for the street-level facade of their Rookery Building in Chicago of 1886. The prime iconographic difference between the two, aside from Loos's simplified capitals, may be said to reside in the inset bay window, which, in the *Looshaus*, are as much indebted to the English Arts and Crafts as they are to the utilitarianism of Chicago. More significant, however, is the treatment of the upper rented floors, the non-public parts of the Goldmann and Salatsch building, which, being 'without qualities', are reduced to silence, that is, stripped. They are, in fact, abstract rental space, and as such exemplary of those mute, degree-zero facades that Loos would have liked to see imposed throughout the length of the Ringstrasse. A similar double standard appears in the unreal urbanistic setting that Loos devised for a monument to Franz Joseph in 1917, a project for Vienna wherein the stripped 'silence' of two prismatic 17-storey office towers, replete with nothing but punched windows, would have stood in uncanny contrast to the rhetorical pathos of the neo-Schinkelesque colonnaded forecourt enclosing and preceding the statue itself – an involuntary monument, as Gravagnuolo has put it, 'to the *finis Austriae*, the swan song at the sunset of an age'.[43]

Adolf Loos, competition entry for Chicago Tribune Tower, Chicago, 1922, elevation showing stone coursework.

Five years later Loos would return to a similar contradictory double in his famous entry for the Chicago Tribune competition of 1922, wherein a colossal *hollow* Doric 'column', comprising 22 floors of rentable space, imposes an ironic qualification on the three-storey-high *solid* Doric columns in antis that flank the main entrance to the 'pedestal' block beneath. This academic historicism is qualified not only by the giant parody soaring above, but also by the stripped silence of the 11-storey orthogonal pedestal that, as opposed to the megacolumn, was destined to house the editorial offices of the newspaper itself – the part that Loos ambiguously called the *Zeitungspalast*. Unlike the historical architectural expression accorded to the craft of tailoring in the Goldmann and Salatsch store of 1910, this paradoxical silencing of the media, i.e. journalism (which Kraus despised), affords Loos a mean term, so to speak, in which the transhistorical giantism of the modern American metropolis is seen to relate to silence (the press!) as silence relates to the conventions of history (the columns in antis). This ratio patently renders the giant hollow column a negative sign, an anti-monumental monument, comparable in its ontological consequences to all the other pre-existing 'inhabited monuments' of the modern North American metropolis.

None of this was lost on Loos, who remarked in his competition report that the most successful models of American skyscraper architecture derived from monuments that were never meant to be lived in – from antique Greek monuments such as the famous Mausoleum of Halicarnassus, to the pinnacled glories of the Gothic cathedral. In the first instance, he is apparently alluding to the Metropolitan Building in New York of 1909; in the second, to Cass Gilbert's Woolworth Building, completed in Lower Manhattan in 1912. Lest we retain doubts as to Loos's ironic intent here, it is important to note that he intended to face the entire fabric of his Chicago Tower in polished black granite. Surely this eccentric choice confirms the underlying negativity of his outlandish exploitation of historical form, his pushing of an accepted bourgeois precept to subversive extremes. Moreover, what is an anti-monument if not the ultimate sign of the modern apocalypse, the final indication, as it were, that there is nothing left that merits commemoration? To recall what he said in his essay 'Architecture': '... for us [the colour of mourning] is black'. This was Loos's way of pushing a paradox to the point where it breaks apart and opens to another vista that is at once liberative and tragic. In this matter his work at every scale oscillates constantly between conformity and violence. On the urban scale he had exhibited this sensibility earlier, in his Franz Joseph monument proposal of 1917, when he expressed some concern as to the height of the twin towers in relation to the spire of St Stephen's cathedral. But in Chicago, in the midst of the great plains and surrounded by timeless secular 'rental towers' of inordinate height, he felt free to proceed with impunity. However, his confidence was misplaced. For given the underlying insecurity and provinciality of North American culture at the beginning of the century, it is hardly surprising that his Archimedian essay was to prove altogether too American for the Americans. Loos was beside himself when he learned that his design was not even placed in the competition, and so he wrote, as much in anger as in prophecy, 'The Big Greek Column will be built, if not in Chicago, elsewhere, if not for the Chicago Tribune, for someone else, if not by me, by some other architect.'[44]

Previously unpublished, written in 1986.

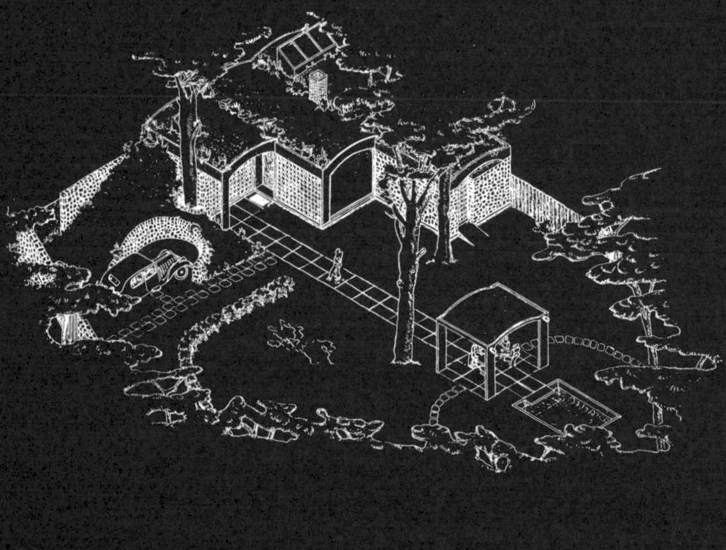

The Other Le Corbusier: Primitive Form and the Linear City, 1929–52

> *Contemporary society suffers from a devastating sickness. Mechanization, which should have been a remedy for all its ills, has been misplaced. We allowed it to upset our traditional mode of life with which it was unable to come to terms. In spite of isolated miracles, the machine age has not yet got into its stride. It has not been able to achieve its proper measure of abundance nor learnt to bridge the gap and establish a new tradition of human happiness. Thus, what should have been toiling humanity's means to freedom has come to be considered by many as little less than a calamity.*
>
> Le Corbusier, *The Four Routes*, 1941[1]

Le Corbusier's name is so bound up with the white modern architecture of the first half of the twentieth century and with that category which ever since the early Fifties has been known as the International Style that it has become difficult, if not impossible, to characterize the architect's career in any other way. And yet there is evidence that, between 1950 and 1955, Le Corbusier made a decisive break with the Purist–machinist vision that he had elaborated so ingeniously with the painter Amédée Ozenfant immediately after the end of World War I. It is my contention that after 1950, Le Corbusier no longer believed in the Purist project as the manifest destiny of the machine-age civilization. Thus, he came to realize that far from heralding a new golden age, the machine was at best an ambivalent instrument or, if not that, then certainly an insufficient cause for the realization of utopia.

Something close to this recognition had already been intimated in the opening pages of *Vers une Architecture* of 1923, where the author was to make it clear that architecture cannot be reduced simply to unadorned engineering technique, as both the Futurists and the Constructivists had been wont to proclaim in the first two decades of the century. Nonetheless, Le Corbusier maintained throughout the 1920s that the machine, while not the sole cause for the imminent triumph of the Enlightenment, was certainly the prime agent for its potential realization. This much is evident in his frequent appeals to the 'captains of industry'. He had in mind those Saint-Simonian industrialists who had secured the ascendancy of France as a modern nation during the second half of the nineteenth century.

Le Corbusier's disillusionment with the machine as the inevitable demiurge did not occur overnight. It came into being gradually, as the result of a series of checks and disappointments, and its emergence may be seen as the chequered course of a creative struggle in which Le Corbusier came to terms with the historical reality in which he was operating. There is, for example, the famous disappointment he suffered as the result of a commission that he received, in the late 1920s, for the design of mass-produced housing, initiated under the terms of the Loi Loucheur. Whether justified or not, he expressed his disillusionment about the fate of his Loucheur project in a letter to the Minister himself: 'We shall not make a single one ... Because your law has no real basis. There is no point of contact between the two sides involved: my plan (which is a way of life) and those for whom the law is made, the potential clients who have not been educated.'

This check put an end, so to speak, to his dream of achieving a Taylorized house comparable to the Model T Ford or the Citroën car – first *fully* articulated in his famous Maison Citrohan of 1920 – with which he had hoped to be able to transform the petit bourgeois, working-class suburbs into an inhabited green belt of cultivation and light; his ambition of civilizing the rustic Anglo-Saxon garden city through the 'classic' urban rationality of the French Enlightenment. This vision was first demonstrated, after a great deal of bureaucratic obstruction, in the small garden settlement that he realized at Pessac, near Bordeaux, in 1925–8 for the industrialist Henry Frugès.

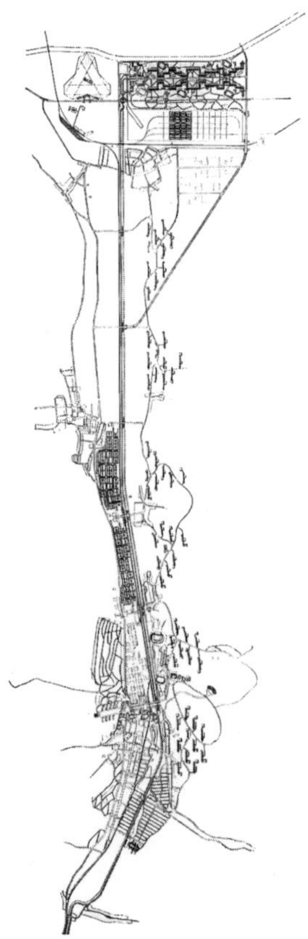

Le Corbusier, plan of Zlín, 1935. Note that here a linear industrial city is superimposed over traditional urban fabric.

The Maisons Loucheur project was not the only setback of the late 1920s, however, as we may tell from his gradual abandonment of the anthropomorphic ideal city, derived as it was from the geocentric metaphysical paradigms of the Renaissance. This centralized neo-humanist model, evident in Le Corbusier's Ville Contemporaine of 1922 and even in his marginally more linear and hence extendable Ville Radieuse of 1930–5, is finally discarded in his plan for the industrial town of Zlín, projected for the Czechoslovakian shoe manufacturer, Jean Bat'a, in 1935. As far as my present theme is concerned, 1935 is the *annus mirabilis* of Le Corbusier's life, for it sees the realization of two works which were to be highly influential for the remainder of his career: first, the linear city of Zlín, which was, in effect, the substitution of an Aristotelian open-ended model for the closed Platonic ideality of his previous urban paradigms; and second, the 'proto-Brutalist' Petite Maison de Weekend, built in the suburbs of Paris out of a significant mixture of machine-made elements and vernacular materials.

It remains somewhat unclear as to how Le Corbusier finally assimilated the idea of the linear city, although this model as a regional instrument had already been formulated by 1882, with the Spaniard Soria y Mata's famous *Cuidad Lineal*. This concept was to be transformed into a regional city model, made up of parallel sectors allocated to different uses, in Léon Jaussely's 1902 plan for the extension and reorganization of Ildefonso Cerdá's Barcelona grid. Le Corbusier would have no doubt been familiar with these proposals through the French garden city movement and its publications as promulgated by the French garden city theorist Charles Benoit-Lévy. Whatever the ultimate source for this idea, it is significant that this model (appropriate in the sense that it was compatible with the global suburbanization which was already taking place) should come to be incorporated into Le Corbusier's repertoire at exactly the same time as he reconciled himself to the fact that materials, other than the gleaming seamless products of industry, would still have to be used in a great deal of building and that this unavoidable condition should be seen as a desirable mediatory factor, rather than as a negative, disagreeable imposition, to be avoided at all costs.

Primitive building techniques and rustic materials begin to appear as consciously expressed elements in Le Corbusier's work from 1929 onwards: first, in the little-known, vaulted 'Ma Maison' project, sketched out on the *SS Massilia* en route to Brazil in 1929; then, in the pitch-roofed, rough-hewn timber and rubble-stone Errazuriz House projected for Chile in 1930 and in the equally rustic villa that he built for Madame de Mandrot, near Toulon, in 1931; and finally in two remarkable works of 1935 and 1937 respectively – the concrete-vaulted Petite Maison de Weekend and the lightweight, canvas-covered Temps Nouveaux Pavilion erected for the Paris International Exhibition. While the roof of the former recalls not only Le Corbusier's Maison Monol of 1919 but also the traditional Catalan vault, the latter evokes the nomadic tent as this had been rendered in a reconstruction of the Hebraic temple in the wilderness, an axonometric of which had appeared as a didactic illustration in *Vers une architecture*. With this series of works, the burden of expression in Le Corbusier's work shifted from the neo-Platonic form to the means of construction itself; in contradistinction, let us say, to the Villa Stein–de Monzie of 1926–8 where a reinforced concrete frame and block in-fill structure was rendered over so as to produce a seamless, totally abstract surface appearance. This was the impression of 'polished, naked steel' which Le Corbusier had ascribed in *Vers une architecture* to the entablature of the Parthenon. Nothing could be further removed from this than the intent of the 1935 Petite Maison de Weekend, as Le Corbusier was to make clear: 'The designing of such a house demanded extreme care since the elements of construction were the only architectural means. The architectural theme was established about a typical bay whose influence extended as far as the little pavilion in the garden.

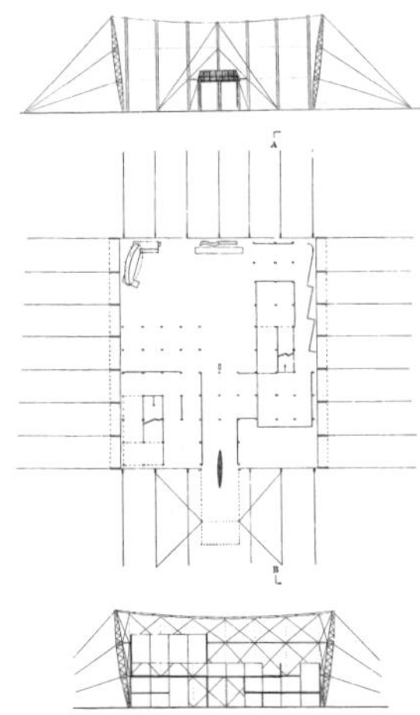

Le Corbusier, Temps Nouveaux Pavilion, Porte Maillot, Paris, 1937, elevation, plan and section.

Here one was confronted with white ceramic tiles on the floor, Nevada glass block walls and a table of Cipollino marble.'

On occasion, Le Corbusier was to excuse this lapse into constructional expressivity and his way of combining old and new materials on the grounds of the remoteness of the building site. This was the line that he adopted, for instance, in accounting for the unpainted timber framework and rubble-stone masonry used in the Maison aux Mathes, which was another weekend house realized near Bordeaux, also in 1935:

The impossibility of supervising the construction and the necessity of employing a small contractor from the village led even to the conception of the plan itself. The house had three successive and absolutely separate stages of work:

a. *the masonry built at one time*

b. *the carpentry built at one time*

c. *the joinery, comprising windows, doors, shutters and cupboards, all to a standard and to a unitary principle of construction; assembled independently and variously panelled in glass, plywood and asbestos cement.*[2]

Despite the archaic and vernacular references, all these works still made extensive use of advanced technology; the weekend houses variously employing reinforced concrete, plywood, plate glass and glass lenses, and the tented exhibition pavilion making a spectacular demonstration of a steel-cable suspension structure in such a way as to allude to jointing techniques that had become familiar in aeronautical and dirigible engineering. Unlike the four large-scale Constructivist curtain-wall buildings which Le Corbusier and Pierre Jeanneret succeeded in realizing between 1930 and 1933 (the Maison Clarté, the Pavillon Suisse, the Cité de Refuge and the block containing his own apartment at 24 rue Nungesser-et-Coli in Paris), these other, incidental, works seem to have served as sophisticated metaphors for a non-doctrinaire future in which men would be free to combine primitive and sophisticated techniques according to their needs and resources. Something of this same archaic spirit is surely detectable in the polychromed reproduction of a Greek *kore*, set up by Le Corbusier in his studio as part of Louis Carré's 'Exposition d'art dit Primitif' of 1935, or in Le Corbusier's exhibition of primitive art staged in Paris in 1940 under the colonialist title, 'La France d'outre-mer'.

Le Corbusier, painted plastercast of a Greek kore, *'Exposition d'art dit Primitif', Paris, 1935.*

An equally direct recourse to primitive methods appears repeatedly in his work throughout the late Thirties and the early Forties, initially in an unrealized 'log cabin' projected for the Jaoul family in 1937 and then in the rubble-walled, pitch-roofed Lannemezan workers' low-rise housing projected in 1940, this being the first occasion on which he was to depict a roof permanently covered in grass. His technical approach became even more primitive in the Murondins, projected in the same year as a model housing type to be used in temporary postwar reconstruction, in which Le Corbusier, the hitherto Modernist, turned his deft hand to a modern adaptation of traditional *pisé* rammed earth construction. Something equally traditional, from a tectonic point of view, is intended in his barrel-vaulted Peyrissac House projected for Cherchell, North Africa in 1942. This last is all too obviously the prototype for the Roq et Rob housing designed for Cap-Martin in 1949, just as the Lannemezan project anticipates the more sophisticated temporary housing designed at the end of the war. In this, the low-rise, barrel-vaulted housing projected for La Sainte-Baume in 1948 and the all but simultaneous Roq et Rob project are seminal. They link back to the Petite Maison de Weekend of 1935 and assert, at the same time, the tectonic and organizational basis for both the first designs for the Maison Jaoul in 1952, and Siedlung Halen, realized outside Bern, Switzerland in 1960 to the designs of the Swiss team Atelier 5 and adhering closely to the low-rise 'carpet' housing prototype advanced by Le Corbusier 12 years previously for La Sainte-Baume.

Le Corbusier, sketch of Roq et Rob Housing, Cap-Martin, 1949.

This is surely the other Le Corbusier, the figure, in fact, who seems to go to ground as the golden promise of the machine age ends in the disastrous apocalypse of World War II. This, I would submit, is the architect who, despite his opportunism during the Vichy regime, nonetheless responds with astonishing sensitivity to the existential strand evident in the emerging poetic realism of the time. As James Stirling was to write in 1956, the Maison Jaoul, with its claustrophobic fenestration, its rough concrete structure and its *briques apparentes*, was an affront to those sensibilities which had been nurtured on the myth that modern architecture should manifest itself as smooth, machine-wrought planar surfaces within an articulated structural frame.

As far as linear planning is concerned, it seems that Le Corbusier was first caused to abandon his ideal utopian urban model because of the obdurate character of the *topos* itself; that is to say, by the narrow volcanic contours of the Rio de Janeiro corniche, which he first experienced when he visited Brazil in 1929. He seems to have realized on this occasion that in many instances it would be inappropriate, if not impossible, to impose idealized urban grids on highly contoured, irregular sites. This would account for his instant adaptation of Edgar Chamberless's Roadtown project of 1910 in his proposals of 1929 for Montevideo and Rio de Janeiro. These grandiloquent visions led in the following year to his remarkable Plan Obus for the corniche of Algiers, in which he combines together for the first time both the linear city concept and the notion of 'artificial sites'; the latter being tiered empty lots on which people would be free to erect houses, designed according to their personal taste. The lesson learned about the inaccessibility of modern architectural form, dating from the Maisons Loucheur, seems to be assimilated here into a project of Boullée-like grandeur and ambition.

Le Corbusier, Maison Jaoul, Neuilly, 1956, exterior view.

In retrospect, one witnesses Le Corbusier's ideal city disintegrating before one's eyes: first in the Antwerp plan of 1935, then in the project for L'Oued-Ouchaia, Algeria of 1934, and finally in the proposals for Nemours and Zlín of 1934/5, where the *redent*, or zig-zag block, as the metaphorical residential 'lung' of the anthropomorphic Ville Radieuse is finally relinquished. Le Corbusier's acceptance of the reality of the suburban megalopolis comes soon afterwards when he first visits the United States and sets down his critical but realistic reflections on the problem of New York City in *Quand les Cathédrales étaient blanches* of 1936. Even if one remains unconvinced by the Corbusian counter-proposal of high-rise residential slabs set in idyllic parkland, his critical indictment of the petit bourgeois nature of normative suburban settlement is surely no less apposite today than when it was first written 50 years ago:

Manhattan is so antagonistic to the fundamental needs of the human heart that the one idea of everybody is to escape. To get out. To avoid wasting one's own life and that of one's family in that hard implacable atmosphere. To see the sky. To live where there are trees and to look out on grass. To escape forever from the noise and racket of the city.

This dream of the millions has been realized. Millions of city dwellers have moved out to the country. They arrive and settle down and in so doing they cause the destruction of the country. The result is a vast, sprawling, built-up area encircling the city – the suburbs. All that remains is the dream – the dream of being free, the dream of being master of one's destiny.

This suburban development makes necessary the hours spent daily in the metros, buses and Pullmans and causes the destruction of that communal life which is the very marrow of a nation. Yet all this only makes a life of very little real freedom – front doors side by side on the edge of the road, windows overlooking each other, neighbouring roofs shutting out the sky, and an occasional tree which has survived this onslaught. (I am speaking here of those masses who have not succeeded in doing very well for themselves and who are the vast proportion of the populations of New York and Chicago.)[3]

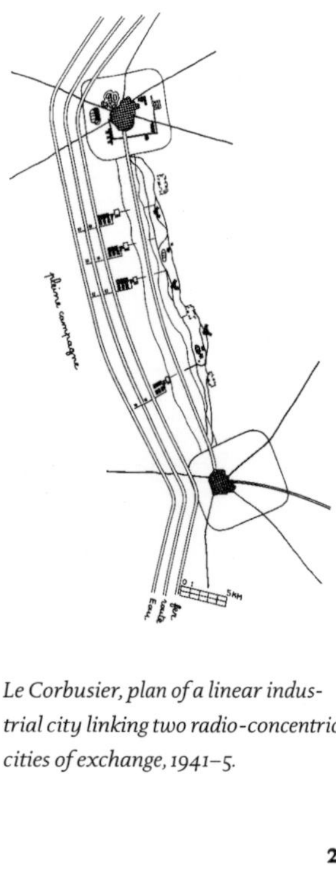

Le Corbusier, plan of a linear industrial city linking two radio-concentric cities of exchange, 1941–5.

After his visit to the United States in 1936, Le Corbusier gravitated even more decisively towards the evolution of a viable 'open-city' form of urban development, one which would correspond more closely to the reality of the generic megalopolis then spontaneously emerging in the areas surrounding every major capital city. The primary unit of Le Corbusier's regional planning thesis had first, in fact, been formulated in 1934. It may be thought of as being prime in more ways than one, since it corresponds directly to the first term in the economic taxonomy that divides our modern productive economy into primary, secondary and tertiary industry, and Le Corbusier was to evolve the functional units of his new urban model in exactly this order. The first unit emerged with Le Corbusier's Syndicalist proposal for an architectonic and Taylorized reorganization of agriculture. This project, known as the Ferme Radieuse, was further developed by him as the Village Coopératif in 1938 and later became the quintessential unit of agricultural exploitation in his book *Sur les Quatre Routes*, first published in a limited edition in 1941; the thesis was later reworked as *Les Trois*

Etablissements humains (1945). This last publication posited the three generic units of Le Corbusier's regional urbanism, one for each sector of the economy: the Ferme Radieuse of 1934, the green factory or Usine-Verte of 1944 and the traditional radio-concentric city of exchange.

The final form of Le Corbusier's industrial linear city owes much to the Soviet comprehensive linear city model, and above all to the generic model advanced by N A Miliutin in his book *Sotsgorod* of 1930. Le Corbusier had already started to move in the direction of linear organization in the earliest version of the Ville Radieuse, presented in the Soviet Union as the *Réponse à Moscow* of 1930. Although the plan of Zlín (1935) does not correspond exactly with the Miliutin paradigm, the generic 'linear industrial city', published in *Les Trois Etablissments humains* of 1945, follows precisely the first four zones of Miliutin's six-zone system. These zones are: 1. The heavy transport (in Miliutin's case the railway, in Le Corbusier's the three freight routes of road, rail and canal); 2. The industrial sector; 3. The green band with an axial high-speed civic autoroute, and 4. The residential area with the various supporting facilities. Miliutin's fifth zone, the park, is eliminated from Le Corbusier's linear model, since it is integrated with the residential zone, which is Miliutin's sixth zone. At the same time, the agricultural sector, treated as a continuous linear strip in the Miliutin model, has been transformed into another element entirely, namely the hexagonal domain of agricultural production. This unit, with the 'radiant village' at its centre, corresponds, geometrically and logistically, to Walter Cristaller's hexagonal regional planning model advanced in 1935 in Cristaller's book *Die zentralen Orte in Süd-deutschland*.

Cristaller, an urban geographer rather than a planner in the strict sense, found, through studying the topographical distribution of urban settlements in southern Germany, that traditional radio-concentric settlements happened to be located according to the coordinates of a triangular or hexagonal grid. While we do not know how Le Corbusier came to be familiar with this work, it would seem that the Cristaller concept was the catalyst for Le Corbusier's ultimate regional planning model, wherein existing radio-concentric towns are to be linked by linear industrial cities and where the remaining triangular interstitial areas, allocated to agriculture, are to be subdivided into the hexagonal mosaic previously described. The neo-humanist centralized finite city, as in the Ville Contemporaine, has finally been dissolved, just as the seamless white architecture has been totally abandoned. It is 1944 and Le Corbusier is 57 years old. He has come to terms with the Pandora's box of the infinite megalopolis and a further 21 years of 'open-city' practice and thought still lie ahead of him.

First published in *Le Corbusier: Architect of the Century*, London: Arts Council of Great Britain, 1987, pp.29–34.

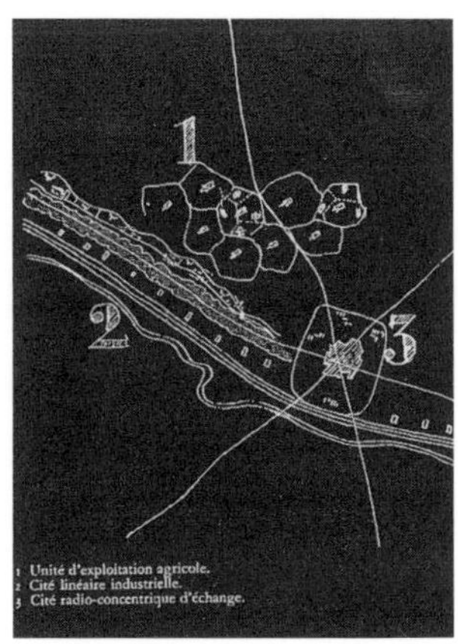

Le Corbusier, diagram of Les Trois Etablissements humains, *1945: 1) unit of agricultural exploitation; 2) linear industrial city; 3) radio-concentric city of exchange.*

Perhaps one of the most surprising things about Los Angeles is that one can easily spend a month travelling around the megalopolis, and still not exhaust the rich seams of modern architecture that lie embedded there. In this regard it is not only a modern architectural mecca but also an improbable North American paradox, for in many respects this is a city where architecture is of little consequence. Unlike Chicago, this is the media capital of the world, where film and television dominate public life and where architecture is, at best, only a poor relation.

Nonetheless, LA is still an astonishing cultural centre where the ethos of what was most vital in American modern architecture is still alive. And when all the dust has finally settled in the great debate that surrounds the rise and fall of a suspect Postmodernism, we may possibly look to Los Angeles, to begin again, with an 'other' modernity, that has been nurtured in this city for well over 80 years – certainly since Irving Gill's Bailey House and Wilson Acton Hotel, both built in La Jolla around 1908.

Gill inaugurated another important tradition in LA which has unfortunately suffered a serious eclipse everywhere, except possibly in Latin cultures, and that is a concern on the part of the profession for a socially committed, bio-climatic architecture. This progressive approach was first advanced by Gill in a perimeter block of workers' housing that he realized in Sierra Madre in 1910. Esther McCoy's sensitive and succinct description of this block, known as Lewis Courts, can hardly be improved on:

One cottage was separated from the next by a long shallow porch intended for lounging or sleeping. On the south and east sides were cottages spaced in such a way that they did not interfere with garden areas or light and sun for the row houses. Each unit had its own private garden, leading

Rudolph Schindler, El Pueblo Ribera, site plan.

into a community garden, with a large pergola in the centre. Less than a third of the land was used for dwellings. There was a reverence for the individual in the plan that has never been equalled in the field of minimum housing.[1]

Gill was the first in a whole succession of transplanted Prairie Style architects who first worked in Chicago and then migrated to the West. The émigré Austrian Rudolph Schindler was the next of the Prairie progeny to come to southern California via Chicago, and his arrival in Los Angeles in 1920 (to work on Wright's grand mansion for Aline Barnsdall) was to be followed with a similar migratory pattern by his fellow countryman Richard Neutra, who in the space of two years worked first for Holabird & Roche in Chicago and then for Wright in Taliesin before coming to Los Angeles in 1925.

This transmigration of Prairie culture to southern California was reinforced by a genial climate and by a number of other sympathetic factors, such as the indirect influence of the Prairie Style on Kim Weber and J R Davidson (both of whom were from Berlin and were active in the area from 1923 onwards) and by the direct presence of Wright himself – who built almost continually in the region, from the Barnsdall House of 1920 to the Sturges House, erected in Brentwood Heights in 1939. It is critical that this last was a Usonian house since nothing could have been closer than Wright's Usonian model to the principles of the other modernity that flourished in the LA region from he late 1920s onwards. Something similar may also be claimed for the Barnsdall House, a cultural project that in any event served as a training ground for both Schindler and Neutra.

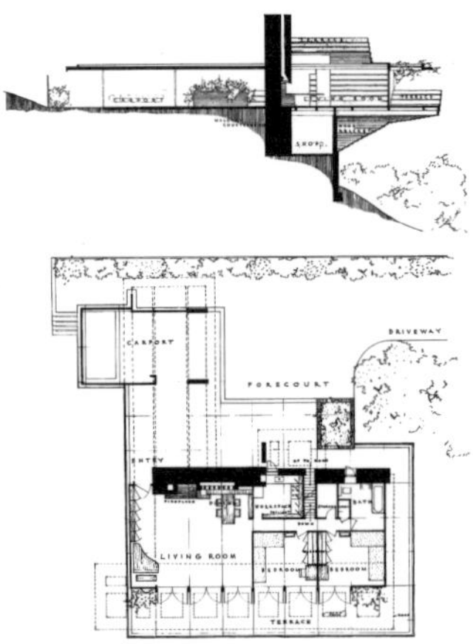

Frank Lloyd Wright, Sturges House, Brentwood Heights, California, 1939, section (above) and plan (below).

It is sobering to have to recognize that Wright's generic house represented the last serious effort to evolve and establish a truly civilized typology for American suburban development. With the exception of the southern Californian school the whole progressive undertaking seems to grind to a halt with Wright's death in 1959, which happened to coincide with a series of articles in *House and Home* popularizing Wright's Usonian notions. In retrospect it was an ironic combination of popular triumph and almost immediate eclipse – the double movement coinciding with Wright's own demise. Of this widespread but limited Usonian influence John Sergeant has written:

It didn't matter that the whole message of Wright's popularizing activity was rarely communicated. North Americans all over a continent encountered it in one garbled form or another, through magazines and radio, often locally produced or syndicated or by the example of local Wrightian design. Advances were made, and the American home of the late 1950s and early 1960s does represent a distinct architectural achievement.[2]

Sergeant reminds us that Wright's definition of the organic was ecological, that it favoured a symbiotic, metabolic relation with nature rather than one of wilful domination involving air conditioning and the optimization of energy consumption. As Sergeant put it: 'Wright's attitude welcomes intermediate technology and the use of indigenous materials, rather than being reliant on increasingly distant, impersonal products of centralized technology.'

While neither Schindler nor Neutra publicly subscribed to specific Usonian precepts and while they resisted belabouring the term *organic* in the same way as Wright, they remained, none the less, continually subject to his influence in the most creative way imaginable. They were thus able to develop their own European-based modernity along extremely reflexive regional lines. In terms of the cultural continuity of southern California, it is important to note how Schindler's El Pueblo Ribera development, completed in La Jolla in 1925, really picks up where Gill's Lewis Courts left off and recasts the whole generic project in more Wrightian micro-spatial and tectonic terms. At the same time nothing could be more middle European than the collective paradigm of the *Siedlung*. Here the idea of a socially conscious land-settlement pattern is transplanted and then transformed by being combined with the Californian bungalow tradition. This creative operation was to yield a socio-cultural result of exceptional richness and life-enhancing potential. It is already the essential inspiration that carried Schindler through the rest of his career and it, in turn, sustained a number of LA courtyard settlements of a similar order and intent, above all, perhaps, Neutra's own Strathmore apartments, built in Westwood in 1938. El Pueblo Ribera is as relevant a pattern of land settlement today as it was when it was first completed over 60 years ago. In the interim, save for our current petit-bourgeois consumerist cupidity (facilitated by the stylistic degeneracy of Postmodernism) little has changed the fundamental socio-economic and technical need to integrate the automobile with low-rise high-density megalopolitan housing, for, given the distributive capacity of the freeway it is highly unlikely that we will ever return to the dense pattern of the traditional city.

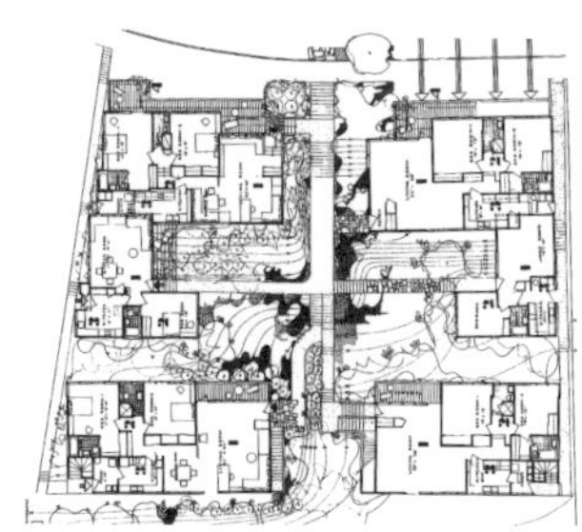

Richard Neutra, Strathmore Apartments, Westwood, California, 1938, exterior view (above) and ground floor plan (below).

The luxury and economy of El Pueblo Ribera certainly has to be experienced to be fully appreciated, but something of its appropriateness to the site and its setting may be gleaned from David Gebhard's appraisal:

The Pueblo Ribera community is definitely one of the most original urban designs of the period. It is a success in almost every regard – in its blend of coherence and irregularity which it presents as a streetscape, in its provision for maximum privacy for each unit, its use of roof terraces so that each dwelling enjoys a view of the sea, and finally in its adventuresome use of concrete which was formed into walls through the employment of moveable forms.[3]

This last brings to our attention Schindler's significant critique of the American balloon frame that, much like Gill, he deemed to be a tectonically degenerate method of construction. He once described it with ironic disdain as 'an inorganic, unelastic plaster slab supported by means of an organic swelling and shrinking skeleton'. In this regard Schindler, like Wright, constantly tried to ground the poetic of his work in a direct revelation of the way in which it was built.

Inspiration of Neutra

It is to be greatly regretted that Schindler's long overdue re-evaluation (starting with Gebhard's Los Angeles County Museum retrospective of 1967) should have been achieved at the expense of Neutra's reputation, despite recent ambiguous reparative efforts made on Neutra's behalf by the Californian historian Tom Hines. Far from being little more than a ruthlessly competitive plagiarizing egoist, which is how he has been commonly represented in recent years, Neutra was an architect of extraordinary commitment, sensitivity and power. His role in the cultivation of a modern regional school of architecture in LA throughout the Thirties and Forties was seminal, and the careers of many distinguished southern Californian architects of the second generation are virtually inconceivable without Neutra's inspiring influence. I am thinking of the brilliant work produced by Gregory Ain, J R Davidson, Harwell Hamilton Harris, Raphael Soriano and last but not least, the pre-Miesian career of Craig Ellwood (1952–8) as this is evidenced in Ellwood's Hollywood Courtyard Apartments of 1953 or in his finely tuned and delicately detailed Case Study House, built in Beverly Hills, California, in 1958.

Neutra's initial contribution to southern Californian architecture lay in four main areas: in the compelling dynamism of his topographically inflected Neo-Cubistic compositions; in the programmatic introduction of new building techniques; in the formulation of a metabolic, liberating, almost therapeutic approach to the organization of space; and, finally, in the pursuit of a proto-ecological sensibility towards the climate and topography of the region. With regard to the last, it should be noted that Neutra is one of the great unrecognized landscape architects of the first half of the twentieth century. Trained in plant materials by the Swiss landscape designer Gustav Amman, it was Neutra rather than Schindler who designed the diminutive seaside cactus garden below Schindler's elevated Lovell Beach House, built at Newport Beach in 1926.

Caught in the disenchanted labyrinth of the late twentieth century, it is hard for us to imagine the existence of clients like Philip and Leah Lovell who were progressive from almost every conceivable standpoint, be it radical politics or preventive medicine. If they were not quite so insistently anarcho-socialist as Rudolph and Pauline Schindler, with whom they were intimate friends, they were certainly equally therapeutic in their attitude toward the maintenance of psychological and physical well-being in modern industrialized society. Thus, as Gebhard has written of Lovell, 'Lovell was a characteristic southern California product. It is doubtful whether his career could have been repeated anywhere else. Through his *Los Angeles Times* column, "Care of the Body", and through "Dr Lovell's Physical

Culture Center", he had an influence which extended far beyond the physical care of the body. He was, and he wished to be considered, progressive, whether in physical culture, permissive education, or architecture.'

Theory of biorealism

The ideology of Lovell and its direct expression in Neutra's Health House, designed for Lovell in 1926, was to exercise a decisive influence over the rest of Neutra's career. From now on his work was at its best where the building programme could be interpreted as making a direct contribution to the psycho-physiological well-being of its occupants. The central theme of both Neutra's work and his writings was the beneficial impact of a well-designed environment upon the functioning of the nervous system. And while his theory of 'bio-realism' sometimes rested on dubious causal arguments linking architectural form to overall health, it is difficult to discredit the extraordinary sensitivity and supra-functional attitude that coloured his whole approach; let alone the direct evidence that has accumulated since his death that there is indeed a direct connection between our increasingly abrasive post-industrial environment and the incidence of cancer. Nothing could be further removed from the exclusively formal motivations attributed to the International Style by Hitchcock and Johnson than the overall biological concerns addressed by Neutra in his book *Survival Through Design* (1954) where he wrote, 'It has become imperative that in designing our physical environment we should consciously raise the fundamental question of survival in the broadest sense of the term. Any design that impairs or imposes excessive strain on the natural human equipment should be eliminated or modified in accordance with the requirements of our nervous, and more gradually, our total physiological functioning.'

Thus, the primary concern of Schindler and Neutra (both of whom had served their American apprenticeships with Wright) was not abstract form as such, but rather the articulation of sun and light, combined with a sensitive integration of vegetation and tectonic form into the existing fabric. This ambient hedonism was never more subtly expressed than in the Sachs Apartments, Los Angeles, built to Schindler's design in 1928; or in Neutra's second masterwork, his Kaufmann Desert House built at Palm Springs, California, in 1947.

That an architect could conceive of his work as transcending both self-conscious aesthetics and the needs and resources of the middle-class client on whom he or she would invariably depend for patronage is as about as foreign to us today as it was normal for southern Californian architects in the period of the New Deal. Thus we find Neutra writing in the Fifties of his interest in progressive educational methods and of their dissemination to the Third World:

The briefly illustrated Ringplan school designed in 1926 has rooms in which by monitor-like ceiling openings and the guarded influx of light from above, brightness differentials were kept down with care throughout the enclosed space. This space is . . . extended to an open-air classroom, with many activities possible on the equally extended ground and floor, so naturally close to children. Undoubtedly the first teaching of geometry and geography took place on the ground, not just on vertical blackboards.

The ideas presented in these designs have now been broadly accepted in California and in other states. To be commissioned to give thought to the design of an entire school system of a country like Puerto Rico is indeed a fascinating task; and to consider herein a most economical

Richard Neutra, Kaufmann Desert House, Palm Springs, California, 1947, evening view.

budget gives it world significance, because the world consists mostly of poor countries, where means are not as plentiful as in the State of New York or even in Stockholm or Zurich.[4]

The Usonian legacy was never more prominent in Neutra's work than in his inflected elaboration of single-storey residential accommodation with internal volumes fusing into planted patios at every turn and with bedrooms and corridors being invariably treated as incidental living space, as galleries, libraries, storage walls and the like. He was, in this particular respect, the prime mentor of the southern Californian school and those who worked for him in the Thirties and Forties – architects such as Ain, Pfisterer, Harris, Soriano and even Ellwood (who, as a young man, was to supervise the construction of some of his houses) – followed him faithfully in this regard, designing residences that were always ingeniously articulated in terms of their micro-space. Certainly one cannot claim that there are decisive masterpieces among the highly civilized houses realized by this group of architects, but this hardly justifies our current snobbish tendency to dismiss the level of domestic civility generally achieved in southern California during the Forties and Fifties, and still evident, as continuing culture, even today.

Usonian superiority

In our search for more socially accessible and economic patterns of land settlement the Usonian model surely still surpasses the virtues of the only other prevalent residential paradigm that is available for future megalopolitan development. Certainly one may claim that it is *ecologically* superior to the Anglo-Saxon suburban garden city pattern, above all for its tendency to proliferate interstitial micro-climatic conditions throughout the built-up area. Other cultural differences between the two are equally apparent, for where Ebenezer Howard's Rurisville is a compensatory petit-bourgeois pattern of private land settlement that still simulates the nostalgic iconography of an idealized but lost agrarian past, Wright's Usonia continues to project a hedonistic and ecologically viable post-industrial future. And where the former invariably results in an unending expanse of free-standing, pitched-roofed brick boxes, relieved only by puritanical over-worked lawns and flowerbeds and by the generally meaningless lacunae of leftover space, the latter results in a semi-collective pattern of carpet housing where built/unbuilt, culture/nature and public/private all continually interpenetrate each other throughout the built-up area. The socio-familial and bio-regional advantages of this last have already been convincingly advanced many times since Wright's death (above all by Roland Rainer), but this unfortunately has not led to its widespread adoption as the normative mode of our time. The reactionary and ultimately uneconomic prejudices of mortgage companies, banks and bureaucrats continue to prevail more or less everywhere, and it is these forces rather than the critically creative intellect that continue to determine the received image of home as this is reflected on the market and in the general pattern of land settlement. As Antonio Gramsci was to put it, 'The old is dying and the new cannot be born and in this interregnum many disturbing symptoms appear.'

Among the very few exceptions to this depressing rule, vestiges of sensitive, low-rise, high-density development may still be found in southern California today, above all in the recent planned unit-developments built on a relatively small scale by young architects and developers. I am thinking of a whole series of condominium terrace houses recently built in Santa Monica to the designs of such architects as David Cooper, Michael Folonis, James Stafford, Ricky Binder and Steve Andre. Of these works perhaps the most spectacular and generic, from the point of view of positing a model for future development, are the so-called Sun-Tech townhouses realized in Santa Monica to the designs of Andre in 1981. While Wright's Usonian house can no longer be claimed as the conceptual origin of this work, and while prewar European housing models are as much an influence on the Sun-Tech houses as Schindler's El Pueblo Ribera block, there nonetheless remains that particular interpenetration of interstitial interior and exterior micro-space that has become the hallmark of the southern Californian school.

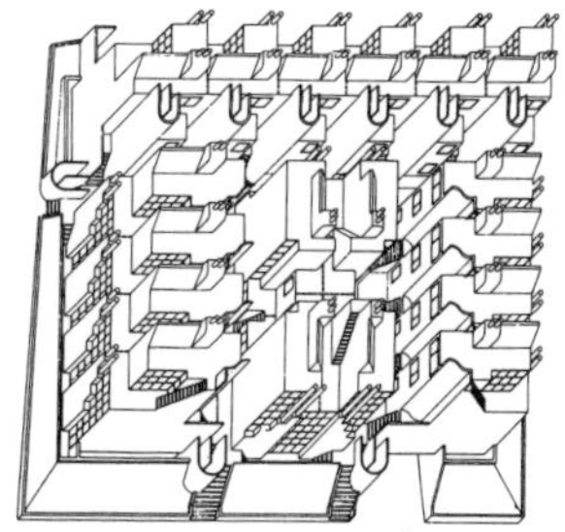

Steve Andre, Sun-Tech Townhouses, Santa Monica, California, 1981, axonometric.

First published in *Architectural Review*, vol.182, no.1090, December 1987, pp.26–31.

The Legacy of Alvar Aalto

The structures which were means to create a new architecture have been wrested from us and turned into commercialized decorative ends in themselves with no inner value. There was a time when a misconstrued, lifeless traditionalism was the chief enemy of good architecture. Today its worst enemy is the superficial decorative misuse of the means acquired during the breakthrough . . . The contrast between deep social responsibility and decorative 'surface effects' is perhaps the oldest and certainly the most topical issue in the debate on architecture. Please do not think that I wish to disparage beauty in rejecting decorativeness. Architecture must have charm; it is a factor of beauty in society. But real beauty is not a conception of form which can be taught, it is the result of harmony between several intrinsic factors, not least the social.

Alvar Aalto, 1936[1]

The view that the final significance of an architect's career must ultimately depend upon his or her long-term influence is one that is at variance with the contemporary cult of the star. It stems from the conviction that, in architecture, the creative capacity of the culture as a whole is of more consequence than the contribution of any particular individual – a sentiment that Aalto himself endorsed when he accorded credit, as he did on many occasions, to the 'anonymous', highly experienced architects who had assisted him over the years. This acknowledgment gives priority to the social cultivation of the art rather than emphasizing the presence of any singular talent. Thus, irrespective of Aalto's indisputable status as a master architect, a position of which he was fully aware, of greater import in the last analysis, both for him and for the culture of this century, was and still is the more general implication of his contribution at both a practical and theoretical level.

As Demetri Porphyrios has shown in his revealing study, *Sources of Modern Eclecticism* (1982), Aalto's architecture after 1934 was a total antithesis to the *homotopia* of Western European rationalism. Whereas the homotopic model was based on order, regularity, symmetry, recurrence and familiarity, irrespective of whether this assumed a neoclassical or a functionalist format, Aalto's *heterotopic* approach was one that favoured fragmentation, layering, multiplicity and a more or less continual state of organic growth. Porphyrios characterized this approach as one in which order arises haptically out of juxtaposition, rhythmic repetition and asymmetrical inflection without any evident unifying or universal principle. As Porphyrios put it, 'If the homotopic mind set out to establish frontiers of an uninterrupted continuity, heterotopia was to destroy the continuity of syntax and to shatter predictable modes of the homogenous grid.'[2]

Some 40 years younger than Frank Lloyd Wright and approximately a decade younger than the generation of Le Corbusier and Mies van der Rohe, Aalto may be seen as being doubly fortunate in terms of the place and the date of his birth, in the first instance, because he inherited the rich cultural tradition of Finnish national romanticism just as it was entering its decline, and, in the second, because he came upon the Modern Movement when its pioneers had already established a zero degree functionalism against which he could react in humanist and organic terms.

As the architect Colin St John Wilson has written, Aalto may be seen as having expanded modern functionalism to include within its rubric a psycho-neurological response to different levels of stimuli arising from a single cause, as filtered simultaneously through the visual, aural and tactile senses.[3] In this sense, in an age in which we are overwhelmed by ephemeral images of every kind, we may justly see him as an architect whose œuvre was totally antithetical to the reduction of building to modular spatial arrangements largely determined by proximal or productive considerations, or to provisional assemblies predominantly conceived to provide a spectacular image – the cult of the 'decorated shed', against which he reacted throughout his life. While this did not render him immune to the picturesque in European culture, Aalto's predisposition towards asymmetrical compositions was always qualified by a deep concern for an appropriately organic aggregation of the parts and for the integration of the resultant assembly into the site.

Aalto belonged to that 'existential' generation of northern European intellectuals in which, to put it in terms of Martin Heidegger, 'building, being, dwelling and cultivating'[4] were seen as part and parcel of the same socio-organic response to the conditions of existence. And while he was too democratic and realistic to have anything to do with the chauvinistic politics that were fatally associated with this view, Aalto's ecological propensity brought him nonetheless close to Hugo Häring's *Neues Bauen* movement, that is to say, to that alternative line in modern architecture identified by St John Wilson as 'the other tradition'.[5] This tradition, loosely associated with northern European Expressionism, would be more precisely defined through the work of Häring and Hans Scharoun and, above all, perhaps through Häring's famous Gut Garkau farm complex of 1924, which came closest to anticipating Aalto's heterotopic syntax.

The work of Aalto is of critical import at the end of the twentieth century because, while he was by no means antithetical to the manifest advantages of modern technoscience and industrial production, he was, simultaneously, far from sanguine about the tendency to regard technological advance as an end in itself rather than as a means to a liberative end. He thought that the habitat in general should be able to respond easily and freely to cyclical life changes and to fluctuations in the daily pattern of existence, particularly as these affected psychic mood as well as physical well-being. Like the Franco–Irish architect Eileen Gray, he thought that 'a window without a shutter was like an eye without an eyelid'[6] and that the interior of the living volume should, within limits, be freely modifiable by the occupant. On these grounds, like Giancarlo de Carlo, he was opposed to the very notion of cheap housing.

As de Carlo put it in 1968 in his pamphlet *Legitimizing Architecture*, 'We have a right to ask "why" housing should be as cheap as possible and not, for example, rather expensive; "why" instead of making every effort to reduce it to minimum levels of surface, of thickness, of materials, we should not try to make it spacious, protected, isolated, comfortable, well equipped, rich in opportunities for privacy, communication, exchange and personal creativity.'[7] A decade earlier Aalto had already pursued a similar line of reasoning in bitterly ironic terms. Thus, in 1957 he argued:

Then there is our old enemy the speculator in real estate. That is the enemy number one of the architect. But there are other enemies too who may be even more difficult to defeat. For instance, we have in my country . . . the theoretical line of building economy, which is popularly stated in this way: 'What form of house is the most economical . . . How deep should it be? How long? What is the cheapest way we could give people badly needed dwelling houses?' Of course, this may be called science. But it is not. The answer is very, very simple – the deepest house is the cheapest. That is clear. One can go further and say that the most inhuman house is the cheapest, that the most expensive light that we have is daylight – let us eliminate that, and then we will get cheaper housing . . .

Real building economy cannot be achieved in this ridiculous way. The real building economy is how much of the good things, at how cheap cost, we can give . . . It is the same in all economy – the relationship between the quality of the product and the price of the product.

But if you leave out the quality of the product, the whole economy is nonsensical in every field.[8]

However, Aalto's concept of building economy was not restricted to housing. It extended, as we shall see, to the economy of the built environment as a whole. Thus, elsewhere in the same speech of 1957, we find him stating, 'The most expensive thing is fresh air, because it is not only a question of ventilation, but also a question of city planning. Fresh air for human beings costs acres of ground and good gardens and forests and traffic and meadows.'[9] In short, he cited everything that cannot be readily achieved in dense urban environments, which are fed by the carcinogenic automobile and other equally polluting late-modern technologies.

For Aalto, building culture was to be given the widest possible interpretation rather than be narrowly understood in a classical or modern avant-gardist sense. Hence, despite his lifelong attachment to Italy, he displayed almost no interest whatsoever in humanistic proportional systems or, for that matter, in any radically hermetic intellectual proposition. And, while he was not averse to employing organizing grids and modules, and indeed would frequently do so, he was totally opposed to the use of modular systems as ends in themselves. His intuitive, biomorphically inspired approach to environmental design caused him to place an enormous emphasis on the capacity of built form to modify equally both the landscape and the urban fabric. In this regard he would have been sympathetic to the architect Mario Botta's slogan, 'building the site'.[10] All of Aalto's sites were built in this topographical sense, and his achievements as an architect cannot be separated at any stage of his career from his capacity as a designer of landscapes.

Aalto's mature career seems to break down into two interconnected but distinct episodes: on the one hand, the early *constructivist* work that he designed and realized in Turku in close collaboration with Erik Bryggman, such as the Turku 700th Anniversary Exhibition and Trade Fair of 1929, and, on the other, the shift towards *organicism*, as this was first unequivocally expressed in his own house and studio, completed in the Helsinki suburb of Munkkiniemi in 1935–6.[11] In retrospect, it is clear that the laconic character of Finnish Constructivism derived from its origin in the severity of Nordic classical form.[12] In Aalto's case, this is at once evident in the Southwestern Finland Agricultural Cooperative Building in Turku of 1927–30 and in the different phases of his competition entry for the Viipuri City Library of 1927–35, wherein one may witness the gradual evolution of classical norms into constructivist tropes. However, unlike the extravagant engineering forms adopted by the Russian Constructivists, Aalto eschewed the technological rhetoric of the Soviet avant-garde in the name of an objective propriety. This much is at once clear when one compares the main elevation of Aalto's Turun Sanomat building of 1928–30 to the Vesnin brothers' project for the *Pravda* newspaper building in Moscow of 1923,

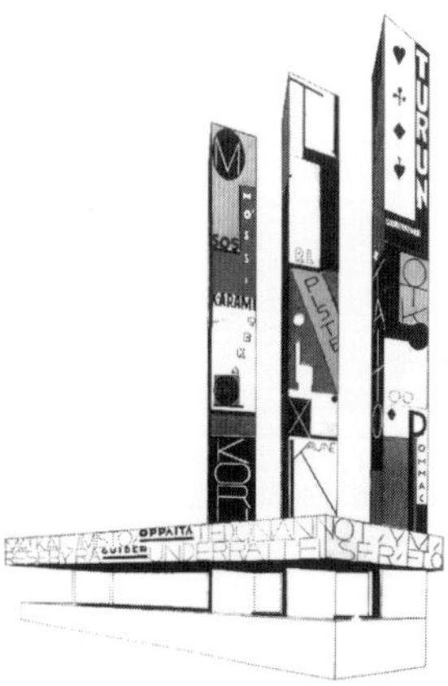

Alvar Aalto and Erik Bryggman, Pavilion for the Turku 700th Anniversary Exhibition, 1929, perspectival drawing.

with which Aalto was surely familiar. We find the same singular display device in both, namely the projection of the front page of their respective newspapers onto a large glass wall facing the street. While the Russians augmented this ultra-modern gesture with all sorts of technological paraphernalia, from transparent elevator cabins to digital clocks, the large display window of Aalto's building was simply juxtaposed with sober, steel-framed, ribbon windows, typical of a functionalist facade of the late 1920s.

Alvar Aalto, Turun Sanomat building, Turku, 1928–30, streetfront perspective. Note the large picture window displaying enlarged front page of the newspaper.

Aalto's gradual recasting of neoclassical tropes into the sobriety of the *Neue Sachlichkeit*[13] may be readily perceived if we not only follow the stages of the Viipuri City Library but also if we observe the development of the Southwestern Finland Agricultural Cooperative Building at the level of its interior detailing, particularly the treatment devised for its 500-seat theatre. While the first version of this auditorium was a Nordic classic essay after the manner of Erik Gunnar Asplund's Skandia Cinema in Stockholm of 1922–3, the second was an objective, prismatic volume of similar proportions, wherein discrete technical components assumed the space-modulating role that had been previously afforded by the classically romantic mural depicted in the initial perspective. Where the mural had previously articulated the wall surface and the volume into upper and lower zones, this division now depended upon the virtual plane established by Poul Henningsen's light fittings, hung in a U-formation around the sides of the auditorium. A similar functional articulation, in ornamental terms, is evident in the retractable footlights that pop out of the stage and in the severe reveals of the vomitoria leading into the hall.

The subtle shift that occurs in Aalto's work at this time, as he passed from the neoclassical formality of Nordic classicism to the 'product-form' of the *Neue Sachlichkeit*, was never more evident than in the Tapani Standard Apartment Block in Turku of 1927–9. Commissioned by Juho Tapani of the Tapani Construction Company, this block was constructed out of standard precast, lightweight concrete units, namely 50 cm wide beams and 30 cm thick wall units, both components being hollow in order to lighten their weight and accommodate mechanical services within the void. Of the technologically progressive character of this work, Göran Schildt has written:

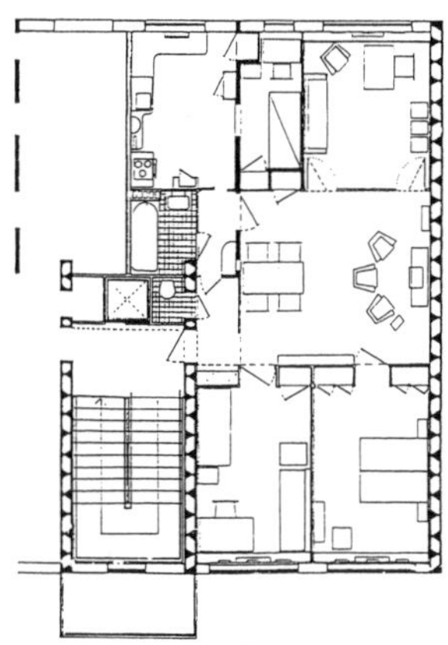

Alvar Aalto, Tapani Standard Apartment Block, Turku, 1927–9, plan.

The building has shops on street level and three stairways, with lifts to the five residential floors. The structural principle of transverse bearing walls between non-load-bearing facades was borrowed from Mies van der Rohe's house at Stuttgart's Weissenhof exhibition of 1927, and provides flexible variation of secondary walls and windows, allowing for varied apartment size, from studio flats to three-room apartments with kitchen and servant's room. Some apartments contain a living room which can be partitioned in various ways. When the building was completed in 1929, Aalto furnished one of the flats with high-quality standard furniture, some of it made by the Thonet company, some designed specially by Aino

Aalto. This model apartment was exhibited to the public during the Turku 700th anniversary exhibition.[14]

Immediately after completing this building, the Aalto office began to produce a series of standard drawings, featuring normative solutions for windows, doors and a wide range of other components, with the ostensible aim of reusing these solutions in future work. Thus, while Aalto's typological approach had its roots in Nordic classicism, it became technologically focused through the work of the German and Dutch left-wing functionalists with whom he became familiar between 1929 and 1932.

As Elina Standertskjöld has shown, the effects of this influence are particularly evident in Aalto's emerging sense of the creative potential of the typical object in the evolution of modern environmental culture.[15] Aalto's interest in perfecting quasi-industrial prototypes was stimulated further by his decision to attend the second Congrès Internationaux d'Architecture Moderne (CIAM), held in Frankfurt in 1929. Aside from the ingenious solutions he devised for light fittings, handrails and doors, together with the standard signs that he developed for both the Turun Sanomat Building of 1928–30 and the Paimio Tuberculosis Sanatorium of 1929–33, Aalto also evolved standard solutions for prototypical casement and sliding double-glazed windows, in both timber and steel, which were subsequently exhibited at the Frankfurt congress.

This preoccupation with norms reached its apothesis with the Stockholm Exhibition of 1930, held under the auspices of the newly constituted Swedish welfare state. Aalto wrote of the exhibition with great enthusiasm and perspicacity on two occasions. In May 1930, he wrote:

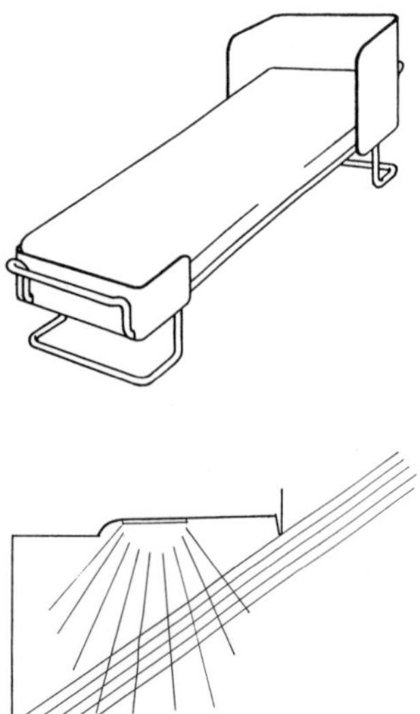

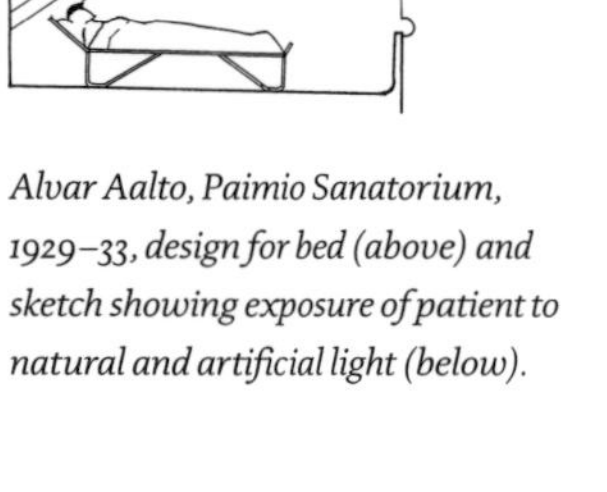

Alvar Aalto, Paimio Sanatorium, 1929–33, design for bed (above) and sketch showing exposure of patient to natural and artificial light (below).

I see it as a very positive manifestation that the artist is in a sense denying himself by going outside of his traditional sphere of work, that he is democratizing his production and bringing it out of a narrow circle to a wider public. The artist thus steps in among the people to help create a harmonious existence with the help of his intrusive sensibility, instead of obstinately upholding the conflict between art and non-art which leads to acute tragedies and a hopeless life.

The biased social manifestation which the Stockholm Exhibition wants to be has been clad in an architectural language of pure and unconstrained joy. There is a festive refinement but also a childish lack of restraint to the whole. Asplund's architecture explodes all boundaries. The purpose is a celebration with no preconceived notions as to whether it should be achieved with architectural or other means. It is not a composition in stone, glass and steel, as the functionalist-hating exhibition visitor might imagine, but rather is a composition in houses, flags, searchlights, flowers . . . and clean tablecloths.[16]

In a second article he adopted a more critical attitude, discriminating between the evolutionary character of a refined material culture as opposed to the pursuit of superficial radicalism as an end in itself. This was already an articulation of the ethical position that he would assume throughout the remainder of his career.

The international socialist challenge to provide decent minimum residential accommodation for all was patently the inspiration behind Aino and Alvar Aalto's 60 square metre, one-bedroom apartment designed for the 'Rationalization of the Minimum Dwelling' exhibition staged in Helsinki in 1930. In addition to modern furnishings, this exhibition featured a range of prototypical products pioneered by Finnish manufacturers, including rubber and linoleum floor finishes and the Enso-Gutzeit Company's standard plywood doors, which served as the prototype for the plywood doors that Aalto installed in Paimio. Aalto's first plywood and tubular-metal chair, the so-called Hybrid Chair, also dates from this time, making its debut in the furnishing of Paimio. His general preoccupation with standardized serial production at this time led finally to the development of the Paimio Chair of 1931–2, made entirely out of bent, laminated plywood. This chair, with its cantilevering organic form, was poised on the dividing line between Aalto's early constructivism and the organicism of his later career.

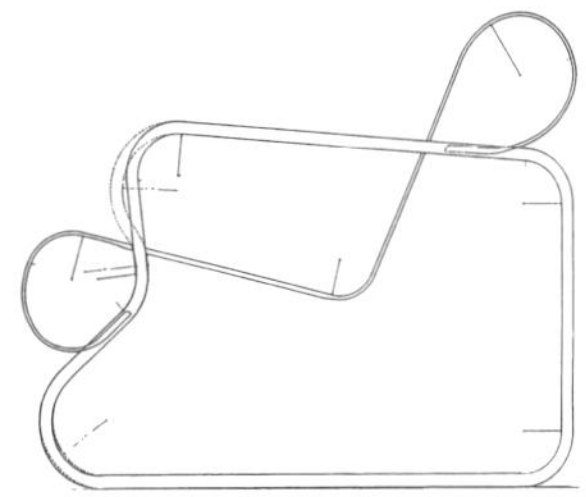

Alvar Aalto, Paimio Sanatorium, elevation of sprung plywood armchair, 1931–2.

Aalto's next attempt at an organic inflection of structural form came with his 'bent-knee' leg of 1933, which was the key to the production of his famous three-legged, stackable stool, first shown in London that year.[17] This leg was produced by inserting slivers of wood into a series of saw cuts and then bending and gluing it into position. With this diminutive 'column', as the architectural critic Gustaf Strengell termed it, Aalto was able to transform not only his furniture but also his entire architectural syntax, even though he continued to design the occasional piece in tubular steel, such as the convertible sofabed, specially designed for Sigfried Giedion's *Wohnbedarf* furniture store in Zurich in 1932. From this date onwards, however, Aalto's furniture tended to be exclusively of wood, with an ever-expanding repertoire of birch pieces, ranging from the triangular laminated bookshelf brackets to the so-called sledge tea trolley of 1937.

Alvar Aalto, stackable three-legged footstool, c.1933.

In his 1940 essay 'The Humanizing of Architecture', Aalto returned to his rationale for abandoning tubular steel as an appropriate material for the production of furniture:

The tubular steel chair is surely rational from technical and constructive points of view: it is light, suitable for mass production, and so on. But steel and chromium are not satisfactory from the human point of view. Steel is too good a conductor of heat. The chromium surface gives too bright reflections of light, and even acoustically it is not suitable for a room. The rational methods of creating this furniture style have been on the right track, but the result will be good only if rationalization is exercised in the selection of materials which are most suitable for human use.[18]

Viipuri City Library, as completed in 1935 in what is now Vyborg, Russia, testifies to a similar transposition in a shift from the classical ashlar of the main entrance to the constructivist character of the steel-framed glass doors set back from the stone front and braced by welded, tubular struts. Similarly, the vestigial Neoclassicism of the top-lit reading rooms (compare Asplund's Stockholm Public Library of 1926) are enriched throughout by a number of carefully inflected details, from the familiar conic lantern lights first pioneered in the Turun Sanomat Building to the serpentine, double-scaled, biomorphic character of the timber stair rails that lead down into the lending area, together with the plywood-faced checkout counter centrally situated between the main reading room and the lending section. At the same time, despite the Asplundian functionalist character of the detailing, it would be hard to imagine a more organic element than the undulating acoustical timber ceiling suspended within the orthogonal prism of the Viipuri auditorium.

A comparable concern for ergonomic inflection had been evident in the inclined splash-backs of the washbasins in the Paimio Tuberculosis Sanatorium, which were angled to minimize the noise of water discharging into the basin, the patients' rooms being doubly occupied. Aalto adopted an equally nuanced attitude towards the quality of the artificial light so as not to expose the recumbent patient to direct illumination. A similar concern for the modulation of natural light led him to crank up the floor slab at an angle close to the window to provide a transitional zone between the glare of the window surface and the softer light of the room. While the angled soffit obviated the effect of glare at the ceiling, the cranked floor at the window afforded a place for the installation of radiant heating below a continuous top.[19]

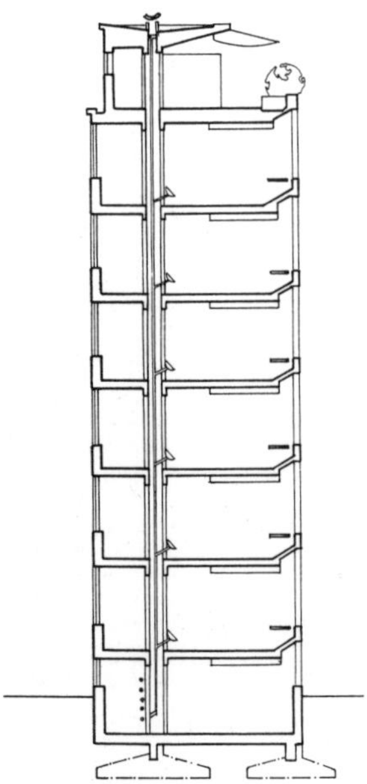

Alvar Aalto, Paimio Sanatorium, cross-section of hospital wing showing service runs and chamfered anti-glare window section.

Aalto extended these bio-realist concerns to the design of the minimum dwelling, wherein he linked them to the issue of flexibility. His 1930 essay 'The Dwelling as a Problem' was his prompt response to the idea of *Existenzminimum*, as this had been posited by the *Neue Sachlichkeit* architects in the 1929 CIAM conference. To this end, we find him writing, with the Stockholm Exhibition still fresh in his memory:

No family can live in one room, not even two, if they have children. But any family can live in an equivalent area if this area is divided up with particular attention to this family and its members' lives and activities. A dwelling is an area which should offer protected areas for meals, sleep, work and play. These biodynamic functions should be taken as points of departure for the dwelling's internal division, not any out-dated symmetrical axis or 'standard room' dictated by facade architecture.

Modern man – and the family – are more mobile than before. This is reflected in furniture's mechanical characteristics. Sixty square meters – and morning exercise for the whole family: this assumes furniture can be easily moved and folded up …

Moveable and foldable furniture enlarge a minimal dwelling. And in fact, the whole method of designing the interior that I have mentioned aims at enlarging the dwelling by developing its use possibilities.

In and of themselves, large dimensions are no advantage, but rather a drawback. If we take a minimal dwelling as our point of departure and strive to increase the use possibilities of its various parts with the purpose of psychologically making the dwelling appear roomier, then we arrive at a concept, no longer of a minimal dwelling, but of a universal dwelling – a dwelling which in its characteristics is better and more correct than the one where an emotional handling of the space has led to an unorganic totality.

The biological conditions for human life are, among others, air, light and sun. Air does not have to do with the size of the rooms or their number. It is an independent concept. We can surely build a dwelling with a large cubic footage of air without using the floor area uneconomically and affecting the ceiling height. The air space is a question of ventilation. On the other hand one must give a great deal of consideration to the air's quality. And this is a question that is dependent on the city's internal organization, the town plan.[20]

While Aalto had by no means relinquished the idea of standardization at this stage, one cannot help remarking on his pejorative use of the term *standard* in this text. By the mid-Thirties, Aalto tended to value standardization only at a relatively small and incremental scale. As far as the larger whole was concerned, particularly in respect to housing, he moved away from the *Zeilenbau* row house pattern of the *Neue Sachlichkeit* to adopt a more organic, aggregated dwelling form. He now tended to favour fan-shaped housing clusters rather than east–west rows of terraces of the same height, width and length, set a standard distance apart. After 1932 he tended to regard such orthogonal east–west orientation as being over-determined by normative criteria, not to mention its excessive optimization of cross ventilation.

Thus, despite his continued sympathy for the socially committed functionalism of the Swedish *Acceptera* group,[21] Aalto distanced himself from both the formalist and materialist wings of the international avant-garde, particularly during the first half of the Thirties, when he was completing the first three canonical works of his career: the Turun Sanomat Building, the Paimio Tuberculosis Sanatorium and the Viipuri City Library. By 1935 he had begun to question the techno-scientific and productive criteria that were still being insisted upon by materialist architects and intellectuals. In a lecture, 'Rationalism and Man', given in that year, he once again sought to extend the concept of rationality into the psycho-physiological domain:

We can say that one of the ways to arrive at a more and more humanely built environment is to expand the concept of the rational. *We should rationally analyse more of the requirements connected with the object than we have to date … As soon as we include psychological requirements, or, let us say, when we can do so, then we will have already expanded the rational method to an extent that has the potential of excluding inhuman results . . .*

A standard article should not be a definitive product; it should on the contrary be made so that the form is completed by man himself according to all the individual laws that involve him. Only in the case of objects that have a neutral quality can standardization's coercion of the individual be softened and its positive side culturally exploited. There is a civilization that, even in its traditional phase, its handicraft era, showed enormous sensitivity and tact towards the individual in this regard. I mean parts of the Japanese culture, which, with its limited range of raw materials and forms, inculcated a virtuoso skill in creating variations and almost daily recombinations. Its great predilection for flowers, plants and natural objects is a unique example. The contact with nature and its constantly observable change is a way of life that has difficulty getting along with concepts that are too formalistic.[22]

It is remarkable that someone who had never been to Japan and who, as far as we know, had little contact with Japanese culture,[23] should turn to the Orient for a model during his passage from the functionalist emphasis on constructivism to the critical potential of an organic architecture, in which a more flexible range of forms could be recombined according to the metabolic needs of everyday life. Henceforth, the principles of combination and recombination were to be the main qualifying factors for Aalto as far as standardization was concerned. Thus, as he put it in a lecture at the Nordic Building Conference in Oslo in 1938:

In nature standardization appears, above all and almost exclusively, only in the smallest units, the cells. This results in millions of elastic combinations in which there is no trace of formalism. Furthermore this give rise to the enormous wealth of organic growing shapes and their eternal change. Architectonic standardization must follow the same path.[24]

At the same time, there was nothing willfully anti-rational in Aalto's organicism, for, as he wrote in 1960, 'It is not the rationalization itself that was wrong in the first and now past period of modern architecture. The wrongness lies in the fact that the rationalization has not gone deep enough.'[25]

There is no single work in Aalto's long career that is more synthetically symptomatic of his critical response to all these issues than his Apartment Building for the Interbau Exhibition in the Hansaviertel, Berlin, 1954–7, for it is here, perhaps more than anywhere else, that he brought together two ostensibly opposed impulses. On the one hand, there was his lifelong recognition that the most urgent problem confronting the species was some satisfactory solution to the perennial social problem that Friedrich Engels had identified as the 'housing question'; on the other hand, there was his growing conviction that the vernacular in general and the Finnish vernacular in particular embodied within its form a key to the solution of this crisis. As far as Aalto was concerned, this potential stemmed from the fact that the Karelian agrarian tradition was quintessentially additive in character and, therefore, perennially open to the process of agglutinative growth. He returned to this theme in the midst of the Continuation War of 1941–4, when eastern Karelia was occupied by Finnish troops, in an essay simply titled 'Architecture in Karelia':

The first essential feature of interest is Karelian architecture's uniformity. There are few comparable examples in Europe. It is a pure forest-settlement architecture in which wood dominates, . . . in most cases naked, without the dematerializing effect that a layer of paint gives. In addition, wood is often used in as natural proportions as possible, on the scale typical of the material. A dilapidated Karelian village is somehow similar in appearance to a Greek ruin, where, also, the material's uniformity is a dominant feature though marble replaces wood. By making this comparison I am not in any way trying to fan some kind of Finnish chauvinism; it is a purely instinctive association whose justification experts surely could recognize.

Another significant feature is the manner in which the Karelian house . . . is in a way a building that begins with a single modest cell or with an imperfect embryo building, shelter for man and animals and which then figuratively speaking grows year by year. 'The expanded Karelian house' can in a way be compared with a biological cell formation. The possibility of a larger and more complete building is always open.[26]

From this, he went on to argue that the inevitably tight economic constraints governing the period of postwar reconstruction would, by definition, necessitate a similar additive approach. As he put it:

The task presupposes an architectural system according to which houses can grow and be enlarged over the years. We cannot accomplish our work with the conventional cultural loans or the 'technocratic' rationalism and buildings that have been dominant in Europe in recent times. The system must be created here and must take our own circumstances into consideration; but certain features in the Karelian building system that I have just mentioned can give us some excellent help in finding the right system, at least to the extent that larger population groupings, thanks to this architecture, become accessory to the necessary self-confidence and feeling that we are not taking the wrong path.[27]

With these words, Aalto categorically rejected the technocratic rationalism of the early modern movement as unacceptably reductive, while recognizing that without the popular support of society one cannot achieve anything of lasting consequence as far as habitat is concerned. This Karelian thesis evidently implied some form of topographically inflected, low-rise, high-density housing, such as Aalto had already achieved in his Sunila Pulp Mill and Housing of 1936–8 and the stepped terrace housing for Kauttua of 1937–8. Thus, while he was not totally

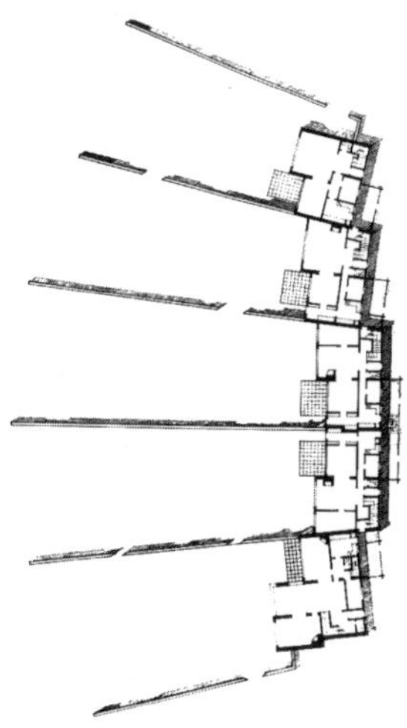

Alvar Aalto, Sunila Pulp Mill, Sunila, near Kotka, 1936–8, terrace housing with canted walls aligning with the contours.

opposed to high-rise construction, it is clear that for him, as for Frank Lloyd Wright, the preferred line was horizontal, since, as he put it in 1946, 'High-rise apartments must be regarded, both socially and architecturally, as a considerably more dangerous form of building than single-family houses or low-rise apartments.'[28] Last, but not least, there was the clear implication that the key to ecologically responsible housing production in the future lay in the 'ready-made' model of the Finnish vernacular, just as this had once served as the point of departure for the Finnish national romantic architects of the 1890s. It was just this Finnish tradition that led Aalto back to the L- and U-shaped plans of the English Arts and Crafts house, and to type plans that, in their turn, had been derived from vernacular forms. His own house in Munkkiniemi signalled this return as early as 1935, and this would find further elaboration in the adjacent timber ambulatory and courtyard that was designed to receive Aino Aalto's grave after her premature death in 1949.

It is virtually the same Finnish vernacular paradigm that resurfaces with full force in his high-rise Hansaviertel Apartment Building of 1955–7. In this instance, each apartment is, in effect, a small single-storey patio house, and we may say that their syncopated aggregation creates the semblance of a diminutive village on each floor. The basic apartment is an assembly of three bedrooms, plus a bathroom and a kitchen, grouped around three sides of a central living room that opens directly to the exterior through a generously proportioned terrace partially inset into the corpus of the building. Each terrace is shielded from the next, and from the ground, by virtue of the way it is incorporated into the staggered plan of the block. A galley kitchen gives direct access to this terrace for the purposes of eating outdoors, while the kitchen is directly accessed from a generously proportioned internal foyer. Acoustical and visual privacy is facilitated throughout by a pattern of circulation that serves the flanking bedrooms while being partially screened from the central living volume. This carefully modulated arrangement is matched by the generosity of the glazed elevator hall, which is wide, naturally lit and well ventilated. It is a room, rather than an access corridor in the usual sense. In ergonomic terms, this apartment layout is one of the most brilliant middle-class apartment plans invented in the entire span of the twentieth century, and the mystery is that neither Aalto nor anyone else would have the occasion or the desire to replicate its form or to develop a further variation of its patio organization.[29]

While Le Corbusier displayed comparable ingenuity in the development of his typical high-rise dwelling units, these were invariably too spartan to be accepted at a popular level or alternatively, where luxurious, were too expensive to be made available to society at large. Hence the fundamental limitations of his heroic Unité d'Habitation in Marseilles of 1948–54, which, while occupied today, was never fully available for either working-class or lower-middle-class accommodation.

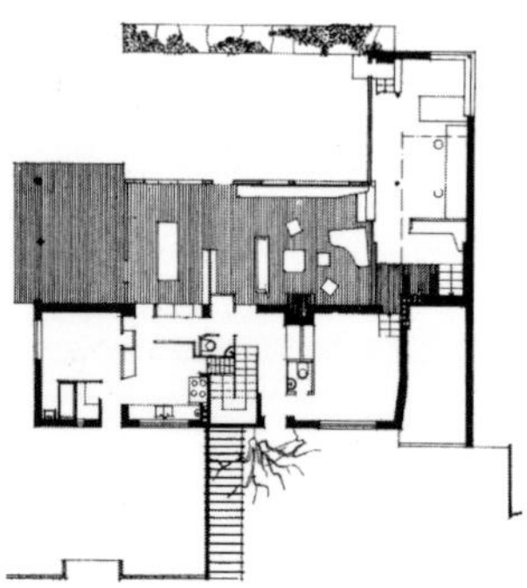

Aino and Alvar Aalto, Villa Aalto, Munkkiniemi, Helsinki, 1934–5, ground floor plan.

The virtues of Aalto's Hansaviertel prototype do not end with the units themselves, for the modular rhythm of the block, established through its precast concrete modular wall system, sets up a significant interplay with the inset terraces that are automatically incorporated into its form. These terraces are rhythmic at another scale in that the raised soffits above the living rooms impart a 'noble' identity to each apartment. Furthermore, the grey concrete panels, cast from steel formwork, are rhythmically jointed, so as to create a coursed effect reminiscent of stone facing on a gigantic scale – the merest hint, one might say, of a latent Nordic classical sensibility. At the same time, the partially protruding terraces, opening towards the south and thereby imparting a direction to the massing, serve to distance the overall form from any sense of classical propriety, except for the entry portico, which, framed by a peristyle of concrete columns, imparts a classic touch to the entrance. Aalto's intention in developing this apartment type and block formation is confirmed by the description that appears in the first volume of his complete works, published in 1963:

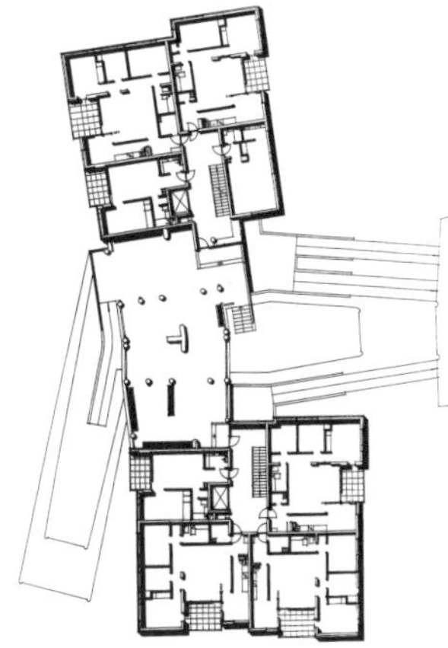

Alvar Aalto, Hansaviertel Apartment Building, Berlin, 1955–7, ground floor plan with clustered apartments.

The conventional apartment house is a sort of collective dwelling; it can never possess the same qualities as, say, a private house, which has a direct relation to the landscape. Nevertheless, the private house, which is often placed as a box in a small garden without a protected interior court, has its negative sides, while, on the other hand, the apartment block can present some positive advantages. Therefore an attempt should be made to combine, in an ideal manner, the specific advantages of an apartment block with the merits of the individual house …

The conventional small corridor-like balconies were here transformed into patios around which the rooms of the apartments were grouped. This grouping around the open-air room created an intimate, private atmosphere.[30]

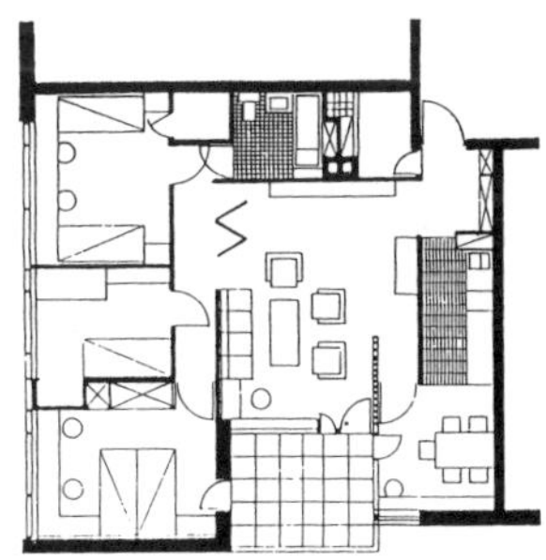

Alvar Aalto, Hansaviertel Apartment Building, Berlin, 1955–7, plan of standard apartment clustered around the living room and inset balcony.

This cluster organization entailed the provision of balconies, which, by virtue of the manner of their enclosure, ensured both privacy and a sense of being in the open air. At the same time, their chevron formation implied a biomorphic organization similar to that analysed in D'Arcy Thompson's *On Growth and Form* of 1917.[31] Unlike the modular cubic character of Le Corbusier's Pavillon de l'Esprit Nouveau at the Exposition Internationale des Arts Décoratifs et Industriels Modernes in Paris of 1925 (which was also designed as a prototypical high-rise dwelling), Aalto's Hansaviertel apartments could have been readily adapted to form clusters of single-storey houses at grade, aggregating into picturesque assemblies with each house stepping down to follow the contours of the site, much like the format that Jørn Utzon adopted in his Kingo Housing, completed near Helsingør in Denmark in 1956.

Like Mies van der Rohe and Ludwig Hilberseimer, both of whom were subject to the influential proto-ecological writings of Raoul Francé,[32]

Aalto envisaged a more-or-less continual urbanization of the earth's surface, one in which his all but mythical 'forest town' would come to be universally adopted in northern Europe and, to some extent, elsewhere as a kind of regional Gaia system,[33] equally devoted to agrarian and industrial development, the one continually fusing into the other. Aalto first posited his concept of the forest town in his 1936 masterplan for the industrial community of Sunila, near Kotka, of which he remarked in a lecture of 1956, 'The housing is placed wholly on the southern slopes leaving the northern slopes to the forest ... Both the housing developments and the factory itself are designed to grow without disrupting their harmony.'[34] Here, the heroic monumental Sunila Pulp Mill, built for a consortium of major paper producers as a gridded, brick-faced matrix on an island promontory facing the sea, was complemented by low-rise workers' housing laid out in a fan formation on an adjacent mainland site. This terraced housing was integrated into the contours of the undulating ground, as opposed to the orthogonal row house (*Zeilenbau*) planning principle of the *Neue Sachlichkeit*, which had influenced Aalto's masterplan for Ahlström's Varkaus factory projected in the same year. Aalto's subsequent planning work for the Ahlström Corporation in the late Thirties (owing to the patronage of Harry Gullichsen) would confirm the distance he had gone from both the row house tradition and the perimeter-block models of urban development, the one stemming from Otto Häsler's pioneering row house paradigm, first realized in Celle, near Hanover, in 1926, the other deriving from Eliel Saarinen's plan for Munkkieniemi and Greater Helsinki of 1915. The exclusion of these paradigms from Aalto's urban form is first evident in his Kauttua site plan for the Ahlström Corporation of 1938.

Aalto's green-city ideology seems to have been informed by a number of countervailing open-city planning models developed during the first four decades of the century, from N A Ladovsky's formalistic planning precepts – which seem to have influenced a prototypical new town, 'An American Town in Finland', designed by MIT students under Aalto's direction in 1941 – to the Anglo-Saxon garden-city model refined by Clarence Stein and Henry Wright in Radburn, New Jersey, and in their green-belt New Towns. Aalto would have become familiar with the latter through his friend Lewis Mumford, whose influential *The Culture of Cities* had been published in 1938. The other primary influence on Aalto's approach to planning at this time was unquestionably the Tennessee Valley Authority (TVA) Regional Plan promulgated under the auspices of Franklin Delano Roosevelt's New Deal after 1933. This was surely the inspiration behind Aalto's Kokemäenjoki River Valley Regional Plan of 1940–2, when Harry Gullichsen persuaded several river-based municipalities, from Pori to Kokemaki, to unite in commissioning Finland's first regional plan from Alvar Aalto. To all intents and purposes, this was a linear industrial city at a regional scale, wherein the

Alvar Aalto, 'American Town in Finland', 1941, design developed with MIT students.

traditional livelihood of agriculture would be supplemented by timber-related light industry, with a new main road and rail line following the river's course as an efficient transportation spine throughout the length of the region. Of this layered proto-megalopolitan plan, Aalto wrote:

The principle governing the housing areas is that they should not be developed into separate, heavy, indivisible entities, but instead grow like star-shaped figures from the existing agglomerations, with belts of farmland, forests, and parks between ... The natural landscape itself is valuable as a means of architectural characterization in the planning of the communities.[35]

Aalto's regional planning strategies had been influenced by the work of Frank Lloyd Wright, particularly in his Usonian phase – above all, surely, by Wright's Galesburg Country Homes in Galesburg, Michigan, of 1946–9, which seem to anticipate almost to the letter the cellular layout of the residential quarters in Aalto's plans for Rovaniemi of 1944–6 and Imatra of 1945–53. Of Imatra, Göran Schildt has written:

Aalto planned for a projected population of 100,000, of whom some 37% were to live in single-family homes and 63% in apartment houses no more than four storys high. The goal of small, organically integrated residential districts with their own heating plants, day-care facilities, health centers, sports fields, shops, etc., bears witness to Aalto's interest in American neighborhood theories. The plan, completed in 1953, was implemented by and large, but the high cost of land in the densely-built areas led to an undesirable scattering of new construction to peripheral areas.[36]

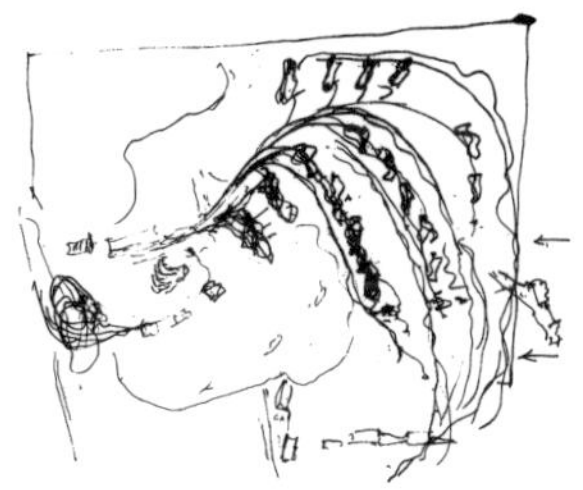

Alvar Aalto, Forest Town, sketch plan for Summa residential quarter for Enzo Gutzeit, 1954–9.

Aalto's masterplan was, in his words, a 'formation of trees, planted areas, meadows and fields, providing a distinctive feature characteristic of Imatra and separating the built-up areas'[37] thereby obviating the need for formal parks of any kind. This diffusion of tended woodland justified the title 'forest town'. As Jussi Rausti has written of the Imatra plan, 'There is thus no need to plan artificial parks in the midst of settlement, especially as the forest often penetrates all the way to the central areas. The Finnish character of the parks must be preserved, even further accentuated. The unique beauty of Finnish nature is not based on luxuriant growth or colours or enormous scale. Our nature is marked by a realistic beauty, and should be kept that way.'[38]

Aalto justified his forest town approach in terms that were reminiscent of Bruno Taut's de-urbanizing thesis, as set forth in his 1920 publication, *Die Auflösung der Städte oder die Erde eine gute Wohnung* (The Dissolution of Cities). Thus, we find Aalto writing of the Kokomäenjoki River Valley Regional Plan:

Exactly as the medieval cities once upon a time lost their fortification walls and the modern city grew out beyond them, the concept of the city today is in the process of shedding its constraints. But this time it is happening, not to lead once again to the creation of a larger unit, but rather so that the city will become part of the countryside. The underlying meaning of such regional plans is that they synchronize country and city.[39]

Despite their organic flexible character, Aalto's regional plans remained largely unrealized due to speculation and other economic constraints.[40] Such interests did not prevent the realization of Aalto's smaller civic complexes, however, where the geological metaphor assisted him in establishing the identity of the place through the way in which the profile of the built form extends itself into the site. This is at once evident in the case of Säynätsalo Town Hall of 1948–52, where the municipal structure is the cumulative element in the chevron formation of low-rise structures running through the centre of the town. Here, Bruno Taut's concept of the 'city crown'[41] returns in the mono-pitched roof of the council chamber, which rises up as an indicator, so to speak, of the way in which the town ought to grow. A similar roof crowned most of Aalto's later civic centres with the same basic intention, namely, to serve as a symbolic core around which the rest of the municipality would develop.

Resisting closure around either a classical paradigm or a technological norm, Aalto strove for an organic flexibility wherein function and production would play their appointed roles without being over-determined and where, within the megalopolis, agriculture and industry would interact with nature in such a way as to create an environmental ecology satisfying to fundamental human needs. Aalto's overall socio-cultural attitude was close to that of the physician–philosopher Alexis Carrel, whom he was to cite on more than one occasion. Aalto made explicit reference to Carrel in his 1940 obituary for Erik Gunnar Asplund and again in his essay, 'National Planning and Cultural Goals' of 1949.[42] Carrel, a Franco–American research doctor and Nobel Prize winner, was one of the first scientists to mount a full-scale critique of industrial civilization, particularly with regard to the priority given to mass production and consumption at the expense of other deeper psycho-cultural needs. Complex and contradictory, and in some respects profoundly pessimistic, Carrel was a rather atypical figure for Aalto to identify with. For, although he was as preoccupied as Aalto with regional decentralization and with what he called a nominalist mediation of any kind of universal principle, he was, at the same time, elitist and sceptical as to the prospects of democracy. However, like Aalto he was opposed on biological grounds to large areas of glass, regarding overexposure to the sun as debilitating for both mind and body, and, to this end, he wrote with gratifying prejudice for anyone coming from the Baltic, 'We must not forget that the most highly civilized races – the Scandinavians, for example, are white, and have lived for many generations in a country where the atmospheric luminosity is weak during a great part of the year.'[43] It is interesting to note that Carrel was already part of Aalto's intellectual milieu by the late Thirties, as we may judge from the inclusion of Carrel as a prospective author in the first ten issues of the unrealized Anglo–Swedish magazine, *The Human Side*, which was to have been edited by Gregor Paulson and Alvar Aalto on the eve of World War II.[44]

It is one of the ironies of the history of the modern movement that while the de-urbanizing[45] principle of Aalto's forest town was directly inspired by the regional planning paradigms of the TVA and by the Green-belt New Towns realized in the United States in the Forties, the full welfare state potential of these pioneering prototypes was ultimately realized in Finland rather than in North America. The reasons for this are many and complex: on the one hand, the Finns were confronted with a major rebuilding programme at the end of the war; on the other, the country benefited from having a mature government, while America, simultaneously triumphant both from winning the war and overcoming the Depression, in exactly the same period, began to sell the government-financed New Deal Green-belt New Towns back into private ownership.

An additional tragic irony of this moment resides in the fact that Aalto, who had everything to give to the idea of the forest town and who had, in any case, prepared the ground for its coming into being as a generic form of regional urbanism, was almost totally excluded from its actual realization. The ultimate reason for this is suggested by Jere Maula in his article 'The Growing Perspective in Urban Planning', where he argues that the bureaucratic aspect of Finnish social democracy favoured Swedish productive norms for its large-scale housing programmes to the 'neglect of the local tradition', as he put it, by which he surely means Aalto and the school of Aalto.[46]

In June 1977, in the commemorative issue of *L'Architecture d'aujourd'hui* following Aalto's death, the Italian architect, Leonardo Mosso, analysed the underlying substance and method of Aalto's work in the following profound and moving terms:

Each project has a double system of requirements: those that are material and those that are social. Material requirements must absolutely be resolved or else the very reasons for a project's existence are compromised ... As for the social requirements, Aalto attempts to solve the material problems of the individual within the framework of social organization, by inserting qualities of sociability into the system of objective requirements. He seeks to overcome man's egoism (in the sense of a primacy of self over others) by combining functions that tend to be more collective than individualistic, while at the same time, he fights against alienating aspects by including insulating and protective qualities. Aalto incorporates physically into his spaces the basic attributes of this dialectic ... The aphorism 'to achieve Paradise on earth through the sole means of the art of the building' means (as the whole of Aalto's practice demonstrates) the recreating of a unity between urban tissue and natural surroundings. In other words, permitting the entire population to recover urban spaces colonized by capitalist commercialism and profit seeking, by all that destroys the identity of man and of social man.[47]

Now, 20 years later, on the occasion of the centenary of his birth, we have cause to reassess, in comparable terms, the relevance of Aalto's work to the architecture of the emerging future, above all, because of the fragmented character of contemporary development and the ever-widening domain of the megalopolis in the late modern world. As far as this last is concerned, it is clear that Aalto embraced a critically realistic view in which ecologically tempered tracts of regional urbanization would become the universal norm, however much they may be layered and inflected, as his vision of the forest town implies.

Aside from the general relevance of his ecological critique, it is equally necessary to acknowledge the pertinence of Aalto's heterotopic method, given the fragmented, not to say chaotic, character of urban development as it currently prevails. The way in which this method may serve as a counter principle of rationalism has never been better defined than by Demetri Porphyrios in 1982, wherein he characterized the heterotopic principle as achieving cohesion 'through adjacency: where the edges touch, where the fringes intermingle, where the extremities of the one denote the beginning of the other, there in the hinge between two things an unstable unity appears'.[48] Porphyrios proceeded to argue that it was just this sensibility that enabled Aalto to distance himself from all forms of positivism and from the latter's secret alliance with consumerism inasmuch as rationalized production presupposes the equal but opposite 'irrationality' of unbridled consumption. By a similar token, Aalto distanced himself from any kind of vulgar populism and from the perennially romantic myth of individual genius. As Porphyrios put it, 'The heterotopic sensibility of Aalto ... was neither an individual expressionism (that is, a secretly lodged *maniera*), nor a Dionysian irrationalism, and even less a liberating transformation of Modernism.'[49] It was, as we have seen, in many respects, a return to the fragmentary aggregational manner of the English Free Style and, hence, to the ethos of Scandinavian national romanticism in all its multifarious forms. This seemingly retrograde move enabled Aalto not only to integrate topographic idiosyncracies but also to meet the specificity of a brief in an appropriate way without sacrificing either rhythmic drive or functional performance. Above all, it facilitated the realization of buildings that were laid into their surroundings in such a way that one could not discern with certainty where building ended and context began.

While Aalto exploited the sensuous potential of the heterotopic method for what he called its unpremeditated style-creating power, the significance of this strategy at the end of the century resides in its categoric antipathy to building a proliferation of free-standing objects. Like the comparable architecture of Hugo Häring and Hans Scharoun, with whom, as

Colin St John Wilson reminds us, there was always an affinity,[50] Aalto's buildings were either landscapes in themselves, as in the case of the Wolfsburg Cultural Centre of 1958–62 or, alternatively, they extended into the surroundings in such a way as to transform the pre-existing ground, as in the case of the Maison Carré of 1956–9 or Seinäjoki Civic Centre of 1958–87. Of parallel ontological consequence was the way in which his buildings were constituted as topographic structures rather than as gratuitous sculptural gestures, which, by definition, can never transcend their free-standing isolation. This is the paradox of Aalto's heterotopic legacy, for while it is an idiosyncratic response to the specificity of both site and programme, it remains open, almost by design, to the subsequent collective transformation of the work across time. It anticipates, in terms of the larger future, that which is already inherent in the design process itself. It is the precondition, one might say, for Alvaro Siza's insistence that the main task of architecture resides in transformation rather than invention.[51]

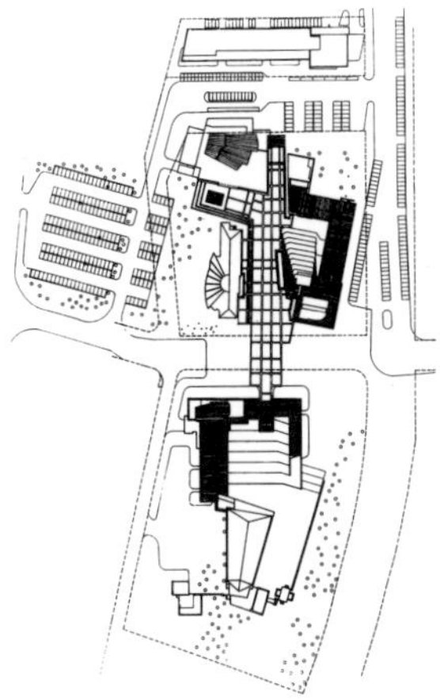

Alvar Aalto, Seinäjoki Civic Centre, 1958–87, plan showing (from top to bottom) an office building, theatre, town hall, library and church.

Thus, the ultimate significance of Aalto's work for the coming century resides in his conviction that built work always has to be rendered, in large measure, as a landscape, thereby fusing and *con*fusing both figure and ground, in a ceaseless interplay between natural constraint and cultural ingenuity. This surely is the critical essence of what Aalto leaves to us, as we contemplate a totalizing limitless environment in which we can no longer say where city ends and country begins. And, while the ruthless rapacity of late-modern development takes us further and further from the ecological ethic of Aalto's forest town, the hope remains that all the ill-considered, ill-related, half-abandoned objects of our time may, one day, be redeemed through an ad hoc creation of layered, topographic assemblies, irrespective of whether these be roofworks or earthworks or, as is more often the case, an inseparable mixture of both.

This is an edited version of an essay first published as 'The Legacy of Alvar Aalto: Evolution and Influence', in Peter Reed, ed., *Alvar Aalto: Between Humanism and Materialism*, exh. cat., New York: Museum of Modern Art, 1998, pp.119–39.

theory

history

criticism

Introduction

The initial pieces of criticism were texts written in 1964 and 1965 for the British magazine *Architectural Design* on which I served as Technical Editor from 1962 to 1965. The first of these essays is devoted to James Stirling and James Gowan's 'New Brutalist' Leicester University Engineering building, while the second deals with Hans Scharoun's equally canonical late expressionist tour de force, the Philharmonie in Berlin.

My subsequent move to New York, in 1965, provided the occasion for my more incisive critique of Kevin Roche's Ford Foundation building, published in 1968, once again in *Architectural Design*, under the title 'The House of Ivy League Values'. In this piece I allude to the criteria for critical analysis outlined in Christian Norberg-Schulz's book *Intentions in Architecture* (1966): that is, the opposition between the *physical milieu* and the *social milieu* in the appraisal of a building, with the former stressing functional considerations and the latter focusing on the symbolic. Norberg-Schulz proceeds to argue that there should exist a semantic correspondence between the building task and the means by which it is achieved; one has to ask, he writes, 'whether the task has been defined properly and the form articulated adequately'. These were indeed the questions I attempted to ask in the case of the Ford Foundation – and I found the building wanting in respect of a non-correspondence between the explicit symbolic charge of the building as an institution, and the nature of its form.

These initial pieces are followed by a hitherto unpublished essay of 1981 on Rafael Moneo's Bankinter, Madrid, which dates from 1973. This building, designed with Ramon Bescos, has continued to preoccupy me over the years for many reasons. Not least of these is the fact that Moneo first entered into his maturity with this subtly organic work, which is at once ingeniously conceived, sensitively modulated and beautifully executed. I recall visiting this building while Moneo was in residence at the Institute for Architecture and Urban Studies in New York. During the second half of the Seventies Moneo was primarily appreciated in the States as a critical intellectual; few of my colleagues at the Institute had any idea of Moneo's already proven prowess as an architect.

There follows short appraisals of three contemporary architects: Herman Hertzberger, Alvaro Siza and Tadao Ando. Their separate contributions to late modern culture seem to me to have been particularly prescient.

The piece on Hertzberger, written in 1986, appeared in Dutch, in the magazine *Archis* in December of that year. In this essay, as elsewhere, I tried to show how Hertzberger was in effect the most fertile architect of the Dutch Structuralist movement, realizing works that, in their typological range, scale and structural elaboration, went beyond Aldo van Eyck's interpretation of his quasi-ethnographic concept of 'labyrinthic clarity'.

The essay on the work and thought of the Japanese master Tadao Ando, written for the Museum of Modern Art's exhibition of Ando's work in 1991, is paralleled here by a critique of the Portuguese architect Alvaro Siza's Duarte House, completed in Ovar, Portugal in 1985. These two architects remain for me the twin magi of the late modern movement in architecture. While the overall plastic character of their respective works could hardly be more different, they parallel each other closely in the marked continuity and consistency of their architectonic development. They also display a similar responsiveness to both the character of the native landscape and the ambient feeling of the local light. Moreover, they each exemplify in their own way a critical culture of architecture that pertains to the distinct regions of the world in which they are predominantly active.

'In the Name of the Father' turns on the fact that the German Ambassador's Residence in Washington, DC, realized to the design of Oswald Mathias Ungers in 1997, was, in fact, built opposite Egon Eiermann's German Embassy of 1964. Thus, the 'father' in question is first, Eiermann, who had been Ungers's professor in Karlsruhe, and second, Peter Behrens, whose atectonic preoccupations with quadratic geometry, his neo-Quattrocento manner, may be sensed as a presence in the interiors of the building.

First published in *Scroope 9*, the magazine of the Cambridge University School of Architecture, 'Minimal Moralia' attempts to differentiate in a cursory way between different manifestations of late modern minimalism as these have appeared in recent Swiss German architecture. In so doing, it begs the question as to whether this phenomenological aesthetic, taken to artistic extremes, may not at times lead to extremely reductive results.

Leicester University Engineering Laboratory

Any major work built today is inherently placed in an extremely vulnerable position, for we spontaneously look to such a work for a possible demonstration of a general principle through which a vigorous and integrated environmental culture might again be achieved. Once we have acclaimed our 'model', our immediate reaction is to question why this work, rather than any other, should constitute a break with the present *impasse*. No satisfactory answer can be given to such a question unless a critical, if premature, historical assessment be first attempted. In the case of this engineering laboratory such an assessment seems to be even demanded by the work itself, as it appears to possess an in-built historical context that may be readily appreciated by students of the Modern Movement. This context, with few exceptions, is not evident in the form of either direct or adapted quotations, and herein resides the building's true integrity and distinction – for in almost all aspects both its formal and conceptual influences have been fully absorbed into the total abstraction of its final form.

In making a historical appraisal it is only reasonable to give the greatest importance to obvious allusions and to influences that are admitted by the designers themselves. In the first instance it is evident that many of the forms employed derive directly from late nineteenth-century marine and civil engineering. Where these forms are functionally appropriate, they serve to further the historical continuity and the technical validity of the work as a whole. The overall sheath of patent glazing, the engineering-brick podium, the faceted steel balustrades and stairs, the tubular handrails, the lattice roof trusses, the exposed pipework and the snorkel vent are all integral elements of a particular functional tradition. The resultant effect, if not the conscious intent, is polemical. For the exact manner of the detailing and assembly indicates a preference for a direct engineering approach to design problems. Apart from all the anonymous nineteenth- century works in which Britain still abounds – the train sheds, the bridges, the warehouses, etc. – certain individual pieces appear to be evoked: Paxton's Crystal Palace, Brunel's Paddington Station, Burton's greenhouse at Kew, Peter Ellis's Cook Street building in Liverpool. As the number of possible attributions grow, one realizes that without the presence of a single specific quotation the building almost comprises a compendium of early modern constructional development. Even when certain derivations appear to be unconscious or highly unlikely, the mainstream of the functional tradition always appears to be in evidence. Thus the set-back blocks of Sant'Elia's Città Nuova appear in the raked glazing of the administration tower, and in the workshop escape stairs we may see the interior of Poelzig's water tower at Posen.

The cultural complexity of this work is not to be underrated, however. Both in detailing and in planning it is relatively simple, functional and consistent, and thus it may easily be misinterpreted as a continuation of a prewar European functional tradition. This, however, is not the case, for its true spiritual affinity lies well within that great romantic American tradition that stems from Frank Lloyd Wright and remains most vividly alive today in the work of Louis Kahn. Stirling and Gowan have simply used, out

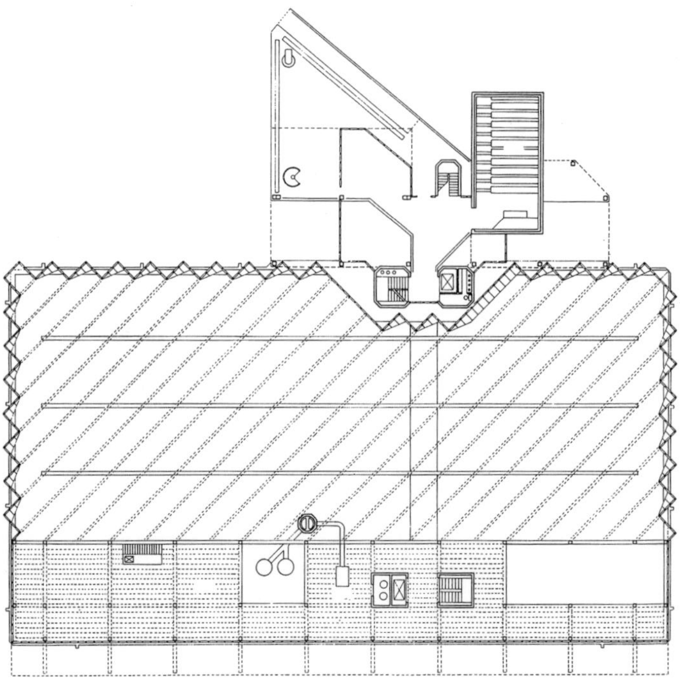

James Stirling and James Gowan, Leicester University Engineering Building, first floor plan.

of a realistic preference, the vocabulary of the 'Engineers' Aesthetic' to create a self-contained dream; a dream that both in style and effect is almost as hermetic as Wright's Midway Gardens of 1913.

The architects themselves acknowledge Wright's Johnson Wax building at Racine, Wisconsin, as the one dominant influence underlying the conception of the whole work. The completely tiled interior of the landings within the tower, the continuous glazing of the brick laboratory block, the extensive use of translucent glass, the glazed bridge links and finally the brick podium that embraces the entire complex, all testify to this influence. The podium motif is after all a recurrent element to be found variously throughout Wright's work, and its presence here provides an iconographic as opposed to a functional explanation of the whole *parti*.

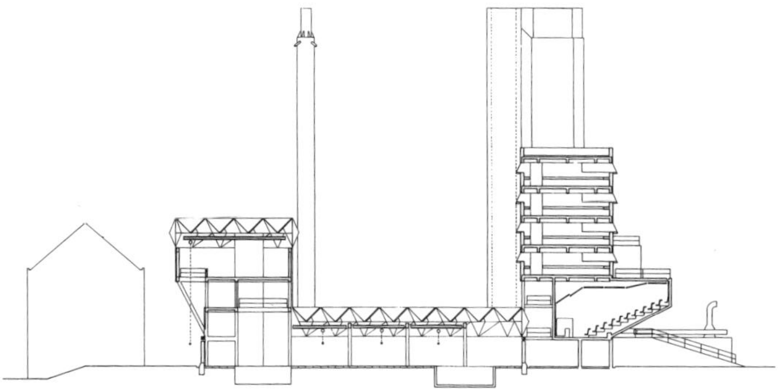

James Stirling and James Gowan, Leicester University Engineering Building, section through research laboratories and small lecture theatre.

In most of Wright's work, suppressed entry is made through a podium wall under a *piano nobile* which then naturally receives great horizontal stress from the deep base of the composition. In this building, the use of a 'podium element' has the similar effect of stressing the potential horizontal character of the workshop block, through emphasizing its roof, and as this roof coincides with the first floor of the tower complex, an architectural rationale is immediately established which stresses this floor as a *piano nobile*. This architecturally rationalizes the two-level entry into the tower complex, the second entry being made by a ramp to the first floor level. There is no inherent reason in either the brief or the site for this additional entry, and the solution, once stripped of its Wrightian context, only partially argues a case for it on the grounds that mass entry into the lecture halls is more easily affected by a ramp. The argument is not sustained, however, for while the small hall is completely served by the ramp, the larger volume still requires for its entry the negotiation of either stairs or a lift. A small lecture theatre, a gallery foyer space and a terrace are in effect inadequate justification for the additional entry, and after climbing the ramp a sense of spatial anticlimax is unavoidable. The fact that the brief was without a 'social core', as such, appears to have been unacceptable to the architects, and in consequence the gallery foyer has been promoted to become an inflated 'social core' at this level. In addition the podium solution stresses a *piano nobile* which is for its greater part an inaccessible roof, and this emphasizes still further the ambiguous nature of the solution adopted. Although the continuous podium imparts an architectural unity to the whole complex, its presence obstructs any consistent expression of volume and surface within the workshop block itself, for whereas the brick-screen support walls of the third-floor workshops are clad in plyglass, those surrounding the ground-floor workshops are expressed in the brick of the podium. The change in the character of the space enclosed by the podium as it passes from under the tower out to enclose the workshops creates a further feeling of ambiguity.

The regulating order established by the architects consists primarily in the geometry of the plan, which automatically profiles the configuration of any part according to the interaction of two systems – the one an orthogonal system deriving from site shape, and the other a 45 degree diagonal system arising primarily out of the orientation of the north light trusses. Here we have the imposition of an overall Wrightian discipline (compare the Paul R Hanna House of 1937). It is used here to govern the expression or suppression of any architectural event, depending upon the contribution it may or may not make to the initial image of the building – that is, to an essentially semi-solid tower hovering over a sea of glass. To maintain this image certain elements of the structure are deliberately suppressed. The tower, for instance, rests on supports of deliberately minimized dimensions, and the surface relation between these exposed concrete supports and the tiled skin of the concrete/cantilevered lecture hall is left ambiguous. Similar ambiguities occur in the support conditions for other volumes within the tower complex and this amounts to a dissipation of a potential structural order which is scrupulously observed elsewhere, particularly in the workshop roof where it forms an integral part of the overall geometry.

The culture and the calibre of this faculty building at Leicester render it at once a subject for searching criticism; yet its achievement is not to be underrated, for very few buildings since the end of the war have been conceived and realized with such authority and precision. It is an extraordinary development from the architects' previous work, and both in the professionalism of its execution and in its informed originality it is quite exceptional. It is an achievement that is rendered all the more remarkable by the circumstances under which it was designed. It was an exacting programme on a small site which for most of its area had to be covered with workshops, and after receiving the commission the architects were given only a year in which to start it in the ground.

The stature of its architectural achievement is inseparable from its historical significance, for it is the first building to be erected in this country which is profoundly influenced by Wright, and indeed it is probably the only building to be so influenced which does not indulge at some point or other in the essentially Art Nouveau aspects of his style. Nevertheless, in spite of its utilitarian detailing the building remains the embodiment of a dream. It is a dream with marine associations. The floodlit control tower

James Stirling and James Gowan, Leicester University Engineering Building, aerial view.

floats over the park and on over a sea of translucent ever-changing glass, which at night becomes a long crystal of glowing light. Its aspirations are those of Louis Kahn's young architect who said, 'I dream of spaces full of wonder. Spaces that rise and envelop flowingly without beginning, without end, of a jointless material white and gold ...'.[1] Yet if the accessibility of an architectural syntax to the general culture as a whole is ultimately to be dependent upon the establishment of a system which permits within a rational discipline the controlled functional distortion of form by the programme itself, then the achievement of this building may well be limited on a wider cultural level. It was the strength of the *Esprit Nouveau* and of Constructivism that their systems were open to programmatic distortion and to the admission of non-aesthetic standard elements, and thus their output was related to the technological capacity of the whole society. In Wright's work all distortions and elements are incorporated within one closed individual aesthetic. Thus this engineering building may be seen as a heroic and liberating attempt to reconcile the essential conflict existing between two distinct cultures of the environment.

First published in *Architectural Design*, vol.34, no.2, February 1964, p.61.

Genesis of the Philharmonie

The Philharmonie is a phoenix born in the Tiergarten out of the soil and the culture of Berlin. It is the genuine article as opposed to the imported and now faded flowers of seven years ago, the buildings of the Hansa Viertel. It owes its vitality and authenticity to its septuagenarian designer Hans Scharoun, who has been a Berliner without a break for the last 40 years of his life.

The Philharmonie is not only a phoenix, it is the fulfilment of a vision first dreamt of in the Berlin of 1919. It is at one and the same time the end of a long road, the realization of a dream and a challenge to the future.

The challenge that it offers to the future is complex. Indeed it is a challenge on more than one level, for its successful realization tentatively proffers again the possibility of an organic topological architecture that would be both utilizable and capable of a wide application. In this respect the Philharmonie may well not be the end of a road but rather a beginning. Both in its structure and its spatial organization it tentatively relates different generations and modes of thought that would otherwise remain, as at present, extreme poles apart. Model for model there is not too much separating the Philharmonie from the largely unrealized suspension projects of Frei Otto and Conrad Roland Lehman. The development of new materials and techniques will surely see more of these light suspension projects realized, and should this happen, the Philharmonie will then appear in retrospect to be a prototype solution, an all-embracing tent structure, within the web fabric of which, warped or flat surfaces could be irregularly suspended for human use.

Whether or not the Philharmonie holds any promise for the future, as opposed to being a singular monument realized out of a past utopian dream, turns largely upon this issue of utilizability. Hardly any case can now be made against it as a general model, on the grounds of it being ultimately an irrational conception from the point of view of modern production techniques. The promise and present performance of both sprayed and moulded plastic argues to the contrary – as does the fact that Frei Otto's suspension structures are always built up out of the assembly of a few simple repeated elements. On the grounds of utility, however, it is certainly arguable that, taken as a whole, the Philharmonie has a future as a model only for building on a public level. Scharoun himself would surely make no broader claim for his concert hall than this.

To understand more fully this one-off public work, to determine its monumentality or conversely its lack of it, one needs to examine in more detail the development of Scharoun's own thought. There is no doubt that this is his masterwork, the tardy realization of an inner concept with which he has been struggling all his life. It is surely as much the essence of Scharoun's thought as is his almost equally masterly model housing for the Breslau Werkbundsiedlung of 1929, yet it would be a gross oversimplification to see it simply as an extension of German Expressionism, now flowering into the present. Scharoun's position is at once more complex. It comprises a compound of apparently irreconcilable attitudes, almost as though he had inherited from the 'Der Ring' group of 1924 (of which he was the youngest founder member) the joint irreconcilability of the different views then held by its various members. For 'Der Ring' – comprising initially Häring, Mendelsohn, Mies, Gropius, the brothers Taut, Bartning and Hilberscheimer, as well as the young Scharoun – failed understandably to generate a common approach. It was in the last analysis simply the banding of an 'us' of young 'moderns', against a reactionary 'them', which was then almost totally omnipotent. Although it met frequently and discussed at length, it failed to develop a unified aim as a group. The rebuff that Hugo Häring received as secretary of 'Der Ring' at the first CIAM congress held at La Sarraz in 1928 appears to have only had the effect of promoting the cause of the *Neue Sachlichkeit*, presumably causing further differences between the various factions of 'Der Ring'. These differences were similar no doubt to those which divided the schools of Rotterdam (Brinkman and Van der Vlugt) and Amsterdam (De Klerk and Wendigen school) at the same time. The differences that then divided 'Der Ring' still divide architects today. It is doubtful whether these differences will ever be resolved collectively, as they may well prove to be rooted in those poles of human thought which are fundamentally apart – the age-old schism which on occasion we see in terms of the classic versus the romantic.

In all this Scharoun has held and still holds a special position; a position that, at its most responsible, is close to the teachings of his friend and mentor Häring, and, at its most exotic, is to be found in his own contribution to Bruno Taut's *Die Gläserne Kette*. This position, which Scharoun has gradually established through his work over the years, has been sharply analysed by Margit Staber in her essay on Scharoun in *Zodiac* no.10. She writes, 'One of the most important aspects of Scharoun's work is that he has enlarged the necessary ascetism of the "functional building" of the Thirties, deriving from an objective thinking, into an architectonic art, not by the use of decoration or ornament, but by morphogenetic means, and by this means achieving greater richness and liberty in the disposition of his buildings.'

Essentially Scharoun's thinking is mystical and pragmatic at the same time. He has inherited from Häring, and developed in close collaboration with him, the notion of an 'organic' architecture, in which space acts as a positive force upon the life it contains, and vice versa. Their joint conception of an 'organic' architecture seems to turn upon the manner in which the human will is used collectively to create the form of the environment. It is a conception that immediately promotes a confrontation of the traditional Eastern and Western conceptions with regard to man's relation to nature. Häring places himself firmly in the Eastern camp. Two typical quotations from Häring's writings leave us in no doubt as to his views and sympathy. In favour of the tilted roof he wrote, 'It covers, roofs, protects and accompanies a man striding forward, his elevation to the sun. Rising from the horizontal of the earth, starting therefrom, it at the same time lifts towards the sun; this shape of roof is in complete harmony with nature.' And of standardization he wrote (more extremely) in 1948, 'Standardization promotes the might of machinery, meaning the might of the owner of machinery. Machinery creates a compulsion leading to imperialism. Standardization runs on the tracks of power. Supremacy is achieved by non coordination. The people are difficult to lead because their superiors overdo it. The more laws and orders there are, the more thieves and robbers there are (Laotse). Suggest, do not command.'

The intense mysticism and the social commitment of both Häring and Scharoun, developed jointly in periods of great political and social unrest, have brought them to make statements with regard to art, form and life which are essentially religious in the faith that they both place in universal forces. Thus in 1919, Scharoun wrote to the members of *Die Gläserne Kette*, in a letter addressed to 'You who fight with me', as follows: 'We are throwing around coloured rags which a genius above and within us all, someday – who knows when – will bring into a convincing unity and shape.' In 1947 Häring wrote, 'Organic building has naturally nothing to do with the imitation of the created world. The determinant requirement which emanates from the opinion of organism, is that the form of objects is no longer to be governed from the outside, but must be sought within the essence of the object ... An order will come to exist, as it exists in nature itself.'

The genesis of the Philharmonie can be traced back through Scharoun's two unbuilt projects for the state theatres of Mannheim and Kässel (1952–3), to watercolour sketches that he made in the isolation of his Berlin 'retreat' during the period 1939–45. (See also his evocative design for a cinema dating from 1923.) In these sketches, Scharoun visualizes vast mountainous aspirational public structures, reminiscent of icebergs, flooded with light and crowded with people. Once a real problem of a public structure presented itself however, he returned in collaboration with Hugo Häring and Margot Aschenbrenner to a consideration of the 'essence of the object' – the inner form or space. Out of these two projects (Kässel being premiated but remaining unbuilt owing to local opposition), Scharoun constructed his essay on the architectural structure of the theatre in which he contrasts the 'nordic' German theatre, the theatre of the Greeks and the medieval mystery plays, the theatre of the irrational and the modern theatre of the absurd, with the proscenium arch theatre of the Renaissance as exemplified in the French classical school. For Scharoun, the irrational theatre raises man from the level of perspective to 'aperspective', to become one of 'a community of affected and touched persons'.

Hans Scharoun, project for a cinema, 1922–3, watercolour.

The projects for the theatres of Mannheim and Kässel and the Philharmonie were designed practically as a continuous series, the latter taking almost eight years to be realized after initial designs were made. In the Philharmonie, the Greek theatre is once again a model. Scharoun's own words more than adequately convey the manner in which he has attempted to achieve 'a community of affected and touched persons'. In a talk entitled 'Musik im der mittlepunkt' given before work was started on site, he said:

One questions whether it is any coincidence that in any place where music is improvised that people gather themselves into a circle ... The orchestra is not exactly at the centre of the space, but on a podium placed in such a way that it is encircled by a rising row of seats in a kind of 'vine-yard-mountain-system'. The actual concert hall of the Philharmonie is a raised-up, built-in valley created through the gentle depression of the ground above the foyer and the elevation of the vineyard mountains on either side of the orchestra ... At the same time, the grouping of the orchestra and the performance of the conductor can be observed from various points in 'essence' and in 'action', and the uniting aspect of an all-embracing relationship replaces a former stage-like 'picture aspect' only.

Of the conception of the foyers in the same talk he remarked, 'They thus serve as preparatory spaces for the latter musical event enjoyed in community. In this way the transitory, ephemeral aspect stands in a tensional relationship to the permanent abiding aspect, i.e. to the essential festive spirit, the climax of the whole building – the Konzertsaal.' (See *Architectural Design*, June 1963.)

The spaces of the Philharmonie, the foyer and the auditorium itself conform exactly to these design aims and confirm the mastery of its architect. Staircases spring lightly out of the foyer floor and flow and straddle across and around the irregular flanks of the auditorium in a continuous sweep of space. The total colour tone here is cold: the concrete walls and columns are painted pale grey or white, the lowest foyer level is finished in cut grey limestone and slate mosaic and the foyers and stairs are carpeted in grey fabric above, while the whole is flooded with muted light, either reflected or direct. On occasion brightly coloured glass blocks are introduced in large panels to create zones of bright 'colour-as-light' within the grey foyer area. The whole effect is of a cool, indeterminate and almost immaterial space, encircling under and around the auditorium. The auditorium itself is equally indeterminate volumetrically, an inner space composed of shifting 'dynamic' slabs or banks of seating, the apparent relative positions of one slab to another continually changing as the observer moves around the inside of the auditorium. The tent form of the roof bellows out and down over the orchestra podium carrying suspended from its 'belly' an 'immaterial'

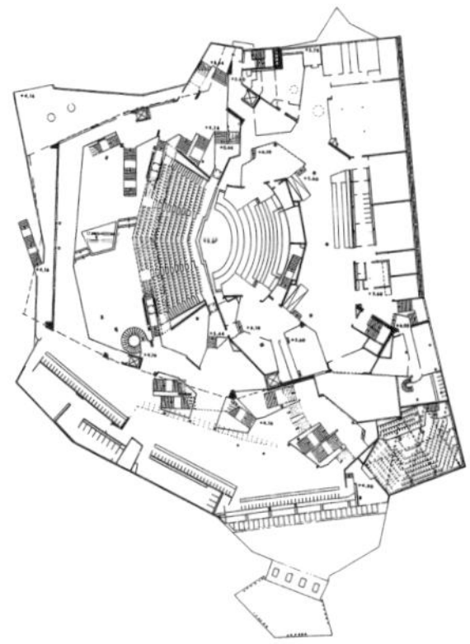

Hans Scharoun, Concert Hall for the Berlin Philharmonic Orchestra, first floor plan (above) and ground floor foyer (below).

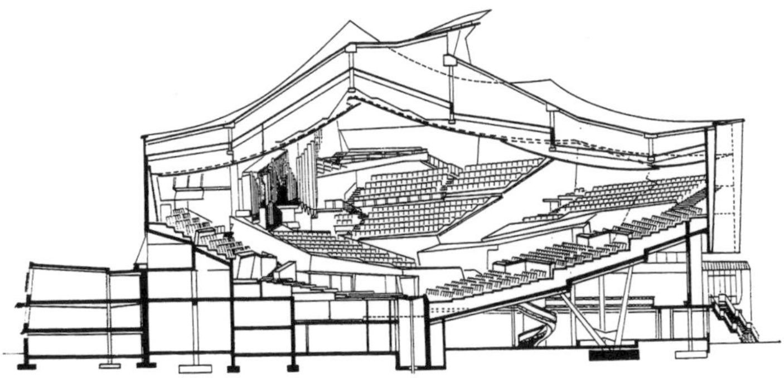

Hans Scharoun, Concert Hall for the Berlin Philharmonic Orchestra, south–north section along the axis of the hall.

layer composed of curved sound reflectors and lights. The tone of the auditorium interior is warm; generally the wall and ceiling surfaces are either faced extensively in plywood or painted white in small areas. The seats themselves are built of a matching plywood and covered with a yellow ochre-coloured fabric. The flat-topped balustrades of the tiers of seating are faced in pale grey limestone. Very little strong colour is used and the whole effect is of a contained, intimate, dynamic space, whose tone is established by the warmth of the light wood and the ochre fabric offset by white metal organ pipes and enriched by ochre and white paint.

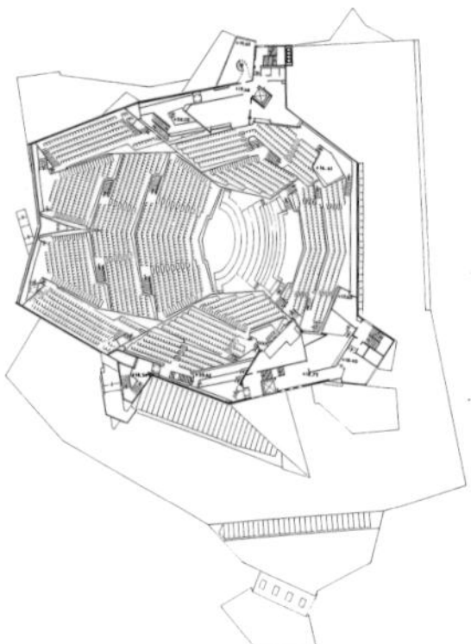

Of the outside of the Philharmonie, succinct comments are always made and rarely are they complimentary. Equally succinct and significant is Scharoun's own interrogative reply when once pestered by a student for a justification of its somewhat awkward exterior. The oracular retort was, 'It has an outside?', and the conversation ended. Undoubtedly it does have an outside and its swelling bulky irregular form has not been rendered more explicit and unified through the naive decision to paint the main bulk – the auditorium – yellow ochre, and the outside walls of the ground-floor foyer white. An already critical composition is dissipated further by this change of colour. This, the colour of Berlin, the colour of the East as they say, is yellow ochre – or the 'Brandenbergischer' colour which was used on the walls

Hans Scharoun, Concert Hall for the Berlin Philharmonic Orchestra, third floor plan (above) and view of the auditorium (right).

of the eighteenth-century Charlottenberg Palace. Here plinth, pilasters, window surrounds and pediments are all picked out in white, while the walls remain in yellow ochre. In following a Berlin tradition so crudely and slavishly, Scharoun's 'phoenix' in the Tiergarten has not been well served.

Scharoun has always set great store by the choice of site. It forms a consistent part of his theory, and on occasion, as in the 'Romeo or Juliet' flats at Stuttgart or in the girls' gymnasium in the small town of Lünen, he has achieved his aim with economy and clarity. Here in Berlin, however, the choice is not so clear or so felicitous, and until the western tangential motorway is built there will be very little for the building to 'work with' in plastic terms. The Tiergarten is virtually a zero space, today flat and lifeless. The other buildings scheduled to join the Philharmonie and form a 'cultural centre' to be wilfully implanted on the site, do not promise to serve it well from a plastic–urban point of view, in spite of the fact that one of these buildings, the state library, has been designed by Scharoun himself.

Hans Scharoun, Concert Hall for the Berlin Philharmonic Orchestra, exterior view.

A final and fundamental townscape conflict will be set up once the New National Gallery designed by Mies van der Rohe is erected to face, across an irregular space, the opposing Philharmonie. It will be an uneasy polemical confrontation between two distinct and age-old poles of thought, between the classic and the organic; a 'building out' of a conflict of little mutual benefit to either buildings or people. Scharoun's precepts about the sociological importance of the choice of a theatre site hardly seem to apply here, and one remains profoundly doubtful that the Philharmonie does in fact stand at that mystic point where 'it naturally possesses its necessary spiritual relevance to the town' (to quote Scharoun's own words).

The erection of the Philharmonie raises all the old problems once more, and demonstrates that the conflict between the two poles of thought within 'Der Ring' is by no means settled. Since the building was first opened just over a year ago, appropriately with Beethoven's Ninth Symphony, it has been nothing but an unqualified and even popular success. Few buildings built outside Finland have achieved such unity to the extent that all applied art, light fittings, etc., appear as from a single hand yet are in fact from many. In the Philharmonie a number of artists worked jointly under Scharoun's direction. In addition it has scored on almost every other level: socially, economically (cost £1.5 million), technically, acoustically (reverberation time 2–2.4 seconds), and finally musically. This success only serves to strengthen the challenge jointly made by Scharoun and Häring (the one built, the other largely theoretical) to standardization and to classicism. The Philharmonie is not a historicist tour de force in style, a phenomenon with which we are today so much inflicted. It cannot be written off as a monument because it is not in the least monumental. It is a piece of living design and although it is the idiosyncratic creation of a powerful individual, its importance lies in the fact that it does offer an alternative choice that appears to be valid. In its foyers, one quickly becomes aware of the potential that this non-Euclidean architecture possesses for being erected out of lightweight prefabricated plastic parts held in suspension. Although it is unlikely that such an architecture will ever have a general application, the total success of the Philharmonie, the point of balance which it holds between an organic and an objective architecture, compels us to reassess a forgotten school of architecture, to look again at Bruno Taut's utopian dreams and to read, perhaps for the first time, the theoretical writings of Hugo Häring.

First published in *Architectural Design*, vol.35, no.3, March 1965, pp.111–12.

A House of Ivy League Values: The Ford Foundation Headquarters

The new Ford Foundation headquarters in New York is, without question, the finest urban work yet produced by the successors to the firm of the late Eero Saarinen, the architects Kevin Roche and John Dinkeloo. Few modern institutional buildings can equal it for its authority and sober sense of decorum. It is equally distinguished by virtue of its restrained elegance, the daring of its basic conception and the precision of its elaboration and realization.

The building is an uncanny response to Sigfried Giedion's 1944 appeal to the *Zeitgeist* for a 'new monumentality' – a custom-made monument down to the very last door spring. No expense has been spared. So much so, that one can only be sceptical of the published contract figure of 16.5 million dollars (excluding furnishing and the site), rumour having it that the real figure is almost twice the amount.

That the Ford Foundation has built itself a prestigious building of the highest possible quality no one can doubt, even if some might take exception to such institutional self-indulgence. Kevin Roche, even more than his predecessor Eero Saarinen, is a proven heir to the 'high' architectural tradition in North America, which runs, in New York at any rate, as far back as the Racquets Club by McKim, Mead and White, about which Peter Smithson has commented that no Renaissance palace was ever so well detailed. The tradition includes the high calibre skyscrapers of the Twenties and Thirties by Harrison, Hood, Fouilhoux, Van Ellen & Co.; the SOM mid-town buildings of the Fifties; and the Mies van der Rohe/Philip Johnson Seagram Building, completed in 1958. Within this tradition the achievement of the Ford Foundation building is assured, although it may well be the penultimate palace of the North American 'Renaissance'.

One can hardly begin to question its achievement without questioning the programme and, by implication, the self-image and operating persona of the Ford Foundation itself. But such questioning must depend upon an acceptance of John Summerson's dictum that twentieth-century architecture is primarily to be distinguished from that of the past by the emphasis it inherently places upon the programme.

The Ford Foundation is evidently an institution so prestigious that when embodied in built form, it requires no name. It simply exists as an unemphatic brown granite outcrop, between Second and Third Avenue; an imposing megalith of stone, steel and glass, occupying the full depth of a sloping site between 42nd and 43rd Street. The site is effectively occupied by the built volume. This volume rises for 12 floors above 42nd Street and for 11 floors above 43rd Street; accommodating, in its first nine floors, a stack of double-banked offices on two of the adjacent sides of its square plan, and, for the remaining two floors, offices on four sides. The bulk of this office space thus wraps itself (on the north and west faces) around the remainder of the site, amounting to one-third of an acre in area, enclosing a vast glazed conservatory of some six million cubic feet. The sloping floor of this conservatory is ramped, paved and planted with shrubs and trees, which in some instances, notably the eucalyptus and cryptomeria, will eventually grow to 200 feet. This, then, is the patio–house solution on a colossal scale, eccentrically extended in height. (For such a *parti* there is some precedent, particularly in North America.)

On entering this 'patio–conservatory' from 42nd Street, one feels that one has been privileged to enter into the 'private' realm of a large and benevolent family institution. Here one may take a very constricted turn around the 'garden', gape briefly at the greenery, at the vast space above, watch the diligent 'family workers' behind their hermetic glass, and then leave – for other than going up for a 'grant' or a 'guided tour', there is nothing else to do and no point of arrival or rest.

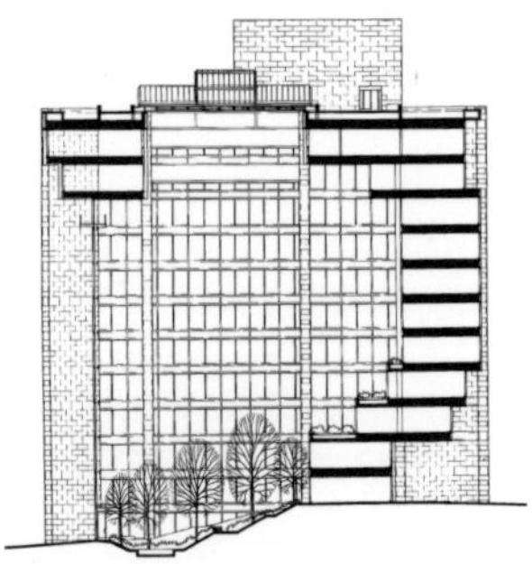

Kevin Rocbe John Dinkeloo Associates, Ford Foundation Headquarters, section through conservatory-cum-entrance foyer looking west.

It is at this juncture that the irresolution of the building's programme is to be felt most keenly. To walk in, to look briefly around and to walk out – one cannot but question whether this unavoidable procedure symbolizes adequately the rapport that the Ford Foundation conceives of itself as possessing in respect of the general public. There is even less of a public *agora* here than in the average Park Avenue bank or in the street-level foyer of a Wall Street corporation building. Are we to conclude from this that in our Western society, the house of private profit is more naturally rendered 'public' than the house of private, non-profit, public benevolence?

To the dilemma of twentieth-century architecture as a whole and, in this instance, to that posed by the Ford Foundation building in particular, the architectural theory of Christian Norberg-Schulz provides a critical point of departure. In his discussion of the role of the programme or the *building task*, Schulz argues that it may be analysed broadly as two interdependent aspects, expressed as dualities; firstly, the *physical milieu* and the *functional frame* and, secondly, the *social milieu* and *cultural symbolization*.[1]

It is in the second aspect that the Ford Foundation building is to be seen as problematic. For Schulz, 'the building task is the point of departure of the architectural solution. While a classification in terms of formal and technical factors would isolate architecture, a classification in terms of tasks unites the architectural totalities to the form of life in general. An architecture determined by the need for a "symbol milieu" could be denominated as *monumental*.'[2] Schulz elsewhere states that 'an architecture where the formal dimension is unduly stressed is "formalistic", a term which implies that the forms are unsatisfactorily coordinated with the building task.'[3] In this situation, turning upon the possible invention of new building tasks, there are two possibilities: either the forms are inappropriate to the inherent reduced building task, or the building task has been inadequately developed through the agency of the building programme.

In the case of the Ford Foundation building, a critique may be sustained on the two fronts at once; for, formally, from the two street facades, the building promises a hierarchy that may only be interpreted as first 'public' and then 'private'. To a degree, this promise seems to be momentarily fulfilled on entry – but almost at once it becomes apparent that what promised to be a public space is in essence an *anti-agora*, invaded by the vegetative processes of nature, and that there remains nothing for man to do but to leave. As realized then, the building is formalistic, for the forms are far from adequately coordinated with the building task.

From formal evidence alone, one may only construe the building as being monumental, yet its present task or programme is far from being so. The second *post facto* alternative is that the Foundation and its architects should jointly have amplified the building task, so as to embody a valid public element, through which to establish symbolically and actually a correct 'contractual' relation between the Foundation and the public it serves.

As it is, the one element which could have effectively fulfilled this public contractual role, the 175-seat auditorium in the basement, has been rendered exclusively private. The building is thus totally devoid of a public realm that is in any way appropriate to the scale of its volume, its institutional content and its prominent location. The bulk of the Ford Foundation's direct grant goes to educational institutions, for the purposes of education. Surely then the introduction into the programme of an adequate auditorium for public use would not only have been within the capacities of the site and the budget but would also have symbolized, through actual use, the Foundation's main public function.

This paradox of an exclusively private monument (of public import) is further emphasized by the conscious egalitarian symbolism of the building's internal detailing and finish. One standard of high-quality furnishing is maintained throughout the office space. Be it secretary, programme director or president, the same range of high-quality equipment, designed by Kevin Roche and Warren Platner, is placed at their disposal. The clear implication is of a working team, which in spite of different roles is symbolically equal. The 'house style' is consistent throughout, and the floor-to-ceiling glazing to both the office space and the 'conservatory' mutually permits that every act on every floor (with the exception of the chairman's) is observed and witnessed by all, testifying to an exclusive, private, closely interrelated vigilant *élite* functioning collectively in the service of the public.

It is ultimately in the small-scale detailing of the furnishing of its fabric that the Ford Foundation building acquires its full cultural significance. For here we are presented with an identifiable taste which is to be directly associated with a particular lifestyle and a particular accepted system of values. That this value system may be seen as the direct opposite to that evoked by the Carpenter Art Center at Harvard is not without significance with regard to the ultimate values aspired to by these very different buildings. Apart from its pale mauvish-brown granite 'shell', selected so as to harmonize with the brick facing of Tudor City, the Ford Foundation building is a study in Corten 'weathering' steel both inside and out. This sombre, opaque, non-reflective frame is complemented by an equally sober range of elements – ranging from the granite itself to black ceramic tiles in the public galleries and parquet floors in the offices, from dark brown, pale grey and beige fabrics and carpets to the occasional muted sparkle of mauvish-red Florentine marble, plate glass and polished bronze. The wooden furniture throughout is of dark Honduras mahogany, the upholstery is in restrained earth-coloured fabric, the walls of the offices and staffrooms are decorated with modest prints selected by the director of the Yale Art Gallery. The public gallery balustrading is finished in brown cowhide, as are the lift carts and certain wall panels. An atmosphere of indestructible decorum reigns throughout, with a persistence and a level of craftsmanship only to be matched, in its all-pervasive sense of confidence and stability, by the high institutional styles of the nineteenth century. In this, paradoxically, resides its underlying sense of *insecurity*. As at the macro scale, so at the micro scale; for at all scales this building admits to no intrusion by a single part of any *general* current system of value. Its egalitarianism is totally introverted. Unlike the rigorous generosity and stoicism of the Carpenter Arts Center, it cannot welcome the public presence and worlds beyond its own realm. The *Third World* would have no place here, for the building is at once private, custom-made, exclusive and hermetic. The *objet trouvé* and the *objet type* of civilization at large cannot be welcomed into its *consensus* system of order. The presence of a cheap mass-produced wire wastepaper basket would, unavoidably, have to be regarded as an object of subversion.

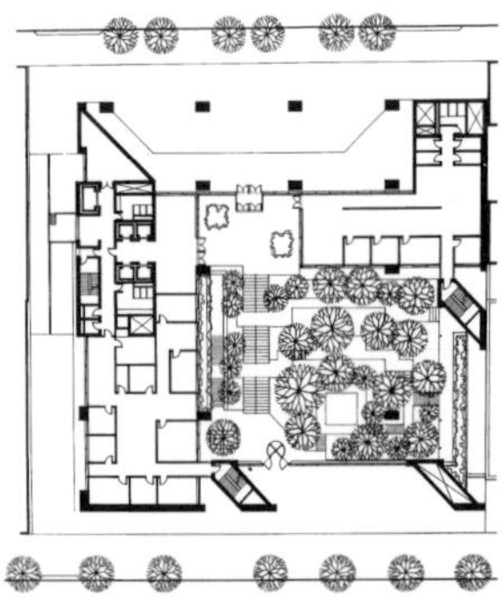

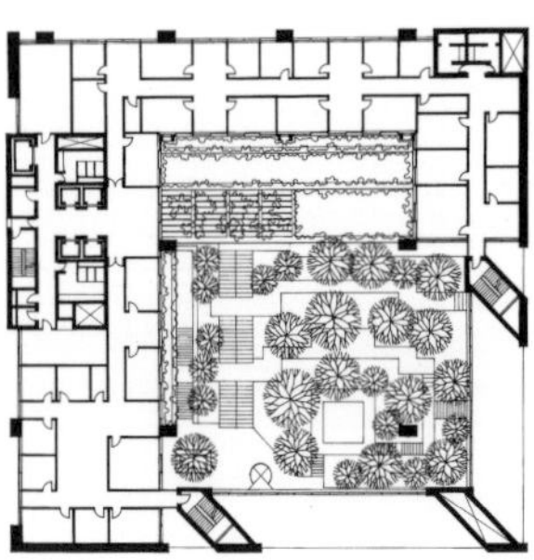

Kevin Rocbe John Dinkeloo Associates, Ford Foundation Headquarters, ground floor plan (above) and typical floor plan (below).

One cannot but conclude that consciously or unconsciously, the Ford Foundation and its architects knew what they were doing. The public, like the more ordinary objects of our industrial civilization, must be ministered to, but

Kevin Roche John Dinkeloo Associates, Ford Foundation Headquarters, offices flanking the conservatory.

kept constantly at a distance. It is a wholly regrettable and highly dangerous symbolic stance for a great benevolent institution to adopt. For what remains is a superbly organized Shangri-La housed with impeccable technique. A house of Ivy League values and good intentions, dedicated to the dispensation of private profit for the public good, hermetically sealed in an unreal world, which is not only open to unfortunate external misinterpretations but which may well also distort, through its all-pervasive yet delusive sense of security, its own internal perception of the reality in which it must operate.

First published in *Architectural Design*, vol.38, no.7, July 1968, pp.305–11.

BANKINTER

Moneo's Paseo: The Bankinter

Buildings are appropriated in a twofold manner: by use and by perception – or rather, by touch and sight. Such appropriation cannot be understood in terms of the attentive concentration of a tourist before a famous building. On the tactile side there is no counterpart to contemplation on the optical side. Tactile appropriation is accomplished not so much by attention as by habit. As regards architecture, habit determines to a large extent even optical reception. The latter, too, occurs much less through rapt attention than by noticing the object in incidental fashion. This mode of appropriation, developed with reference to architecture, in certain circumstances acquires canonical value. For the tasks that face the human apparatus of perception at the turning points of history cannot be solved by optical means, that is, by contemplation, alone. They are mastered gradually by habit, under the guidance of tactile appropriation.
Walter Benjamin, 'The Work of Art in the Age of Mechanical Reproduction', 1936[1]

As far as late modern architecture is concerned, Spain still remains the unknown continent despite the boom that architectural publishing has enjoyed in recent years. The reason for this may well reside in the fact that, by and large, modern Spanish building has remained resistant to the camera. The architecture of José Rafael Moneo has been no exception in this regard, for, from his earliest commission – his remarkable brick-faced Diestre Factory, built outside Zarazoga in Spain in 1965 – the architectonic presence of his work has denied summation in terms of photography. And what was the case with the solemn whale-like profiles of this enormous industrial complex was to be equally true of his next work of international importance, the Bankinter Building in Madrid, designed with Ramon Bescós in 1973 and completed in 1977.

The triangular plan form of the Bankinter, eased into the confines of an awkward site, has so far refused to respond to the blandishments of the camera. Even where it has been photographed with consummate skill, the unavoidable optical distortions have prevented any real fidelity to the tactility of its form, above all perhaps because with each movement of the viewer the building radically changes. Thus, although faced externally in a single material, namely brick, it is nonetheless not a singular mass but a contentious irregularity – a faceted escarpment whose character changes with the varying incidence of the light, thereby transforming the texture of its monolithic surface from one instant to the next.

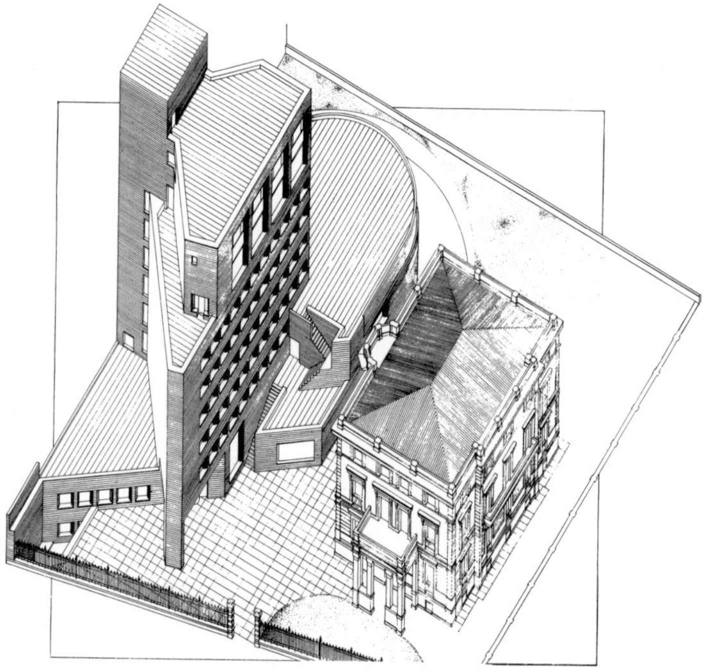

Rafael Moneo, The Bankinter, axonometric.

The *parti* of the Bankinter seems to have its origins in an impossible proposition, in an effort to combine into a single whole the rationality of a frontal scheme with the irrationality of a picturesque disposition. The problem that the architect posed for himself (once the client had been persuaded to retain an existing nineteenth-century villa) was how to establish a mediatory position between the old and the new, or rather, how to arrange the building's entry in such a way as to turn subtly towards the new development while still acknowledging the presence of the old. The architect's solution was to circumvent the driveway and *porte cochère* of the existing villa and to enter between the two structures on the line of a new car entrance. However, since this new opening in the boundary was nec-

Rafael Moneo, The Bankinter, view of office slab from the Calle Marquès de Riscal.

essarily normal to the line of the Calle Marquès de Riscal, the visual approach was automatically inflected towards the new development. And yet at the same time, the old palazzo was the only building to actually confront the street, thereby leaving the status of the existing development unchanged by the impact of the new form.

On inspection the Bankinter proves to be ordered about a series of incidental inflections, the building asserting itself as a kind of inverted perspective, predicated on the conjunction of various found elements within the site. Thus, both the thin escarpment of the slab and prow-like form of the podium seem to be the product of a number of converging factors: the rise of the land from the Paseo de la Castellana, the angle of the service road in relation to the geometry of the site, the favourable orientation toward the south, and last but not least, the existing tree planting. One should add to this Moneo's profound respect for the original nineteenth-century grain of the city, for the time when this area was inlaid with large free-standing bourgeois villas, of which the existing building is one of the few survivors. Aside from this respect for tradition and the topographic idiosyncrasies of the site, the tectonic of the building derives from a need to filter these heterogeneous factors through a rational schema or *parti* and to render the result in terms of traditional brickwork, distantly related to the context of other brick structures in the Paseo.

In reading the Bankinter one moves back and forth between the two most disjunctive aspects of its composition; that is, between the inverted visual cone of its prow-like entry foyer and the frontal deportment and modelling of the facade. It is clear that any claim which this facade may

Rafael Moneo, The Bankinter, view of office slab in relation to the wrought iron gateway giving onto the existing villa (above), and detail of entry into the bank under the portico (right).

make to its own primacy is at once countermanded by the curious fact that rather than confront the street, it presents itself to the side elevation of the existing villa (although the honorific 'Gothic' top of the slab is, in fact, frontally readable from the Paseo della Castellana). The formal tension that arises between the displaced frontality and the thrust of the salient prow towards the street is plastically mediated, or at least counterbalanced, by the service core bustle behind the building. It is also mediated by the semi-circular, two-storey podium situated to the rear of the composition. It is exactly at this prow that an American referent is first brought to mind, above all in the thick-topped T-fenestration to the main entrance, patently reminiscent of the work of Louis Kahn. At the same time, the minimalist conjunction of the primary elements – the stump of the prow, the singular rotating door – takes one away from the judicious proportioning of the facade and back to a brutal confrontation between primary elements.

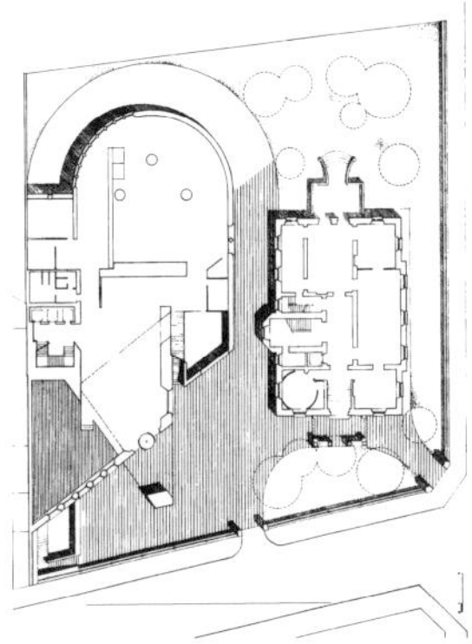

Rafael Moneo, The Bankinter, ground floor and basement plan.

Aside from the possible debt to another American – Robert Venturi, and his more monumental Yale Mathematics Building project of 1971 – one has sufficient grounds for suggesting that the schism in the composition of the Bankinter may derive from a split that runs through the architect's formation, for while Moneo respects the Mediterranean rational tradition, he is nonetheless affected by a passion for the organic in modern architecture. At the same time, the source of the organic in Moneo's work varies considerably from a strong susceptibility to the work of Frank Lloyd Wright – acquired no doubt while Moneo was still a student in Madrid, working under Javier Saénz de Oíza – to an affinity for the late northern European Romanticism so evident in the post-1939 work of Alvar Aalto or in the mature achievements of Jørn Utzon, for whom Moneo worked in the early Sixties. As Gabriel Ruiz Cabrero has pointed out in his essay 'Sobre Bankinter o un Americano en Madrid?', the presence of Aalto is perhaps never more evident than in the ceiling illumination of the banking hall, although the handling of the brick mass as a whole is decidedly Aalto-esque.[2]

The rational versus romantic schism in Moneo's work also has its roots in a cultural exchange between England and Spain in the late Fifties, for at that time, with the liberalization of Franquista culture, British New Brutalism exerted a decisive, if brief, influence on the development of Spanish architecture. In the case of the Bankinter the seminal building seems to have been Stirling's Leicester University Engineering Laboratory of 1959–63, for the paradigm of Leicester lies as much at the root of the Bankinter as does the work of Venturi. This connection tends to be confirmed by the fact that the *parti* for Leicester also informs the plan of Moneo's Logroño City Hall dating from 1973, a work which was developed and built between 1977 and 1981. What Leicester, Bankinter and Logroño have in common is a triangularly structured composition radiating out from a single centre. In each instance this centre is a condensed mass asymmetrically disposed in relation to the main bulk of the building. However, certain critical differences clearly obtain, for at Leicester and Logroño the focus of the composition is the public core of the institution – the stacked lecture halls in the case of Leicester and a compact, multi-use municipal complex in the case of Logroño. In the Bankinter, however, these public components are missing owing to the nature of the programme, although the architect has been at pains to compensate for this in a number of ways. It was Moneo, after all, who persuaded his clients to build a multipurpose public room on the *piano nobile* directly above the ground-floor banking hall – a provision which, as might have been predicted, has not received

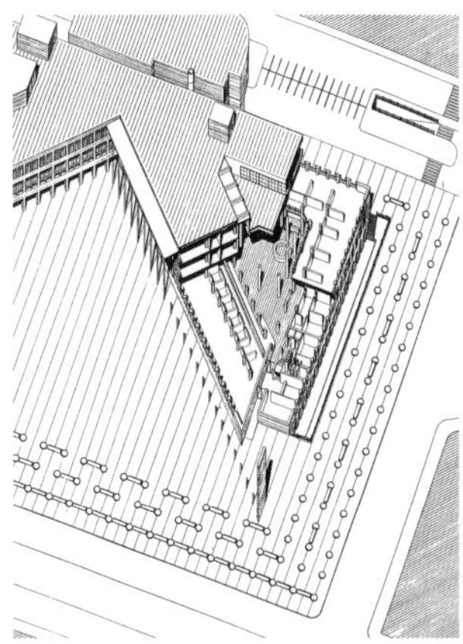

Rafael Moneo, Logroño City Hall, Logroño, 1973, axonometric.

much use in the subsequent life of the building.

One is reminded here of Frank Lloyd Wright's efforts to transform the place of corporate activity into the house of public sacrament – evident, say, in his incorporation of an organ into the nave of the Larkin Building (1904), or in his partly frustrated efforts to introduce a theatre into the ground floor of his Johnson Wax Administration building (1936). And it is surely a similar concern to represent an all but absent public realm that motivated the architects of the Bankinter. A comparable motivation led to the application of four ornamental, cast-bronze spandrels to the elevation of the directors' offices on the top two floors. It is surely no accident that these recessed spandrels misleadingly suggest the presence of a double-height honorific space.

Stirling's Leicester building may also be cited as the precedent for the Bankinter at the level of the facing material, above all, in terms of its assertion of engineering brickwork as the shiny opaque substance of a dense yet dynamic form. Here, as at Leicester, one encounters brick used with the plastic boldness of concrete, and here again the common origin is Wright's Johnson Wax building, for the plastic brick membranes used in the Bankinter and at Leicester speak at once of the concealed frame which is essential to their support.

Stirling may also be adduced as the touch of the neo-Corbusianism which is latent in the Bankinter, for, as Peter Eisenman has demonstrated in his essay 'Real and English',[3] the Leicester University Engineering Laboratory was derived in its turn from Le Corbusier's Pavillon Suisse of 1933. It was, it seems, an inversion of the *parti* for the Pavillon Suisse: where in Paris the slab was primary and the service tower secondary, in Leicester it is the tower which is primary while the slab, transformed into a horizontal shed, is treated as a secondary form. In the Bankinter, on the other hand, the slab assumes the primary role even though it is reduced to a screen, a thick 'billboard', and the unifying vectors of the composition seem to stem not from the slab but from the two-storey podium; the latter is the location of diagonal intersections from which the guillotine slab seems to take its precarious limits.

It is a measure of Moneo's poetic sensibility that he should differentiate at a tectonic level between different faces of the slab, thereby compensating for its disconcerting narrowness and for the fact that the body of the slab, that is, the available office space, is at once both polygonal and limited in area. It is no doubt this contradiction which prompted Moneo to differentiate between the ontological density of the slab in its frontality and the unexpected diminution of its return facades. This differentiation is largely achieved through tectonic articulation, so that the 'thin front' of the slab is treated as though it were a 'thick wall', while the return walls to the office space are treated as though they were of normal thickness. As in all wall architecture, the tectonic depth of the masonry mass is made evident through modelling. The window plane of the main facade is in fact set back in stages through rebates, while its depth in section is indicated by a straight reveal faced in cast bronze; a sill below and a lintel above. This modelling principle runs throughout the south facade, including the apparently double-height opening accommodating the directors' offices on the top two floors. On the return facades, however, the shallower penetrations are simply cut into the surface with reveals of uniform depth except for the podium, where a rotated brick pier imparts a comparable depth to the circular, brick-faced perimeter. This variation in modelling also suggests that the 'thick facades' are to be read as representative elevations appropriate to such public features as the banking hall, the public room, or the principal facade which is representative of the institution as a whole. At the same time, while the windows are lined with bronze reveals throughout, the actual apertures are empirically yet rationally positioned once they are separated from the main facade or the semicircular podium; in fact, they are so ordinary in their treatment as to echo the fenestration of the adjacent party wall.

The most extraordinary space in the Bankinter is unquestionably the inverted perspectival cone of the foyer, which apart from unexpectedly expanding instead of diminishing as it recedes from the eye, also affords distant vistas into the banking floor at the rear. This unexpected spatial expansion prompts the visitor to turn back towards the framed views of the adjacent villa and its environs, towards the traditional forms of the boundary fence and wrought iron gateway. The Wrightian quality of this interior, that is to say, its sense of lateral expansion recalling Wright's Avery Coonley and Hanna houses, is emphasized here through the use of exotic, rich and striated revetment, by the application of long diagonal bands of polished travertine to the floor, and by the equally syncopated linear panelling of the walls in figured oak. The satin finish common to both travertine and oak affords a calm sense of material refinement, while at the same

Rafael Moneo, The Bankinter, interior entrance hall.

time implying – through the pitted and gnarled surfaces – the Piranesian quality of an enrichment which has been apparently achieved through erosion over time. Needless to say, this is in strong contrast to the precise, normative brickwork in which the building is faced. And yet this is not the only contrast, nor for that matter is it the only allusion to Wright, for Wright is again present in the abstract décor of the intaglio plaster ceiling and in the dense pile of the foyer carpet, since both surfaces have been enriched by Wrightian decorative treatments designed by the painter Pablo Palazuelo. The contrast here resides in the fact that the plaster and the pile are absorbent, as opposed to the matt, hard finish of the travertine and the oak.

This interior treatment is inflected by another reference which, in contrast to the first, is initially suggested in a subtle way by the brass highlights of the foyer railings and light fittings, whose gleaming edges shoot through the space to combine with the luxurious depth of the black furniture, and in so doing immediately evoke the spirit of *fin-de-siècle* Vienna. Such elements also testify to the presence of a Doricist sensibility in Moneo's work, to his penchant for that atectonic allusion which was once the touchstone of Scandinavian neoclassical eclecticism. This nostalgia for what Henry-Russell Hitchcock once categorized as the New Tradition is, of course, equally evident in the ornamental cast-bronze spandrels applied to the front facade. These are decorated with stylized orange trees designed by Francisco Lopez Hernandez, which remind one, in their placement and their scale, not only of Louis Sullivan's Wainwright Building, as Ruiz Cabrero has pointed out, but also of Gunnar Asplund's penultimate principal facade for his Gothenburg Law Courts of 1934–7. But this naive symbolization of gold is discreetly absent in the rest of the fabric. Instead, a pattern of Viennese revetment *à la* Hoffmann or Loos becomes apparent as one penetrates deeper into the interior, into the elevator lobby and main stairs, where on finally attaining the director's suite at the top of the building, one is again confronted by walls lined in figured oak, illuminated by the diffused inner glow of the onyx clerestory above. This amber environment is sharpened in its intensity by the thin chromium-steel frames containing the onyx. Like certain Japanese minimalist architects, Moneo is able to maintain his control over these exotic finishes largely through the use of reductively simple – not to say abrasive – profiles, and through an angular geometry, which is evident in the solid balustrading of the main stair and in the guillotine-like placement of the mezzanine balustrade across the trapezoidal space of the foyer.

Rafael Moneo, The Bankinter, interior of executive suite with onyx clerestory.

It is clear that Bescós and Moneo manipulated the site in a manner which was at once pragmatic and yet geometrically controlled. Evidently their task was to accommodate a compact mass on a severely limited site. The 'organicism' with which they approached this charge was closer to Wright than to Aalto, for to predicate a *parti* on the intersection of an equilateral and a right-angle triangle is to evoke Usonian principles rather than the organic expressiveness of, say, Aalto's Neue Vahr apartments built in Bremen in 1958–62. On the other hand, the tight orthogonal planning of the basement parking together with the ingenious insertion of two interlocking levels of radial car ramps under the semicircular podium is rationalist rather than organic, testifying once again to the multivalency running through the entire work.

How are we to interpret this organic cast, which, despite a constant recourse to rational devices, persists in permeating the entire fabric of the building, and moreover, what is the significance of a Spanish building in which recurrent references are made to the culture of northern Europe – to the ascetic or playful moods of the Doricist sensibility and to the fractured, geological mass forms which characterize the later forms of Aalto and Utzon?[4] Is this not what Paul Ricoeur had in mind when, in his essay 'Universal Civilization and National Cultures',[5] he evoked the prospect of a world culture; and does not Moneo reiterate in his own work the art of contradictory synthesis between East and West, between old and new, that he once must have discerned in the work of his Danish master? For Utzon's career has turned on this paradigmatic synthesis of opposites: of platforms and pagodas, of forms which may generically transcend the limits of their temporal and cultural origins – the podium being as much Meso-American as Mediterranean, and the pagoda, when conceived as a floating roof, being as much a Chinese precedent as a triumph in reinforced concrete.

Ever since its impregnation during the Islamic conquest, Spain has never been able to ignore the cultural relativity of Humanist culture and the inevitability of having to revitalize it through contact with the 'other'. While Moneo does not create in terms of the opposites assumed by Utzon – the Occident versus the Orient – there nonetheless remains in his work a comparable drive towards a contradictory synthesis, wherein the transfigured conjunction will be the sign of a vital cultural meaning, the substance of *répétition differente*, because it consciously deconstructs and reassembles its alien ingredients into a compound of universal significance. This is surely what Paul Ricoeur had in mind when he wrote, 'No one can say what will become of our civilization when it has really met different civilizations by means other than the shock of conquest and domination.'[6] This, then, is the ultimate significance of the Bankinter; for the West, despite the example of Louis Kahn, has yet to rediscover the subtlety, the rigour and the richness of a more Oriental and tactile approach to building. When it does so, the way will be open towards a future wherein architecture will be mixed with a wider history, without falling into the dead end of repetition or into the gratuitous vagaries of kitsch.

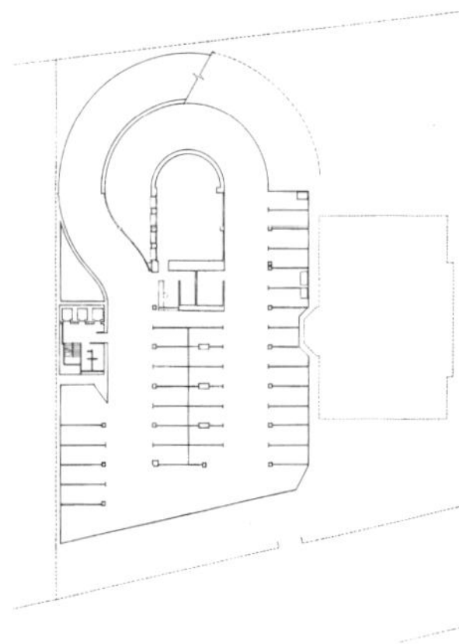

Rafael Moneo, The Bankinter, basement parking plan.

Previously unpublished, originally written in 1981 for the journal *Oppositions*.

It is a cause of considerable pride for Herman Hertzberger that his buildings are rarely, if ever, photographed without people, as opposed to the photogenic uninhabited purity which is so evidently sought after in a great deal of current architectural photography. For Hertzberger a building is primarily a context for life, a work which, as Walter Benjamin reminds us, is usually perceived in a state of distraction by the ordinary man. And yet Hertzberger can no more predicate his work on an intellectual distanced mode of beholding than he can accept the aesthete's perspectival illusion. For him architecture must be ultimately based on the tactile appropriation of the environment by the user. Thus what has to be represented, or rather presented, is not so much the purity of abstract or organic form, but rather the potential of his work for a constantly changing interplay between tectonic structure and human action. Perhaps no two works condense the range and complexity of this socially committed attitude more intensely and completely than the Apollo Montessori and Willemspark schools recently completed in Amsterdam.

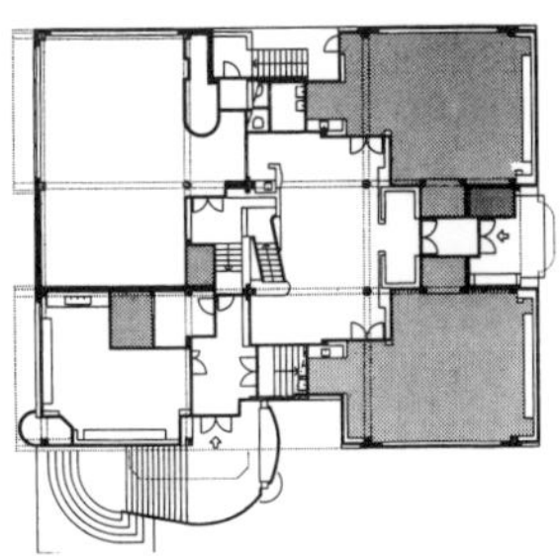

Herman Hertzberger, Apollo Montessori School, 1980–3, ground floor plan.

Of these twin schools, set diagonally to each other about a common forecourt, the Apollo Montessori school affords by far the most intense and elaborate rendering of Hertzberger's vision to date. In recognizing this distinction one is compelled to acknowledge the different cultural aspirations projected by the different educational ideologies involved. For it is ultimately more correct to describe the Montessori method as a vision of life rather than just as an alternative pedagogical technique. It is, one may argue, an end rather than a means to an end, for it displays an evident belief in the untapped sovereign potential of the individual which transcends the operative methods which generally pass for education in the disenchanted Western world. The Montessori method is, one might say, a living extension of nineteenth-century utopianism at its best. And here one needs to remark in passing on the manner in which the Hertzberger family are steeped in the Montessori ethos; one should note the way in which, in one form or another, every member of the household has been formed by this pedagogy, continuing in some instances through two generations of pupils and teachers. This is nowhere more evident than in the fact that Hertzberger's wife and daughter are both Montessori teachers.

This subculture, Dutch by assimilation, is integrated in Hertzberger's own work with two later utopian strands of modern thought: on the one hand the existential phenomenological tradition stemming from Husserl and Kierkegaard and passing through Heidegger and Sartre to culminate today in writings of Paul Ricoeur, on the other the school of anthropological structuralism whose origin lies in the linguistics of Ferdinand de Saussure and the anthropology of Claude Lévi-Strauss. Hertzberger's affinity for this compound of French and Germanic thought stems not only from the Dutch condition of being situated geographically and culturally between these two countries but also from his formation as an architect under the tutelage of Aldo van Eyck.

Four aperçus seem to have determined the critical character of Van Eyck's thought from 1945 onwards. These may be characterized as follows. In the first place there is the underlying assumption that the modern world can only be endured if it is constantly challenged and that this existential critique is in itself a creative act. For Van Eyck and Hertzberger alike the critical intellectual is a militant who is engaged in a perpetual struggle against the perennial positivism of industrialized society. This militancy owes something to Guy Debord's Situationism of the early Fifties and the related poets and painters of the Dutch Cobra group, with whom Van Eyck had close contact in its formative years. Cobra strongly influenced Van Eyck in his early maturity and one way or another this critical-anarchic ethos has sustained itself in Dutch culture for nearly 40 years. It was revitalized in the Sixties by Roel van Duijn's Provo movement which anticipated in many ways the European student revolt of 1968.

Second, while Van Eyck was sympathetic to Situationism he rejected its latent negativity. Thereafter the Dutch Structuralist movement strove to combine Lévi-Strauss's structural anthropology with Sartre's existentialism, so as to posit an anthropologically oriented architecture appropriate to the critical restructuring of modern life. This synthesis gave rise to that paradigm which Van Eyck characterized as 'labyrinthine clarity'.

Third, Van Eyck committed himself implicitly to the necessity of 'place-creation' in all architecture and in so doing espoused the belief that a place-oriented environment has to be structured in terms of 'twin-phenomena'. What Van Eyck intended by this term is best explained in his own words: 'Life flourishes only to the degree to which the two contradictory principles governing human nature can be brought into a state of harmony: the individual and the collective.' Elsewhere he remarked, 'It is not possible for a habitat conducive to life to be created from the mistaken belief that the individual and the community represent two antagonistic opposites. The individual and the community are ambivalent and together form a twin-phenomena.' Later in the Otterloo meeting of 1959 he gave a rhetorical example of the twin phenomena at work: 'What then, I ask, is the greater reality that frames your coming and going, for it's a vital experience not only for those that do so, but also for those encountered or left behind. *A door is a place made for an occasion*. A door is a place made for an act that is repeated millions of times in a lifetime between the first entry, and the last exit. I think that's symbolical.'

Finally Van Eyck mounted a fundamental critique of the time-obsessed trajectory of the Western Enlightenment together with its delusional myth of progress. This double-headed attack has never been better expressed than by Van Eyck himself, above all when he wrote in 1962, 'Western civilization habitually identifies itself with civilization as such, on the pontifical assumption that what is not like it, is a deviation, less advanced, primitive, or at best exotically interesting at a safe distance.' Five years later he wrote in the magazine *Forum*: 'I dislike a sentimental antiquarian attitude towards the past as much as I dislike a sentimental technocratic one toward the future. Both are founded on a static, clockwork notion of time (what antiquarians and technocrats have in common). So let's start with the past for a change and discover the unchanging conditions of man.'

It is to Hertzberger's credit that he has continued to extend and to refine through successive realizations the precepts of his mentor, and one may claim that the continuity of this master/pupil relationship is unique in the annals of twentieth-century architecture. It says something for the inherent 'interpretability' of Van Eyck's approach that his prime pupils have not followed him slavishly and that they have felt free to develop and elaborate much which remained open in his thought and work. This is perhaps more true in the case of Hertzberger than in the subsequent careers of Hertzberger's contemporaries, those other prominent members of Van Eyck's *Forum* circle in the late Fifties, such as Piet Blom or Joop van Stigt, who have either given their work an unduly formalistic cast or have built comparatively little.

For those who know the inside story, all of this is at once evident in Hertzberger's Apollo Montessori school of 1983 where the principles of Dutch Structuralism find themselves subtly inflected and richly elaborated under a single roof. The multi-layered complexity of this building demands that we accord it some attention before proceeding to consider Hertzberger's larger and more ambitious 'labyrinthine' works. Considered from the point of view of its plan, nothing could be more surprising than this simple four-square layout with its four classrooms per floor, one in each corner of the all-embracing orthogonal volume. This planimetric simplicity is deceptive, however, as is at once evident from the split, east–west section, linked by free-standing staircases; the whole engendering a dynamic spatial interconnection between one level and the next. This diagonal spatial interpenetration is in no way formalistic, however, since it serves to establish the school as a community, as though it were an encapsulated introversion of a Cycladic village, wherein each house and patio is visible from the next, as the community piles up about a harbour inlet or a steep mountain slope. The internal artificial site in this instance is a steeply raked wooden amphitheatre which is the ultimate spatial focus and symbolic place-form of the entire school; a stepped 'space of public appearance' which is consummated by casual encounters, school assemblies and theatrical performances. This is the school as a city-in-miniature, as a compensation, one might say, for the loss of a public forum in the community as a whole. It is difficult to imagine a more specifically political gesture than this, and it would be hard to find any school built during the last 20 years that is of comparable critical subtlety and depth.

Hertzberger's Apollo Montessori school reveals in a most singular way the presence of a model which has been perennially implicit in all his work, but which has never been declared so forcefully as on this occasion. I am alluding to the way in which the architect has remained obsessed, throughout his career, with the introverted paradigm of the Maison de Verre as this was realized in Paris in 1932, to the designs of Pierre Chareau and the Dutch architect Bernard Bijvoet. This influence manifests itself in the Apollo Montessori school in three specific ways: first, in the filtered sub-aqueous light which descends into the main volume of the building from the translucent glass-fibre vaults above; second, in the similar filtration of side-light through glass block panels; and third, in the 'constructivist' detailing of the main metal stairways, both internally and externally. Here, as in all works of quality, the details make multiple references so that the glass treads and perforated metal risers are as much a tribute to the main stair of Le Corbusier's Maison Clarté, Geneva (1935), as they are a testament to the Maison de Verre. This is hardly surprising since the Maison Clarté was, in its turn, influenced by the Maison de Verre.

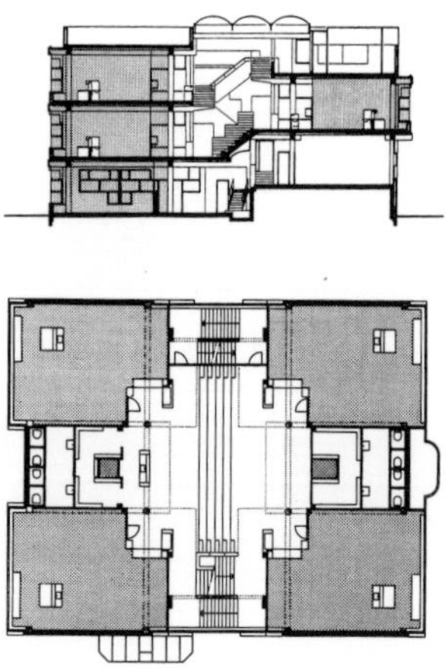

Herman Hertzberger, Apollo Montessori School, section (above) and first floor plan (below).

Prewar Dutch Constructivism is a general influence on Hertzberger's work, not only in terms of the Dutch input to the Maison de Verre due to Bernard Bijvoet's collaboration but also in terms of Bijvoet's partner, Johannes Duiker. The latter emerges as a latent presence in both the Apollo Montessori and Willemspark schools not only in the detailing of the metal stairs and the ferro-vitreous canopies, but also in the basic reinforced concrete skeleton used in both buildings, with its outriding beams cantilevering east–west. The constructivist 'model' here is patently Duiker's famous Open Air School realized in Amsterdam in 1930, an influence that is equally evident in the main classroom elevations with their symmetrical emblematic character and their cantilevered concrete beams.

Like the Montessori school realized in Delft in 1966 and the De Drie Hoven old people's home built in Amsterdam in 1974, the Apollo Montessori school is elaborated in terms of a double interlocking syntax which is present to different degrees in almost all of Hertzberger's work. This syntax arises out of two interrelated systems of articulation: on the one hand, a constructional logic which presents itself as a series of permutable elements, i.e. variations on the beam–column–in-fill syndrome; and on the other, a hierarchical concatenation of thresholds ranging from amplified entryways to intimately inflected thick walls, the latter comprising wide transoms, windowsills, inset-benches, etc. While these two systems meet only intermittently they are, in a sense, the mirror image of each other. In this respect two spatial themes are particularly prominent in the Apollo Montessori school: the point of classroom entry and the 'space of public appearance'. As in De Drie Hoven the former is amplified through a series of complementary 'activity settings' while the latter establishes its presence in the amphitheatrical atrium of the school. On entering the thresholds of each classroom one first encounters the work recess, which serves as a direct extension of the teaching space itself. Adjacent to this recess but on the other side of the entry door is a 'museum' display case provided for the work of each classroom. It is as though each teaching unit were regarded as a pre-industrial village-dwelling in which the threshold may be used both for production and display. Of a similar transitional nature is the shift from the frosted glass of the clerestory to the clear glass of the re-entrant corner glazing which flanks the combined entrance into the bathroom core.

Herman Hertzberger, Apollo Montessori School, interior view of class rooms opening off central stair hall.

Inflections of a similar macro–micro order abound throughout the interior, such as the 'inaugural windowsill' which is tiled with individually glazed ceramic tiles, each one being designed by a different member of the first class to use the school. Of a more intimate order perhaps are the inset balcony benches, the built-in emblematic block-lights (four glass blocks arranged in a square), the constructivist, colour-toned light fittings, and the highly articulated planar approach taken towards the detailing of the tubular handrails. As Hertzberger puts it, alluding to a certain North American neo-Corbusian practice, 'I don't want my handrails looking like sausages.'

This seemingly innocuous aside is extremely revealing inasmuch as it indicates the presence of a quintessentially Dutch tradition which, while it surely predates Berlage, is intensely articulated and elaborated in Berlage's work. I have in mind the way in which Berlage develops and, in a sense, realizes the Structural Rationalism theorized by Viollet-le-Duc. The same kind of tectonic tactility, deriving from the logic of the construction, is patently decisive in shaping the tenor of Hertzberger's architecture. It is paradoxical that this should now be seen as lying in opposition to North American practice inasmuch as Berlage was influenced at different times by both H H Richardson and Frank Lloyd Wright and inasmuch as Hertzberger himself has been inspired by this 'tectonic' line in American architecture – a rich strand which, as far as American contemporary practice is concerned, now seems to have fallen into abeyance. This transatlantic line of cross-cultural exchange (one thinks quite literally of the Holland–American line!) is of the utmost importance to our understanding of Hertzberger not only because it permits us to establish the common roots linking Hertzberger's work to the paradigmatic architecture of Wright and Louis Kahn, but also because it serves to ground Hertzberger's own architecture in that we may identify it as the Dutch structuralist elaboration of the Dutch tectonic tradition. This is particularly so as the tradition reached its apotheosis in the work of Berlage and his contemporaries, not to mention the successive generations of colleagues and students who followed essentially the same line, figures such as J H de Groot, J L M Lauweriks, K P C De Bazel and even in their early careers, Bijvoet and Duiker who were influenced to an equal degree by both Berlage and Wright.

All of this is only too evident in the Centraal Beheer insurance building, the first stage of which was realized in Apeldoorn in 1972, for here the 'transatlantic connection' makes itself manifest at many levels, ranging from the tectonic to the typological. What is paramount here is the canonical importance of Wright's Larkin Building of 1904, which played an equally seminal role in the work of Louis Kahn. Here in Apeldoorn, as opposed to Philadelphia, the Larkin Building has been remembered not so much for its megalithic monumentality as for its introspection and for the way in which it posited a new way of working as part of a new way of life. For Wright's Larkin Building was not so much an office structure as it was a compensatory microcosm, a surrogate for the loss of communality and collective value in society at large. Nothing less than this is able to account for the layered tiers of open office floors, for the improving inscriptions on the spandrels trimming the central atrium and for the organ which was eventually installed in the uppermost part of the volume. This surely is the place of work as the house of sacrament, and for all the implicit anarchy of Hertzberger's structuralist approach, something of Wright's initial intention still remains in the cantilevered offices and interstitial top-lit atria of the Centraal Beheer.

Frank Lloyd Wright, Larkin Building, Buffalo, New York, 1904, interior.

In the Centraal Beheer the tectonic and the typological – that is to say, structural syntax and spatial order – are mutually fused together into an inseparable whole, so that the orientation of generic T-columns, the pattern of occupation and the cruciform voids generated by the cantilevered office bays are all related in terms of module, dimension and typologic structure to the standard norms of open office layout as these may be broken down into operational subsets. As in Wright's Martin House, Buffalo, of 1904, the tartan structure weaves its way in and out of the labyrinthine spatial subdivision, its immutable nature being literally enlivened by the constantly changing permutability of its appropriation. Something of the same kind of openness within the law can be found in Hertzberger's Diagoon houses of approximately the same date, and it is this surely that he had in mind when he wrote:

What we must look for, in place of prototypes which are collective interpretations of individual living patterns, are prototypes which make individual interpretations of the collective patterns possible; in other words we must make houses alike in a particular way, such that everyone can bring into being his own interpretation of the collective pattern . . . Because it is impossible (and it always was) to make the individual setting that exactly suits everyone, we have to create the possibility for personal interpretation, by making things in such a way that they are indeed interpretable.

Herman Hertzberger, Centraal Beheer, Apeldoorn, 1968–72, aerial view.

In his essay 'Architecture for People' of 1979 Hertzberger was to elaborate this notion through an analogy with structural linguistics. Thus he was to write, 'We don't have knowledge of everybody's personal images and associations with forms, but we assume that they can be seen as individual interpretations of a collective pattern. The relationship between collective pattern and individual interpretations can perhaps be likened with the relationship between language and speech.'

The multi-storey network of square platforms separated by cruciform voids which constitutes the essential body of Centraal Beheer affords a labyrinth of potential activity spaces that may be appropriated as either individual or group working stations, through the rearrangement of modular elements such as desks, seats, light fittings, cabinets, couches and espresso machines. According to Hertzberger this bunker-like labyrinth has been left deliberately unfinished so as to encourage the 'spontaneous' appropriation and decoration of the space by its immediate users. Hertzberger's antipathy to the mechanistic provision of flexibility, as found in the sophisticated infrastructural propositions of both John Nikolaas Habraken and Yona Friedman, seems to have been vindicated here by the apparent spontaneity and ease with which the working spaces have been taken over and modified. And while one can only be circumspect about the rhetorical comparison that Hertzberger draws between the appropriation of space in the Centraal Beheer and the Saussurian linguistic distinction between *langue* and *parole*, there is little doubt that his approach has done something to overcome the inaccessibility of architecture in a Taylorized age.

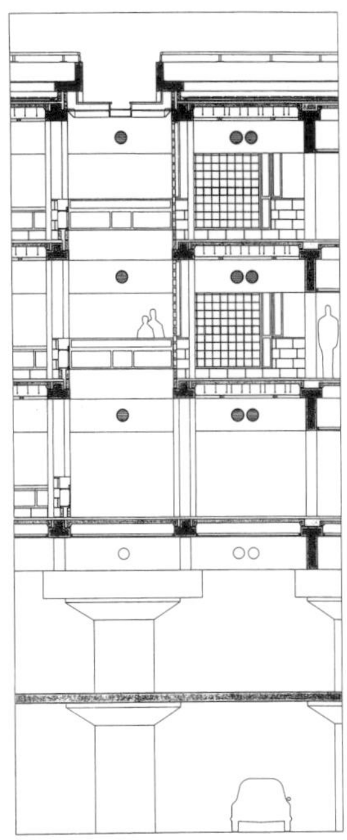

Herman Hertzberger, Centraal Beheer, Apeldoorn, section of structure showing transfer of the structure to mushroom columns beneath.

In two major civic works of recent date, Hertzberger seems to have overcome the anti-monumental consequences of the structuralist approach. These works are the music centre at Utrecht, completed in 1985, and the still-evolving project for a new Ministry of Social Welfare in The Hague, dating from 1979. Some of the more negative aspects of Centraal Baheer need to be noted if we are to appreciate the way in which Hertzberger has been able to swerve away from the atomizing tendency of Van Eyck's labyrinthine approach, in which the emphasis always tends to fall on the internal structuring of the work at the expense of its capacity to represent itself as a civic institution.

From the point of view of public representation the Centraal Baheer may be said to display the following negative characteristics. The first arises from its assertion as a 'city in miniature', evident in its resemblance to an

Italian hill-town and, rather paradoxically, in the absence of a clearly perceivable perimeter. This conjunction of hermetic urban form with a weakly defined boundary not only challenges the urban value of the surrounding city fabric but also questions the status of an office building as a civic institution. This induced 'doubt' is exacerbated by the fact that while this is an important national insurance company it remains barely legible within the overall fabric of the city. This illegibility is compounded by the fact that one can only identify the point of entry with difficulty. In fact graphic signs have been added in order to enable the unfamiliar visitor to find the main entrance. Over and above all this, articulation of the stepped structural elements is such as to render them incapable of representing the body of the building as a civic entity.

These shortcomings have been largely overcome in both the music centre and the project for The Hague. Indeed, with the exception of the trabeated facades of De Drie Hoven and the newly completed old people's home in Almere, the Utrecht music centre seems to be one of the few occasions in which Hertzberger has been able to combine his structural components in such a way as to generate an urban elevation. Here successive concrete elements such as floor slabs, solid and perforated block in-fill panels, square mushroom column heads, cylindrical columns and mullioned industrial glazing have been adequately stacked together in such a way as to constitute the 'body' of the building in a traditional sense. Indeed one is reminded of classical concatenations (stylobate, colonnade, entablature) when looking at the exterior of the music centre.

Herman Hertzberger, Centraal Beheer, view of central area (above) and partial floor plan showing different furniture layouts in each bay (below).

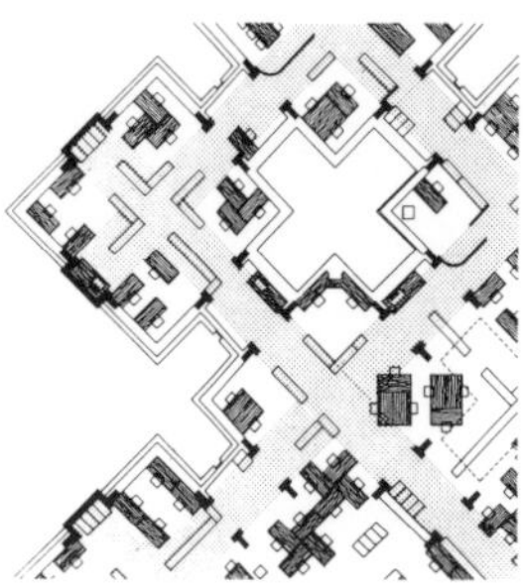

Something similar seems to occur in the Ministry of Social Welfare proposal, where the structure is still frontally and tectonically expressed despite the fact that a great deal of the perimeter is faced in transparent curtain walling. Unlike the Centraal Beheer, where the scale of the syncopated spatial network is incapable of generating an adequate hierarchy, the Ministry of Social Welfare opens out from a clearly defined central point, in terms of much larger and more generous increments. As one might expect this point coincides with the main entrance, and from here the 'city-in-miniature' unfolds as a series of set-back internal terraces linked by escalators. Compared with Centraal Beheer the number of light wells per usable square metre has been reduced and the atria now assume an elongated and irregular form in order to unite a wide range of bureaucratic units throughout the length of the extended east–west axis. Closer, typologically speaking, to the nineteenth-century department store with its complex hierarchy of internal voids (compare Gustave Eiffel's Bon Marché store of 1876) and linked by virtue of this to both the Larkin Building and Norman Foster's Willis Faber building of 1974, Hertzberger's proposal for The Hague is surely the finest and most sophisticated public 'cellular' work which he has projected to date. Should the government fail to realize this masterpiece, it would be a cultural loss of unprecedented magnitude.

As I have tried to indicate elsewhere, Hertzberger's work has to be regarded as 'regional' because it is, in a sense, unthinkable in any other context. Dutch Structuralism is hardly to be associated with this nationalistic rubric gratuitously, for it is clear that despite Arnulf Lüchinger's laudable attempt to establish Structuralism as a universal phenomenon (plausible perhaps in the case of the Japanese) its most able and convincing exponents remain uncompromisingly Dutch.

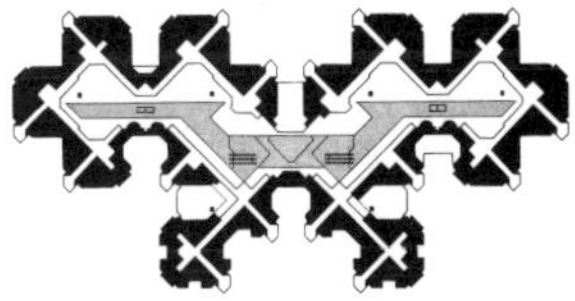

Herman Hertzberger, Ministry of Social Welfare and Employment, The Hague, 1979–90, plan. The black areas are the offices and the grey is the common circulation spine comprised of passerelles and escalators.

It is hard to come up with a satisfactory explanation for this national predilection except, at the risk of redundancy, to remind the reader, once again, of the long-standing Dutch collective tradition, of their capacity as a people to act in unison to an equal degree against the rapacious inroads of the sea and the acquisitive proclivities of men. It is this, perhaps, combined with the Dutch people's unique feelings for the 'other', which has imparted to Dutch Structuralism its uniquely anti-Eurocentric cast – although it is to be doubted whether this other hypothetical modern civilization, neither Western nor Eastern, neither new nor old (in a historicist sense) will be able to prevail in the long run against the degenerative inroads of the postmodern media machine as it continues to erode the 'cause of architecture' from within. However, the fact that this struggle is so passionately enjoined in Hertzberger's work makes this Dutch architect one of the most consistently critical practitioners in the field today, and one can only hope that, when the current stylistic 'hype' has exhausted itself, this legacy will be appropriately assumed as an inspiration for the generations to come, not only in Holland but also elsewhere.

First published in Dutch as 'Het structurele regionalisme van Herman Hertzberger' in *Archis*, no.12, December 1986, pp.8–13.

Alvaro Siza: Duarte House and the Teixeira Apartment

At the still point of the turning world. Neither flesh nor fleshless;
Neither from nor towards; at the still point, there the dance is,
But neither arrest nor movement.
And do not call it fixity, Where past and future are gathered . . .
T S Eliot, *Four Quartets*[1]

Alvaro Siza belongs to that generation of modernists who have understood that the liberative legacy of the Modern Movement resides in its potential for ambiguity and in its capacity for being articulated in terms of spatial fluidity and mechanical transformation. This much is evident from Siza's earliest houses, from the otherwise typically cubistic house, built in the Av. dos Combatentes, Porto in 1970, wherein mobile, glazed partitions, meeting at right angles, act both to separate and unify the foyer, the kitchen and the main living volumes. These sliding and pivoting elements are not just conveniences, for they serve to express the confluence of these spaces; emphasizing through their potential and actual motion the diurnal significance of their interrelationship. This '*poésie d'équipage*' is a recurrent theme in Siza's syntax and this singularly dynamic element is often closely related to another constant concept in his work: namely, the 'fan-seam' which invariably facilitates the transformation of a given volume into a totally different kind of space. We are witness to such an Aalto-esque transformation in the rotating and expanding volumes of the banking hall of the Pinto Bank built in Oliveira de Azemeis in 1974. Here the *fixed* point of the conceptual pivot lies outside the confines of the building; a geometric reference which not only inscribes the radial curve of the corner but also 'rotates' the contingent volumes and planes, in such a way as to diminish and shift in two rifts the width of the stair serving the upper mezzanine.

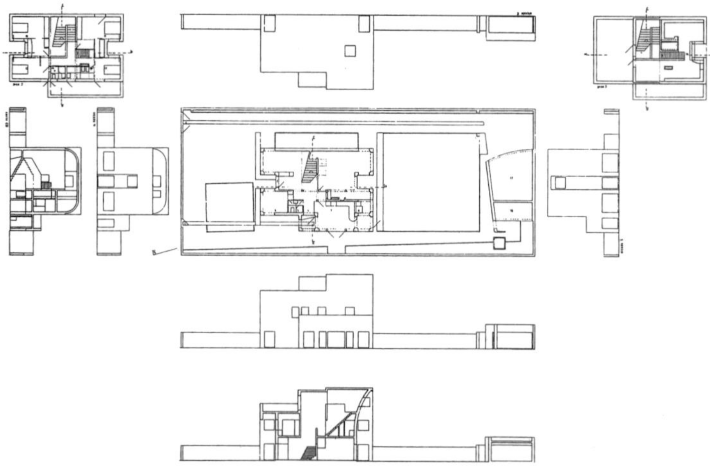

Alvaro Siza, Duarte House, Ovar, 1980–4, plan, sections and elevations.

In the recently completed Duarte House in Ovar, Siza has now added three further operations to this disjunctive 'repertoire'. The first of these, which is fundamental to both the volume and the mass of the house, turns on the manipulation of the classic Palladian rhythm of ABABA in such a way as to omit the last A bay (it registers only at the boundary) and to reduce the adjacent B bay to a single-storey addenda. The result of this is a largely symmetrical body (ABA) centralized about the remaining B bay which naturally serves as the main entrance to the house.

The two other operations, which are even more disjunctive, seem to derive ultimately from Adolf Loos: the strategy of the *Raumplan* and the concept of a collaged and fractured revetment. The first of these asserts itself unequivocally in the entrance hall, where a terraced stairway, faced in marble, rises towards the first floor, serving to remind one of the main living volume of Loos's Müller House in Prague (1930). The second occurs primarily in the way in which this same marble is used throughout the remainder of the house, above all in the free-standing column and surround to the main living room fireplace, where it is treated as a fragment of an eroded, archaeological stratum; the marble giving way to mirror as it 'fractures' across the upper part of the chimney breast.

The net effect of this tripartite orchestration – Palladianism, Raumplan and Collage – is to transform a modest suburban house into a 'palazzetta', Siza conjuring up a unique expression here, combining the necessary sense of intimacy with a feeling for high bourgeois, aristocratic grandeur rarely to be found in a contemporary house. If one seeks for precedents for this subtly lit and richly furnished interior, then surely, other than Loos, one looks to the early houses of Neutra and Mies van der Rohe. This luxurious sense of encasement is augmented, as one penetrates into the interstitial recesses of the house, by richly veneered and precisely wrought joinery; elements which deepen and enclose every 'secret' cabinet and chamber, affording not only comfort and convenience but also the sense of an erotic labyrinth which one can never fully know. This is particularly true on the first floor of the house where the main and second bedrooms may be linked to form a continuous suite, with the principal bathroom and terrace (facing west) over the vestigial B bay, and where the twin bedrooms for the children are similarly interconnected with the aid of a common study and a secondary bathroom. It is significant that both bathrooms are provided with two means of access (pivoting doors set at right angles to each other) thereby permitting discrete individual use without passing, as the case may be, through either the semi-public or private circulation. This complex mechanized joinery epitomizes Siza's 'poetry of equipment'.

Alvaro Siza, Duarte House, note the marble revetment of the fireplace and columns in the living room (above) and the main stair seen from above (below).

To analyse the Duarte House in terms of Loos's Raumplan alone is somewhat misleading, however, since the floor planes are never broken in themselves. The sense of rift or fracture seems to arise instead from the way in which the stone revetment is applied in relation to the broken profile which surrounds the first-floor perimeter of the triple-height stair hall. Here the stepped soffit of the open gallery, leading to the bedrooms, is echoed by the profile of the marble veneer to the 'threshold' of the second-floor staircase, which gives way, as it penetrates, to wood-lined treads and door reveals. This hierarchically finished spatial progression loses its eventual focus on the top floor where the open-planned study/library falls all too loosely into the triple-height volume of the stair hall and where an emblematic window sits awkwardly in the curved upper profile of the central bay, situated to the rear of the house.

In general, despite a surprising reversal in the massing (from a three-storey rear to a two-storey front), formal and informal formats are conventionally employed in ordering the principal and secondary facades – the approach elevation being absolutely symmetrical, and the back elevation being subtly and asymmetrically inflected by the additional B bay so as to accommodate the fusion of the living volume with the laundry and kitchen spaces situated at the extreme corner of the garden parterre. Beyond this gridded order Siza returns to his earlier organic approach, above all in the fan-shaped plan and curved front of the free-standing garage block situated to the rear of the house.

Alvaro Siza, Duarte House, exterior view.

Many of the syntactical and material themes elaborated in the Ovar house are returned to in the seaside penthouse apartment at Póvoa do Varzim, designed at around the same time, for the industrialist J M Teixeira. Here an otherwise subtly balanced plan has been compromised by the client's ill-advised insistence on providing a full bathroom for every bedroom. This ostentatious but curiously 'hidden' luxury has been accomplished at the expense of the main living volume, which is patently inadequate given the total coverage and proportion of the unit. This unnecessarily cramped space has been compensated for, partly, by an upper-level music room situated on top of the penthouse.

As in the Duarte House singular foci stand as symbolic pieces, as *axes mundi*, and serve, at the same time, as iconographic condensers for the entire composition. Thus in both works a solitary cylindrical column emerges as a nexus; that is to say as an attendant tectonic presence standing beside the realm of a symbolic *aedis*. This last, which is quite literally

Alvaro Siza, Teixeira Apartment, Póvoa do Varzim, 1979–86, interior of discotheque.

a hearth in the case of the Ovar house, is transformed in the Teixeira Apartment into a shallow circular recessed ceiling over the hypothetical centre of the penthouse dance floor. An inclined knife-edge blade, which unexpectedly penetrates the perimeter of this domed ceiling, acts as an antithesis to the adjacent cylindrical column – the two forms dancing together, as it were, within the charmed circle of the discotheque. In each instance the free-standing symbolic column is appropriately finished: plaster in the transitory environment of the penthouse and marble in the suburban residence where it surely represents the presence of protective household gods. In this work, the idea of the Lares is symbolized by a complex relief of mirror, marble, plaster and stone, a still point, so to speak, in what is otherwise an unavoidably fractured and constantly whirling universe.

First published as 'Casa Duarte e Appartamento Teixeira', in *Casabella*, vol.49, no.514, June 1985, pp.4–11.

festival
festival

Born in Osaka in 1941, Tadao Ando first came to the fore in 1976 with his prize-winning Row House (Azuma Residence), Sumiyoshi. Self-taught, save for a brief apprenticeship with a Japanese carpenter, Ando emerged almost overnight as an architect of world stature without ever attending a school of architecture or serving as an assistant to a master architect. Pressed to give an explanation of his unusual development as an architect, he will only admit to two influences: the spiritual depth of Japanese building culture and the study tours that he made during the second half of the Sixties. His output has been prolific: well over 40 buildings since he opened his own office in 1969.

More than any other contemporary figure, Ando has been the architect of the reinforced concrete wall, creating volumes delimited by such boundaries not only in order to define space but also to form it in such a way as to admit and reveal an ever-changing pattern of light. Aside from employing walls as domain-defining planes, Ando has also exploited the wall as a datum against which to read an internal armature of free-standing columns and beams.

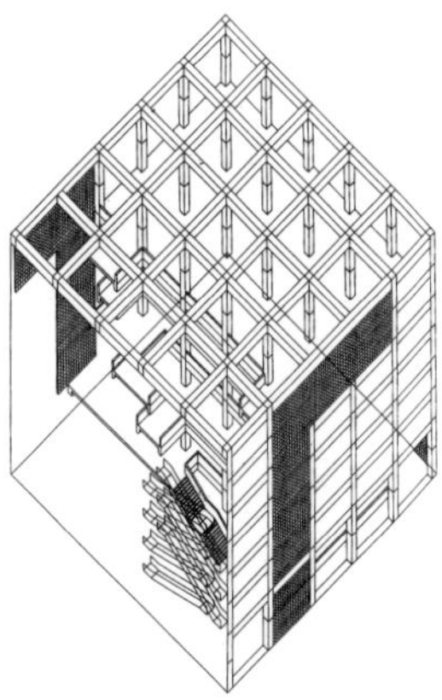

Tadao Ando, Festival Building, Naha, axonometric.

From his self-consciously cross-cultural position, Ando sees the reinforced concrete frame as a universal twentieth-century technique, which for all its manifest advantages, has robbed the central Shinto column – the so-called *diakokubashira* – of its symbolic potency and the classical colonnade of its plastic rhythm. At the same time, he regards the wall as a protective shield that is categorically opposed to the infinite space-field of the modern megalopolis. In Ando's work the court house is seen as the provider of a calm, character-forming, restorative domain wherein the individual may escape the turmoil of the tertiary-industry city and regain some sense of domestic tranquillity. In his seminal essay of 1978, entitled 'The Wall as Territorial Delineation', Ando wrote:

The cheap sprawl and crowded conditions of the modern Japanese city reduce to a mere dream the liberation of space by modern architectural means and the resulting close connection between interior and exterior. Today, the major task is building walls that cut the interior off entirely from the exterior. In this process, the ambiguity of the wall, which is simultaneously interior on the inner side and exterior on the outer side, is of the greatest significance. I employ the wall to delineate a space that is physically and psychologically isolated from the outside world . . .

I think walls can be used to control walls. In the Matsumoto house, for example, walls standing independent in the world of nature delineate a territory for human habitation. Inexpressive in themselves, the two major bounding walls are protective devices for the interior. At the same time they reflect the changes taking place in the world of nature and help to introduce this world into the daily lives of the inhabitants. The limiting operation of the walls directly reveals the boldness of the house itself. . .[1]

Within the Japanese philosophical tradition, nature manifests itself as two interrelated but opposed aspects, the tangible and the ineffable, that is to say, the palpability of the natural forest landscape as it literally encroaches onto the terrace of his Wall House (Matsumoto Residence) at Ashiya, Hyogo, and the equally apparent intangibility of light and other changing climatic elements as these are consciously integrated into all of Ando's work. As he was to write of the Koshino House, completed in the pinewoods of Ashiya in 1981, 'Light is a mediator between space and form. Light changes expressions with time. I believe that the architectural materials do not end with wood or concrete that have tangible forms, but go beyond to include light and wind which appeal to our senses.'[2] And, moreover, not only light and wind but also rain, snow and fog are to be directly experienced as one traverses, for example, the open courtyard of the Azuma Residence, Sumiyoshi, in order to pass from one room to the next. Although this is the most extreme of Ando's houses, it nonetheless testifies to an underlying stoicism that is evident in all of his architecture. Paradoxically for one who has been frequently commissioned by the Japanese fashion industry, Ando remains opposed to the ubiquitous triumph of modern comfort and consumerism that is as prevalent in Japan as elsewhere. In this respect, functionalism is a contradictory concept for Ando, an ergonomic value that first has to be satisfied and then partially denied:

I am interested in discovering what new life patterns can be extracted and developed from living under severe conditions. Furthermore I feel that order is necessary to give life dignity. Establishing order imposes restrictions, but I believe it cultivates extraordinary things in people.

I believe in removing architecture from function after ensuring the observation of functional basics. In other words, I like to see how far archi-

tecture can pursue function and then, after the pursuit has been made, to see how far architecture can be removed from function. The significance of architecture is found in the distance between it and function.[3]

This idea of a gap, be it physical or metaphysical, is constantly present in all of Ando's architecture, and the level and nature of its appearance varies considerably from one work to the next and even among different sectors of the same work. Seen in this light, a courtyard becomes a space within which the ubiquitous void may be rendered perceivable, partly through changes of light and climate, and partly through the changing ethos of the space itself. This is close to the idea of *yugen* in Japanese poetry, wherein the ineffable presence of living nature is sensed through such things as a faint drizzle or a sudden unexpected breeze, the onset of twilight or the premonition of dawn.[4]

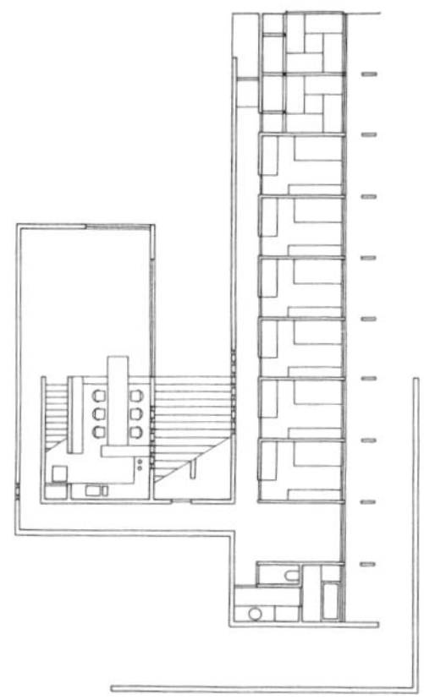

Tadao Ando, Koshino House, Ashiya, 1980–1, plan of main living area (above) and living room interior (below).

All of this is implied in the layered plan of the Koshino House, which is inscribed into the surrounding topography in such a way as to expose the principal rooms to the full trajectory of the sun. However, sunlight enters more precipitously into this house from above, through a narrow slot cut into the roof at its junction with the wall. From this aperture a single interrupted shaft of light descends to run its ever-changing luminous course across the adjacent concrete wall that runs the full length of the living room. The concrete face of this plane seems to have been treated in such a way as to effect its dematerialization under the impact of sunlight, to illuminate, through the continual movement of the sun, the latex sheen of its subtly undulating surface. A similar light slot is let into the roof of the radial studio, added to the northern face of the house in 1984. In this instance, the pattern of changing light becomes increasingly organic in shape as it falls onto a continuously curved wall.

The Koshino House features a totally different kind of luminosity within its interior, where a shadowy darkness of somewhat uncertain depth emanates from the concrete-lined corridor linking the living volume to the bedroom block. Here we are close to that traditional Japanese space of darkness, characterized by the novelist Jun'ichirō Tanizaki in his highly influential critique of Westernization, which first appeared in print under the title *Inei raisan* (*In Praise of Shadows*) in 1934. Tanizaki was to describe the symbiosis between Japanese secular and sacred light in terms that seem to parallel the varying levels of luminosity to be found in many of Ando's interiors:

Whenever I see the alcove of a tastefully built Japanese room, I marvel at our comprehension of the secrets of shadows, our sensitive use of shadow and light. For the beauty of the alcove is not the work of some clever device. An empty space is marked off with plain wood and plain walls, so that the light drawn into it forms dim shadows within emptiness. There is nothing more ... We are overcome with the feeling that in this small corner of the atmosphere there reigns complete and utter silence; that here in the darkness immutable tranquility holds sway ...

In temple architecture the main room stands at a considerable distance from the garden; so diluted is the light that no matter what the season, on fair days or cloudy, morning, midday, or evening, the pale, white glow scarcely varies. And the shadows at the interstices of the ribs seem strangely immobile, as if dust collected in the corners had become a part of the paper itself... The light from the pale white paper, powerless to dispel the heavy darkness of the alcove, is instead repelled by the darkness, creating a world of confusion where dark and light are indistinguishable. Have not you yourselves sensed a difference in the light that suffuses such a room, a rare tranquillity, not found in ordinary light? Have you never felt a sort of fear in the face of the ageless, a fear that in that room you might lose all consciousness of the passage of time, that untold years might pass and upon emerging you should find you had grown old and grey?[5]

As susceptible as Tanizaki is to the transformation of traditional light under the impact of modernization, Ando has constantly tried to render his work as a subtle interface in which the two civilizations are brought to confront each other. To this end, he has created an object-world in which the value of the one, the proliferating Occident, is brought into opposition with the value of the other, the sequestered Orient. This dialogue is expressed in the living room of the Koshino House by two features: by a dining table that cantilevers beyond the dining recess above a portion of the main living floor so that occidental and oriental sitting postures may be adopted at the same table, and by the heights of two windows giving onto the garden and patio, respectively. Where the first of these windows extends to head-height in the usual occidental manner, the second brings the opening down to just below the average standing height, that is, to a level more in keeping with Japanese stature and posture.

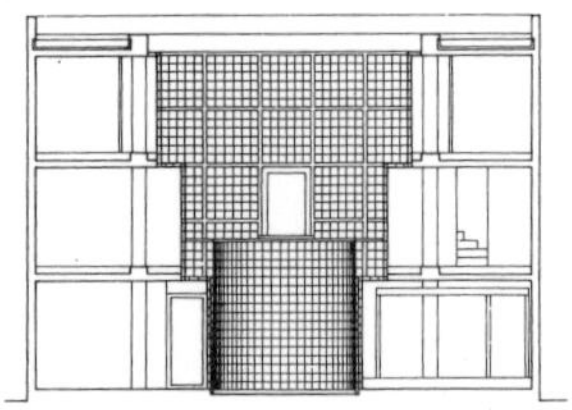

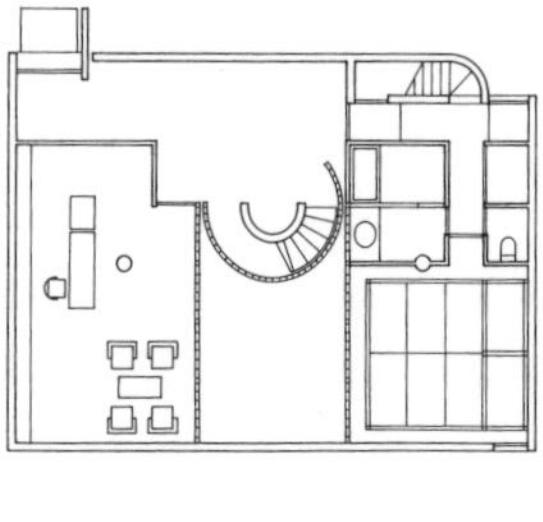

Tadao Ando, Glass Block House (Ishihara Residence), Osaka, 1978, exterior view (top), section (middle) and ground floor plan (below).

This occidental/oriental dyad constantly crops up in unexpected ways throughout Ando's architecture. It is patently evident in the sameness and difference evoked by the juxtaposition of glass block fenestration with traditional *shoji*, in the inner and outer facades of the *tatami* room on the ground floor of the Glass Block House (Ishihara Residence), completed in Ikuno, Osaka, in 1978. A similar dialogue is present in the first phase of his Rokko Housing complex, realized on a precipitously steep site overlooking Kobe Bay, in 1983. Here, as in the so-called Step development built at Takamatsu, Kagawa, in 1977–80, Ando tries to combine two totally different kinds of public spaces: the oriental *roji*, or narrow alley, as drawn from the residential labyrinth of the traditional Japanese city, and the occidental plaza, which appears in modified form half-way up the inclined access spine running vertically through the centre of the Rokko complex. This hybrid space is further enriched by being deliberately organized, in Ando's phrase, as a 'discontinuous-continuity' in which, save for climbing a nine-storey stairway, one can only traverse the full height of the stepped settlement by changing elevators at

Tadao Ando, Glass Block House (Ishihara Residence), interior view across the atrium towards the tatami room.

mid-point and crossing from one to the other across the *roji*/plaza (compare the Row House, Sumiyoshi). For Ando this discontinuous-continuity is seen as an essential attribute of the elusive concept *Ma*, which not only signifies place but also the idea of the consummation of space through the action of a body crossing from one point to another, in much the same way as an electric spark jumps across a gap.

Discontinuous-continuity may be said to characterize the confrontation between occidental and oriental values that permeates Ando's architecture at every conceivable level. This disjunctive principle is made even more explicit in the Chapel on Mount Rokko, built in Kobe, Hyogo, in 1985–6, as part of a resort–hotel complex. Here two countervailing notions of the spiritual are juxtaposed side by side, so as to effect an abrupt contrast between the significance of the crucifix and the empty silence of the void; to oppose, that is, the sign of the West with the non-sign of the East.

In this work, the only ordained space is the basilica itself. However, this form is preceded by an intercolumniated arcade, lined and roofed with large sheets of frosted glass. Affording a visually contained approach from the hotel to the chapel, this perspectival space terminates in a void at the crest of the hill, thereby focusing on the datum between sky and ocean that has long been an embodiment of the sacred in Japan. Only a stepped descent at the end of this long, processional Shinto-esque volume gives any indication as to the transitional space that will open onto the chapel at the end of the arcade. Ando himself has remarked on the referential nature of this volume to the Fushimi Inari Shrine in Kyoto, where hundreds of *torii* (Shinto post-and-lintel gates) line the route to the sacred precincts.

Once one enters the chapel, the presence of nature is reasserted through a full-height glass wall let into one side of the basilica. Divided by an inverted concrete cruciform into four large panes, this window-wall

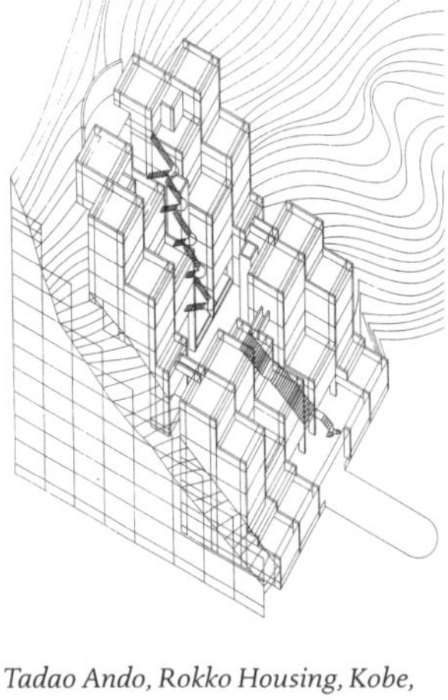

Tadao Ando, Rokko Housing, Kobe, 1983, axonometric.

opens onto a banked courtyard, bounded by a dwarf wall known by the name *tsukiji*. As in the famous rock garden of Ryoanji Temple, Kyoto, this wall extends for a seemingly infinite distance to the right-hand side of the space. In representing nature as the ultimate repository of the divine, Ando splits the focus of the chapel between a steel crucifix suspended at the end of the nave and the tranquillity of an embanked court covered with gardenias. The entire sequence thus breaks down into three interrelated spiritual domains: arcade, basilica and court.

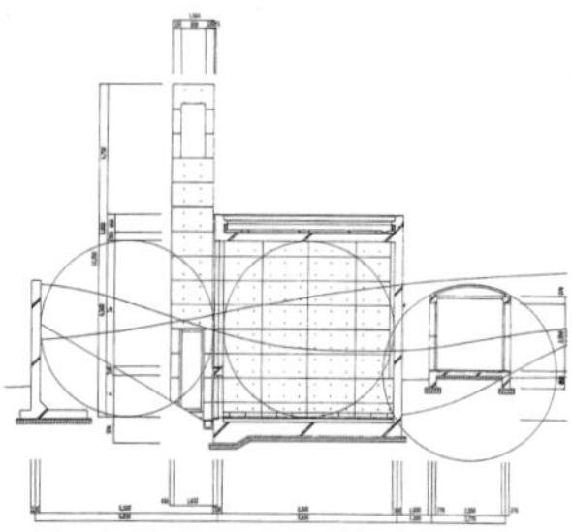

Tadao Ando, Chapel on Mount Rokko, Kobe, 1985–6, section with superimposed circles.

Ando's habitual reliance on geometry is particularly in evidence here, where three circles of the same radius control the interval and the sectional profile of these spaces. Similarly, the dimensions of the basilica are precisely related to the square modular bay of the arcade. The chapel is thus two-and-a-half bays wide by five bays deep while the arcade extends for 15 bays in length, ten of which elapse before the floor steps down to continue with the last five bays of the total run. The double-square plan of the basilica divides in length into three different parts – entry, nave and altar – having the proportions of one–two–one, respectively, with the window-wall lining one side of the nave for its full extent. This glazed wall is divided vertically into a complementary three-to-one modular proportion, the underside of the cruciform transom being one-quarter of the total height.

Fushimi Inari Shrine, Kyoto, founded AD 711.

Ando's involvement with nature becomes more topographic and expansive as the scope of his practice changes and as the sites become increasingly bucolic. This shift is particularly noticeable in the so-called Church on the Water, completed at Tomamu, Hokkaido, in 1988, which is positioned so as to take maximum advantage of the undulating, forested prospect which it faces. While the sign of the cross is even more prominent in this composition, its traditional significance is weakened through its quadruplar repetition within a glass enclosure. Since the four crosses are absolutely symmetrical and equal on all their respective axes, and since they also almost touch each other at their extremities, they deny the traditional orientation of the Christian Church and in so doing imply a totally 'other' idea of the godhead. The resultant spatial figure, voided at the centre, insists upon a totally panoramic reading of the landscape.

To enter the church, the visitor climbs up within this ferro-vitreous prism to the level of the crosses, and after traversing this stair, completes the descent via a curved staircase into the half-cubic volume of the chapel itself. Here we are presented with the contemplative space of the chapel, which opens onto a subtly articulated vista comprising a free-standing steel cross standing in the midst of a shallow artificial pool. Patently influenced by Kaija and Heikki Sirén's Otaniemi Chapel of 1957, this highly symbolic vista is separated from the outside by a 50 by 25 foot glazed wall capable of being moved away in summer so as to expose the chapel totally to the open air. Since the track of this sliding wall is sustained by a concrete frame that outlines, as it were, the absent elevation of the church, we seem

Tadao Ando, Church on the Water, Tomamu, Hokkaido, 1985–8, exterior view at night.

to lie suspended here between two divergent references, that is to say, between the parallel domains of the Ise Shrine, the one in use, the other lying fallow, and the Romantic animistic visions of Caspar David Friedrich, wherein the mirage of a cross becomes assimilated to a pine tree.

The development at Tomamu is intended to embrace an even more complex cultural synthesis in the form of Ando's proposal for a Theatre on the Water, also to be located on a wooded site, some 1,300 feet to the northwest of the church. Built around a fan-shaped artificial pond, fed from the same stream as that of the church, this 6,000-seat amphitheatre is intended to be used for a wide range of public events, including concerts and fashion shows. Once again, occidental and oriental references are equally in evidence as the poles of a double dialogue. The amphitheatre is clearly Greek in origin except for the fact that the orchestra and stage are absent, their traditional locations being flooded with water. Their place is assumed by a suspended runway cutting across the amphitheatre and intersecting, as it does so, a row of free-standing columns that serve to establish the diameter of the theatrical space. These intersecting trajectories would seem to derive from two different cultural memories. Thus, where the colonnade stands in place of an absent proscenium, the interpenetrating runway alludes to the traditional 'pontoon bridge' of the Kabuki stage. Once again we encounter Ando's practice of deploying oriental type-forms in such a way as to qualify the Western paradigms with which they are integrated.

Much the same phenomenon occurs in the Church of the Light, built at Ibaraki, Osaka, in 1987–9, where, despite the traditional eastern end, radiating light, the form as a whole stems as much from the concrete Tea House – which Ando added in 1982 to his 1976 Soseikan Houses (Yamaguchi Residence) – as from the truncated basilica form that snugly accommodates the congregation of this small church. Both tea house and church are enclosed by a *roji*, or alleyway, that, in each specific instance, turns out to

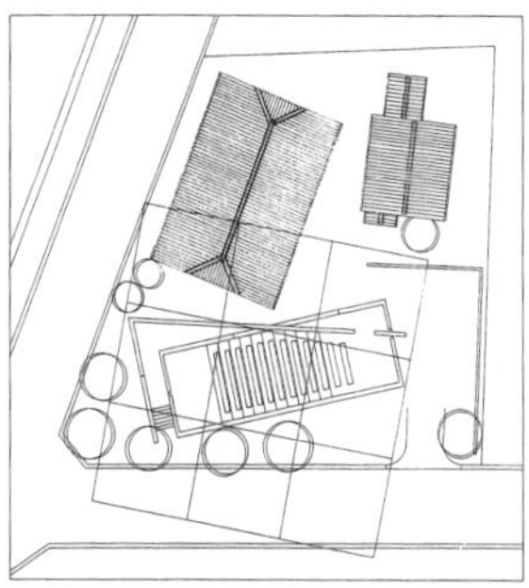

Tadao Ando, Church of the Light, Ibaraki, Osaka, 1987–9, site plan.

Tadao Ando, Children's Museum, Himeji, Hyogo, 1987–9, aerial view.

be a 'vestigial' approach to the space. In the Soseikan Tea House, the *roji* leads to a *nijiriguichi*, or traditional 'crawl door', that, since it is not a door but a fixed sheet of plate glass, both invites and precludes entry. Similarly, in the Church of the Light, steps leading down into the *roji* imply an approach that is abruptly denied by an angular space that instantly terminates in a plate-glass window-wall, which, while it gives onto the interior, fails to provide access.

In contrast to the introspective character of his earlier work, the Tomamu complex and the Time's Shops, built along the banks of the Takase River, Kyoto, in 1983–8, testify to Ando's growing interest in extending the influence of his work into the surrounding topography, even if the *shakkei*, or borrowed scenery, of the Church and Theatre on the Water remains as yet incomplete.

What was intended in the case of the two buildings at Tomamu was to be more fully realized in the Children's Museum, completed in 1989 on a dramatic site near Himeji, Hyogo. Carefully positioned on a promontory overlooking a large lake, the principal museum building assumes the form of a prow-like acropolis facing southwest towards the water and approached by a serpentine road traversing the northern reach of the lake.

The inspiration in this instance could hardly be more Greek, the museum appearing like an isolated citadel as one approaches it from the north to arrive finally at an elevated parking court situated to the south of the main complex. The subsequent pedestrian approach is equally imposing since one descends from the high ground via a monumental flight of steps, all the while looking over the full length of the lake as it loses itself in the foothills lining its southern shore. That this grand staircase is paralleled by a water-stairway cascading down over virtually the same section, only adds to the monumental aura of the approach. Compared to Tomamu, the *shakkei* waterscape is brought to a finer level of resolution at Himeji, as the tiered reflecting pools fan out against the curving prow of the museum, fusing the metallic sheen of their surfaces with the distant waters of the reservoir.

The museum is entered after this dramatic descent through an open, but covered, cruciform court that divides the twin slabs of the institution into four separate blocks. The stepped section of the open-air amphitheatre crowning the assembly appears to echo the profile of the nearby mountains and thus evokes the sense of *oku* permeating much of Ando's recent work.[6] This traditional sensibility implies a certain spatial and spiritual depth extending from the domestic *tokonoma*, or alcove, to the outer reaches of the paddy fields and then beyond to a shrine in the foothills, and ultimately to the vastness of the peak itself.

Tadao Ando, Forest of Tombs Museum, Kumamoto, 1989–92, model. Note prehistoric tumulus in the background.

Surrounded on all sides by reflecting pools, the museum engages in a subtle proportional play comprised of squares, cubes and golden sections that serves to define and articulate the various halls and mezzanines of which its volume is composed. This strictly orthogonal prism is offset by outriding diagonal walls and paths that extend into the undulating topography to link eventually with a workshop building situated to the northeast. The resultant trajectory, pre-Columbian rather than Greek, runs out through a nine-square, sixteen-column belvedere from which one looks back over the museum and the reservoir. This dynamically structured landscape, traversing a more or less virgin site, will be soon complemented by a Seminar House, or children's hostel and observatory, situated some 1,000 feet to the southeast of the museum and comprising a small cluster of free-standing buildings rising out of a fractured acropolis.

The Children's Museum initiates a whole series of topographic projects by Ando that are now in various stages of development. These include the Chikatsu-Asuka Historical Museum, Osaka; the Forest of Tombs Museum, Kumamoto; and the so-called Water Temple for Hompukuji monastery on Awaji Island in Osaka Bay.

Part necropolis and part amphitheatral stairway, the Chikatsu-Asuka Historical Museum amounts to a visitors' centre for the study of some 200 ancient tumuli that are scattered throughout the region. The work is thus conceived as a 'time machine', that is to say, as a subterranean device for experiencing the past rather than as a museum in the conventional sense. To this end, the undercroft of the esplanade-stairway is rendered as a sarcophagus in which the excavated relics of the various tumuli will be exhibited. Nothing could be further from this telluric gloom than the observation tower planted in the midst of a stepped podium, which affords views over the entire region. Since the podium steps will be dedicated to occasional performances of various kinds, the entire complex will serve as a place of pilgrimage.

Tadao Ando, Chikatsu-Asuka Historical Museum, Minami-Kawachi, Osaka, 1990–4, view of roof.

Once again, a dialogical play with opposites permeates the work so that the square atrium let into the podium is complemented by a square tower of exactly the same dimensions in plan. This opposition is paralleled by the dialogue between the stepped podium and the diagonal ramp, and by the contrast between the open atrium and the shadowy void within the space of the tower.

A work of comparable subterranean intensity is to be found at the heart of the Awaji Water Temple, as we may appreciate from the three stages of the approach to the nexus of the composition: first a large concrete wall concealing the presence of the precinct, then a labyrinthine path terminating in an elliptical pond covered with water lilies. The supplicant descends by stair through this lotus-covered surface, into a subaqueous space that will be largely occupied by a cylindrical volume filled with columns. In the most recent version, these have been reduced to a skeleton of columns lining the perimeter. In the centre of this pillared hall, the visitor will finally encounter the image of a Buddha back-lit from the west, the low afternoon sun heightening the luminosity of the traditional red interior.

Tadao Ando, Water Temple, Awajishima, Awaji Island, Osaka Bay, 1989–91, aerial view.

Such womb-like chambers have appeared elsewhere in Ando's recent work, most notably perhaps in his comprehensive proposal for the redevelopment and refurbishing of Nakanoshima, situated in the middle of downtown Osaka. This elaborate, partially subterranean project, reminiscent of Étienne-Louis Boullée (famous for his 500-foot-diameter spherical monument to Sir Isaac Newton), culminates in a cosmic 'egg' that is deftly inserted into the shell of an existing nineteenth-century structure. This ultra-modern auditorium is lit by a myriad of recessed lights set into the inner surface of the shell, suggesting the presence of a science fiction volume dropped into a classical box.

As the Japanese critic Koji Taki has remarked, Ando is a builder rather than an architect, with all the ontological implications that this has, in a profound sense, for the art of building rather than architecture.[7] Against the classical humanist values inseparable from architecture, Ando sets the palpability of things in all their characteristic purity, whether this is precision casting in concrete or a discrete assembly of hand-crafted components built to exacting standards. As the architectural historian Masato Kawamukai has written:

Material is an extremely important part of his 'concept'. It would not be an exaggeration to say that, in his case, a concept is correct only if it suggests a way in which the real character of a material might be expressed, as well as a consequent form of spatial expression. He tries to use material, whether it be natural or factory-produced, in its pure, solid form, without working it. Standardized products such as tiles, concrete blocks and glass blocks are not fragmented but used full-size. Moreover, each material must be an autonomous compositional element even as it serves to shape the space he intends.[8]

In the tradition of Ludwig Mies van der Rohe, Ando tries to take the intrinsic character of any given material and enhance its expressive potential to the highest possible level, to bring to it an essential, indisputable density or radiance. This intention is provoked to extreme limits in the fabrication of concrete where certain strict principles are observed in order to guarantee both density of material and precision of surface. In the first place, the mix itself is of engineering quality, Ando never using a 'slump' (the degree to which the concrete settles) greater than approximately six inches. Since complete and thorough vibration of the pour is an absolute prerequisite if one is to produce a concrete free from 'pocketing', no reinforcing bar may be set closer than one and a half inches from the inside face of the formwork. To all this must be added the precision joinery of the formwork itself. Ando employs different teams of select carpenters to this express end and even encourages these teams to engage in rivalry with regard to their collective capacities as craftsmen. As a result, Ando's concrete is remarkably stable and, unlike the concrete produced from weaker mixes, it resists the penetration of moisture and thus takes a long time to become stained with rain, even in the heaviest downpour. In this particular regard, it is easy to see why Kawamukai claims that, 'Ando has no need of costly or rare materials, since any material will become radiant if it is used in the right way.'[9]

Even more astonishing is Ando's rather Zen-like approach to the act of creation itself, conceiving of the entire work in a single instant after a relatively short period of gestation. During this inner formation of the concept, nothing is drawn, at least not by Ando himself. All the constraints of the project are internalized either by Ando alone or, more commonly, in collaboration with his staff who will elaborate and test a number of tentative schemes, suggested by the architect almost in passing. Ando sharpens his concentration, waiting for the moment in which the concept will suddenly reveal itself in its entirety. When that point arrives, the scheme is engendered in a very short period of time, and a single assistant is selected to develop it and to carry it through to completion.

This method produces a kind of absolute architecture – what Ando calls an 'original form of space' – wherein geometry and nature are precisely balanced with respect to each other and where, once the die is cast, the purity of the volume housing the accommodation is no longer negotiable. Where there is conflict with the client beyond this point Ando will either carry the day through persuasion or abandon the job.

The fundamental dyad underlying Ando's work comprises the opposition between geometry and nature, although for him nature is as artificial in its meditation as abstract form. This opposition has another level of significance, however, in that Ando regards occidental form-making as irreducibly geometrical, volumetric and vertical, in contradistinction to the traditional Japanese mode of building which can be seen as natural, horizontal and spaceless. In this respect, Ando's architecture implies a particular synthesis in which, while geometry determines the built, nature either infiltrates the enclosed volume from above, be it open or roofed, or alternatively extends the bounded domain into a recessive landscape.

Ando conceives of our being as the third term, as the living catalyst without which the bond between geometry and nature can never be made. Of this indispensable agent, conceived as the indivisible *shintai*, he has written:

Man articulates the world through his body. Man is not a dualistic being in whom spirit and the flesh are essentially distinct, but a living, corporeal being active in the world. The 'here and now' in which this distinct body is placed is what is first taken as granted, and subsequently a 'there' appears. Through a perception of that distance, or rather the living of that distance, the surrounding space becomes manifest as a thing endowed with various meanings and values. Since man has an asymmetrical physical structure with a top and a bottom, a left and a right, and a front and a back, the articulated world, in turn, naturally becomes a heterogeneous space. The world that appears to man's senses and the state of man's body become in this way interdependent. The world articulated by the body is a vivid, lived-in space.

The body articulates the world. At the same time, the body is articulated by the world. When 'I' perceive the concrete to be something cold and hard, 'I' recognize the body as something warm and soft. In this way the body in its dynamic relationship with the world becomes the shintai. *It is only the shintai in this sense that builds or understands architecture. The* shintai *is a sentient being that responds to the world. When one stands on a site which is still empty, one can sometimes hear the land voice a need for a building. The old anthropomorphic idea of the genius loci was a recognition of this phenomenon. What this voice saying is actually 'understandable' only to the* shintai. *(By understandable I obviously do not mean comprehensible only through reasoning.) Architecture must also be understood through the senses of the* shintai.[10]

As the above would indicate, Ando seeks nothing less than a tectonic transformation of our being through space and time. Set against the profligate waste of our consumerist culture, his art proffers an extremely subtle response to Hölderlin's untimely challenge as to the role of poets in a destitute time.[11]

First published as 'Tadao Ando', in Harriet Schoenholz Bee, ed., *Tadao Ando*, New York: Museum of Modern Art, 1991, pp.10–22.

In the Name of the Father:
O M Ungers's German Ambassador's Residence

Oswald Mathias Ungers is a scholastic architect who ever since his Berlin days has always been searching for the ultimate statement of principle. In one meticulously drawn project after another he has constantly pursued the sublime; a goal that has proved to be strangely elusive in his realized work for reasons that are not easy to determine. In this ultimate honorific villa for a representative of the State – namely the German Ambassador to the United States – he has finally found the perfect vehicle for his vision. Set on the very crown of a natural if modest acropolis, this villa enjoys a commanding view over the inner suburbs of the city. The building is judicious in its placement to the point of perfection: the access from Foxhall Road is abrupt, giving almost at once onto an absolutely flat turning ellipse, bracketed on one side by a low garage block recalling livery stables, and on the other by the Ambassadorial Residence. The two buildings, having the same length, are precisely aligned with each other across the forecourt, although they are respectively one and two storeys in height.

In terms of the initial approach the Ambassadorial Residence is modesty itself. Executed in simple, stretcher-bonded stonework, it is at first glance little more than an asymmetrically fenestrated prism with a neo-Palladian porte cochère set assertively off axis. With its concatenation of shallow-pitched, hipped copper roofs, as a demonstration of the metal-smith's art, the exterior of the buildings has the aura of an understated, impeccably cut lightweight suit, with every seam and thread in place. As one approaches one senses the presence of a formidable intellectual obsession, for this is a rigorously atectonic game of stones and squares – immediately evident, let us say, in the typical, fully fenestrated window-door, which is organized about a proliferation of squares. The basic unit is a square, two stone courses (63 cm) high, that yields a door opening of ten stone courses or five squares in height. In the horizontal direction the length of each stone conforms to the same 63 cm module, while the face proportions of the stones are either double square or (at the quoins) a square, just as each door leaf is two squares wide. (In point of fact it is actually 1.25 m wide as opposed to the theoretical 1.26 m, since an allowance has to be made – even in the best of all possible worlds – for the thickness of things.) Further to this the double door, as a total unit within the centre of the opening together with its central stile, sets up a geometrical pattern of four squares each measuring 1.25 m on its side.

This is Ungers in the apotheosis of his *quadrat* mode – to such an extent as to make Josef Hoffmann look like an amateur, for almost everything in the interior of this building is determined in terms of major and minor squares. The square ladies' living room is a case in point for its central square carpet is surrounded by two bands of marble squares, amounting to 76 squares in all. The two pairs of double doors giving access to the room are each three squares wide, while the four light columns in the four corners of the carpeted area are, needless to say, also square in plan. The proliferation of the square in terms of steel-framed fenestration reaches its ultimate dematerialization in the main facade of the building, where one encounters a double-layered curtain wall facing east over the view. Thus in the ladies' living room (where the preordained circular quorum is such that no more than eight ladies may be seated at any one time) we find a battery of elongated glass doors reminiscent of Wittgenstein's Stoneborough House in Vienna. This glass wall is subdivided into 11 square panels at the clerestory level – which, needless to say, also conforms to the 11 panels of the square frieze running around the rest of the room at the same height, thereby providing an enclosure of 44 squares. The perfection of this arrangement is only partially compromised by the fact that here, at the outer limit of the building, the re-entrant 33 squares are solid while the remaining 11 are glazed.

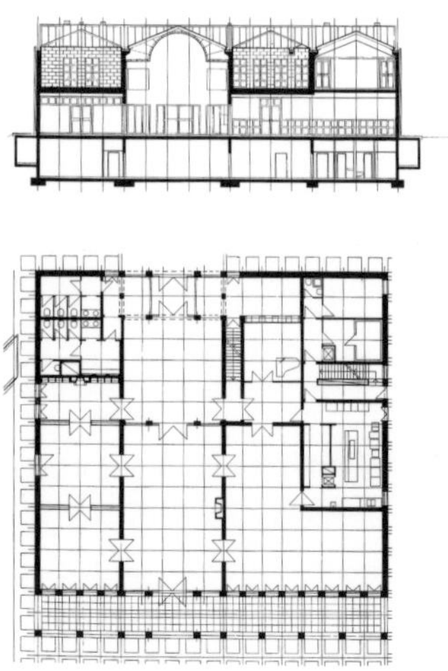

Oswald Mathias Ungers, German Ambassador's Residence, elevation (above) and plan (below).

All of this is nonetheless an impressive tour de force, sufficient one might say to stir the soul of a Beuronic monk.[1] However, a more sublime intellectual system seems to be attained in the curtain wall itself, where there is a simultaneous interplay between masonry and glass and between the modern provision of a continuously glazed membrane and the more archaic value of a pierced wall that, in an Albertian manner, gives rise to a sequence of free-standing piers. And as if this interstitial counterpoint were not enough there is a further alternation between the outer, wider piers of the monumental loggia that crowns the east facade and the inner, narrower piers and end walls that lie embedded, as it were, within the two layers of the curtain wall. The same 63 cm module, used in the double-layered curtain wall, continues without interruption inside and out for the entirety of the eastern elevation, while the counter-rhythm of the 'imprisoned' piers

Oswald Mathias Ungers, German Ambassador's Residence, interior.

and walls occupies every third module of the glazed membrane. In between this beat are full-height double doors, permitting both human passage and the maintenance of the glass. This sequence – where masonry infiltrates glass and glass envelopes masonry and where our perception is incapable of deciding, as in a magic square, which of the two readings is the dominant – is, in many respects, the most modernist episode in the entire work.

All in all this building embodies an atectonic dematerialization of sublime intensity. It appears as the climax of Ungers's unique vision where the impulse of modernity, charged with pathos, has come full circle to reinsert itself within the petrified abstraction of an inaccessible classicism. It is a touchstone of the atectonic that there is no lintel, stylobate or podium in sight. There is, indeed, a monumental barrel vault but there is no abutment or evident means of support. The wide spans are miraculously achieved thanks to the concealed structure, and the bottom stone course of the facade simply rests on and/or descends into the ground: the denial of the alpha of the tectonic through the omega of the atectonic. Does not this frozen representation of the state hint at some strange predestination that Ungers's first sketches for this building should issue from his hand in the very year that follows the demolition of the Berlin Wall and the precipitous reunification of Germany?

What shall we make of this peculiarly ambivalent expression, for this clearly is not the Ungers of the late Forties when he studied under Egon Eiermann in Karlsruhe, nor is it the Ungers of his early Brutalist brick building manner, when in 1959 he completed his own intimate house in

Müngersdorf in Cologne? At some point (it is hard to say exactly when) there was a decisive shift towards the ethos of the Italian Tendenza. This was an absolutely irrevocable move away from the tactile *matière* of his earlier brick building; an abandonment of the ontologically tectonic, in favour of a dimensionless, dematerialized square grid of a hypothetically reconstructed classicism. This shift was already accomplished in the metaphorical Russian doll that constituted the original scheme for the Deutsches Architekur museum in Frankfurt (1981–4), and it is equally in place, with similar romantic overtones (note the evocation of Weinbrenner), in the Badische Landesbibliothek, projected for Karlsruhe in 1979.

Until now, Ungers's intellectuality has enabled him to keep his distance from the Prussian past, to which he is not, in any event, an heir. Nevertheless his open admiration of Karl Friedrich Schinkel has long been there, dating back to his first years in Berlin as a professor at the Technical University in the early Seventies. It is this deeply felt affinity that has now come home rather surprisingly to roost in the solemn halls of this diplomatic residence. However, we are not confronted here with the reinterpreted Schinkel of the Prussian Enlightenment but rather Schinkel as revisited through the *Machtstaat* of Wilhelmine, Germany; that is to say we face the Schinkel of Peter Behrens rather than the Schinkel of Mies. The presence of Behrens in the interior of this building is nothing short of astonishing, for what do we have here if not Behrens's German Embassy in St Petersburg of 1912, only now totally recast, stripped of any sense of pathos?

This game of minimalist recall is pursued with a formidable relentlessness, to such an extent that the distant evocation of the past finally turns into something else. Thus while we may be in awe, let us say, of the Behrensonian rigour of the ladies' room, the dining room and the reception room we are also constrained to recognize that this intellectual rigour finally dissolves into a kind of metaphysical modernity that has more to do with the mysticism of Ad Reinhardt or the minimalism of an artist like Sol LeWitt than it does with the Zarathustrian spirit of Behrens's megalomania. One notes at this juncture the sublime 'smoky' mural by Christa Nüher that adorns the wall of one of the first-floor drawing rooms, the equally abstract minimalist wall ornamentation by Gerhard Merz at the first-floor atrium, and the metaphysical dissolution of the first-floor corridor which, like the inner court and pool of the Barcelona Pavilion, may be rotated readily as an image, whether in error or for didactic effect. Thus we seem to be confronted with a hermeticism that, despite the allusion to classicism, Theodor Adorno would have appreciated.

The spiritual distance that separates Eiermann's German Embassy in Washington (1959–64) from Ungers's Ambassador's Residence assumes an unbridgeable ideological dimension. It is hard to believe that such very different values could be advanced by virtually the same nation over such a relatively short period of time. The neo-humanism of Eiermann's techno-

Egon Eiermann, German Embassy, Washington, DC, 1959–64, exterior.

cratic, organic embassy, stepping down the slope rather than crowning it, surely represented only too well the welfare state values of the German social democracy – so much so that it takes its modest place among the concourse of nations as though it were a progressive Nordic state. Thirty years later, consciously or not, Ungers's Ambassador's Residence reflects the values of a totally different, emergent epoch and seems to evoke in the name of reunited Germany the dreams of a lost imperial past. We are returned, as in a trance, to the Apollonian *mise en scène* that held the stage before World War I and the iniquitous Versailles Agreement, before the collapse of 1929 and the Third Reich plunged Germany into a protracted nightmare within which the Marshall Plan was the first glimmer of light. After the first 15 years of the *Wirtschaftswunder* Eiermann conceived of his building as a delicate tectonic fabric in steel running through a screen of trees, merging with nature at many different levels, metaphorically and otherwise. Ungers, on the other hand, has now realized his ambassador's house as a perfect atectonic statement in stone, totally removed from nature. Thus where Eiermann proffered us the harmonious poetics of an empirically mastered technique, the shifting elision of a building process that is, in principle, forever unfinished, Ungers achieves the disturbing challenge of an absolutely hieratic *Gesamtkunstwerk* determined down to the last centimetre by the law of the square. Where the one looks to mix itself symbiotically with nature, the other stands aloof to look out over a supposedly compliant and pacified world. Are we reading too much here into these phantom signs or do we perceive correctly the neurasthenic nerve of our fragile time?

First published in *Domus*, no.766, December 1994, pp.21–2.

Minimal Moralia:
Reflections on Recent Swiss German Production

One can share Frampton's fear, but one must also admit that there has never been a less favourable time for setting architecture into motion. Firstly because of the (de)nature of materials, secondly because of the effective separation between interior and exterior, and thirdly because of the insignificance of a discipline whose only content is in its own perfection. After the Second World War the frontiers between art and architecture were not blurred intentionally, but because the Modern Movement had failed in its mission to change society. Artistic processes in an architectural context do not aim to make aesthetic objects out of buildings, but to place them, by working on the formation of meaning, in a cultural framework.

For the architects of the 'New Simplicity', Bill's case presents a chance: he manages to include what they exclude. Either one accepts this inheritance or one gives oneself completely to the artistic direction Frampton fears. The simple must not be confused with the position of the reduced, in which one finds refuge when fleeing indifference. The simple is the formula of a process rich with a great number of possibilities.
Hans Frei, 'Neuerdings Einfachheit'[1]

Peter Zumthor, Thermal Baths, view of sun terrace.

The current prestige of contemporary Swiss German practice is to be gauged by the fact that Peter Zumthor's Thermal Baths at Vals of 1996 came within a hair's breadth of being awarded the 1997 Fundación Mies van der Rohe European Prize for Architecture. Ten years separates this cavernous stone-cut achievement from Herzog and de Meuron's lightweight Ricola warehouse constructed out of Eternit, built at Laufen in Switzerland in 1987; a building that enjoyed universal acclaim and established the reputation of its authors overnight. During the ensuing decade, Swiss German minimalist production has risen to the fore within the annals of contemporary architecture. However, during this period it has also diverged into subtly diverse, one might even say totally unpredictable, modes of expression derived from the same basic minimalist *parti pris*. On the one hand, then, we have the ontological focus of an architect like Peter Zumthor, whose work is not without its own unevenness; on the other hand, we have the superficial concerns of the 'younger' Swiss German school, although in this instance, age is not so much a matter of generation as it is a measure of the stage of a particular development. Zumthor, after all, is only seven years older than Herzog and de Meuron. And in fact, the main difference between these practices is not so much age as differences in their fundamental formation. In this respect, Zumthor is a man apart, above all because of his five-year apprenticeship as a cabinet-maker and his subsequent ten years of service as an architect in the Graubünden Cantonal department dedicated to the preservation of historic monuments. This fairly unique beginning, at least by today's standards, no doubt goes a long way towards explaining Zumthor's unique approach to both time and material; to his desire, particularly evident in the case of the thermal baths, to create a work that looks as though it has always been there. Can we say perhaps, in this regard, that time and material are the two intrinsic attributes of built form that tend to separate a work of architecture from a work of art? While these may only be indicators, so to speak, they are particularly crucial in the work of Zumthor, as the architect himself makes clear:

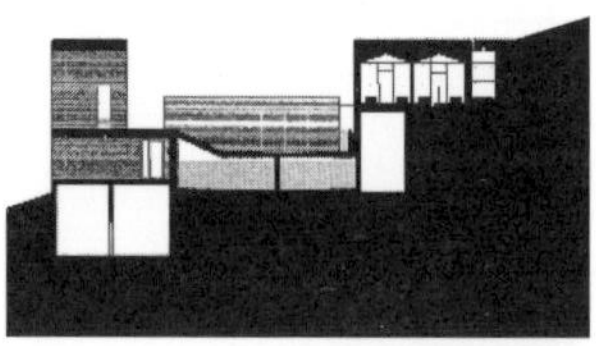

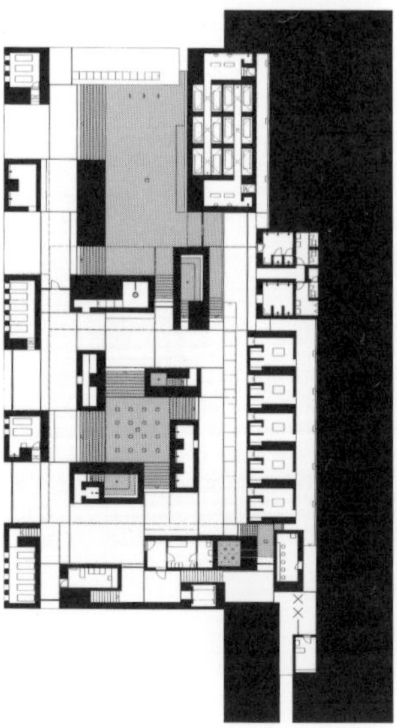

Peter Zumthor, Thermal Baths, section (above) and plan (below).

. . . The building takes the form of a large, grass-covered stone object set deep into the mountain and dovetailed into its flank. It is a solidarity building, which resists formal integration with the existing structure in order to evoke more clearly – and achieve more fully – what seemed to us a more important role: the establishing of a special relationship with the mountain landscape, its natural power, geological substance and impressive topography. In keeping with this idea, it pleased us to think that the new building should communicate the feeling of being older than its existing neighbour, of always having been in this landscape.

Mountain, stone, water, building in stone, building with stone, building into the mountain, building out of mountain, being inside the mountain – our attempts to give this chain of words an architectural interpretation, to translate into architecture its meanings and sensuousness, guided our design for the building and step by step gave it form.

Consequently the design process was a playful but patient process of exploration independent of rigid formal models. Right from the start, there was a feeling for the mystical nature of the world of stone inside the mountain, for darkness and light, for the reflection of light upon water, for the diffusion of light through steam-filled air, for the different sounds that water makes in stone surroundings, for warm stone and naked skin, for the ritual of bathing. From the start, there was the pleasure of working with these things, of consciously bringing them into play.

That minimalism compels the subject to discriminate, albeit unconsciously, between the province of architecture and that of art may be perceived particularly sharply in the mature work of Luis Barragán. One thinks in this respect of a canonical piece like Las Arboledas, where one may spontaneously distinguish between those parts that belong all too categorically to the discourse of art – such as the abstract interplay between the blue door and the white wall – and those elements that are more embedded in the tradition of the Mexican vernacular: a horse trough charged to the brim, a flanking gravelled yard and a stand of eucalyptus trees.

This deceptively simple yet complex *synthesis*, simultaneously uniting the polarities of 'architecture versus art', 'tradition versus innovation' and 'nature versus culture', is largely absent in the work of Herzog and de Meuron, who seem to insist on being recognized as artists rather than as architects, that is to say as artist/architects rather than craftsmen/architects who happen to practise the art of architecture rather than art as such. That this a priori stance has imposed a limit on the trajectory of their production seems to be borne out by the fact that they have been at their best in relatively small, one-off pieces, or in handling large, undemanding industrial volumes, since in both circumstances the building may be rendered as an artwork writ large. I have in mind such works as the stone house at Tavole and the Goetz Museum, or alternatively the Ricola warehouse in Laufen, with which they made their name, or the copper-clad signal box that they recently realized in Basel for the Swiss railways. In each instance the object derives its power as a *Gestalt* from the tectonic character of the revetment which, needless to say, envelops the entire structure. This strategy may be distinguished from their more dandified impulse 'to draw or write' on the surface of their work as though the structural material itself, however dramatically wrought in respect of its origin, cannot be given a sufficiently emotive 'charge'. This partly explains their understandable rhetoric about the disappearance of traditional categories and about the unavoidable degeneration of craft in the face of our ever-escalating division of labour. Despite this familiar lament, and despite a critical recourse to the phenomenological under the influence of Joseph Beuys in their earlier work, they now tend increasingly towards the effete, particularly when it comes to silk-screening photographic images onto glass – as though in a world rendered destitute by technology, all one can do is to enrich the surface of things with distracting iterations, with Warhol-like glyphs that will hopefully pass as some kind of critically significant image.

Herzog and de Meuron, Signal Box, Auf dem Wolf, Basel, 1994, exterior view.

In this way, following in the line of the latter-day avant-garde, the poet/architect bestows upon the people the *zaumy* innocence that they have inadvertently lost. All of which might be to our cultural benefit were it not for the fact that the once spontaneous virtue of the 'new' has now become so ambiguous that today one may easily end up living in the brutal context of a *transrational* poem, as we find in, say, Herzog and de Meuron's Pilotengasse housing in Vienna or in their student dormitories in Dijon, these last being hardly redeemed by the appliqué artwork of Remy Zaugy. It is a fact that should one choose to compare Pilotengasse to the prewar Siedlung Neubuhl completed outside Zurich in 1932, one is compelled to acknowledge the passage of some kind of inescapable decadence. Strange that the vision of the radical should depend upon a gratuitous impoverishment of the act of dwelling. What was it Adolf Loos said? 'There is no point in inventing anything unless it is an improvement', and elsewhere, 'The house is conservative and the work of art is revolutionary and so the man loves his house and hates art.' We would do well, would we not, to dwell once again on these paradoxical distinctions and to listen specifically, once more, to Loos's critical, ironic distinction between architecture and art.

Herzog and de Meuron, Pilotengasse Housing, Vienna, 1986–91, exterior view.

Werner Moser, Rudolf Steiger et al, Siedlung Neubuhl, Zurich, 1932, general view.

The latter-day Swiss German 'school' seems subtly divided today between those architects who aspire to the Neues Bauen tradition and thus keep alive Max Bill's distinction between Konkrete Architektur and Konkrete Kunst – as we find, say, in a figure like Roger Diener – and those architects, like Herzog and de Meuron and the partnership of Christian Sumi and Marianne Burckhalter, who appear to be increasingly seduced by the hallucinatory surface effects of the mediatic world. Distantly influenced by what one can only call the rise and fall of Aldo Rossi, the more 'artistic' members of the Zurich school seem to have opted, in one way or another, for that which Martin Steinman once identified as the 'empty sign'. Only occasionally of late have they pursued single-mindedly the presence of things in an ontological sense. Thus, unlike Zumthor at Vals where an elemental 'thingness of things', of water, steam and stone, compels one to re-experience the nature of one's 'being in the world', the Zurich school seems to gravitate with high sophistry towards the indifference of a value-free sign or its aestheticized equivalent. Thus, as Sumi puts it:

> *. . . certain manipulations emphasize similarities amongst materials. I would use the concept of* indifference *in a positive sense [my emphasis]. One achieves an equilibrated relationship amongst diverse materials. And furthermore new technologies, better insulation values and load-bearing potential have changed the perception of glass for example. It is a matter of the degree of transparency, of cast shadow, or of reflection. This is perhaps the decisive moment, the impulse away from materials to those materials' effect. By effect, I mean immediate effect, uncorseted by semantics . . .*

Here a talented architect seems determined to pursue surface effect to the exclusion of all other values, thereby presumably to arouse the benumbed late modern populace at large who, after the commodification of architecture, could hardly care less how much the shed comes to be decorated. Thus Burckhalter and Sumi's Lustenau Kindergarten larch wood window frames are to be audaciously combined with the asphalt 'street' tiles, along with other synthetic novelties, as though the classless connotations of asbestos cement had never been pursued by Hannes Meyer and Hans Wittwer in their entry for the League of Nations competition of 1927 (as opposed, that is, to Le Corbusier's palatial design for the same competition, faced in stone). One may note in passing that tectonic hierarchy still played a key role in the work of Meyer, as it did in the prewar work of Max Bill and Karl Egender. Today, however, in Burckhalter and Sumi's Lustenau Kindergarten, both structure and space suffer from 'deliberate' neglect one might say, in favour of producing a decorative, toy-like surface. Subjected, it would seem, to the influence of Robert Venturi, we are confronted here with nothing less than a highly sophisticated version of the 'dumb and ordinary'. Sophistry aside, one would never know that this is a building for small children, particularly since there seems to be no provision whatsoever for differentiating between the scale of the adult and that of a child. Is this too much to ask in terms of specific socio-culture value at a time when we seem to no longer know what architects are for? One thinks in this regard of Heidegger's rhetorical question after Hölderlin, 'What are poets for in a destitute time?'

We may oppose the effete effects of the Lustenau school to the Kirchner Museum in Davos, completed to the designs of Annette Gigon and Mike Guyer in 1992. Of this work, Annette Gigon remarked:

We envisioned very simple, unassuming exhibition spaces which would almost erase themselves from the visitor's perception to the benefit of Kirchner's work. They recall the exhibition spaces of the nineteenth century with their parquet floors, white walls and glazed roofs. Our spaces are as such as a kind of spatial quotation, although simplified to prismatic spaces without cornices and baseboards. These spaces were the basis for a kind of structural and material 'deviation' of facades. The exhibition halls, comprising structural concrete walls, are juxtaposed to one another. The resultant interstice becomes the fair-faced concrete circulation hall. The exhibition spaces' glazed roofs transpose themselves in the subdividing grids and materials of the building's facade.

Here, irrespective of the shift between tectonic and atectonic, we are returned to the notion of a *répétition differente*: to a stance that despite the repetition, is capable of sustaining architecture as a critical culture. Thus she continues:

... To see things, materials, substances, to regain an ability to see them, to observe, touch, compare, appropriate and implement, is one way to establish a relationship to one's environment. There are things

recalled, positively or negatively, which present a challenge to this approach. The use of generally negatively valued things seems perhaps provocative, or perhaps conciliatory. It is, however, interesting that at those points where the indigenous materials are disparate and urban structures splinter, the possibilities of making something new are increased.

Gigon/Guyer, Kirchner Museum, Davos, 1989–92, exterior view.

Elsewhere we read that Gigon and Guyer strove for a facade which could be simultaneously read as both a museum and as an analogy to industrial building and its conditions of production. This ethical-cum-critical attitude seems to be reinforced by Guyer's insistence that 'For us any building material must have a certain directness. That's why it would never occur to us to silk screen onto glass if the image's subject was visible below the panes.' It is just such a delicate balance that enabled Gigon and Guyer to detail their Kirchner Museum in a way that was rigorous without descending into brutality, as opposed to, say, the work of Rem Koolhaas who, on occasion, has justified his indifference to details on the grounds that they are too expensive! While one may discriminate between the lyricism of Koolhaas's Villa dall'Ava in Paris and the more arbitrary formalism of his Kunsthalle in Rotterdam, on balance the primary motivation remains the graphic image rather than the phenomenological presence of either structure or material.

Gigon/Guyer, Kirchner Museum, interior exhibition hall.

Architecture's perennial search for legitimacy in the face of techno-scientific modernization, which no sooner undermines one field than it promptly proceeds to transform another, is perhaps the most poignant manifestation of the way in which our ever-escalating rate of change creates a level of destabilization that the species can hardly assimilate. Over the last 40 years architecture has turned first this way and then that in an effort to validate its socio-cultural role. Thus architects have constantly shifted their ideological ground from *science envy* to *art envy* and back again, crossing the hypothetical frontier between C P Snow's two cultures with impunity and opting eventually for either one side or the other of this divide, that is to say electing to practise either as architect/engineers (Renzo Piano) or as architect/artists (Frank Gehry). As Nicola di Battista has written, the constant play between these poles has been detrimental for architecture for in so doing it has removed itself from the world-creating potential of its craft:

It was thought that to contrast the dominion of engineering it was sufficient to exalt the sphere of art. Now whilst this may have saved some, it rendered the majority ineffective, and has in point of fact practically dissolved the discipline. It was erroneously believed that the aesthetic quality of a single product could be enough to go forward. But we know that if it cannot be transfigured into collective aspirations and interests, it remains in reality only a personal experience, serving that purpose but no other... Finally, as far as the relation between art and architecture is concerned, even though quite different considerations would be necessary here, we seem to be living today in a colossal paradox. While many contemporary architects look to the world of art for material and inspiration to solve problems within their own discipline, there are just as many artists who look, conversely, to the sphere of architecture – a realist art if ever there was one – for the realism which they can't find any more in their own craft. Everything would be fine, were it not for the fact that the artists have turned to architecture at a time when realism is no longer appropriate to it, and architects have turned to art at a time when the latter refuses to converse with terms like aesthetics or creativity. The paradox is that both the artists and the architects seek solutions to their problems in disciplines that have by now changed and which can only offer a parody of themselves...[2]

It is difficult to add anything to the perspicacity of this critique, save to remark that the work of a number of the architects that I have briefly touched on here would seem to fall under its stricture. One can only hope that others will be able to sustain their early capacity or, alternatively, to reveal an untapped potential for the pursuit of the art of architecture in all its anachronistic fullness. One perhaps needs to add that one does not indulge in critique for the sake of a gratuitous negativity, but rather to spur the critical sensibility, to sharpen the debate, to overcome, as far as this is feasible, the debilitating dictates of fashion, and above all to guard against the ever-present threat, in a mediatic age, of sliding into an intellectual somnambulance where everything seems to appear to be for the aestheticized best in the best of all commodified worlds.

First published in *Scroope, Cambridge Architecture Journal*, no.9, 1997, pp.19–24.

Notes

Introduction: On the Predicament of Architecture at the Turn of the Century

1 Hans Magnus Enzensberger, *The Consciousness Industry: On Literature, Politics and the Media*, New York: Seabury Press, 1974, pp.36, 40 and 41.
2 Marshall Berman, *All That Is Solid Melts Into Air*, New York: Simon and Schuster, 1982, pp.134–142. See also Hilda Heynen, *Architecture and Modernity: A Critique*, Cambridge, MA: MIT Press, 1969, pp.8–24.
3 Hal Foster, 'Why All the Hoopla', *London Review of Books*, 23 August 2001, pp.25–6.
4 Peter Rice, *An Engineer Imagines*, Zurich: Artemis, 1994, pp.76–7.
5 Geoffrey Alan Jellicoe, *Motopia*, New York: Praeger, 1961.
6 Jean Gottman, *Megalopolis*, Cambridge, MA: MIT Press, 1961.
7 Serge Chermayeff and Christopher Alexander, *Community and Privacy*, Garden City, NY: Anchor Books, 1969.
8 Roland Rainer, *Livable Environments*, Zurich: Artemis, 1972 (Verlag for Architecture).
9 Peter Buchanan, *Ten Shades of Green*, New York: Architectural League of New York, 2000, p.9.
10 See *Towards an Urban Renaissance: Final Report of the Urban Task Force, Chaivel by Lord Rogers of Riverside*, London: Urban Task Force, 1999.
11 See John Tillman Lyle, *Design for Sustainable Development*, New York: Wiley, 1994. The larger part of this study is addressed to the cultivation of landscape in terms of energy flows and hydraulic conservation. See also Steven Moore, *Technology, Place & Architecture*, Austin: University of Texas Press, 2001.
12 Manuel de Solà Morales, *Progettare città/Designing Cities, Lotus Quaderni Documents*, no.23, Mirko Zardini, ed., Milan: Electa, 1999.
13 Melvin Webber, *Explorations in Urban Structure*, Philadelphia: University of Pennsylvania, 1964.
14 Georgia Warnke, *Gadamer: Hermeneutics, Tradition and Reason*, Stanford, CA: Stanford University Press, 1987, p.39.
15 See David Chipperfield, 'Tradition and Invention', *2G Revista Internacional de Arquitectura*, no.1, Barcelona: Gustavo Gili, 1997, p.131.
16 Eugenio d'Ors, cited in Luis Bunuel, *My Last Sigh*, New York: Alfred A Knopf, 1984, pp.69–70. I am indebted to Juhani Palassma for this reference to Eugenio d'Ors.

The Status of Man and the Status of his Objects

1 Hannah Arendt, *The Human Condition*, Chicago, IL: University of Chicago Press, 1958, p.7.
2 Ibid.
3 *The Shorter English Dictionary*, 3rd edition, Oxford: Clarendon Press, 1947.
4 Arendt provides the following etymological footnote on p.136 of *The Human Condition*: 'The Latin word *faber*, probably related to *facere* ("to make something" in the sense of production), originally designated the fabricator and artist who works upon hard material, such as stone or wood; it also was used as translation for the Greek word *tekton*, which has the same connotation.'
5 Adolf Loos, 'Architecture 1910', in Tim and Charlotte Benton, eds, *An International Anthology of Original Articles in Architecture and Design, 1890–1939*, New York: Watson Guptill, 1975, pp.41–5. In her essay 'Thinking and Moral Considerations' Arendt directly relates representation with thought in her footnote on Augustine: 'The image, *the representation of something* absent is stored *in* memory and *becomes* a thought object, a "vision of thought" as soon as it is wilfully remembered.' See *Social Research 38*, no.3, Autumn 1971, p.424.
6 Arendt, *The Human Condition*, p.53.
7 Ibid., p.201.
8 See Melvin Webber, *Explorations into Urban Structure*, Philadelphia, PA: University of Pennsylvania, 1964. See also his article in Lowdon Wingo, Jnr., ed., *Cities and Space*, Baltimore, MA: Johns Hopkins University Press, 1963.
9 Robert Venturi, *Complexity and Contradiction in Architecture*, New York: Museum of Modern Art, 1966, p.133.
10 Arendt, *The Human Condition*, p.204. See also her essay 'Thinking and Moral Considerations', pp.430, 431. In this text Arendt opposes the house to the nomadic tent. 'We can use the word house for a great number of objects – for the mud hut of a tribe, the palace of a king, the country home of a city dweller, the cottage in the village, or the apartment house in town – but we can hardly use it for the tents of some nomads. The house, in and by itself, *auto kath'auto*, that which makes us use the word for all these particular and very different buildings, is never seen, neither by the eyes of the body, nor by the eyes of the mind; ... the point here is that it implies something considerably less tangible than the structure perceived by our eyes. It implies "housing somebody" and being "dwelt in" as no tent could house or serve as a dwelling place which is put up today and taken down tomorrow.' This recognition of the house as a *place of dwelling* is fundamentally Heideggerian and as such relates to the 'darkness' of the *megaron*. As in Martin Heidegger's 'Building, Dwelling, Thinking', the argument implicitly links 'house-building' to agriculture and to rootedness.
11 Camillo Sitte, *City Planning According to Artistic Principles*, trans. George R Collins and Christiane Craseman Collins, New York: Random House, 1965. As the translators point out, Sitte made pointed use of the term *Platz* ('place') rather than the word 'square', which has geometrical connotations antipathetic to Sitte's urban principles. Sitte's work was polemically against the normative gridded city as advocated by Reinhard Baumeister.
12 Arendt provides the following etymological footnote on p.71 of *The Human Condition*: 'The Greek and Latin words for the interior of the house, *megaron* and *atrium*, have a strong connotation of darkness and blackness.' She cites Theodor Mommsen, *Römische Geschichte*, 5th edition, Berlin: Weidmann, Book 1, pp.22, 236.
13 Arendt, *The Human Condition*, p.38.
14 Ibid., p.39.
15 Ibid., p.59.
16 Luis Barragán, quoted in Clive Bamford-Smith, *Builders in the Sun: Five Mexican Architects*, New York: Architectural Book Publishing Co., 1967, p.74.
17 Arendt, *The Human Condition*, p.122.
18 Luis Barragán, quoted in Bamford-Smith, *Builders in the Sun*, p.77.
19 Arendt, *The Human Condition*, p.45.
20 Ibid., pp.173–4.
21 Ibid., pp.167–8.
22 G C Argan, *The Renaissance City*, New York: Braziller, 1969, pp.25–6.
23 Arendt, *The Human Condition*, pp.282–3.
24 Ibid., p.307.
25 Michel Parent and Jacques Verroust, *Vauban*, Paris: Editions Jacques Fréal, 1971, p.60.
26 The horse-drawn tram of the Ringstrasse gave way to the electric tram in the early 1890s. In his *Teoría general de urbanización* (1867), Ildefonso Cerda, the planner of modern Barcelona and inventor of the term *urbanization*, argues that 'the form of the city is, or must be, derived from the necessities of locomotion'. From this date onwards the city becomes inundated by mechanized movement.
27 Arendt, *The Human Condition*, p.304.
28 See Robin Evans, 'Regulation and Production', *Lotus*, no.12, September 1976.
29 Arendt, *The Human Condition*, pp.125–6.
30 See Reyner Banham, *Theory and Design in the First Machine Age*, New York: Praeger, 1960, p.135.
31 For the complete text see Constant Nieuwenhuys, 'New Babylon', *Architectural Design*, June 1964, pp.304–5.
32 See Stanley Buder, *Pullman: An Experiment in Industrial Order and Community Planning*,

1880–1930, London: Oxford University Press, 1967. George Pullman, founder of the Pullman Palace Car Company, had, in fact, made his start in Chicago in 1855 raising buildings above the then-existing ground level.

33 Arendt, *The Human Condition*, p.132.

34 Innumerable examples exist of the specific displacement of the public realm in contemporary building. Among the more recent instances, one might cite the following: The Ford Foundation Building, New York, for its provision of a false 'public' foyer which is programmed in such a way as to assure that no public realm may be allowed to come into existence. The Centre Pompidou, Paris, for its reduction of its 'users' to the same status as the 'services' – the users being piped-in, so to speak, on one side, and the services fed into the structure on the other. In short, the reduction of a museum to the status and the model expressiveness of an oil refinery! The Richards Laboratories at the University of Pennsylvania has service towers rendered as monumental elements and the whole structure is pervaded by a sense of 'religiosity' inappropriate to the processal nature of a laboratory building. In this last example a misplaced monumentality fails to transcend the manifest absence of an appropriately 'representative' or 'commemorative' programme, whereas in the first case the presence of a 'representative' programme is rendered null and void by the rhetoric of the machine. Consciously designed as a cultural supermarket, art in the name of populism is reduced to a commodity.

35 See Herman Broch, 'Notes on the Problem of Kitsch', in Gillo Dorfles, ed., *Kitsch: The World of Bad Taste*, New York: Universe Books, 1969, p.54.

36 Arendt, *The Human Condition*, p.131.

37 Ibid., pp.307–8.

38 Ibid., p.154.

39 Ibid., p.171. Arendt's distinction between 'thought' and 'cognition' is worth repeating here: 'Thought and cognition are not the same. Thought, the source of art works, is manifest without transformation or transfiguration in all great philosophy, whereas the chief manifestation of the cognitive processes, by which we acquire and store up knowledge, is the sciences.' Ibid., p.170.

40 Ibid., pp.117–18.

41 For a historical account of the Frankfurt School and Institute of Social Research see Martin Jay, *The Dialectical Imagination*, Boston, MA: Little Brown, 1973.

42 Earl F Murphy, *Governing Nature*, Chicago, IL: Quadrangle Books, 1967, p.31. See also p.118 for an interesting comment on the nature of industrial consumption: 'Men have assumed that there was a direct line from production to consumption to disappearance. Now it is evident that man, whether as producer or consumer, is part of a cycle. The residue streaming from his production and consumption do *not* disappear.'

43 Arendt, *The Human Condition*, p.169. See also p.127 and Johan Huizinga, *Homo Ludens: A Study of the Play Element in Culture*, Boston, MA: Beacon Press, 1950. As to the limits of play in respect of art we find Huizinga writing: 'The "music" arts live and thrive in an atmosphere of common rejoicing; the plastic arts do not' (p.167).

44 The history of the Proletcult movement in the Soviet Union and its cult of production has yet to be written. For an introduction to the founding principles of the movement and work of Alexander Malinowsky, otherwise known as Bogdanov, see James B Billington, *The Icon and the Axe*, New York: Knopf, 1968, p.489.

45 See Annette Michelson, 'The Man with the Movie-Camera: From Magician to Epistemologist', *Art Forum*, March 1972.

46 Arendt, *The Human Condition*, p.181.

47 Herbert Marcuse, *Eros and Civilization*, New York: Vintage Books, 1962, p.139.

48 Ibid., p.141.

49 Hannah Arendt, *On Revolution*, New York: Viking Press, 1965, p.268.

50 Jürgen Habermas, *Towards a Rational Society*, trans. Jeremy Shapiro, Boston, MA: Beacon Press, 1970, pp.118–19.

Apropos Ulm: Curriculum and Critical Theory

1 Tomás Maldonado, quoted in Roberto Segre's review of *Design, Nature and Revolution* by Tomás Maldonado, in *Arquitectura Cuba*, no.34, 1973.

2 Donald Drew Egbert, *Social Radicalism and the Arts*, New York: Alfred A Knopf, 1970, p.700. Egbert makes it clear that John McCloy was involved in the founding of the school. It is evident that in the late 1950s the HfG still received American financial support. 'In the last few years the industry of West Germany gave an average of DM100,000 per year for further expansion of the school, for the scholarship fund, and to balance the budget. The Rockefeller Foundation donated DM40,000 for the completion of school buildings and workshops. The Ford Foundation gave DM65,000 for the establishment of an Institute for Visual Perception.' (Appendix to *Ulm*, no.2, October 1958.) If Wachsmann is correct in asserting that the original intent had been to found a school of politics then an interesting parallel would emerge with the Frankfurt School of Social Research, since this was re-established in Frankfurt under the auspices of McCloy in July 1949. See Martin Jay, *The Dialectical Imagination*, Boston, MA: Little, Brown & Co., 1973, p.282.

3 The founding of the Grand Ducal School of Arts and Crafts at Weimar in 1906, under the directorship of Henry Van de Velde, was a direct outcome of the German *Kunstgewerbeschule* reform movement, as was Peter Behrens's appointment to the head of the School of Applied Art, Düsseldorf, in 1903.

4 Hans Maria Wingler, *The Bauhaus*, Cambridge, MA: MIT Press, 1969, p.125. The Bauhaus newspaper also bore the name *Zeitschrift für Gestaltung*.

5 Max Bill, 'The Bauhaus Idea from Weimar to Ulm', in Trevor Dannatt, ed., *Architects' Yearbook*, no.5, trans. P Morton Shand, London: Elek, 1953, pp.29–32.

6 *Ulm*, no.1, October 1958, p.1.

7 Tomás Maldonado was born in Buenos Aires in 1922. Trained at the Fine Arts Academy of Buenos Aires from 1938 to 1942, he thereafter worked as a painter and a writer. From 1951 he was editor of the magazine *Nueva Vision*, an Argentine publication dedicated to art, typography, architecture and industrial design. He joined the foundation faculty of the Hochschule für Gestaltung at Ulm in 1954 and became chairman of the triumvirate board in 1956. The initial contact would seem to have been established during the preparation of Maldonado's monograph on the work of Bill, *Max Bill* (Buenos Aires: Editorial Nueva Vision, 1955). Maldonado, who was present at some of the earliest planning meetings with Inge Scholl, has confirmed the Wachsmann thesis that the idea for a 'new Bauhaus' had come from Bill. Maldonado's own position in the mid-1950s is evident from his text on the school published in *Nueva Vision* in 1955. 'In the years following the First World War the necessity for a generic modern culture was strongly felt. This programme now seems too vague and deficient: we could not use it as a basis for a current programme, or at least, not without certain reservations ... The HfG we are building in Ulm intends to redefine the terms of the new culture. Unlike Moholy Nagy in Chicago, it does not merely want to form men who would be able to create and express themselves. The school at Ulm ... wants to indicate what the social goal of this creativity should be; in other words, which forms deserve to be created and which do not. That is, generic modernity and creativity hold no place in its programme ... An example can better clarify the nature of the phenomena to which we are referring. It is a widespread belief, at least, in certain circles, that the industrial designer, the planner who works for mass production, has only one function: that of catering to the sales programme of large scale

industry, while simulating the mechanism of competition. In contrast to this view, the HfG proposes that the designer, even while working for industry, must continue to absolve himself of his responsibilities with regard to society.' It is obvious that Maldonado sensed from the outset the contradiction of industrial design in a neo-capitalist society; although at this date, it is clear that the prime hope was to evolve a workable strategy for the mediating role of design.
8 For a detailed breakdown of the 1957 curriculum see *Ulm*, no.2, October 1958.
9 Hanno Kesting, *Technik und Industriearbeit* and *Das Gesellschaftsbild des Arbeiters*, Tübingen: Mohr Siebeck, 1957.
10 Tomás Maldonado, in *Ulm*, no.2, October 1958, pp.29–30.
11 Ibid., p.30.
12 Ibid., pp.31–2.
13 Since it was the left-wing Swedish art historian Gregor Paulson who largely introduced objective functionalism into Scandinavia, under the name *funkis*, and who was thereby partly responsible for the *Neue Sachlichkeit* style of the Stockholm Exhibition of 1930. In English-speaking circles the importance of Paulson is still unappreciated. His untranslated text, *Die Soziale Dimension der Kunst*, of 1955, was evidently a major influence on the structure of Christian Norberg-Schulz's book, *Intentions in Architecture*.
14 Tomás Maldonado, in *Ulm*, no.2, October 1958, p.35.
15 Ibid., p.40.
16 Anatol Rapoport, *Operational Philosophy*, New York: Harper & Row, 1953.
17 Tomás Maldonado, 'Colloquium con Maldonado e Ohl', *Design-Italia III*, September 1972, p.32.
18 Max Bense, *Aesthetica*, Stuttgart: Verlag-Anstalt, Baden-Baden, 1954; *idem*, *Aesthetische Information*, Krefeld/ Baden-Baden, 1956. In a recent letter to the author Maldonado has attempted to clarify something of Bense's relation to the HfG. 'As for Max Bense, I am convinced that he played an extremely important role in the first years of Ulm, with his tremendous interest in the application of scientific disciplines to the various areas which we dealt with. Probably for generation reasons he sided with Bill in our conflict, even if his own attitude – given his interest in the scientific approach etc. – should have placed him among the younger faculty members, of whom I was one.'
19 See Charles William Morris, 'Scientific Empiricism', *International Encyclopedia of Unified Science*, vol.I, no.1, 1938; *idem*, 'Foundations of the Theory of Signs', *International Encyclopedia of Unified Science*, vol.VII, no.2, 1938.
20 From a conversation between the author and Tomás Maldonado.
21 Gunter Schmitz, 'Education, Research and Development in Industrialized Building at the School of Design, Ulm, Germany', *AIA/ACSA Teachers' Seminar*, Montreal, 1968.
22 Ibid.
23 Tomás Maldonado, 'Design-Objects and Art-Objects', *Ulm*, no.7, January 1963, pp.18–22. Review of an exhibition of consumer products designed as though they were art objects.
24 Claude Schnaidt, '200 Years of Modern Architecture', *Ulm*, no.7, January 1963, pp.24–6. This review concludes, 'this recent book of Leonardo Benevolo offers modern architects a new opportunity to return to the origins of their tradition'.
25 Gui Bonsiepe, 'Information/Machines/ Consciousness', *Ulm*, no.7, January 1963, p.24. Bonsiepe quotes from Georg Klaus's book *Kybernetik in Philosophischer Sicht*, Berlin, 1961.
26 Theo Crosby, ed., *Uppercase*, no.5, London: Whitefriars Press, 1963, p.60.
27 Ibid., pp.47–60. In addition to the Maldonado text and the semiotic glossary, this special issue of *Uppercase* also featured an article by Gui Bonsiepe on verbal and visual rhetoric.
28 Ibid., p.9.
29 Paul M Fitts, 'Engineering Psychology and Engineering Design', in Stanley S Stevens, *Handbook of Experimental Psychology*, New York: Wiley, 1951; Alphonse Chapanis, 'Engineering Psychology', *Annual Review of Psychology*, vol.14, Palo Alto, CA: Annual Reviews, Inc., 1963. See also the pioneering work of Frederick Winslow Taylor, *The Principles of Scientific Management*, New York and London: Harper, 1911.
30 Tomás Maldonado and Gui Bonsiepe, 'Science and Design', *Ulm*, no.10/11, May 1964, p.29.
31 Tomás Maldonado, 'Design Education', in Gyorgy Kepes, ed., *Education of Vision*, Vision and Value Series, New York: George Braziller, 1965.
32 Ibid., p.132.
33 Ibid., p.133.
34 Claude Schnaidt, 'Prefabricated Hope', *Ulm*, no.10/11, May 1964, pp.8–9.
35 Tomás Maldonado, 'The Emergent World: A Challenge to Architectural and Industrial Design Training', *Ulm*, no.12/13, March 1965, p.6.
36 Otl Aicher, 'Planning All Awry?', *Ulm*, no.17/18, June 1966.
37 Tomás Maldonado, 'How to Fight Complacency in Design Education', ibid., p.20.
38 Abraham Moles, 'Functionalism in Crisis', *Ulm*, no.19/20, August 1967, p.24.
39 Claude Schnaidt, 'Architecture and Political Commitment', ibid., pp.30–32.
40 Ibid., p.26.
41 Gui Bonsiepe, 'Communication and Power', *Ulm*, no.21, April 1968, p.16.

The Volvo Case
1 The Norwegian Works Research Centre was started by Elinor Thorsrud, who had previously been trained at the Tavistock Institute in London and who had already helped to create a number of experimental situations in Swedish industry.
2 Frederick Taylor, *The Principles of Scientific Management*, New York: Harper, 1911: 'This work [pig iron handling] is so crude and elementary in its nature that the writer firmly believes that it would be possible to train an intelligent gorilla so as to become a more efficient pig-iron handler than any man could be.' Antonio Gramsci, in that section of his *Prison Notebooks* dealing with 'Americanism and Fordism', writes: 'Taylor is in fact expressing with brutal cynicism the purpose of American society – developing in the worker to the highest degree automatic and mechanical attitudes, breaking up the old psychophysical nexus of qualified professional work, which demands a certain active participation of intelligence, fantasy and initiative on the part of the worker ...'.
3 See Emma Rothschild, 'GM in Trouble 1. The Vega', *New York Review of Books*, 25 February 1971, p.15. 'Foreign manufacturers produce cars cheaply, then, because they have a high level of productivity, and because they accept smaller profits than American corporations. GM makes about three times as great a profit on each vehicle it produces as its foreign competitors: a profit of $239 per vehicle worldwide in 1969, compared to $75 per vehicle for Toyota, $59 per vehicle for VW, and $57 per vehicle for Datsun/Nissan.'
4 Rolf Lindholm and Jan-Pedler Norstedt, *The Volvo Report*, Stockholm: SAF/Swedish Employers Confederation, 1975.
5 See Melvin Webber, *Explorations in Urban Structure*, Philadelphia, PA: University of Pennsylvania, 1964. Webber first coined the term 'non-place urban realm' as a general paradigm for megalopolis in 1961 in the essay 'Order in Diversity: Community without Propinquity', which appears in Lowdon Wingo, Jnr., ed., *Cities and Space*, Baltimore, MA: John Hopkins University Press, 1963.
6 Jürgen Habermas, 'Technology and Science as an Ideology', in *Towards a Rational Society*, Boston, MA: Beacon Press, 1971, p.118.
7 Ibid., pp.119 and 120.

Towards a Critical Regionalism: Six Points for an Architecture of Resistance

1 Paul Ricoeur, 'Universal Civilization and National Cultures' (1961), in *History and Truth*, trans. Chas A Kelbley, Evanston, IL: Northwestern University Press, 1965, pp.276–7.

2 That these are but two sides of the same coin has perhaps been most dramatically demonstrated in the Portland City Annex completed in Portland, Oregon in 1982 to the designs of Michael Graves. The constructional fabric of this building bears no relation whatsoever to the 'representative' scenography that is applied to the building both inside and out.

3 Ricoeur, 'Universal Civilization and National Cultures', p.277.

4 Fernand Braudel informs us that the term 'culture' hardly existed before the beginning of the nineteenth century when, as far as Anglo-Saxon letters are concerned, it already finds itself opposed to 'civilization' in the writings of Samuel Taylor Coleridge – above all, in Coleridge's *On the Constitution of Church and State* of 1830. The noun 'civilization' has a somewhat longer history, first appearing in 1766, although its verb and participle forms date to the sixteenth and seventeenth centuries. The use that Ricoeur makes of the opposition between these two terms relates to the work of twentieth-century German thinkers and writers such as Osvald Spengler, Ferdinand Tönnies, Alfred Weber and Thomas Mann.

5 Hannah Arendt, *The Human Condition*, Chicago, IL: University of Chicago Press, 1958, p.154.

6 Clement Greenberg, 'Avant-Garde and Kitsch', in Gillo Dorfles, ed., *Kitsch: The World of Bad Taste*, New York: Universe Books, 1969, p.126.

7 Clement Greenberg, 'Modernist Painting' (1965), republished in Gregory Battcock, ed., *The New Art*, New York: Dutton, 1966, pp.101–2.

8 See Charles Jencks, *The Language of Post-Modern Architecture*, New York: Rizzoli, 1977.

9 Andreas Huyssen, 'The Search for Tradition: Avant-Garde and Post-modernism in the 1970s', *New German Critique*, vol.22, winter 1981, p.34.

10 Jerry Mander, *Four Arguments for the Elimination of Television*, New York: Morrow Quill, 1978, p.134.

11 Herbert Marcuse, *One-Dimensional Man*, Boston, MA: Beacon Press, 1964, p.156.

12 Alex Tzonis and Liane Lefaivre, 'The Grid and the Pathway. An Introduction to the Work of Dimitris and Susana Antonakakis', *Architecture in Greece*, no.15, 1981, p.178.

13 Ricoeur, 'Universal Civilization and National Cultures, p.283.

14 Aldo van Eyck, *Forum*, vol.16, no.3, 1962.

15 Hamilton Harwell Harris, 'Liberative and Restrictive Regionalism', address given to the Northwest Chapter of the AIA in Eugene, Oregon in 1954.

16 Jørn Utzon, 'Platforms and Plateaus: Ideas of a Danish Architect', *Zodiac*, no.10, 1962, pp.112–14.

17 Jean Gottmann, *Megalopolis*, Cambridge, MA: MIT Press, 1961.

18 Martin Heidegger, 'Building, Dwelling, Thinking', in *Poetry, Language, Thought*, New York: Harper Colophon, 1971, p.154. This essay first appeared in German in 1954.

19 Hannah Arendt, *The Human Condition*, p.201.

20 Melvin Webber, *Explorations in Urban Structure*, Philadelphia, PA: University of Pennsylvania Press, 1964.

21 Robert Venturi, *Complexity and Contradiction in Architecture*, New York: Museum of Modern Art, 1966, p.133.

22 Stanford Anderson, 'Modern Architecture and Industry: Peter Behrens, the AEG, and Industrial Design', *Oppositions*, no.21, summer 1980, p.83.

Rappel à l'Ordre: The Case for the Tectonic

1 Hans Sedlmayr, *Art in Crisis: The Lost Centre*, New York and London: Hollis and Carter Spottiswoode, Ballantyne & Co. Ltd., 1957, p.164.

2 Clement Greenberg, 'Modernist Painting' (1965), republished in Gregory Battcock, ed., *The New Art*, New York: Dutton, 1966, pp.101–2.

3 Giorgio Grassi, 'Avant-Garde and Continuity', in *Oppositions*, no.21, summer 1980, pp.26–7.

4 Ignasi Solà Morales, 'Critical Discipline', in *Oppositions*, no.23, winter 1981, pp.148–50.

5 Gunter Nitschke, 'Shime: Binding/Unbinding', *Architectural Design*, no.44, 1974, pp.747–91.

6 Vittorio Gregotti, 'Lecture at the New York Architectural League', *Section A.*, no.1; February/March 1983.

7 Marco Frascari, 'Technometry and the work of Carlo Scarpa and Mario Ridolf', Proceedings of the ACSA National Conference on Techdoom, Washington, 1987.

8 Marco Frascari, 'The Tell-the-Tale Detail', in *VIA*, no.7, Philadelphia: University of Pennsylvania and MIT Press, 1984, pp.23–37.

9 See Joseph Mali, 'Mythology and Counter-History: The New Critical Art of Vico and Joyce', in *Vico and Joyce*, Donald P Verene, ed., Albany: State University of New York Press, 1987.

The Humanist versus the Utilitarian Ideal

1 The projects are referred to as the Meyer and Le Corbusier entries, although all evidence suggests that Hans Wittwer, as Meyer's collaborator, played an equal part as designer, and that Le Corbusier could not have brought such precision to his design had not his genius been matched by Pierre Jeanneret's technical ability.

2 Colin Rowe and Robert Slutzky, 'Transparency: Literal and Phenomenal', *Perspecta*, no.8, 1963, pp.45–54.

3 Claude Schnaidt, *Hannes Meyer*, London: Alec Tiranti, 1965, p.25.

4 Le Corbusier and Pierre Jeanneret, *Oeuvre complète 1910–29*, vol.1, 5th edition, Zurich: Girsberger, 1965, p.165.

5 Ibid., pp.128–9.

6 Le Corbusier, *Une Maison, un palais*, Paris: Editions Crès, 1928.

7 Mircea Eliade, *The Sacred and the Profane*, trans. Willard R Trask, New York: Harcourt Brace, 1961.

8 Claude Schnaidt, *Hannes Meyer: Buildings, Projects and Writings*, London: Jovanovich Tiranti, 1965, p.95.

9 The article was reprinted in *L'Architecture d'aujourd'hui*, no.10, 1963, pp.38–61, and dedicated by Le Corbusier to '*Alexandre Vesnine, fondateur du Constructivisme*'.

10 Le Corbusier and Jeanneret, *Oeuvre complète 1910–29*, pp.190–7.

11 Hannah Arendt, *The Human Condition*, Chicago, IL: University of Chicago Press, 1958, pp.52–3.

The Work and Influence of El Lissitzky

1 Chimen Abramsky, 'El Lissitzky as Jewish Illustrator and Typographer', *Studio* (International Journal of Modern Art), October 1966, pp.182–5.

2 'World of Art' was at one time the name of a magazine and a group extending from the late 1890s to the outbreak of World War I. See Camilla Gray, *The Great Experiment: Russian Art 1863–1922*, New York: Harry N Abrams, 1962.

3 See Camilla Gray, *The Great Experiment*, p.227: 'Malevich renamed the Vitebsk school "Unovis", which is short for College of the New Art.' From this Lissitzky derived the compound name *Proun*, i.e. Pro and Unovis.

4 For Malevich's original designs for *Victory over the Sun* see Gray, *The Great Experiment*, plate 99.

5 El Lissitzky, 'The Electrical-Mechanical Spectacle', trans. Standish D Lawder, *Form*, no. 3, 15 December 1966, pp.12–14.

6 Subsequent documentation by Lissitzky's wife has made it evident that Lissitzky also used a much richer colour range on occasion. See Sophie Lissitzky-Küppers, *El Lissitzky*, London: Thames & Hudson, 1968.

7 See *Typographia*, no.16, 1967, p.33 (old series). Translation by Camilla Gray. Principles listed in

Merz, no.4, July 1923.
8 According to Lubetkin's article in the *Architectural Review* (vol.LXXI, May 1932, pp.199–208), the ASNOVA group was first formed by Ladovsky in 1923. This group appears to have been re-established on an international basis by Ladovsky and Lissitzky in 1926. A cover design for an ASNOVA journal by Lissitzky, exhibited in London at the Grosvenor Gallery in 1966, indicates that the Association was founded in 1926 with Mart Stam, Le Corbusier and Karel Tiege amongst others as its corresponding members.
9 El Lissitzky, 'K und Pangeometrie', reprinted in *Russland: Architektur für eine Weltrevolution, Ullstein Bauwelt Fundamente*, no.14, 1965, pp.122–9. In this essay Lissitzky traces the evolution of Western spatial conceptions in painting.
10 El Lissitzky, 'Prounen Raum', reprinted in *Russland: Architektur für eine Weltrevolution, Ullstein Bauwelt Fundamente*, p.118.
11 Ibid., p.120.
12 El Lissitzky, 'Alte Stadt-Neue Baukorper', in ibid., pp.32–8.
13 El Lissitzky, 'Demonstrationsraume', in ibid., p.130.
14 Ibid.p.131.
15 El Lissitzky, 'Alte Stadt-Neue Baukorper' in ibid., p.38.
16 El Lissitzky, 'Alte Stadt-Neue Baukorper' in ibid., pp.33 and 34.
17 El Lissitzky, 'Zukunft und Utopie' in ibid., pp.46 and 48.
18 'NASCI' from *Merz*, no.8/9; reprinted in Sophie Lissitzky-Küppers, *El Lissitzky: Life, Letters, Text*, London: Thames & Hudson, 1968, p.351.
19 El Lissitzky, 'Ideologische Überban', in *Russland: Architektur für eine Weltrevolution, Ullstein Bauwelt Fundamente*, p.52.
20 'GEAM' programme for mobile building, in *Russland: Architektur für eine Weltrevolution, Ullstein Bauwelt Fundamente*, pp.160–61. Members of the initial GEAM group included Emmerich, Frieden, Friedman, Gunschel, Pecquent and Ruhnau.

Team 10, Plus 20: The Vicissitudes of Ideology
1 This manifesto was the product of a post-mortem on the 9th CIAM Congress held at Aix-en-Provence in 1954. Compiled in Doorn, Holland, it is a manifesto without signatories although one may assume that the Smithsons, Van Eyck, Bakema and Voelcker had a strong hand in its composition. The articles are largely structured about the Geddes valley section and they appear to constitute an argument for the ecological and physical integration of the habitat into the landscape. For a complete account of Patrick Geddes's Valley Section see David Lewis, ed., *Architect's Year Book*, no.12, London: Elek, 1968, pp.65–71.
2 Alison and Peter Smithson, eds, *Team 10 Primer*, Cambridge, MA: MIT Press, 1968, p.27.
3 Alison and Peter Smithson, *Team 10 Primer*. See p.76 for the main quotation from George Candilis. Candilis clearly played a major design role in the whole of the ATBAT Afrique work documented in *Architectural Design*, January 1955. The importance of this work should not be underestimated but it is not dealt with in this outline. One may assume that Candilis and Woods worked in very close collaboration between 1952 and 1955. For Voelcker's contribution to the *Primer* see pages 29, 33, 45, 46, 49 and 87. John Voelcker's most typical contribution of the late 1950s – an 'ordinary' atrium house – is documented in Oscar Newman, *CIAM'59: Otterlo*, Stuttgart: Kramer, 1961, pp.157–159.
4 Bye-law housing was in fact a euphemism for building closely packed worker's dwellings on large tracts of land. See J N Tarn, *Working-class Housing in 19th Century Britain*, AA Paper, no.7, London: Lund Humphries, 1971.
5 Le Corbusier's slum clearing proposal exhibited in the Pavillon des Temps Nouveaux in the Paris World Exhibition of 1937. See *Le Corbusier and P Jeanneret, Oeuvre Complète 1934–38*, 6th edition, Zurich: Girsberger Editions, 1958, pp.48–55.
6 The term Ville Radieuse is used generically to refer to Le Corbusier's planning models of the 1920s and the early 1930s, namely the Ville Contemporaine, 1922, the Ville Radieuse, 1930, and the Plan Obus for Algiers of 1931.
7 Ulrich Conrads, *Programs and Manifestoes on Twentieth-Century Architecture*, Cambridge, MA: MIT Press, 1970, pp.137–145.
8 The vestigal 'yard' in the Golden Lane project of 1952 opened off the street-in-the-air and seems to have been conceived as being an addendum to the house that could be converted into closed living accommodation.
9 Built under the auspices of Sheffield City Architect's Department between 1961 and 1966. Chief architect J Lewis Womersley, designers Jack Lynn, Ivor Smith and Frederick Nicklin.
10 See Newman, *CIAM'59 in Otterlo*, pp.140–149. Kenzo Tange's extremely perspicacious critical remarks may be found on p.220.
11 See Ernst May's plans for Autostroi Magnitogorsk and Tirgan, all of the period 1930–31. See Kenneth Frampton, *Notes on Soviet Urbanism 1917–32*, Lewis, *Architect's Year Book*, no.12, pp.238–252.
12 See Arthur Korn and Felix Samuely, MARS Group London Reconstruction Project, *Architectural Review*, June 1942, pp.143–150.
13 The phrase 'nonplace urban realm' was first coined by Melvin Webber in his book *Explorations in Urban Structure*.
14 The spirit of Prussian Baroque and German Neoclassical space seems to have had an appeal for the Smithsons in the late 1950s. The Mehringplatz proposal suggests a direct reference to the notion of 'Bauhof'. See 'Aesthetics of Change', *Architect's Year Book*, no.8, 1957. See also Bakema's reference to the 'Bauhof' in the *Team 10 Primer*, p.23.
15 Alison and Peter Smithson, *Urban Structuring*, London: Studio Vista, 1967, pp.85–7.
16 Kenneth Frampton, 'The Economist and the Hauptstadt', *Architectural Design*, January 1965.
17 Alison and Peter Smithson, *Ordinariness and Light*, Cambridge, MA: MIT Press, 1970, pp.187–195. For more complete documentation see *Architectural Design*, September 1972 and also Peter Eisenman, From 'Golden Lane to Robin Hood Gardens, etc', *Oppositions*, no.1, 1973, pp.27–56.
18 See Francis Strauven, *Aldo Van Eyck, The Shape of Relativity*, Amsterdam: Architectura & Natura, 1998, pp.143–149.
19 Alison Smithson, *Team 10 Primer*, p.22.
20 Alison Smithson, *Team 10 Primer*, p.12.
21 Newman, *CIAM'59 Otterlo*, p.197.
22 Alison Smithson, *Team 10 Primer*, p.31.
23 Yona Friedman, *L'Architecture Mobile*, privately published in 1958 and 1962. This was one of the first work papers of the *Groupe d'Etudes d'Architecture Mobile* (GEAM) founded by Friedman, Eckard Schultze-Fielitz, Runau and others in 1957.
24 See *Team 10 Primer*, p.18.
25 G De Carlo, 'Legitimizing Architecture', *Forum*, vol.XXIII, 1972/1, *Organ van het genootschap et Amicitia*.
26 Jaqueline Tyrnhitt, Jose Luis Sert, Ernesto N Rogers, eds, *The Heart of the City, CIAM*, London: Lund Humphries, 1952.

Constructivism: The Pursuit of an Elusive Sensibility
1 Quoted in Herbert Read and Martin Leslie, *Naum Gabo*, London: Lund Humphries, 1957. See 1956 interview between Naum Gabo, Ibram Lassaw and Ilya Bolotowsky, pp.156–60. The tactic of this present essay has been to pursue the Constructivist sensibility outside its manifestation in professional architectural circles, which so often led, as Lubetkin remarked in 1965, to a reproduction of advanced technique in adulterated form (see Berthold Lubetkin, 'Soviet Architecture: Notes on Developments from 1917 to 1932', *Architectural Association Journal*, no.71, May 1956, p.263).

Instead, I have attempted to concentrate on the primary impulse to found artistic expression in the *real* processes of production. Rising out of the energy of a radical intelligentsia, this impulse seems to have led in two opposed, but complementary, directions: the one towards a natural Primitivism – imbued with a certain fantasy – of which Tatlin's *Letatlin* would be the prime example; the other towards a highly artificial formal language, such as we see in Rodchenko's exercises of permutable, abstract, wooden constructions made out of pieces of the same length. The former was very much emphasized in Ronald Hunt's exhibition, 'Transform the World, Poetry Must Be Made By All', held at the Moderna Museet, Stockholm, in 1969.

2 The term *Sachlichkeit* had been current in German cultural circles long before the art critic G F Hartlaub hit upon the phrase *die Neue Sachlichkeit*, around 1924, to identify a postwar anti-Expressionist school of German painting. In 1929, Hartlaub wrote to Alfred H Barr, Jnr., 'The expression ought really to apply as a label to the new realism bearing a socialist flavour. It was related to the general contemporary feeling in Germany of resignation and cynicism after a period of exuberant hopes (which had found an outlet in Expressionism). Cynicism and resignation are the negative side of the *neue Sachlichkeit*; the positive side expresses itself in the enthusiasm for the immediate reality as a result of a desire to take things entirely objectively on a material basis without immediately investing them with ideal implications. This healthy disillusionment finds its clearest expression in Germany in architecture.'

3 George Rickey, *Constructivism, Origins and Evolution*, London: Studio Vista, 1967.

4 Vladimir Markov, *Russian Futurism: A History*, London: MacGibbon and Kee, 1969, p.41.

5 Ibid., pp.45, 46. '"A Slap" was probably written by David Burluik, Kruchenykh and Mayakovsky together in November or December 1912, in the Romanovka Hotel in Moscow, where they spent their evenings.'

6 Ibid., p.129.

7 Ibid., p.131. The full passage, entitled 'Declaration of the Word as Such' reads, 'Words die, the world stays young forever. An artist has seen the world in a new way, and, like Adam, he gives his own names to everything. A lily is beautiful, but the word "lily" is soiled with fingers and raped. For this reason I call a lily "euy" [pronounced in Russian approximately "ehooee"], and the original purity is re-established.'

8 See Camilla Gray, *The Great Experiment: Russian Art 1863–1922*, New York: Harry N Abrams, 1962, plate 75. Gray's caption reads, 'This film, which appeared in January 1914, was in the form of a "parody on the prevalent genre of the film guignol", according to Jay Leyda. It presented a day in the life of the Futurists; Mayakovsky, the Burliuk brothers, Larionov and Goncharova all took part in it.'

9 Quoted in Markov, *Russian Futurism*, p.202.

10 Quoted in Troels Andersen, ed., *Vladimir Tatlin*, Stockholm: Moderna Museet, 1968. This definitive catalogue on the work of Tatlin contains an English translation of Tatlin's original text, p.69.

11 Markov, *Russian Futurism*, p.202.

12 Quoted in Andersen, *Vladimir Tatlin*, p.86.

13 Ibid., p.6. In connection with a comparison between Tatlin's tower and Boccioni's 1911 drawing for *A Bottle Evolving in Space*, Andersen writes, 'What was for Boccioni a radicalization of a *nature morte* came for Tatlin to be real architecture. Therein lay the change.' See p.8.

14 Read and Leslie, *Naum Gabo*, p.156. This study of Gabo prints the full text of *The Programme of the Productivist Group*.

15 Gray, *The Great Experiment*, p.148.

16 Quoted in Andersen, *Vladimir Tatlin*, p.75. This Tatlin text, written in 1932, was given the title 'Art out into Technology'. Andersen's translation, rendered in English here by Keith Bradfield, gives a slightly different version of the same text. '"Constructivism", in inverted commas, did not reckon in its work with the organic connection between material and concentration. In reality, it is only as a result of these dynamic relationships that form necessary to life emerges.'

17 Ibid., p.57. This text by Punin appeared as an extract in *Veshch*, nos 1–2, 1922.

18 Quoted in René Fülop-Miller, *The Mind and Face of Bolshevism*, London and New York: Putnam's, 1927, p.102. Although Fülop-Miller does not mention Punin by name, he indicates that this passage was originally part of the extract published in *Veshch*, nos 1–2, 1922.

19 Ibid., p.102.

20 Quoted in Andersen, *Vladimir Tatlin*, p.85. Tatlin's text was published under the title 'The Moon on Stage'.

21 Quoted in ibid., pp.77–9. The full text of an interview between Tatlin and Kornely Zelinsky was originally published in *Vechernaya Moskva*, 1932.

22 James Billington, *The Icon and the Axe*, New York: Knopf, 1968, p.489.

23 Quoted in Read and Leslie, *Naum Gabo*, p.156.

24 The exhibition '5 x 5 = 25' was held in 1921. The signatories were the five artists who took part in it, namely, Alexander Rodchenko, Varvara Stepanova, Alexander Vesnin, Alexandra Exter and Liubov Popova.

25 Quoted in Fülop-Miller, *The Mind and Face of Bolshevism*, p.127.

26 Quoted in Marie Seton, *Sergei M Eisenstein*, London: Bodley Head, 1952, p.66. Seton is quoting from Eisenstein's book *Film Form* (New York: Harcourt Brace, 1949).

27 Dziga Vertov, 'Kino-Eye: Lecture II', in Harry M Geduld, ed., *Film Makers on Film Making*, Bloomington, IN: Indiana University Press, 1967, p.102. Quoted by Annette Michelson in her essay '"The Man with the Movie Camera": From Magician to Epistomologist', *Art Forum*, March 1972, p.65. Vertov's real name was Denis Kaufman. His adopted name, which means 'spinning top', seems to be a quintessential 'Constructivist' image when placed in context. Michelson writes: 'In 1924, Vertov made the film we know as *Kino-Glaz* or *Kino-Eye*, the first of a projected series. The *Kino-Pravda* series, his first major work, had involved him for some years in the production of short documents or newsreels on the widest variety of themes. *Kino-Glaz* is a didactic work, centered on episodes which articulate major preoccupations of the young Soviet regime: it deals with the manufacture and distribution of bread, the processing and distribution of meat, celebrates the constructions of youth camps and discusses the problem of alcoholism ... It is near the beginning of *Kino-Glaz* that we first see a peasant woman on her way to market to buy meat. We next see her, walking backwards, propelled by the reversal of that sequence, whence she came. The processing and distribution of meats is then recapitulated in reverse, as well.'

28 El Lissitzky, *Russia: An Architecture for World Revolution*, trans. Eric Dluhosch, Cambridge, MA: MIT Press, 1970, p.32. Original version appeared in German in 1930.

29 Michelson, '"The Man with the Movie Camera": From Magician to Epistomologist', p.64.

30 Lubetkin, 'Soviet Architecture: Notes on Developments from 1917–1932', *Architectural Association Journal*, 1956, pp.260–61.

Louis Kahn and the French Connection

1 Le Corbusier, *Towards a New Architecture*, trans. Frederic Etchells, London: The Architectural Press, 1927. (Originally published as *Vers une architecture*, Paris: Les Editions G Crès et Cie, 1923).

2 Louis I Kahn, *Perspecta*, no.3, 1955.

3 Paul Philippe Cret, quoted in Theo B White, ed., *Paul Philippe Cret: Architect and Teacher*, Philadelphia, PA: Associated University Presses, 1973, p.26.

4 Paul Philippe Cret, citing Dimier in 'The Architect as Collaborator of the Engineer', in White, *Paul*

Philippe Cret: Architect and Teacher, p.64.
5 Vincent Scully, Jnr., *Louis I Kahn*, New York: Braziller, 1962, p.11. Kahn's student design of 1924 for a shopping centre unquestionably displays the characteristic attributes of Beaux-Arts work: the compilation of the plan out of discrete elements, the gradation of major versus minor axes, etc. However, 'moderne' expressive elements are discernible: the curtain wall and the vaguely pre-Colombian frieze applied to the deep fascia at the top of the structure.
6 Paul Philippe Cret, 'The Architect as Collaborator of the Engineer', in White, *Paul Philippe Cret: Architect and Teacher*, p.64.
7 Paul Philippe Cret, 'A Recent Aspect of an Old Conflict', in White, *Paul Philippe Cret: Architect and Teacher*, p.85.
8 See Romaldo Giurgola and Jaimini Mehta, *Louis I Kahn*, Boulder, CO: Westview Press, 1975. Of the influence of Choisy on Kahn the authors write: 'There is a historical aspect to Kahn's concern for composition. Composition of elements was a preoccupation of the Beaux-Arts academic tradition at the turn of the century. Julien Guadet, the respected professor at the Ecole des Beaux-Arts, wrote about it, and his famous pupil, Tony Garnier, may have set in motion forces and attitudes which, no matter how well disguised by subsequent events in architecture, may still be with us. This may explain the association which Kahn is supposed to have with the Beaux-Arts academic tradition. However, it was Auguste Choisy, a contemporary as well as an ideological antagonist of Guadet, who influenced Kahn more – not by his words and ideas (Kahn did not read French and was not a "reader" in the scholarly sense) but by the magnificent illustrations in his book *Histoire de l'Architecture*, which Kahn treasured.' (*Louis I Kahn*, p.184.)
9 See Kenneth Frampton, 'Industrialization and the Crises in Architecture', *Oppositions*, no.1, September 1973.
10 Eugène Emmanuel Viollet-le-Duc, *Discourses on Architecture*, trans. Benjamin Bucknall, New York: Grove Press, 1959.
11 Paul Zucker, ed., *New Architecture and City Planning*, New York: Philosophical Library, 1944. For the 'Nine Points of Monumentality', see Sigfried Giedion, *Architecture, You and Me*, Cambridge, MA: Harvard University Press, 1958, esp. pp.25–61.
12 Louis Kahn, 'Monumentality', in Paul Zucker, ed., *New Architecture and City Planning*, p.577.
13 Ibid., p.578.
14 Ibid., pp.579–80.
15 That Kahn's cognitive concept of structure was related to the structural rationalism of Viollet-le-Duc seems to find confirmation in Hubert Damisch's article 'The Space Between: A Structuralist Approach to the *Dictionnaire*', in which he writes: 'These models are approximate, but even this *imprecision* cannot be seen as a problem if one accepts that in the world of the 'exact' sciences themselves the perfection of any model is conditioned by interpretation ... In this way, structural analysis in its narrowest sense ... rests in fact on operational models which only give an imperfect account of the real behavior of concrete structures ... which is another way of saying that the "truth" of a building is not to be found in bricks and mortar any more than in outer form. No, it lies in the space between them, that which makes them complementary, in that space where style is born, in that gap between things which is intimated in the absence of a logical link between two propositions that open the article on *Construction: Construction is the means; architecture the result* ... And perhaps it is there between those two small propositions separated by an ambiguous semi-colon ... For from this gap between architecture and construction, between a form and a substance which cannot exist separately, the working of stone, of steel or of cement can assume a structural value, can invite meaning and can thereby gain access to style.' See *Eugène Emmanuel Viollet-le-Duc 1814–1879*, New York: Rizzoli, 1980, p.89.
16 Louis Kahn, 'Monumentality', in Paul Zucker, ed., *New Architecture and City Planning*, p.581–2.
17 Heinz Ronner, Sharad Jhaveri and Alessandro Vasella, eds, *Louis I Kahn, Complete Works 1935–74*, Basel and Stuttgart: Birkhauser Verlag, 1977, p.74.
18 Marcello Angrisani, 'Louis Kahn e Storia', *Edilizia Moderna*, no.86, 1966, pp.83–9.
19 Emil Kaufmann, *Three Revolutionary Architects: Boullée, Ledoux, and Lequeu*, Philadelphia, PA: American Philosophical Society, 1952. See also Eduard F Sekler, 'Formalism and the Polemical Use of History', in *The Harvard Architecture Review*, vol.1, spring 1980, esp. p.37. Here Sekler makes fundamentally the same thesis as Angrisani.
20 Angrisani, 'Louis Kahn e Storia', p.87.
21 Marc-Antoine Laugier, *An Essay on Architecture*, trans. Wolfgang Hermann, Los Angeles: Hennssey & Ingalls, 1977, pp.119–20. See chap. IV, 'On the Style in Which to Build Churches'. Other parallels exist of the way in which both Ledoux and Kahn exploited the isosceles triangle, most notably between Ledoux's Hotel Montmorency of 1772 and Kahn's Indian Institute of Management, Ahmedabad, India. As C Kyle Kinsman has observed in an unpublished paper written for Professor William Jordy of Brown University, 'Each has a large entry chamber placed symmetrically on its hypotenuse; at Montmorency, it is circular; at Ahmedabad, it is diamond-shaped. Beyond the entry chamber and within the body of the triangle is a staircase. In Ledoux's case it begins from a half-ellipse; for Kahn, from a half-circle.'
22 Angrisani, 'Louis Kahn e Storia', p.88.
23 Francesco Tentori, 'Ordine e Forma nel l'opera de Louis Kahn', *Casabella*, no.241, 1960.
24 As Scully points out, Kahn's initial use of the term 'order' came from the period when he was most strongly influenced by Buckminster Fuller, when his model of latent 'order' was predicated in part on the idea of natural crystal structure. He later used 'order' to indicate a sort of preordained institutional teleology to be cryptically summed up by the aphorism, 'what the building wants to be'.
25 Louis Kahn, from an article originally entitled 'Structure and Form' for the Voice of America Forum Lectures, a series on Modern American Architecture in 1960; retitled 'Form and Design' and published in *Architectural Design*, vol.31, no.4, April 1961.
26 Maria Bottero, 'Organic and Rational Morphology in the work of Louis Kahn', *Zodiac*, no.17, 1967.
27 Ibid., pp.244–5.
28 Louis Kahn, 'Form and Design', in Scully, *Louis I Kahn*, p.118.
29 Louis Kahn, *Light is the Theme*, Fort Worth, TX: Kimbell Art Foundation, 1975, p.39.

Maison de Verre as Bachelor Machine

1 Dr Jean Dalsace, cited by René Herbst in *Un inventeur, l'architecte Pierre Chareau*, Paris: Éditions du Salon des Arts Ménages, 1954, pp.7–8.
2 In an interview with Robert Vickery in 1965 Bernard Bijvoet stated that no real working drawings were ever done for the house.
3 Kenneth Frampton, *Histoire Critique de L'Architecture Modern*, trans. Renée Rousso, Paris: Philippe Sers, 1985. It is more difficult to account for its omission from the English edition (*Modern Architecture: A Critical History*, London: Thames and Hudson, 1980).
4 For some, the house was too functional. See the account by Julien Lepage in *L'Architecture d'aujourd'hui*, no.9, November/December 1933, pp.14–15.
5 Marcel Duchamp, *The Green Box*, trans. George Heard Hamilton, New York: George Wittenborn, Inc., 1960. One may equally refer to another text by Duchamp where he writes, 'This is no longer a painting: the transparent surface of the glass ceases to play the role of an imaginary screen; the erotic machinery operates in the empiric space.' Arturo Schwarz, *The Complete Works of Marcel Duchamp*, New York: Delano Greenidge Editions, 1997.

6 Michel Carrouges, 'Mode d'emploi', in *Les Machines Célibataires*, Venice: Éditions Alfieri, 1975, p.21.
7 Duchamp, *The Green Box*, 1960.

In Spite of the Void: The Otherness of Adolf Loos
1 Quoted in Kurt Lustenberger, *Adolf Loos*, Zurich: Artemis, 1994, p.19. Taken from Karl Kraus, *Werke III*, Munich: Beim wort genommen, 1965, p.34.
2 Nikolaus Pevsner, 'Introduction', in Ludwig Müniz and Gustav Künstler, eds, *Adolf Loos: Pioneer of Modern Architecture*, trans. Harold Meek, New York: Frederick A Praeger, 1966, p.13.
3 Adolf Loos, 'Architecture', in Yehuda Safran and Wilfried Wang, eds, *The Architecture of Adolf Loos: An Arts Council Exhibition*, trans. Wilfried Wang, Rosamund Diamond and Robert Godsill, London: Arts Council of Great Britain, 1985, p.104.
4 Quoted in Safran and Wang, *The Architecture of Adolf Loos: An Arts Council Exhibition*, p.104.
5 Quoted in Müniz and Künstler, *Adolf Loos: Pioneer of Modern Architecture*, pp.223–5.
6 Quoted in ibid., p.61.
7 Loos, 'Architecture', *The Architecture of Adolf Loos: An Arts Council Exhibition*, p.106.
8 Benedetto Gravagnuolo, *Adolf Loos: Theory and Works*, trans. C H Evans, New York: Rizzoli, 1982, p.117.
9 Quoted in *Adolf Loos Zum 60. Geburtstag Am 10. Dezember 1930*, Vienna: Richard Lanyi, 1930, pp.66–7.
10 Gravagnuolo, *Adolf Loos: Theory and Works*, pp.188–9.
11 Heinrich Kulka, *Adolf Loos: Das Werk Des Architekten*, Vienna: Anton Schroll & Co., 1931.
12 Adolf Loos, *Das Andere*, Jahr 1:1–2, 1903, reproduced in Massimo Cacciari, *Adolf Loos e il suo Angelo*, Milan: Electa, 1981.
13 T S Eliot, 'Burnt Norton', *Four Quartets*, New York: Harcourt, Brace and Co., 1943, p.3.
14 Quoted in Safran and Wang, *The Architecture of Adolf Loos: An Arts Council Exhibition*, p.97.
15 See Hans Richter, *Dada: Art and Anti-Art*, trans. David Britt, New York: Thames and Hudson, 1985, p.84.
16 Boris Podrecca, 'La même inegalité pour tous', *Adolf Loos 1870–1933*, Liège: Mardaga, 1983, pp.111–12. In opposition to Bolshevism, which wished to make Everyman into a proletarian, Loos was a communist who wished to make Everyman into an aristocrat.
17 Adolf Loos, 'Architecture', 1910, quoted in Safran and Wang, *The Architecture of Adolf Loos: An Arts Council Exhibition*, p.104.
18 Ibid.
19 Ibid.
20 Quoted in Müniz and Künstler, *Adolf Loos: Pioneer of Modern Architecture*, pp.226–7.
21 Quoted in Adolf Opel, ed., *Ornament and Crime: Selected Essays*, trans. Michael Mitchell, Riverside, CA: Ariadne Press, 1998, p.187.
22 Ibid., p.187.
23 Adolf Loos, *Trotzdem*, German edition published in 1930; trans. Jane O Newman and John H Smith, ed., Joan Ockman, unpublished.
24 Quoted in Müniz and Künstler, *Adolf Loos: Pioneer of Modern Architecture*, p.231.
25 Ibid., p.229.
26 Quoted in Safran and Wang, *The Architecture of Adolf Loos: An Arts Council Exhibition*, p.105.
27 Ibid., p.105.
28 Ibid., pp.107–8.
29 Hermann Muthesius and Henry Van de Velde, 'Werkbund Theses and Antitheses', in Ulrich Conrads, ed., *Programs and Manifestoes on Twentieth-Century Architecture*, trans. Michael Bullock, Cambridge, MA: MIT Press, 1971, pp.28–31.
30 Yehuda Safran and Wilfried Wang, 'The Architecture of Adolf Loos', in Adolf Loos, 'Architecture', *The Architecture of Adolf Loos: An Arts Council Exhibition*, p.108.
31 Ibid.
32 Ibid., p.108–9.
33 Adolf Loos, 'Review of the Arts and Crafts', in Joan Ockman, ed., *Spoken into the Void: Collected Essays 1897–1900*, trans. Jane O Newman and John H Smith, Cambridge, MA: MIT Press, 1982, pp.104–5.
34 Adolf Loos, 'Glass and Clay', in *Spoken into the Void: Collected Essays 1897–1900*, p.35.
35 Le Corbusier, *L'Art décoratif d'aujourd'hui*, Paris: G Crès et Cie, 1926, p.216.
36 Loos, *Trotzdem*, German edition published in 1930; trans. Jane O Newman and John H Smith, ed., Joan Ockman, unpublished.
37 Paul Engelmann, *Letters from Ludwig Wittgenstein with a Memoir*, B F McGuinness, ed., trans. L Furtmuller, Oxford: Alden & Mowbray, Ltd., 1967, p.97.
38 Quoted in Allan Janik and Stephen Toulmin, *Wittgenstein's Vienna*, New York: Simon and Schuster, 1973, p.193.
39 Ibid., p.199.
40 Quoted in Roland L Schachel, 'Adolf Loos, L'Amérique et l'antiquité', in *Adolf Loos 1870–1933*, Liège: Mardaga, 1983, p.34.
41 Gottfried Semper, 'Science, Industry and Art' (1852), in Hans M Wingler, *The Bauhaus*, Joseph Stein, ed., trans. Wolfgang Jabs and Basil Gilbert, Cambridge, MA: MIT Press, 1969, p.18.
42 Adolf Loos, 'Glass and Clay', in *Spoken into the Void: Collected Essays 1897–1900*, p.35.
43 Gravagnuolo, *Adolf Loos: Theory and Works*, p.167.
44 Quoted in ibid., p.175.

The Other Le Corbusier: Primitive Form and the Linear City, 1929–52
1 Le Corbusier, *The Four Routes*, London: Dennis Dobson, 1947, p.12. Originally published in French as *Sur les Quatres Routes*, 1941.
2 Le Corbusier and Pierre Jeanneret, *Oeuvre Complète 1934–38*, 6th edition, Zurich: Girsberger, 1958, p.135.
3 Ibid., pp.66 and 67.

The Usonian Legacy
1 Esther McCoy, *Five California Architects*, New York: Reinhold, 1960, p.85.
2 John Sergeant, *Frank Lloyd Wright's Usonian Houses: The Case for an Organic Architecture*, New York: Whitney/Watson Guptill, 1976, p.156.
3 David Gebhard, *Schindler*, London: Thames and Hudson, 1971, pp.48 and 50.
4 Richard Neutra, *Richard Neutra Buildings and Projects*, Zurich: Girsberger, 1951, p.144.

The Legacy of Alvar Aalto
1 Alvar Aalto, interview in *Pagens Nyheter*, 28 October 1936; reprinted in Göran Schildt, *Alvar Aalto: The Decisive Years*, trans. Timothy Binham, New York: Rizzoli, 1986, pp.202–3.
2 Demetri Porphyrios, *Sources of Modern Eclecticism: Studies on Alvar Aalto*, London: Academy Editions, 1982, p.2.
3 Colin St John Wilson, *The Other Tradition of Modern Architecture: The Uncompleted Project*, London: Academy Editions, 1995, pp.6, 30, 86–90.
4 Martin Heidegger, 'Building, Dwelling, Thinking', 1954; in English in *Poetry, Language and Thought*, trans. Albert Hofstadter, New York: Harper Colophon, 1975, pp.145–61.
5 Wilson, *The Other Tradition of Modern Architecture*, p.16.
6 See Jean Badovici and Eileen Gray, 'From Eclecticism to Doubt', *L'Architecture vivante*, autumn 1929. See also Wilson, *The Other Tradition of Modern Architecture*, p.117.
7 Giancarlo de Carlo, *Legitimizing Architecture*, Milan: Electa, 1968.
8 Alvar Aalto, 'The RIBA Discourse: "The Architectural Struggle"', speech given to the Royal Institute of British Architects, London, 1957;

reprinted in Göran Schildt, ed., *Sketches: Alvar Aalto*, trans. Stuart Wrede, Cambridge, MA: MIT Press, 1978, p.147.
9 Ibid.
10 See Francesco Dal Co, *Mario Botta: Architetture 1960–1985*, Milan: Electa, 1985, p.17.
11 This break to a kind of organic collage has been seen, in part, as a return to the Finnish national romanticism of the 1890s. This affinity was not missed by Aalto's long-standing friend, the architect and architectural critic Gustav Strengell, who, just prior to his tragic suicide, characterized the architect's house as the new Niemelä farm. This referred to a collection of eighteenth- and nineteenth-century timber structures clustered around a central yard and exhibited in close proximity to their original forest setting. See Göran Schildt, *Alvar Aalto: The Decisive Years*, New York: Rizzoli, 1986, p.130.
12 See Simo Paavilainen, ed., *Nordic Classicism, 1910–1930*, Helsinki: Museum of Finnish Architecture, 1982.
13 The term *Sachlichkeit* had been current in German cultural circles long before 1924, when the art critic G F Hartlaub hit upon the phrase *die neue Sachlichkeit* (the new objectivity) to identify a postwar school of anti-Expressionist painting. *Sachlichkeit* seems to have been first used in an architectural context in a series of articles written by Hermann Muthesius for the journal *Dekorative Kunst* between 1897 and 1903. These articles attributed the quality of *Sachlichkeit* to the English Arts and Crafts movement, particularly as manifested in the handicraft guilds (such as that founded by C R Ashbee) and the application of the craft ethic to early garden-city suburbs. For Muthesius, *Sachlichkeit* seems to have meant an objective, functionalist, eminently yeoman approach to the design of objects, implying the ultimate reform of industrial society itself. In the second half of the 1920s, the term was closely associated with the left-wing functionalist architects of Germany's Weimar Republic, Switzerland and the Netherlands.
14 Göran Schildt, *Alvar Aalto: The Complete Catalogue of Architecture, Design and Art*, trans. Timothy Binham, New York: Rizzoli, 1994, p.224.
15 See Elina Standertskjöld, 'Alvar Aalto and Standardization' and 'Alvar Aalto's Standard Drawings 1929–32', in *Acanthus 1992*, Helsinki: Museum of Finnish Architecture, 1992, pp.84–111.
16 Alvar Aalto, 'The Stockholm Exhibition I', summary of interview in *Åbo Underrättelsen*, 22 May 1930; reprinted in Schildt, *Sketches: Alvar Aalto*, p.16. Inspired by the vision of Gregor Paulsson, the leading figures of the so-called *acceptera* faction were the architects Erik Gunnar Asplund, Uno Åhren, Wolter Gran, Sven Markelius and Eskil Sundahl. They were also the leading designers of the 1930 Stockholm Exhibition. They were closely connected to the socialist *Clarté* movement, which helped develop the programme for the exhibition. Gunnar and Alva Myrdal were part of this intellectural circle, while Viola Markelius was the editor of the group's radical journal to which Aalto contributed. See Schildt, *Alvar Aalto: The Decisive Years*, p.49.
17 This exhibition was organized by P Morton Shand in the London department store, Fortnum & Mason. The success of this show led to the establishment of Finmar, a company that was especially dedicated to the sale of Aalto furniture. See Schildt, *Alvar Aalto: The Decisive Years*, pp.103–28.
18 Alvar Aalto, 'The Humanizing of Architecture', *Technology Review*, 1940; reprinted in Schildt, *Sketches: Alvar Aalto*, p.77.
19 Aalto's biological turn of mind was very much influenced by his contact with the Hungarian Bauhaus master, László Moholy-Nagy, whom he first met in 1930, the year that Moholy-Nagy's *Von Material zu Architektur* (translated as *The New Vision*) was first published. See Schildt, *Alvar Aalto: The Decisive Years*, pp.70–77.
20 Alvar Aalto, 'Asuntomme probleemina' (The Dwelling as a Problem), *Domus*, 1930; reprinted in Schildt, *Sketches: Alvar Aalto*, pp.29–30, 32.
21 See *acceptera*, Berlings: Arlöv, 1980, a facsimile of the original 1931 publication.
22 Alvar Aalto, 'Rationalism and Man', lecture at Swedish Craft Society, Stockholm, 9 May 1935; reprinted in Schildt, *Sketches: Alvar Aalto*, pp.48–51.
23 The only evidence we have of Aalto having had any direct contact with Japanese culture is what we know of his friendship with the first Japanese ambassador to Finland, Hakotara Ichikawa, and his wife. See Schildt, *Alvar Aalto: The Decisive Years*, pp.107–13.
24 Alvar Aalto, 'The Influence of Construction and Material on Modern Architecture', in Bernhard Hoesli, ed., *Alvar Aalto Synopsis: Painting, Architecture, Sculpture*, Basel and Stuttgart, Birkhäuser, 1970, p.13. A slightly different version of the same text appears in Schildt, *Sketches: Alvar Aalto*, pp.62–3.
25 Alvar Aalto, 'The Humanizing of Architecture', in Schildt, *Sketches: Alvar Aalto*, p.77.
26 Alvar Aalto, 'Karajalan rakennustaide' (Architecture in Karelia); reprinted in Schildt, *Sketches: Alvar Aalto*, p.82.
27 Ibid., pp.82–3.
28 Alvar Aalto, 'Rakennuskorkeus sosiaalisesa kysymyksenä' (Building Heights as a Social Problem), *Arkkitehti*, 1946; reprinted in ibid., p.93.
29 Aalto did, in fact, deploy the Hansaviertel block type and apartment plan in his unrealized housing projects for Kampementsbacken, Stockholm (1958) and for Björnholm on the southern Finnish coast (1959).
30 Karl Fleig, ed., *Alvar Aalto*, London: Tiramti, 1963, p.168.
31 D'Arcy Wentworth Thompson, *On Growth and Form*, J T Bonner, ed., Cambridge: Cambridge University Press, 1971. First published in 1917, the book was expanded and revised in 1942.
32 See Fritz Neumeyer, *The Artless Word: Mies van der Rohe on Building Art*, Cambridge, MA: MIT Press, 1991, pp.102–6. Mies was profoundly influenced by Raoul Francé's proto-ecological writings. In the mid-1920s, one finds Mies in total accord with Francé's dictum, 'The best one can do is to find a compromise between the I and this law [of ecology] and to adjust to it according to the variables of the surroundings.' Here we encounter a surprising affinity between Mies and Aalto, particularly concerning their respective attitudes towards regional planning.
33 The name of this hypothesis derives from the Greek goddess of the earth, Gaia. The term was coined by James Lovelock in the 1970s and refers to his hypothesis that the homeostatic balance of the earth's biomass is regulated by a complex network of interwoven feedback systems. See James Lovelock, *Gaia: A New Look at Earth*, London: Oxford University Press, 1979, and *The Ages of Gaia: A Biography of Our Living Earth*, New York: Norton, 1995. See also Max Oelschlaeger, *Postmodern Environmental Ethics*, New York: SUNY, 1995.
34 Alvar Aalto, 'Problemi di architettura', 1956; reprinted in Schildt, *Alvar Aalto: The Complete Catalogue of Architecture, Design and Art*, p.14.
35 Alvar Aalto, *Arkkitehti*, no.1, 1942; cited in Schildt, *Alvar Aalto: The Complete Catalogue of Architecture, Design and Art*, p.16.
36 Ibid., p.22.
37 Alvar Aalto, *Arkkitehti*, nos 1–2, 1957; cited in ibid.
38 See Jussi Rausti, 'Alvar Aalto's Urban Plans 1940–1970', *DATUTOP*, no.13, 1988, p.52.
39 Alvar Aalto, 'Valtakunnansuunnittelu ja kulttuurimme tavoittet' (National Planning and Cultural Goals), *Suomalainen Suomi*, 1949; reprinted in Schildt, *Sketches: Alvar Aalto*, p.100.
40 Jussi Rausti, 'Alvar Aalto's Urban Plans 1940–1970', *DATUTOP*, no.13, 1988, p.55.
41 Bruno Taut, *Die Stadtkrone*, Jena: Diederichs, 1919.
42 For these texts by Aalto, see Schildt, *Sketches: Alvar Aalto*, pp.66–7, 99–102.
43 Alexis Carrel, *Man, the Unknown*, 2nd edition,

New York: Harper & Row, 1939, p.214.
44 See Schildt, *Alvar Aalto: The Decisive Years*, pp.182–86.
45 Soviet regional planning theory in the late 1920s was influenced by the debate taking place between the 'urbanists' and the 'de-urbanists', with the former recommending the housing of the people in large communal blocks (*dom kommuna*) and the latter favouring the redistribution of the urban population throughout the countryside. The de-urbanists recommended the creation of new settlements out of impermanent, prefabricated, free houses. See Anatole Kopp, *Town and Revolution: Soviet Architecture and City Planning 1917–1935*, trans. Thomas E Burton, New York: George Braziller, 1970, pp.168–78.
46 Jere Maula, 'The Growing Perspective in Urban Planning', in *Heroism and Everyday Life: Building in Finland in the 1950s*, Helsinki: Museum of Finnish Architecture, 1994, p.202.
47 Leonard Mosso, 'Aalto: Architect of Social and Cultural Reintegration', *L'Architecture d'aujourd'hui*, no.191, June 1997, p.122.
48 Demetri Porphyrios, *Sources of Modern Eclecticism: Studies on Alvar Aalto*, London: Academy Editions, 1982, p.3.
49 Ibid.
50 Wilson, *The Other Tradition of Modern Architecture*, pp.27–35.
51 See Alvaro Siza, 'Interview', *Plan Construction*, May 1980. 'Architects invent nothing. They work continuously with models which they transform in response to problems they encounter.'

Leicester University Engineering Laboratory

1 Louis I Kahn, 'Form and Design', *Architectural Design*, April 1961, p.145.

A House of Ivy League Values: The Ford Foundation Headquarters

1 Christian Norberg-Schulz, *Intentions in Architecture*, Oslo/London: Universiteks forlaget/Allen & Unwin, 1963/66, pp.112–127. Inspired by the environmental psychology of Egon Brunswick, Norberg-Schulz's text remains one of the most comprehensive theories of architecture attempted in the twentieth century.
2 Ibid., pp.184–185.
3 Ibid., p.185.

Moneo's Paseo: The Bankinter

1 Walter Benjamin, 'The Work of Art in the Age of Mechanical Reproduction' (1936), in *Illuminations*, Hannah Arendt, ed., New York: Schocken Books, 1969, p.240.
2 Gabriel Ruiz Cabrero, 'Sobre Bankinter o un Americano en Madrid?', *Arquitectura*, no.208/209, 1977.
3 Peter Eisenman, 'Real and English: The Destruction of the Box. I', *Oppositions*, no.4, October 1974, pp.5–34.
4 See Jørn Utzon, 'Platforms and Plateaus: Ideas of a Danish Architect', *Zodiac*, no.10, 1963, pp.113–40.
5 Paul Ricoeur, 'Universal Civilization and National Cultures' (1961), in *History and Truth*, Evanston, IL: Northwestern University Press, 1965, p.271–84.
6 Ibid, p.283.

Alvaro Siza: Duarte House and the Teixeira Apartment

1 T S Eliot, 'Burnt Norton', *Four Quartets*, New York: Harcourt Brace and Co., 1943, p.5.

The Work of Tadao Ando

1 Tadao Ando, 'The Wall as Territorial Delineation', *The Japan Architect*, no.254, June 1978, pp.12–13.
2 Tadao Ando, 'Koshino Residence', *Space Design*, no.201, June 1981, p.15
3 Tadao Ando, 'The Emotionally Made Architectural Spaces of Tadao Ando', *The Japan Architect*, no.276, April 1980, pp.45–6.
4 According to Thomas Rimer, the term *yugen*, in Heian and Kamakura poetry, alluded to 'the representation of the ineffable or the unseen, a summoning up of what lies beneath the surface of perceived nature'. See Thomas Rimer, 'Introduction', in *From the Country of Eight Islands*, ed. and trans. Hirokaki Sato and Burton Watson, Seattle, WA: University of Washington Press, 1981.
5 Jun'ichirō Tanizaki, *In Praise of Shadows*, trans. Thomas J Harper and Edward G Seidensticker, New Haven: Leete's Island Books, 1977, pp.20–22.
6 *Oku* indicates a form of deep or folded space. As Fumihiko Maki has put it, *oku* obtains when a spatial arrangement is determined by depth rather than a centre. See Fumihiko Maki, 'Japanese City Spaces and the Concept of Oku', *The Japan Architect*, no.265, May 1979, pp.51–62.
7 Koji Taki, 'Minimalism or Monotonality? A Contextual Analysis of Tadao Ando's Method', in Kenneth Frampton, ed., *Tadao Ando: Buildings Projects Writings*, New York: Rizzoli, 1984, p.11.
8 Masato Kawamukai, 'A Dialogue Between Architecture and Nature', in *Tadao Ando*, London and New York: Academy Editions/St Martin's Press, 1990, p.11.
9 Ibid.
10 Tadao Ando, '*Shintai* and Space', in *Architecture and Body*, New York: Rizzoli, 1988, unpaginated.
11 The reference is to J C F Hölderlin's question: '...what are poets for in a destitute time', as this 1946 address *Wozu Dichter?*, given on the twentieth anniversary of R M Rilke's death. See *Poetry, Language and Thought*, trans. A Hofstadter, New York: Harper & Row, 1975, 'What Are Poets For?', pp.91–142.

In the Name of the Father: O M Ungers's German Ambassador's Residence

1 The reference is to Didier Lenz who entered a Benedictine order in Beuron in 1872 in order to propagate an Egyptoid rigorously geometrical, anti-sensual Christian art. By 1899 the Dutch theosophical artist J L M Lauweriks had become influenced by Lenz's book *Zur Aesthetik der Beuronce-Schule* and he was to adopt Lenz's quadratic proportional method as his own. Peter Behrens assumes this same system for his work after he encounters Lauweriks at the *Kunstgewerbeschule* in Dusseldorf in 1904. See my introduction to Charles Chassé's article, 'Didier Lenz and the Beuron School of Religious Art', *Oppositions*, no.21, summer 1980, pp.98–103.

Minimal Moralia: Reflections on Recent Swiss German Production

1 From the catalogue *Minimal Tradition: Max Bill und die 'Einfache' Architektur 1942–1996*, XIX Triennale di Milano, 1996.
2 Nicola di Battista, 'The Artist's Knowledge', *Domus*, no.773, July/August 1995, p.77.
All other quotations are taken from the collection of interviews, 'Magic of Materials 2', *Daidalos* (special issue), no.56, June 1995.

Select Bibliography

Writings by Kenneth Frampton

Le Corbusier, London: Thames & Hudson, 2001

UIA Bejing Keynote Address, 'Seven Points for the Millennium', *Architectural Review*, vol.206, no.1233, November 1999

'Between Earthwork and Roofwork: Reflections on the Future of the Tectonic Form', *Lotus*, no.99, 1999

Alvaro Siza: Obra Completa, Barcelona: Gustavo Gili, 1999

Kenneth Frampton, ed., *Technology, Place and Architecture*, New York: Rizzoli, 1998

'The Predicament of the Place-Form: Notes from New York', in *Contemporary Architecture and City Form: The South Asian Paradigm*, Farooq Ameen, ed., Mumbai: Marg Publications, 1997

'Intimations of Durability', *Harvard Design Magazine*, Fall 1997

Studies in Tectonic Culture: The Poetics of Construction in Nineteenth and Twentieth Century Architecture, Cambridge, MA: MIT Press, 1995

'Modern Housing Form and the Contribution of Atelier 5: 1895–1992', in *Atelier 5*, Zurich: Birkhauser, 1994

Modern Architecture: A Critical History, 3rd edition, London: Thames & Hudson, 1992

'Richard Meier and the City in Miniature', *Architectural Design*, no.86, July/August 1990

'The Growing Importance of Nature, Culture and History in the Architecture of the Twentieth Century', in *Stadt, Kultur, Natur*, ed. Rudolf Wildennann, Baden Baden: Nomos, 1989

'Peter Eisenman: Three Recent Works', *Domus*, no.686, September 1987

'Gino Valle: Edificio per Uffici', *Domus*, no.683, May 1987

'The Work of Raimond Abraham', *Architecture and Urbanism*, no.199, April 1987

'MOCA, Museum of Contemporary Art, Los Angeles', *Domus*, no.677, November 1986

'Toyo Ito: Semi-Permeable Architecture', *Space Design*, no.264, September 1986

'Moderne versus moderne: affinities transatlantiques', in *Nouvellas Directions de L'Architecture*, Paris: Electa/Moniteur, 1985 (written in collaboration with Michael Kagan)

'The Unknown Mies van de Rohe', in *Mies van de Rohe*, New York: Rizzoli, 1985

'Entre el racionalismo y el regionalismo: la obra de Martorell, Bohigas y Mackay, 1954–1984', in *Martorell, Bohigas, Mackay*, Barcelona: Xarait Ediciones/Electa, 1985

'Asplund and the Legacy of Funkis', in *Asplund*, Stockholm: Arkitektur Forlag, 1985

'Il Museo di Arti Applicante a Francoforte', Casabella, no.515, July–August 1985

L'Architecture Moderne: une histoire critique, Paris: Sers, 1985

'Entre Heroisme et Metier', *Henry Ciriani*, Paris: Electra/Moniteur, 1984

'L'opera di Luigi Snozzi 1957–1984', in *Luigi Snozzi 1957–1984*, Milan: Electa, 1984

'Modern Architecture 1920–1945', *GA Document*, no.3 (special issue), January 1983

'Richard Meier: High Museum of Art in Atlanta', *Casabella*, no.485, November 1982

'Neoplasticism and Architecture: Formation and Transformation', *De Stijl, 1917–1931: Visions of Utopia*, exhibition catalogue, Minneapolis/New York: Walker Art Center and Abbeville Press, 1982

'OM Ungers and the Architecture of Coincidence', *IAUS Catalogue*, no.6, 1982

'Intimations of Tactility: Excerpts from a Fragmentary Polemic', *Art Forum*, no.19, March 1981

'City Without Flags', *Domus*, no.689, September 1980

'The Generic Street as Continuous Built Form', in *On Streets*, Cambridge, MA: MIT Press, 1978

'The Glass House Revisited', *IAUS Catalogue*, no.9, 1978

'Has the Proletariat No Use for a Glider?', *Architectural Design*, no.48, February/March 1978

'Office for Metropolitan Architecture, Two or Three Things I Know About Them: A Note on Manhattan', *Architectural Design*, no.5, May 1977

'Stirling in Context: Buildings and Projects 1950–1975', RIBA Journal, vol.83, no.3, March 1976

'John Hejduk', *A+U*, no.53, May 1975

'On Max Bill', *Oppositions*, no.4, October 1974

'The Evolution of Housing Concepts 1870–1970', in *Another Chance for Housing: Low-Rise Alternatives*, New York: MOMA, 1973. Published in Japanese in *A+U*, no.82, September 1977; and in Italian 'L'evoluzione del concetto di abitazione, 1870–1970', *Lotus*, no.10, 1971

'America 1960–1970: Notes on Urban Images and Theory', *Casabella*, no.359–60, December 1971

'Notes on a Lost Avant-Garde', *Art News Annual*, no.34, 1968; reprinted in *Avant-Garde Art*, New York: Collier Books, 1970 and a revised version in *Art in Revolution*, London: Arts Council of Great Britain, 1971

'Scarborough College, Toronto, Ontario', *Architectural Design*, vol.37, April 1967

'The Economist and the Hauptstadt', *Architectural Design*, vol.25, February 1965 (Spanish version Summa, Buenos Aires, 1965)

'The Works of George Vantongerloo', *Architectural Design*, vol.32, November 1962

Further Reading

Theodor Adorno, *Minima Moralia: Reflections from Damaged Life*, trans. E F N Jephcott, London: New Left Books, 1974

Antonio Angelillo, ed., *Alvaro Siza: Writings on Architecture*, Milan: Skira, 1997

Hannah Arendt, *The Human Condition*, Chicago, IL: University of Chicago Press, 1958

Reyner Banham, *The New Brutalism*, Stuttgart: Kramer, 1966

Reyner Banham, *Theory and Design in the First Machine Age*, London: Architectural Press, 1960

Zygmaunt Bauman, *In Search of Politics*, Stanford, CA: Stanford University Press, 1999

Walter Benjamin, *Illuminations*, trans. Harry Zohn, New York: Schocken Books, 1968

Timothy and Charlotte Benton, eds, *Form and Function: A Source Book for the History of Architecture and Design 1890–1939*, London: Crosby Lockwood Staples, 1975

Barry Bergdoll, *European Architecture 1750–1980*, Oxford: Oxford University Press, 2000

Peter Blundell-Jones, *Hans Scharoun*, London: Phaidon Press, 1995

Peter Bürger, *Theory of the Avant-Garde*, trans. Michael Shaw, Minneapolis, MN: University of Minnesota Press, 1984

Edward Hallett Carr, *What is History?*, New York: Vintage Books, 1961

David Chipperfield, *Theoretical Practice*, Zurich: Artemis, 1994

Alan Colquhoun, *Essays in Architectural Criticism: Modern Architecture and Historical Change*, Cambridge, MA: MIT Press, 1981

Alan Colquhoun, *Modernity and the Classical Tradition*, Cambridge, MA: MIT Press, 1991.

Ulrich Conrads, *Programs and Manifestoes in Twentieth Century Architecture*, Cambridge, MA: MIT Press, 1970

Catherine Cooke, *Russian Avant-Garde: Theories of Art, Architecture and the City*, London: Academy Editions, 1995

William Curtis, *Le Corbusier: Ideas and Forms*, New York: Rizzoli, 1986

Francesco Dal Co, ed., *Tadao Ando: Complete Works*, London: Phaidon Press, 1995

José Paulo dos Santos, ed., *Professione poetica (Poetic Profession)*, Milan: Electa, 1986

Andrew Feenberg, *Critical Theory of Technology*, Oxford: Oxford University Press, 1991

Bent Flyvbjerg, *Rationality & Power: Democracy in Practice*, Chicago, IL: University of Chicago Press, 1998

Hal Foster, ed., *The Anti-Aesthetic: Essays on Postmodern Culture*, New York: The New Press, 1998

Hans Frei, *Konkrete Architektur über Max Bill also Architekt*, Baden: Lars Müller, 1991

Yukio Futagana and Kenneth Frampton, eds, *Tadao Ando*, Tokyo: ADA Edita, 1987

Benedetto Gravagnuolo, *Adolf Loos*, New York: Rizzoli, 1982

Vittorio Gregotti, *Inside Architecture*, Cambridge, MA: MIT Press, 1996

Jürgen Habermas, *Toward a Rational Society: Student Protest, Science and Politics*, Boston, MA: Beacon Press, 1970

David Harvey, *Spaces of Hope*, Berkeley, CA: University of California Press, 2000

David Harvey, *The Condition of Post-Modernity*, Oxford: Blackwell, 1990

Michael K Hays, *Architecture Theory Since 1968*, Cambridge, MA: MIT Press, 1998

Michael K Hays, ed., *Oppositions Reader*, New York: Princeton Architectural Press, 1998

Martin Heidegger, *Poetry, Language, Thought*, trans. Alfred Hofstadter, New York: Harper & Row, 1975

Cheryl Temple Herr, *Critical Regionalism and Cultural Studies: From Ireland to the Midwest*, Gainsville, FL: University of Florida Press, 1996

Hilde Heynen, *Architecture and Modernity: A Critique*, Cambridge, MA: MIT Press, 1999

Fredric Jameson, *The Seeds of Time*, New York: Columbia University Press, 1994

Herbert Lindinger, *Ulm Design: The Morality of the Object, Hochschule für Gestaltung, Ulm 1953–1968*, Berlin: Ernst & Sohn, 1990

Sophie Lissitzky-Küppers, *El Lissitzky*, London: Thames & Hudson, 1968

Christina Lodder, *Russian Constructivism*, New Haven, CT: Yale University Press, 1983

Adolf Loos, *Spoken Into the Void: Collected Essays 1897–1900*, Cambridge, MA: MIT Press, 1982

Tomás Maldonado, *Design, Nature & Revolution*, New York: Harper & Row, 1972

Herbert Marcuse, *Eros and Civilization: A Philosophical Inquiry into Freud*, New York: Vintage Books, 1962

Robert Maxwell, ed., *Stirling James: Writings on Architecture*, Milan: Skira, 1998

Annette Michelson, ed., *Kino-Eye: The Writings of Dziga Vertov*, trans. Kevin O'Brien, Berkeley, CA: University of California Press, 1984

Ignasi Solà Morales, *Differences: Topographies of Contemporary Architecture*, Cambridge, MA: MIT Press, 1997

Kate Nesbitt, ed., *Theorizing a New Agenda for Architecture: An Anthology of Architecture Theory*, New York: Princeton Architectural Press, 1996

Christian Norberg-Schulz, *Intentions in Architecture*, Oslo: Universitetsforlaget, 1966

Joan Ockman, ed., *Architecture Culture 1943–1968: A Documentary Anthology*, New York: Columbia Books of Architecture/Rizzoli, 1993

Juhani Pallasmaa, ed., *Alvar Aalto: Villa Mairea 1938–39*, Helsinki: Alvar Aalto Foundation and Mairea Foundation, 1998

Peter Reed, ed., *Alvar Aalto*, New York: Museum of Modern Art, 1998

Terence Riley and Peter Reed, eds, *Frank Lloyd Wright: Architect*, New York: Museum of Modern Art, 1994, pp.58–78

Claude Schnaidt, *Harmes Meyer: Buildings, Projects and Writings*, London: Tiranti, 1965

John Sergeant, *Frank Lloyd Wright's Usonian Houses: The Case for Organic Architecture*, New York: Whitney Library of Design, 1976

Henryk Skolimowski, *Eco-Philosophy*, Boston, MA: Marion Boyars, 1981

Alison and Peter Smithson, eds, *Team 10 Primer*, Cambridge, MA: MIT Press, 1968

Alison and Peter Smithson, *Ordinariness and Light: Urban Theories 1952–60 and Their Applications in a*

Building Project 1963–70, Cambridge, MA: MIT Press, 1970

Colin St John Wilson, *Architectural Reflections: Studies in the Philosophy and Practice of Architecture*, Oxford: Butterworth Architecture, 1992

Colin St John Wilson, *The Other Tradition of Modern Architecture*, London: Academy, 1995

James Stirling, *James Stirling: Buildings and Projects 1950–1974*, New York: Oxford University Press, 1975

Manfredo Tafuri, *Architecture and Utopia: Design and Capitalist Development*, Cambridge, MA: MIT Press, 1976

Manfredo Tafuri, *Theories and History of Architecture*, New York: Harper & Row, 1980

Peter Testa, *Alvaro Siza*, Basel: Birkhauser, 1996

Luiz Trigueiros, ed., *Alvaro Siza 1954–1976*, Lisbon: Blau, 1997

Luiz Trigueiros, ed., *Alvaro Siza 1986–1995*, Lisbon: Blau, 1995

Gianni Vattino, *The End of Modernity*, Oxford: Polity Press, 1988

Georgia Warnke, *Gadamer: Hermeneutics Tradition and Reason*, Stanford, CA: Stanford University Press, 1987

Michael E Zimmerman, *Heidegger's Confrontation with Modernity*, Bloomington, IN: Indiana University Press, 1990

Index

Bold page numbers refer to illustrations

Picture Credits

© Alvar Aalto Foundation: 239b, 240b, 247, 249; Akademie der Künste, Berlin: 268, 269t, 269b, 270t; © Tadao Ando: 304, 305, 307, 308b, 309c, 310, 311b, 313b, 314; © Architectural Design (November 1963): 142; © Arch Photo Inc / Eduard Hueber: 318, 321; © Hélène Binet: 76, 324; Courtesy of Bundesamt für Bauwesen und Raumordnung: 323; Archive of Rukschcio Burkhardt and Roland Schachel: 204, 212t, 214; © Véra Cardot & Pierre Joly: 147b; Michael Carepetian: 186, 190, 195; John Cava (Ed Pang): 100; Photograph courtesy of Centre Canadien d'Architecture / Canadian Centre for Architecture, Montréal / © James Stirling, Michael Wilford Associates – Photo by Aero Stills (Photography) Ltd: 263; © Alessandra Chemello: 301b, 303; © Roberto Collovà: 298, 301t, 302; Collection Catherine Cooke: 155, 160, 162, 163b, 164; Delftse Universitaire Press, Delft: 212c; © W Diepraam: 296t; Lithograph reproduced in *El Lissitsky*, monograph published by VEB Verlag der Kunst, Dresden: 130; From *Entretiens sur l'architecture*, vol.2, 1872: 169; © Fondation Le Corbusier/ADAGP: 114, 218, 220, 221, 223t, 224; © Fondation Le Corbusier/ADAGP, Paris and DACS, London, 2002: 118, 212b; © Fondation Le Corbusier (*Cahier du Voyage d'Orient*, no.3, p.123): 210; © Fondation Le Corbusier/DACS, 2002: 117; © Fondation Le Corbusier/(*Oeuvre Complète*): 115b; Courtesy of Kenneth Frampton: 46, 88, 163t, 187, 188, 189, 194, 222; © Reinhard Friedrich / Berliner Philharmonisches Orchester: 270b; © Dennis Gilbert / View: 269c, 271; From Gruber's *Die Gestalt der Deutschen Stadt*, 1937: 98; © Heinrich Helfenstein: 330; © Herman Hertzberger: 289, 292, 293, 295b, 296b, 297; Historische Museum der Stadt Wien: 203; Historische Museum der Stadt Wien, 101.162: 198; *Hochschule für Gestaltung, Ulm*, Ernst & Sohn, 1987 / Courtesy of Baseline Archive: 53, 63; Institut für Geschichte und Theorie der Architektur (gta) ETH, Zurich: 328b; Louis I Kahn Collection, University of Pennsylvania, and Pennsylvania Historical and Museum Commission: 168, 177, 178t, 180b; David King Collection: 150; Photo KLM Aerocarto – Arnhem, Holland: 295t; M Lafever, *The Modern Builder's Guide*, 1883: 96; © 2002 The Frank Lloyd Wright Foundation, Scottsdale, AZ: 228, 294; Adolf Loos Archive, Albertina Graphic Collection, Vienna: ALA2267: 196/ALA3149: 200/ALA2580: 201/ALA3101: 202/ALA2440: 213/216; From *Miroir de la Mariee*, Jean Suquet, ed. (Flammarion): 192; © Moholy-Nagy: VG Bildkunst, Bonn / Bauhaus-Archiv, Museum für Gestaltung, Berlin: 126b; Courtesy of Rafael Moneo: 280, 283, 287; Museum of Finnish Architecture, Helsinki: 234, 238, 240t, 241, 245, 246; Photo courtesy of Dion Neutra, Architect and Neutra Papers – UCLA Special Collections: 229b; © Photothèque des Musées de la Ville de Paris / Berthier: 24; Editions A et J Picard / Cliché: Mark Wittmer: 178b; Centre G Pompidou, Documentation Général: 147t; © Christian Richters: 325; Català Roca: 278, 281, 282, 285, 286; Kevin Roche John Dinkeloo and Associates: 272, 274, 276, 277; After Colin Rowe and Robert Slutzky: 113; R M Schindler Collection, Architecture and Design Collection, University Art Museum, University of California, Santa Barbara: 226; G Semper, *Der Stil*, vol.II, p.263: 97; © Shinkenchiku-sha / Photo by Mitsuo Matsuoka: 308t, 309t, 311t, 312, 313t; © Julius Shulman: 229t, 232; Alvaro Siza: 300; © Alison and Peter Smithson Architects: 136, 139, 143; © Sovexportfilm: 165; © Margherita Spiluttini: 327, 328t; © James Stirling, Michael Wilford Associates: 258, 260, 261; Ullstein Bild/Joachim Jung: 264; Ulmer Museum HfG Archiv: 51; Ulmer Museum HfG Archiv / Photo: Otl Aicher: 44; Büro Prof. O M Ungers: 320; University College Santa Barbara: 227; Ger van der Vlugt: 288; Volvo Historical Archive: 64, 69, 70; Drawing by Elizabeth Whitehead: 242, 253; Architekturbüro Peter Zumthor: 326

Photographic sources are listed where possible, but the publisher will endeavour to rectify any inadvertent omissions.

Acknowledgements

In the first instance I have to express my gratitude to my wife Silvia Kolbowski who, apart from offering invaluable criticism, has also had to endure my distracted state of mind throughout the final stages of preparing this anthology. In the second, credit has to be accorded to Vivian Constantinopoulos without whose editorial conviction and persistence this book would never have been realized. I am also greatly indebted to Victoria Clarke and Mari Knutsson of Phaidon Press whose painstaking attention to detail, and picture research, have been essential to the refinement and illustration of the text. Further credit must be accorded to Amanda Johnson, Matthew Perna and Savanah Roberts, whose editorial and research work was indispensable in substantiating this text in its final form.

Apart from these associations, my indebtedness extends further to all those figures who have exercised a decisive influence on me over the years, beginning with Hannah Arendt, to whose memory this book is dedicated, and going on to include many who, directly or indirectly, have shaped the way I have written about twentieth-century architecture and environmental design. In addition to those who are acknowledged in the essays and the bibliography, I have to express my particular debt to the following: Marshall Berman, Francoise Choay, Jean Louis Cohen, Charles Correa, Peter Eisenman, Kurt Forster, Marco Frascari, Alberto Perez Gomez, Vittorio Gregotti, Gevork Hartoonian, Hilde Heynen, Andreas Huyssen, Leon Krier, Helene Lipstadt, Tomás Llorens, Robert Major, Tomás Maldonado, Mary McLeod, Robin Middleton, John Miller, Ignasi Solà Morales, Joan Ockman, Juhani Pallasmaa, Patricia Patkau, Renzo Piano, Demetri Porphyrios, Roland Rainer, Colin Rowe, Joseph Rykwert, Yehuda Safran, Yorgo Simeofiridis, Thomas Stevens, Dalibor Vesely, Anthony Vidler, Wilfried Wang and Gwendolyn Wright. I have also to acknowledge my indebtedness to the editors of those journals in which these essays first appeared.